I0202703

Joseph Coffey
Epistemology or the Theory of Knowledge
An Introduction to General Metaphysics
Vol. 2

EDITIONES SCHOLASTICAE

Peter Coffey

Epistemology
or the Theory of Knowledge

An Introduction to General Metaphysics
Vol. 2

EDITIONES SCHOLASTICAE

Bibliographic information published by Deutsche Nationalbibliothek
The Deutsche Nationalbibliothek lists this publication in the Deutsche Nationalbibliographie;
detailed bibliographic data is available in the Internet at http://dnb.ddb.de

Our books are distributed worldwide by

EUROSPAN

USA & Canada
Independent Publishers Group IPG
E-mail: orders@ipgbook.com
Tel: +1 800 888 4741
www.ipgbook.com

U.K., Europe, Asia and Africa
Eurospan
Gray's Inn House
127 Clerkenwell Road
London EC1R 5DB
info@eurospan.co.uk

©2023 editiones scholasticae
53819 Neunkirchen-Seelscheid
www.editiones-scholasticae.de

ISBN 978-3-86838-282-2

2023
No part of this book may be reproduced, stored in retrieval systems or transmitted
in any form or by any means, electronic, mechanical, photocopying, microfilming, recording or
otherwise without written permission from the Publisher, with the exception of any material
supplied specifically for the purpose of being entered and executed on a computer system, for
exclusive use of the purchaser of the work.

Printed on acid-free paper

Printed in Germany

CONTENTS OF VOLUME II.

PART IV.

THE DATA OF INTELLECTUAL KNOWLEDGE ; SENSE PERCEPTION.

CHAPTER XIII.

SELF-CONSCIOUSNESS AND MEMORY.

CHAPTER XIV.

EXTRAMENTAL REALITY. THE EXTERNAL UNIVERSE.

CHAPTER XV.

VALIDITY OF SENSE PERCEPTION: REAL EXISTENCE OF AN EXTERNAL, MATERIAL UNIVERSE.

CHAPTER XX.

IDEALISM AND THE DISTINCTION BETWEEN "APPEARANCE" AND "REALITY".

CHAPTER XXI.

KANT'S THEORY OF SENSE PERCEPTION, SPACE AND TIME.

PART V.

TRUTH AND CERTITUDE: THEIR CRITERIA AND MOTIVES.

CHAPTER XXII.

RETROSPECT. RELATIVIST THEORIES OF KNOWLEDGE.

CHAPTER XXIII.

TRUTH AND EVIDENCE.

TABLE OF CONTENTS

CHAPTER XXIV.

OTHER INTELLECTUALIST THEORIES OF CERTITUDE. TRADITIONALISM.

CHAPTER XXV.

ANTI-INTELLECTUALIST THEORIES. KANT'S MORAL DOGMATISM. PRAGMATISM AND HUMANISM.

PART IV.

THE DATA OF INTELLECTUAL KNOWLEDGE ; SENSE PERCEPTION.

CHAPTER XIII.

SELF-CONSCIOUSNESS AND MEMORY.

95. TRANSITION TO SENSE PERCEPTION. TERMS AND DISTINCTIONS.—When examining the *terms* and *data* of our general inquiry in the opening chapter, we distinguished (8) between knowledge proper and mere consciousness ; between *reflex* consciousness and the implicit, concomitant awareness which the conscious subject necessarily has of itself in all its conscious states or activities, without which these could not be *conscious*, and which is usually described as *direct* consciousness ; between non-cognitive (volitional, emotional, etc.) and cognitive consciousness ; between the *interpretative* objectivity of those cognitive states of consciousness which fall short of judgment, and the formal or consciously asserted objectivity of the judgment itself. We have also been obliged, in our exposition of the doctrines of Descartes, Kant and Scholasticism (77), to discuss at some length the nature and validity of our awareness of the self as a concrete, existing, individual reality. Presupposing what has been said already in those connexions we may be brief in our present exposition of the cognitive value or significance of the facts of consciousness and memory,—an exposition which will serve as a necessary and natural transition from intellectual knowledge to sense knowledge.

The psychological distinction between *intellectual* consciousness, whereby we are aware of our intellectual activities such as thought and volition,—and *sense* consciousness, whereby we are aware of our external sense functions and the states and conditions of our bodies,—is not itself a *datum* of consciousness, but an inference arising from introspection and based on the diversity of the *objects* presented in the conscious states. As an activity, consciousness of whatsoever kind reveals itself as belonging wholly to the *one* conscious self or *Ego*.

The distinction between direct and reflex consciousness is itself a datum of human consciousness : we are aware of the difference between any direct cognitive act (direct consciousness) and the act whereby we deliberately make our own conscious activities (*psychological* reflection), or their objects (*ontological* reflection), the object of special and distinct contemplation. From the nature of this activity scholastic psychologists infer the immaterial or spiritual nature of the faculty which elicits it,—the intellect,—for the reason that no cognitive power of the sense order, functioning through an animated material organ, could possibly elicit such a reflex cognitive act. Whatever about the nature of the faculty, or the implications of the fact, of reflex consciousness, there can at all events be no doubt about the fact itself.

96. DATA, INTERPRETATIONS, AND IMPLICATIONS OF CONSCIOUSNESS.—Consciousness, of whatsoever kind, makes us *directly* and *immediately* aware of *something*,—which "something" we call the *datum* or *object* of consciousness. This, too, is undeniable. We may, therefore, describe the insight which consciousness gives us into its object as "intuitive," as a direct and immediate awareness of the mental presence of something, or of something as having an *esse ideale*, a "mental existence" for us. This raises two points for consideration.

One is that we must consciously apprehend at least some of the data thus present to us, as *really existing or happening ;* or at all events that we must *intellectually interpret* our consciousness of some data as revealing the *real existence or happening* of such data.[1] Otherwise we could have no conception of real existence, whereas it is a fact of consciousness that we have such a conception. But sense consciousness, or the mere direct awareness of something as present, does not itself analyse the implications of this presence, or reach the distinction between "existing as an object of consciousness" and "existing really". It must be intellect,—or, if we may say so, consciousness as intellectual,—that

---

[1] This does not imply anything more than the recognition that the presence of data in consciousness implies *some real* existence—at least the real existence of the conscious or cognitive process. But even this attribution of real existence requires and implies the operation of intellect.

makes us aware of the " something present " as " something really happening or existing ".

A second consideration, then, is this : Since *all* the objects of consciousness proper are the conscious mental activities, functions, processes, states, and conditions of the conscious subject ;[1] and since these are all *concrete, individual* data,—even those of them that belong to the higher domain of mental life, such as judgments, inferences, volitions, etc.,—it follows that if we describe our direct consciousness of these latter activities as "intellectual consciousness," we are according to intellect (in its capacity as "consciousness") a power of intuitively apprehending "individuals," *viz.* our individual mental acts (thoughts, volitions, etc.) of the higher or spiritual domain (77). If we hold that in exercising the function of external or internal *sense* perception, we are *through the sense faculty* made concomitantly aware of the act of perception,[2] we may and ought to hold, too, that in exercising any conscious *intellectual* function (*e.g.* conceiving, judging, reasoning), we are made, *through the intellect*, indirectly and concomitantly aware of this individual function as actually taking place. Every cognitive act, whether sensuous or intellectual, must thus concomitantly reveal itself *in individuo*, to the knowing subject : not the act apart from its content or object, or apart from its subject or agent, but the whole concrete experience, afterwards analysed into agent, act, and object. Intellect would thus, as consciousness, indirectly reveal an individual thing or event *as existing or happening* (*viz.* the higher mental act in question : judging, reasoning, willing, etc.) ; and would then, as intellect, apprehend the *abstract nature* or *essence* of the act, and go on to analyse its implications as to the nature of the human faculty, and of the human agent, capable of eliciting such an act. If, then, the *proper* object of the human intellect be the *natures* or *essences* of *corporeal* things, considered in the *abstract* and as *universal*, it must be added that all our intellectual cognition has, as *concomitant* object, its own individual acts, not in the abstract,

---

[1] We do not say " I am conscious of a sound," but, " I *hear* a sound," and, " I am conscious of *hearing* it " ; nor, " I am conscious of material substance," but, " I am *thinking* of material substance," and, " I am conscious of *thinking* about it " ; nor, " I am conscious that two and two are four," but, " I *judge* or *understand*, or *see* (intellectually) that two and two are four," and, " I am conscious of *seeing* it ".

[2] Otherwise it would not be a *cognitive* act : *some* degree of such concomitant awareness of the *subjectum cognoscens* is essentially involved in *all* cognition (8).

but as the concrete acts of the individual self-conscious *Ego* apprehending some definite datum or object.

It is commonly said that there are data of consciousness which all philosophers agree in recognizing as such, as being unquestioned and unquestionable, and as forming the starting-points of all philosophical discussion.[1]   And this is quite true.[2]   But inasmuch as from the very dawn of reason in each of us our intellects have been spontaneously scrutinizing these data, it is not easy to distinguish between what are really *data* and what are *interpretations* of, and inferences from, the *data*.   And the difficulty is unavoidably aggravated by the fact that we can discuss these data only as envisaged in introspection by *intellectual* scrutiny.   The very terms we use in describing them are terms which apply to them *as conceived by intellect*.   We have, in fact, no direct conscious experience of these data as they would appear to a being endowed with *sense consciousness alone*,—such as we suppose the lower animals to be.   It is only by a careful and prolonged process of abstraction that we can mentally separate our own intellectual interpretation from the data of sense cognition and sense consciousness, and thus get down to the ever-changing, fluctuating, ebbing and flowing stream of external and internal sense impressions which form the elementary contents of sense consciousness.   From the standpoint of epistemology, however, the difficulty of thus discriminating between the data and our interpretations of them,—or of drawing the distinction between data of *sense* consciousness and data of *intellectual* consciousness, which is just one example of such interpretation, —is not a serious difficulty.   For in regard to every single assertion of ours on the matter we must be prepared to show either that it indisputably expresses a datum of consciousness, or else that it is an interpretation or inference which really has all the rational justification we claim for it.

In classifying the data of consciousness which have an immediate bearing on the questions of epistemology, authors commonly distinguish [3] the *direct* from the *indirect* data or objects of

---

[1] There is another necessary presupposition of philosophical discussion, *viz.* the presupposition on the part of each participant that the data of every other person's consciousness is of the same general nature and order as those of his own (§ 39, vol. i., p. 144, n. 2).

[2] *Cf.* §§ 37, 39, *ibid.*   [3] *Cf.* JEANNIÈRE, *op. cit.*, pp. 358-9.

consciousness. Among the former they enumerate all conscious acts, processes, states, and modes of the conscious subject, not apart from, but as concrete, actually existing modes of, the subject. As indirect object of consciousness they set down *the existing conscious subject* as a consciously acting being ; but not the *nature* of the latter : its nature is revealed not by consciousness but by intellect or reason interpreting consciousness.

Neither, however, is the *existence* of the conscious subject revealed *apart* from the existence or happening of the conscious acts. It is reason or intellect that analyses the whole concrete *datum* into acts, states, processes, etc. (*accidents*), on the one hand, and an agent, subject (*substance*), of these on the other ; and which further interprets this subject or substance as corporeal, living, sentient, rational, etc. And all these interpretations alike have to be justified. Again, some of our conscious, cognitive acts, *i.e.* our external sense perceptions, reveal their objects as located in space outside our bodies ; and others, *i.e.* some of our internal sense perceptions, reveal their objects as located more or less definitely within our bodies. If, therefore, these perceptive acts themselves be said to be the direct and proper objects of consciousness, as being " within " the conscious subject, it must be admitted that the objects of these perceptive acts themselves must, as perceived objects, be also indirectly objects of consciousness—even though they be revealed as "outside" the conscious subject : for by being " presented " or " present " to the conscious subject, in and through the perceptive act, they become also data of consciousness. But here again it is intellect or reason that distinguishes the conscious subject into " mind " and " body " ; that recognizes some of the data or objects of conscious cognition as constituting the *Ego* and others as constituting the *non-Ego* or " external universe " ; and that interprets the real significance of the character of " externality " attaching to the latter, and of " internality " attaching to the former.

97. TRUTHS REVEALED BY INTROSPECTIVE RATIONAL ANALYSIS OF THE DATA OF CONSCIOUSNESS.—We may now proceed to see what objectively true and valid judgments are yielded by psychological reflection on the facts of consciousness. (*a*) They yield first of all the immediate judgment that " *something really exists,*" *viz.* the total, concrete, unanalysed content of the present conscious state or condition of the conscious subject aware of something. No sceptic can deny, or ever has denied, the exist-

ence of something in and for his consciousness. Sceptics have doubted—or denied that they can know—whether there is anything that has a reality or real existence other than the *esse ideale* which the facts of their consciousness have for them in the actual conscious state. But since this *esse ideale* evidently involves the *real existence* of the concrete consciousness, or conscious being,—nay, since this *esse ideale* is itself something, since it is a real state or manifestation of some reality,—it follows that even if such sceptics take up the position of *solipsism* they must at least admit the *real existence* of the concrete conscious self or subject : not of course as distinct from a non-self or object, but simply as something real, and as something revealing this distinction or duality as a problem for investigation.

(*b*) The data of my consciousness yield as certainly valid and objectively true the judgment—" *I, the thinking or conscious being, really exist as subject and agent of my conscious states and activities* ". For my consciousness [1] reveals these states and activities as different from one another,—seeing, thinking, speaking, desiring, grieving, rejoicing, etc.,—but all *in the concrete* as states, conditions, activities of *one* single being, subject, or agent : which I call *myself*, the *Ego*, *self*, or *person*.

No doubt, what consciousness, as a mere faculty of awareness or apprehension, reveals, is one really existing, concrete, complex, heterogeneous whole of subject and states, agent and activities, substance and accidents, etc. My consciousness of my existence does not *commence* with abstract concepts of " self," " existence," "subject," " states," " agent," " activities "; or with a formal act of judgment affirming the " self" to " exist," or the "states," "activities," " accidents," to be those of the " subject," " agent," "substance". But all this rational or intellectual process of analysis and synthesis, of isolating abstract concepts and synthesizing them in judgments, merely expresses and interprets for me intellectually what was really and implicitly given to me in the primitive conscious intuition of the self, consciously existing and acting.

Descartes rightly pointed out that the *Cogito, ergo sum*, is not an inference (31). It is the expression of a self-evident judgment, " I exist," which is virtually contained in the direct intuition of consciousness. And the same is true of the other immediate interpretations of the content of this intuition,—

---

[1] Or my consciousness *plus* my memory, if we take into consideration not only *simultaneous* but *successive* states. *Cf. infra*, § 98.

such as "These are conscious states of which I am the subject," "These are activities of which I am the agent or cause," "These are inhering or 'accident'-entities of which I am the substantive or 'substance'-entity". Descartes was right, too, in accepting the evidence, or "clear and distinct idea," of his existence, as *objectively valid, i.e.* as revealing to him a *really existing* being, though he was inconsistent in questioning the equally cogent evidence in the case of first principles (31). He was right as against the phenomenism of sensists and positivists in their unintelligible and self-contradictory assertion that the *Ego* revealed in consciousness is a *mere* bundle· of "states" *without a subject of these states;* or a *mere* stream of "processes" or "activities" *without an agent or cause of these processes or activities;* or a *mere* ebb and flow of "phenomena," "appearances," or "accidents," *without any substantial Ego or being of which they are the phenomena, appearances, or accidents.* And he was right, as against the phenomenism of Kant, in holding that what the conscious thinking subject apprehends is the *real Ego,* at once phenomenal and noumenal, at once *sensible* and *intelligible,* at once object of sense and object of intellect,—and not merely a "phenomenal" or empirically "appearing" product of a real but "transcendental," "unknowable" *Ego,* for ever hiding itself behind its own miscalled "appearances ".[1] The *Ego* or conscious subject which is revealed in consciousness is identical with the self which our intellect sees to be a necessary condition for the possibility of knowledge. According to Kant, this latter self, in which all our apperceptions must have their unity,[2] can indeed be *thought* as real, as a necessary, *a priori,* transcendental condition of knowledge ; but it cannot be *known* as real, because we have no intuition of it : "The consciousness of myself, in the representation of the *ego,* is not an intuition, but a merely *intellectual* representation of the spontaneity of a thinking subject".[3] In other words, the "I" of the "I think" or "I am aware," which is an essential concomitant of all cognition (and which, for intellectual consciousness, is implicitly "I am" or "I exist"), though it is *thought* as really existing, cannot be *known* as really existing : we know it merely to be something which we are compelled to think as a formal, *a priori* condition or unifying principle of all our conscious apperceptions : "No doubt the representation of *I am,* which expresses the consciousness that can accompany all thought, is that which immediately includes the existence of a subject : but it does not yet include a *knowledge* of it, and therefore no empirical knowledge, that is, experience. For that we require, besides the thought of something existing, intuition also, and in this case internal intuition in respect to which, that is, to time, the subject must be determined."[4] Thus

---

[1] *Cf. infra,* § 134.   [2] *Cf. supra,* § 89, vol. i., p. 337, n.
[3] *Critique* (tr. MÜLLER), p. 781.
[4] *Ibid.,* p. 680. "For that purpose [time determination of the subject in internal intuition]," Kant continues (arguing against the "idealism" of Descartes,—*cf.* vol. i., p. 214, n. 1), "external objects are absolutely necessary, so that internal experience itself is possible, mediately only, and through external experience ". In the same context he speaks of "the *immediate* consciousness of the existence of external things" (*ibid.,* n.), an expression which is intelligible only when we remember that for him "external things" are *mental phenomena.* Again, what this "immediate" "external experience" renders possible, is *not* "the consciousness of our own

Kant repeatedly denies that intellectual consciousness, or introspection, or psychological reflection on the self or *Ego* as consciously functioning in the concrete, gives us any intuition, any direct grasp or apprehension, of the real *Ego* as thus existing and acting. But such denial is purely gratuitous; and can be directly met by the positive counter-assertion,—not gratuitous, but forced upon us both by the most cogent evidence of consciousness and by the most absolute necessity of thought itself,—that consciousness *does* reveal to us intuitively the real existence of the real, consciously acting self or *Ego*, as subject and agent of our conscious states and activities.

(*c*) By reflecting on the conscious and cognitive acts of which I am the conscious subject, and on the objects of these acts, I see both acts and objects to be of various kinds, and I classify them accordingly. The feelings and sensations which I call organic (*e.g.* muscular and motor feelings, bodily aches and pains, hunger, thirst, physical pleasure or discomfort, etc.), and their contents, I am aware of not merely as different from one another, but, in the case of some of them at least, as having *extensity* or *spatial continuity* of parts outside parts, and as spatially distant from others (as *e.g.* headache and lumbago), and yet *all* of them as *mine*, as affections, states, conditions of *myself*, and myself the conscious subject as *spatially extended in and with them*. No doubt, this element of extensity or extendedness, directly revealed in the conscious content of organic feelings, is vague and ill-defined: the definite localization of these feelings being, as psychologists explain, a result of sense development or sense "education" through association of the accumulated sense experiences of the individual, and involving intellectual interpretation and inference. But the element of extensity is there in the concrete from the beginning; and thus it reveals the self or conscious subject as a something which we intellectually apprehend and designate as a substantive reality *having an extended or corporeal mode of being*, or, in other words, as a living, conscious, *corporeal substance.*

Hence Descartes completely misread the immediate data of

existence," *but* the "determination" of this consciousness "in time," or in other words "internal experience" (*ibid.*): this latter, of course, not attaining to reality but only to mental appearances. And what is it that renders *the consciousness itself* of our own existence possible? Nothing; for on Kant's theory consciousness of our own real existence is impossible. We can only *think* this latter as an *a priori*, transcendental condition of knowledge; but we cannot have *knowledge*, or *empirical* consciousness,—or, if we might so put it, *conscious* consciousness as distinct from the Kantian figment of "*transcendental* consciousness" or "*transcendental* apperception,"—of our own real existence.

human consciousness when he regarded them as revealing,—or at least as furnishing grounds for interpreting,—the conscious human subject or self or *Ego*, as a *simple, unextended, incorporeal*, conscious principle which he identified with *soul* or *spirit*.

It is a point of minor importance to observe that it is not consciousness itself, but intellect interpreting its data, that infers the *nature* of the human *soul* to be simple, spiritual, immortal, etc., and the *nature* of the human *self* or *Ego* to be a being composed of body and soul. But it is important to insist, against Descartes and ultra-spiritualists,[1] that among the immediate data of human consciousness is the directly apprehended spatial datum of extensity or voluminousness of the conscious subject,—which latter the intellect must therefore interpret as having the corporeal mode of being, as having in its nature or constitution that which we call body or matter.[2] Whether the distinction which we draw between *our own* bodies and external bodies be valid or not, it is a fact of consciousness that we draw the distinction, and that it is grounded in the consciously apprehended features of *internality* and *externality* attaching respectively to two classes of directly apprehended objects.[3] But if Descartes' contention were true,— that the consciously revealed self or *Ego* is a simple, unextended, spiritual substance or soul,—then, even though we might perhaps be able to *infer* the real existence of a material reality, it is impossible to see how we could apprehend *our* bodies as *our own* and as distinct from *external* bodies: if *consciousness* did not reveal our own bodies as our own no other faculty or mode of cognition could reveal them as such.

Those, then, are the main immediate interpretations of the facts of consciousness that have a direct bearing on epistemology. It must be borne in mind, in reference to them, that mere (sense) consciousness, apart from intellect, simply makes us aware of subjective facts, without interpreting them. But in man this

---

[1] *Cf.* JEANNIÈRE, *op. cit.*, pp. 358, 364-5.

[2] Similarly, it must be emphasized later (116) that in *external* sense perception we are made *directly aware* of *extension, occupation of space, impenetrability*, in that domain of direct sense cognition or awareness, which, by reason of its apprehended feature of *externality* to the self or *Ego*, each of us marks off from the portion (*viz.* his own body) apprehended by *internal* sense perception as characterized by *internality*, and which each of us designates as the (to him) *external material universe*. Here, again, the interpretation of these features of " internality " and " externality " in the data of direct awareness, as revealing a real universe really distinct from the self or *Ego*, is the work of intellect and must be justified by intellect.

[3] *Cf.* preceding note.

awareness is always accompanied by the spontaneous formation of judgments whereby we interpret the facts. These judgments impose themselves on us with spontaneous certitude by a psychological necessity. But we have now seen, by reflection, that these spontaneous assents are not blind or instinctive. "The facts of my consciousness have a *real existence* in and for my consciousness;"[1] "My conscious states are *real states*"; "*I myself*, the conscious subject, *really exist*"; "My conscious states reveal me to myself as having not alone the mode of being which thinks, reasons, judges, but also the mode of being which perceives, and which I mean by *corporeal being*,"—these judgments impose themselves upon my reflecting reason with such cogent objective evidence that I must accept them with reflex, reasoned certitude as indubitably true: on the assumption, already justified as against Kant, that my intellect in its processes of conception and judgment attains not to a subjective, phenomenal disfigurement of reality, but to reality itself.

98. MEMORY, SELF-IDENTITY, AND TIME DURATION.— Memory is described by psychologists as the faculty of *conserving* and *recalling* events experienced in the past; of *recognizing* them as past, and *locating* them more or less definitely in the time series of experienced events. Like consciousness, it is distinguished into *sensitive*, and *intellectual* or *rational*, according to the nature of the events or objects recalled. The distinction is of minor importance for epistemology, inasmuch as in man memory is *always* accompanied by *intellectual* activity,—interpreting the recalled data, of whatsoever kind these may be. And we include in memory, as understood here, this faculty of forming immediate judgments or interpretations of these data. Many of the truths brought to light by the psychology of memory, which is both extensive and interesting, have only a remote bearing on epistemology. But some of the facts and implications of memory, —especially those which bear on our apprehension of *time* and of the *self* or *Ego*,—are of the first importance in a general theory of knowledge.

The process of remembering is itself a conscious process, a

---

[1] It has been pointed out already (18) that "consciousness" is the name of a state or condition of a conscious subject: it is not really "consciousness" that apprehends anything: it is "I, the conscious subject," who apprehends *by* consciousness. We must not hypostasize "consciousness" any more than intellect or reason.

datum or fact of consciousness. It differs from consciousness in this that while the latter reports its facts or objects as *here and now actually present*, the former reports its objects as having been experienced, or present to consciousness, *in the past.* In other words, the act of memory brings into consciousness an object or datum marked by a characteristic which is altogether peculiar and *sui generis*, a characteristic which we *interpret* intellectually as indicating a datum or object *experienced before*, a feeling of *familiarity*[1] whereby we *recognize* the present content of consciousness as being, in part at least, the reproduction or repetition of a *past* or *previous* content of consciousness.[2] And inasmuch as memory reproduces *in the concrete* the past act as it occurred *in the concrete*, it is clear that just as consciousness reveals *the subject* as affected by the present conscious states, so, too, memory reveals *the same subject* as affected both by the past and by the present conscious states. The possibility of thus becoming aware of conscious data endowed with this quality of being "remembered" acts, clearly involves that the subject of such " reproduced " and " recognized " conscious acts apprehends itself as having a real existence extended through *time-duration*, and as remaining or abiding permanently self-identical throughout all the changes which such time duration implies.[3] Just as we immediately judge or interpret the direct data of *consciousness* to imply the real existence, here and now, of an actual substantial subject of the conscious states, so we immediately judge or interpret the direct data of *memory* to imply the reality of the succession and change in conscious states, the reality and abiding self-identity of the *Ego* or subject of those successive states, and the real objectivity of our concept of *time* as the mode of duration of the real existence of the ever-changing real data of our conscious, cognitive experience.

Obviously there can be no question of *demonstrating* the general trustworthiness of memory, in the strict sense of the term *demonstration.* For every single step in the process of demonstration,—from premiss to premiss, and from antecedent to consequent or conclusion,—implies and rests upon the assumed

---

[1] This is analogous to the feeling of *externality* which characterizes the data of external sense perceptions. *Cf.* § 97, p. 9, n. 2.

[2] For distinction between *actually perceived*, and *merely imagined*, and *remembered data, cf.* LAHR, *Cours de philosophie*, p. 132,—*apud* JEANNIÈRE, *op. cit.*, p. 370 n.

[3] *Cf. Ontology*, §§ 74, 75, 85, 86.

trustworthiness of memory.   There can be question only of
reflecting on the concrete data of memory, and on our immediate intellectual interpretations of those data, and convincing ourselves that intellect,—which we have already shown (chaps. viii.,
ix.) to be capable of attaining to objective reality through its
concepts and judgments,—has adequate and cogent objective
evidence for the immediate judgments it forms, from those
data, concerning the real existence of an *abiding Ego*, substantially *self-identical* throughout its really changing states,
and the reality of *time-duration* as a real mode of existence of
these states, their subject, and their contents.

99. TRUTHS REVEALED BY INTROSPECTIVE RATIONAL
ANALYSIS OF THE DATA OF MEMORY.—In addition to the
concepts formed from the immediate data of *consciousness*,—concepts of being, existence, subject, substance, agent, body,
extension, mind, action, state, process, accident, etc.,—we
have furnished by *memory* the data for our concepts of self-
identity, duration, change, succession, time, etc.   These are
the concepts we utilize in interpreting the immediate data of
memory.   Now we have adequate objective evidence for the
following judgments concerning memory, its data, and their
implications ; and these judgments therefore are vindicated by
reflec.ion as objectively valid and certainly true :—

(*a*) My consciousness reveals some of its contents as *familiar*,
as *repetitions :* this character being peculiar to, and inseparable
from, their present appearance in my consciousness.   Now,
when I formulate intellectually what is already implicit in
such data, by the explicit judgments, "*I experienced these
data before : they occurred to me in the past : they are events of
my past experience, recalled and recognized by me as such*,"—my
intellect is determined to such judgments by the clearest objective evidence of the very nature itself of my present conscious
state.   Therefore such judgments are objectively true ; and
their truth is being constantly verified experimentally by their
fitting in with the train of my actual experiences.[1]

_____

[1] The exact *location* of some remembered events in the time series of past
experiences is given immediately; others are located only indirectly and by
reasoning from the present and from already located events.   Here there is room
for error.   Moreover, memory has its limits, it does not retain or recall all past
experiences, but comparatively few.   Nor is it infallible, any more than intellect
itself; except in regard to its immediate data, as intellect is in regard to immediately evident judgments.   Psychology deals with the mistakes and deceptions

(*b*) Since my "remembered" experiences reveal themselves *in the concrete* as having been *actually mine in the past*, and as now actually reproduced in *my present conscious act* of remembering, there is manifestly revealed to me in this act *the concrete duration of my own self-identical existence* as abiding subject and agent of these successive conscious states and activities. I thus form the spontaneous judgment that "*I continue in existence, preserving my substantial, personal self-identity throughout the succession of real but accidental changes to which this my real existence is subject*"[1]; and my certitude of the truth of this spontaneous judgment is confirmed by reflection. For just as I see that at the present moment of *consciousness* I cannot be merely a bundle or collection of states or processes (without any substantial subject or agent), but that I am concrete subject and agent of these states and processes, so I see, in and through my present, conscious act of *remembering*, that I am *the same* self-identical subject who experienced the past datum, and who now reproduce and recognize it as previously experienced.

In other words, just as the attempts of sensists and positivists, such as Locke, Hume, Mill, Taine, etc., to explain *consciousness* (and knowledge generally) without admitting a *real substance*, ends in their *substantializing accidents* (or consciousness itself[2]), so their attempts to explain *memory*, while denying the *real permanence* of the self or subject and holding the latter to be a mere stream or series of conscious states, ends in such fantastic theories of personal identity as that of Professor James: that the present thought (which is the only thinker), or the present conscious state, "appropriates" the content of the immediately preceding state and "transmits" this *plus* its own content to the next succeeding one,—a theory the unsufficiency of which its propounder himself admits by recognizing the necessity of postulating some-

of memory. The theses in the text are in no way influenced by the possibility of such deceptions.

[1] The concept of substance, which I thus find realized in my own being, is not the fanciful notion of an absolutely immutable, hidden, unknowable core or substrate of separate, ever-flowing, evanescent phenomena or accidents,—a fiction falsely attributed to scholastics by modern sensists and positivists (*cf. Ontology*, § 64). It is the notion of a real mode of being which does not inhere in other being for its reality; a mode of being the reality and nature of which are revealed in and through its changing states or accidents; which is subject to (accidental) change and yet persists really (substantially) the same throughout the change (*ibid.*, §§ 63, 80, pp. 302-3).

[2] *Cf. Ontology*, §§ 61, 75.

thing "more than the bare fact of the co-existence of a passing thought with a passing brain-state".[1]

(c) Since the concrete subject or *Ego*, immediately revealed in consciousness and memory, is revealed and intellectually interpreted as a really existing being which persists self-identical throughout a succession of real states, constituting real change, I have in these concrete data the objective and real contents of my concepts of *duration, succession*, and *time*. Since through consciousness and memory I am aware of myself as undergoing *real change*, and of a *real succession* in my conscious states, I am aware in the concrete of my own existence as having *real* and *concrete time duration*. This *concrete awareness* of succession may be described as an internal *perception* of *time*. My intellect, apprehending from this datum successive duration in the abstract, forms the abstract *concept* of *time*. Thus the concept of time is *objectively real*, having its real foundation in the succession involved in real change,—just as we shall see the concept of *space* to be likewise objectively real, having its real foundation in the perceived real extension of bodies.

Time, then, is not a substantive reality, *sui generis*, distinct from real change : its reality is the reality of change, but it is this reality endowed by intellect with the logical features of abstractness and universality, and the logical relation of *measuring* the amount of change : it is, in other words, an *ens rationis cum fundamento in re*.[2] Neither is time, therefore, on the other hand a *mere "ens rationis,"* a mere subjective, *a priori* form of internal cognition or consciousness, as Kant would have it.   The utter untenability of Kant's doctrine on time will be shown below (134).

Kant would, of course, urge against all the intellectual interpretations of the data of consciousness and memory, which we have been vindicating in the present chapter, the general charge that these interpretations are reached *through concepts*, and that concepts can reveal nothing about the *reality* or *real nature* of the self or *Ego*.   Our reply is that they are indeed reached through concepts, and embodied in judgments, but that we have already vindicated, against his theory, the real objectivity of conception and judgment.

[1] *Principles of Psychology*, i., p. 346,—*apud* MAHER, *Psychology*, p. 483. *Cf. Ontology*, § 75, pp. 276-84.   For further developments of the doctrines of substance, person, personal identity, permanence of the *Ego*, time duration, etc., and refutations of sensist theories, *cf. Ontology*, chaps. viii. and ix., chap. xi., § 85, 86; MAHER, *op. cit.*, chap. xxii.

[2] *Cf. Ontology*, § 85, p. 324.

100. CONSCIOUSNESS OF SELF AND COGNITION OF THE EXTERNAL UNIVERSE.—Since we become conscious of the self, and its concrete time-duration, *in and through the conscious activities of the self*, and since these conscious activities are in large part cognitive of that domain of objects or data which we interpret as the *external, spatial, material universe*, or the *non-Ego*, the question may be asked, whether or how far self-consciousness is mediated by, and dependent on, our direct cognition of the non-self or external universe.

Descartes, holding that the *only* immediate object of the mind's awareness is *itself*, failed to explain satisfactorily the possibility of our knowledge of spatial or material reality distinct from the mind : and all subjective idealists we shall find to be in the same condition. Kant made an attempt to prove, against Descartes, that the possibility of empirical self-consciousness presupposes and establishes "the existence of objects in space outside" the mind.[1] But his attempt was futile inasmuch as he, too, had accepted the idealist presupposition,[2] so that the "outside" was for him on his own theory only a department of mental, *i.e.* intramental, phenomena.

Had we no cognitive activities, and therefore no conscious data, of *the sentient order*, it is impossible for us to form any positive conception as to how self-consciousness would take place, or what sort of self it would reveal: we have only a negative and analogical knowledge of the modes of being and knowing with which pure spirits or pure intelligences are endowed.[3] It is in the exercise of cognitive activities of *the sentient order* that we do *de facto* become directly and concomitantly aware of ourselves as conscious beings. Nor, indeed, does it seem possible that *our* intellects, in the total absence of all data of the sort we call *sense*-data from consciousness, could elicit *any* act, or therefore become at all self-conscious. For in such an hypothesis intellect would have *no objects* to apprehend, inasmuch as all the objects of its *direct* activity (including the concrete self or *Ego*) are given to it, and attainable by it, *only in and through the sentient mode of cognition* which apprehends concrete,

---

[1] *Critique*, pp. 799, 705 n. [2] *Cf.* § 97, p. 7, n. 4.

[3] According to scholastic teaching their knowledge of material things would be got not by abstraction but by innate universal concepts. *Cf.* ST. THOMAS, *De Veritate*, Q. viii., art. 9; *Summa Theol.*, I., Q. lv., art. 2.

individual, actually existing sense-data.[1] Of course by *reflex*
action it recognizes itself as immediately given in its direct
functions of conceiving and judging those data of sense ; and it
does so directly and concomitantly even in these direct functions
themselves (95).   But the possibility of these direct intellectual
processes is conditioned by the *sense* apprehension of concrete
data : *Nihil est in intellectu quod non prius fuerit in sensu* (71, 74,
77).   So, too, therefore is self-consciousness.

This expression, " self-consciousness," is perhaps ambiguous. It usually
means the consciousness of self, revealed in psychological reflection or the
deliberate introspective contemplation of our direct mental activities (95).
But these activities themselves are conscious : and *all* consciousness is in a
certain sense consciousness of self, " *con (cum)—scire* " : it is at least the
concomitant awareness of the self or *subject* together with awareness of an
object : not of course an awareness of the self *as such*, but an awareness
which *reveals* the self in the concrete as part of the whole conscious datum.
Reflex consciousness, then, in the sense of introspective contemplation, is not
the first or original revelation of the self ; it rather *recognizes as the self* the
subject which is already *revealed*, but not *recognised* as the self, in the direct
conscious processes of perceiving, conceiving, judging, reasoning, etc.

Now the functions of reasoning and judging are dependent on the
function of conceiving.   And if we call all three functions by the common
name of " thinking " or " thought," then,—since we cannot consciously
" think " *in vacuo,*[2] *i.e.*, without thinking some object, and since we get the
original data or objects, on which to exercise the function of conscious thought,
only in and through sense perception,—it can and must be asserted that
even when the self is concomitantly revealed in our direct *thought* processes,
and recognized in them as the self by reflex intellectual introspection, it is so
revealed and recognized only *dependently on sense perception*, and not otherwise ;—unless, indeed, it be maintained that we do somehow, by direct or
reflex intellectual consciousness, become aware of our *intellectual* acts (and
of the self, in and through them) apart from and independently of the *objects*
of these acts.

Does consciousness, therefore, reveal our direct cognitive acts apart from
their objects ?

Direct concomitant consciousness certainly does not.   This, however,
must be carefully noted, that in at least some of our processes of *external
sense perception* we become,—*through the functioning of the organic, muscular, or motor sense, or feeling of effort,*—directly and concomitantly aware
of what we regard as the *perceptive act itself (e.g.* of seeing, hearing, touch-

---

[1] *Cf.* GENY, *Une nouvelle theorie de perception* (pp. 10 *seq.,—apud* JEANNIÈRE,
op. cit., p. 377 n.) : " No internal conception or perception can take place or have
meaning for us except dependently on an antecedent external perception ; the
Cogito itself is no exception. I do not apprehend myself *in vacuo*, as it were, but
only as knowing an object and first of all an object which is not myself ; the self
' ne se pose q'en s'opposant '."

[2] *Cf.* preceding note.

ing, etc.), at the same time as we become aware of the object of the latter.[1]
And by an effort of attention we may more or less distinctly segregate the
perceptive act, *as an organic event or object*, from the object which *as a
perceptive act* it reveals to us.   But this sort of apprehension of our perceptive
act itself as an organic event or object, is distinct from the concomitant concrete consciousness or awareness of self which is an inseparable and essential
feature of that act *as perceptive*.   For even if our acts of sense perception
did not thus reveal themselves to us, owing to their character as organic
functions of which we become aware through the internal organic and muscular
senses, they would still, *as acts consciously perceptive of objects*, make us concomitantly aware of themselves, or rather of ourselves, in the concrete : as
our direct *intellectual* acts must be held to do, though these are not organic ;
for *every* cognitive act *as such*, must, being conscious, reveal *subject, act*, and
object together in the concrete.

Neither, therefore, can reflex consciousness, or reflection on the whole
direct cognitive process, reveal the direct cognitive act as *cognitive* or *perceptive* (and with it the agent or subject), *apart or in isolation from the object of that act*.   But reflex consciousness or psychological reflection can of
course recognize, more or less in isolation, the *organic process* which was
revealed more or less in isolation by the internal organic and muscular sense,
as accompanying the *perception* (hearing, seeing, touching, etc.), of some object.   If, therefore, this concomitantly apprehended organic event be absent
from any cognitive act, as an index revealing the latter, then no conscious
awareness (whether direct or reflex) of such a cognitive act *apart or in isolation from its object*, would seem to be possible.   And even when the organic
event is present, and apprehended by the internal organic and muscular sense,
it is apprehended not as a *cognitive* act but as an organic event or object
merely ;[2]—nor can the act of the internal sense apprehending the organic event
reveal its own self (or its subject) apart or in isolation from this organic event
as object.

It is important to bear in mind that the concomitant ("direct") consciousness which is an inseparable and essential feature of *all* cognitive
awareness of any datum whatsoever does not reveal the *self* as *formally distinct from the non-self*, or even the conscious *subject* as formally distinct from
the *datum as object*.   Duality of *subject* and *object* is *involved* in all cognition, but it is only by *intellect* that the distinction is *apprehended*.   So, too,
some data of our conscious cognition are marked by a peculiar feature which
intellect interprets as *internality* or *selfness*, and others by an opposite feature
which intellect interprets as *externality* or *non-selfness*,[3] but again it is *intellect* that interprets this internal or external reference of consciously apprehended data as signifying that the former domain of data reveals the *Ego* or
self, and the latter domain the *non-Ego* or external universe.   Psychologists,
moreover, prove that this explicit judgment, whereby the individual explicitly

---

[1] In a similar way we become vaguely aware of the brain-effort, tension, fatigue,
etc., accompanying intense *intellectual* activity, owing to this latter being sustained
and subserved by the organic *sense* activity of the *imagination*.

[2] Having of course the characteristic of *internality* or *selfness*, but not yet
judged by intellect to belong to the *self* in distinction from the *non-self*.

[3] *Cf. supra*, § 97, p. 9, n. 2 ; *infra*, §§ 105, 109.

discriminates his own self or *Ego* from the remainder of the total content of his consciousness, comes comparatively late in the gradual development and growth of his mental experience : that in infancy there is no conscious distinction of self from non-self : that the earlier cognitions and implicit judgments of childhood rather tend to regard *all* their contents indiscriminately as objective and external.[1]

[1] *Cf.* MAHER, *op. cit.*, pp. 361-7, 474-92 ; JEANNIÈRE, *op. cit.*, pp. 379-80 ; *infra*, §§ 106, 107, 109, 116.

CHAPTER XIV.

EXTRAMENTAL REALITY. THE EXTERNAL UNIVERSE.

101. REALITY OF THE COGNITIVE ACTS OR STATES OF THE "EGO," COMPARED WITH REALITY OF THEIR OBJECTS.—We have already adverted more than once to the fact that philosophers generally appear to have experienced much more serious difficulty in explaining how the conscious self or subject can come to know any extra-subjective or mind-independent reality, than in explaining how the subject can apprehend its own reality as self or *Ego*.[1] The possibility of knowing a real, external, material, extended universe, distinct from the perceiving mind, has now to be examined by investigating the significance and validity of external sense perception.

We can, perhaps, best approach this subject by indicating here one reason of the idealist tendency to regard the only direct object of our knowledge as being something essentially mental, —a reason bearing on the nature of the objects of reflex or psychological introspection. These objects are our direct, conscious, cognitive acts. Now these acts are themselves realities : they constitute a domain of reality which we discover by turning our attention inwards from their objects to themselves. When we thus make them objects of our reflex consideration we tend to assimilate them to their own objects, *i.e.* to regard them as realities (or *objects* of cognition) *merely*, and to forget that they are realities of an altogether special kind, quite *sui generis*, inasmuch as they are realities which, unlike other realities, are not merely *objects of cognition* but are themselves *cognitions of objects*. If, therefore, we think of our direct knowledge (or cognitive acts) *merely* as a reality,—of the mental order of course, but yet as something which merely *is*, rather than as something which not merely *is*, but *knows*, or *has* itself *an object*,—we are tacitly accepting the implication that in this direct knowledge

---

[1] Vol. i., §§ 17, 19, 35, 75. *Cf.* PRICHARD, *op. cit.*, pp. 124-6.

2 *

"the world is not, at any rate directly, object of mind, for *ex hypothesi* a reality which merely *is* and is not the knowledge of anything has no object. Hence it comes to be thought that the only object or, at least the only direct object of the mind is this mental reality itself, which is the object of reflection ; in other words, that the only immediate object of the mind comes to be thought of as its own idea. The root of the mistake lies in the initial supposition—which, it may be noted, seems to underlie the whole treatment of knowledge by empirical psychology—that knowledge can be treated as a reality to be apprehended, in the way in which any reality which is not knowledge is a reality to be apprehended."[1]

Now, if the only direct object of the individual mind be assumed to be the mind itself as revealed in its own conscious states, and if some of these conscious states be regarded as " ideas " or " representations " or " appearances " of an external, material universe supposed to have a real being or existence beyond consciousness and independently of the *Ego*,—a universe which men spontaneously believe themselves to be directly aware of through their conscious acts of external sense perception,—the problem at once arises : Can we know with reasoned certitude that any such mind-independent reality exists, any reality whose real existence or *esse reale* is really distinct from the conscious states, or "ideas," "appearances," "representations," etc., of which alone we are assumed to be directly aware, and whose reality or *esse reale* is supposed to consist in their *esse ideale*, in their being objects of awareness, in their " being actually perceived," in their "*percipi*" ?   And if such reasoned certitude of a mind-independent, external, material reality be possible, how do we attain to it ?   This brings out the distinction between the *real* being, which things are supposed to have in themselves independently of our knowledge or awareness of them, or "things-as-they-are-in-themselves," or " things-in-themselves," on the one hand, and " consciously apprehended being," or "the being things have in and for cognition," or consciously apprehended " appearances " or " phenomena," on the other hand.   The distinction, which will recur repeatedly, will be found to have originated for each of us, and to be familiar to each of us, from the ordinarily experienced facts of external sense perception ; and in due course we shall examine its significance.[2]   It seems to suggest that while the reality of directly apprehended facts of consciousness is beyond all possible dispute, being identical with the conscious

[1] PRICHARD, *op. cit.*, p. 126.   [2] *Cf. infra*, chap. xx.

apprehension of them, the reality of anything beyond these is problematical.[1]

102. IS THE REALITY ("ESSE") OF CONSCIOUS STATES IDENTICAL WITH THEIR APPREHENSION ("PERCIPI")?—We may therefore ask what precisely is meant by the common assertion made in regard to all conscious, cognitive states, or data, or acts, —that their "*esse est percipi*," that their being or reality is identical with and consists in their being perceived.[2] A conscious, cognitive act is itself a reality. Now the assertion obviously does not mean that this reality is identical with any second, distinct, *reflex* cognitive act by which the reality of the first or direct cognitive act may be apprehended in its concrete happening. What it does mean is that the directly conscious, cognitive act itself is indeed a reality, but is also, as conscious or cognitive, a reality that is *sui generis*, a reality which differs from every other reality in this that while every other reality is *merely* an *object* of (possible or actual) cognition, this particular reality which is the conscious, cognitive act, is what it is because it reveals an object to a subject and thus *eo ipso* and simultaneously makes the subject aware of *object*, *act*, and *subject* in the concrete ; and that it would cease to be what it is if it failed thus to reveal *itself* (as well as its object) to the subject (or to be itself " perceived " or "known," "*percipi*," by the subject). In other words, it means that the *differentia specifica* of the reality which is a conscious, cognitive act as such,—that which marks it off from all other reality,—is *its being actually apprehended* (not by another act but in and through itself), so that it ceases not only to apprehend or reveal an object, but ceases *to be*, when it ceases *to be directly and con-*

---

[1] " If we apprehended our states of consciousness in a *representation*, and not intuitively and by identity, the question would be raised whether that *representation* faithfully presented them, or falsified them by disfiguring them. Hence we should have to seek for a criterion whereby to determine which states of consciousness *are* as they *are represented* (or *appear*), and which states are otherwise than they are represented; in other words, we should need a Criteriology of conscious representations. But that is just what no one has ever yet felt any need of [Query—What of Kant's doctrine of the '*phenomenal Ego*'? *Cf. infra*, §§ 111, 129]. Our conscious states are given by identity, without the intervention of any representation. They *are* what they *appear*, because for them *to be* and *to appear* are one and the same thing. In the domain of consciousness error is absolutely impossible [96]. And this is the basis of all criteriological research, which takes as undisputed starting-point the reality,—incontestable and uncontested,—of representative states of consciousness."—JEANNIÈRE, *op. cit.*, p. 394 n. *Cf.*, however, *infra*, chaps. xix., xx.

[2] " *percipi* " and " perceived " are understood in the wide sense of " cognosci," " being known,"—*awareness* of any sort.

comitantly apprehended. If other realities can be consciously apprehended, they are supposed to have and retain their reality independently of their being apprehended : they are supposed to have an *esse reale* independently of the *"percipi,"* *esse cognitum, esse ideale, esse intentionale,* involved in their becoming objects of conscious cognition. But the reality or *esse reale* of the conscious, cognitive act, as such, essentially is or includes this *percipi* or *esse cognitum* of the *object* (whatever this be, whether it be matter, spirit, self, non-self, mental acts, forms of thought, etc.) which this act reveals (together with itself) to consciousness.[1]

The whole direct conscious cognitive process may, no doubt, be deliberately made the object of a reflex act of psychological introspection, and may be analysed by acts of the intellect into subject, act, and object ; and in each of these reflex cognitions it gets a new *esse intentionale ;* but the direct act itself, in order to be apprehended in this same act, does not need to get an *esse intentionale* distinct from its own reality : in its own reality, in its *esse reale,* it is present to the conscious subject.

But it is to be noted that all this is true of the *actual existence* or *happening* of the conscious, cognitive act *as cognitive or perceptive of an object.* Every such act, however, besides being essentially conscious or cognitive of an object (under which aspect its *esse* is *percipi*), is in its real nature a vital act of a vital subject, and its real nature as such must be discovered by intellectual analysis of the whole cognitive process. Now if it be an act of sense perception its happening *as an organic event or fact* may be revealed as such to consciousness through the internal, organic and muscular sense (100); and as such it is seen to have an *"esse"* or reality which does not appear identical with its *"percipi"* any more than the *"esse"* of any other non-cognitive reality, such as a mountain, appears identical with its *"percipi"* . Attention to this fact would obviate much confusion and explain much apparent contradiction between statements made by different writers in regard to acts of sense perception.

I consciously judge, for instance, that "two and two are four". To say that the *esse* of that act is its *percipi* means simply that I could not judge

---

[1] Hence a cognitive act, as conscious, and as concomitant object of the mind's awareness, does not need, for such awareness, any *esse intentionale* distinct from its *esse reale,* to make it present to the mind, whereas every other supposed reality, other than a conscious act (which thus concomitantly reveals itself and its subject or agent in the concrete), does need, in order to become an object of awareness, an *esse intentionale* distinct from its *esse reale.*

"two and two" to be "four," I could not apprehend the objective relation between subject and predicate, unless in and by the act of apprehending I were made conscious of the presence of that objective relation to my mind and of myself apprehending it present. It does not mean that the act of judgment is the mere present and apprehended relation, or even the mere presence of the relation,—though without the relation, and its presence, the act of apprehension could not take place,—but that it is an act which essentially and by its nature gives the objective relation its mental presence, and would not be such if it did not give the object this presence and make me aware of myself apprehending the object.[1]

Again, "I see the paper on which I am writing". To say that the *esse* of the seeing is its *percipi* means that unless by the act of seeing the paper I were *aware* of *seeing* it, the seeing would not take place at all : I could not see the paper without being aware of seeing it : by the act of seeing I am concomitantly aware of myself seeing ; though by the mere act of seeing I am, of course, not aware of the *self* and the *seeing* as distinct from the paper, but of all together as one whole. Here, however, I may be simultaneously aware of an additional *datum, viz.* the muscular strain or tension involved in the organic activity of the sense organs, the eyes (100). And if I am, then in addition to my consciousness of seeing as an act *perceptive of an object*, I am simultaneously aware (through the internal, muscular sense) of seeing *as an organic act or event* (and concomitantly aware of this latter awareness).

Finally let us take this example, "I feel a toothache". Now a toothache is a conscious state. Did we not feel it, were we not aware of it, it would not be really there at all. There may be unconscious mental states, —we may leave that to psychologists ;—and there certainly are unconscious organic states,—that is, assuming matter to be a mind-independent reality ; —but a toothache, if and while it is an *ache*, is something of which necessarily we are aware or conscious. As a sentient conscious state or process by which we are aware of something its *esse* is *percipi*. That is, we could not feel or perceive the something without being aware of feeling or perceiving it. Feeling the ache is being aware of feeling it.[2] We could not feel without being aware of feeling. But if the *esse* of a toothache is thus its *percipi*, can it nevertheless be true to say, as Prichard says,[3] "It must in the end be conceded of a toothache as much as of a stone that

---

[1] The act of intellectually apprehending the objective relation, if considered in the abstract, apart from the latter, and from the presence of the latter to the intellect, is nothing that we can become aware of: it is of the concrete act whereby the relation is rendered present to, and apprehended by, the subject, that we assert that its *esse* is *percipi*, in the sense that concomitant consciousness of itself (and its subject) in the concrete is an essential feature of its reality, though not in the sense of denying this "*esse percipi*" to be a real vital process whose nature can be explored by reflection.

[2] If the "aching" or "painful condition" is itself described as a "feeling" we are using this latter term in its objective sense as the object of the conscious act by which we feel or become aware. *Cf.* "I feel (or am aware of) a feeling (or apprehended state or condition)".

[3] *Op. cit.*, p. 118.

it exists independently of the knowledge of it"? That it exists independently of our *reflecting* on it, thinking (judging, reasoning, etc.) about it (and "knowing" it in that sense), *yes :* the reality of my toothache does not depend on what I think or judge it to be, any more than in the case of the stone. That the toothache exists independently of my *feeling* or *being aware* of it (and "knowing" it in that wide sense of the term), *no :* the stone is a reality which I can conceive to exist without my being aware of it ; but the *aching* is a conscious process of an organic sense, a process which is indeed a reality but a reality to which my awareness of it is essential. In that it differs from the stone. Yet even in regard to *mere awareness*, is there not a sense in which a toothache is as independent of this latter as a stone? Yes, if I use the term "toothache" not in its meaning as a *conscious state or feeling*, but in its meaning as *a diseased physical or organic condition.*

The toothache in this latter sense is just as independent of my feeling or awareness as is the tooth itself, or as a stone : the stone, the tooth, and the physical condition of the tooth, we can and do conceive as having each alike a reality which is independent of our awareness of them : whether we are right in thinking them to have such a mind-independent reality being the main question of the significance and validity of sense perception.

All conscious states, processes and activities,—realities of the kind called "mental,"—are at all events realities of whose actual existence or happening the *Ego* is directly and immediately aware. But they belong essentially to the reality of the *Ego :* whether all or any of them bring the *Ego* into cognitive relation with any reality beyond and distinct from the *Ego* is the main point now at issue.

103. ALTERNATIVE METHODS OF JUSTIFYING SPONTANEOUS BELIEF IN THE EXISTENCE OF AN EXTERNAL MATERIAL UNIVERSE. (*A*) TRANSITION EFFECTED BY APPEAL TO THE PRINCIPLE OF CAUSALITY.—The question how we pass from a reasoned intellectual conviction of the real existence of the *Ego* (which has been already vindicated against Kant[1]) to a similar conviction concerning the existence of a material universe really distinct from and independent of the *Ego* (or of a material universe including the individual perceiver's own body, distinct from and independent of the latter's own mind), and the question whether the latter conviction (which exists in all men spontaneously) can be rationally justified, and, if so, how?—is it by reasoning from the implications of the former conviction? or by showing that the real existence of an external material universe is as immediately evident to the knowing subject (in and through external sense perception) as his own real existence is evident to him in and through *all* his conscious processes?—these are questions which can be answered only by

---

[1] *Cf.* vol. i., §§ 77, 89 ; *supra*, §§ 97, 99, 100.

the closest scrutiny of our cognitive processes, both intellectual and sentient, of their respective data, and of the implications of these data.

Nor do those who defend as rationally justifiable men's spontaneous conviction that they have knowledge of the existence and nature of a material universe really distinct from and independent of their own minds, justify this conviction on the same lines. For some of them, holding that the really existing *Ego* is not merely the first but the *only* reality *directly and immediately* apprehended and known by the individual mind as real, and convinced that the immediate data of external sense perception, the data characterized by "extensity" and "externality," can be themselves only intramental states of the *Ego*,—justify our belief in the mind-independent existence and reality of an external material universe by *interpreting* those data of external sense perception as *representing*, and *essentially involving* the existence of, such a universe beyond and distinct from the *Ego*. In their view the transition from knowledge of the real *Ego* to knowledge of the universe as a reality other than and distinct from the *Ego*, while grounded in external *sense perception*, is *effected* and *justified* only by *thought.* They effect the transition by the following line of argument :—

It is by intellect, by thought, that we apprehend, in and through the data of consciousness, the self as really existing, and judge the self to be an existing reality. It is through and from these data (all of which are within the domain of the *Ego*) that we form the concepts of substance and accident, subject and states, permanence and change, agent and action, cause and effect, unity and plurality, identity and distinction, the possible and the actual, essence and existence, being and knowing, etc., and find the objects of these concepts verified in the *Ego*. Reflecting on the judgments we form by means of these and other derivative concepts, we find that these judgments are objectively grounded (chap. viii.) in the nature of the conceived objects, and that the conceived objects themselves represent what is given (chap. ix.) in the concrete, individual data of consciousness. In the concrete *Ego*, therefore, including its whole conscious content, our thought apprehends the existence, and in some measure the nature, of reality. Among the intuitions it has of the nature of reality are the principles of identity, contradiction, sufficient reason, causality, etc. The first three of those enumerated, the *Ego* sees to be of necessary and universal application to whatever *really is*, the fourth to whatever *really becomes* or *happens* (64, 66, 93). Reflecting, in the light of this latter principle, on the conscious data of external sense perception,—data which men spontaneously judge to be external to, and other than, and independent of, the perceiving *Ego* (because of their peculiar feature of "externality"), but which cannot themselves be really anything other than the *Ego* variously affected,—we rationally infer, by the principle of causality, that those data, so characterized by the feature of "external reference," must have an *adequate* cause ; that this adequate cause cannot be the *Ego;* that they are therefore partially caused by an extramental reality beyond the *Ego*, *viz.* the material universe represented by those data of external sense perception or sense consciousness.

It is obvious, these philosophers point out, that if there be a reality beyond and distinct from the *Ego*, this reality, in order to be known, must be somehow really related to the *Ego*, must be *cognitively* identified with the *Ego*, must be somehow ("*intentionaliter*") reproduced in the *Ego*.[1]   This union is originated in sense perception or sense consciousness.   But the objects given in external sense perception, its data, are not *identically* the reality or realities beyond the *Ego*, but are only products of the former in the latter, products which are likewise representations or appearances of the former in the latter.   So that, although we may be said, by and in sense perception, *virtually* to effect the transition from *Ego* to *non-Ego* by becoming aware of *appearances* of the latter in the *Ego*, and by means of this awareness perceiving (though not directly and immediately apprehending) the *non-Ego* (for to "*perceive*"—"*per-capere*"—is to apprehend something *through*, or *by means of*, something else) ; nevertheless, since *perception* merely makes us aware of an *appearing datum*, and does not interpret its nature, or judge of its origin, or distinguish *Ego* from *non-Ego*, it is *thought* alone,—judging, interpreting, reasoning on and from those data,—that *formally* and *by deliberate reflection* effects the transition from knowledge of the *Ego* to knowledge of a real *non-Ego* or external universe.   And while thus justifying, through the aid of the rational principle of causality, our spontaneous conviction that we have genuine knowledge of the existence and nature of a real, material universe beyond consciousness and distinct from the *Ego*, our reason at the same time corrects the erroneous spontaneous conviction of what is called "naif" realism, the conviction, namely, that external sense perception reveals directly and immediately to the *Ego* what sort that material universe *is in itself*, instead of merely revealing, as it merely does, the various representations or appearances produced by that material universe in the consciousness of the *Ego*.

104. CRITICISM OF FIRST ALTERNATIVE.—Now it might, perhaps, be objected to this line of argument that it scarcely achieves its purpose.   Our abstract concept of cause has been shown to be derived by intellect from the individual data of consciousness (65, 75-6, 92-3).   The object of this concept has been shown to be really embodied in these data, and it is therefore validly applicable to them.   These data, however, even those of them characterized by "extensity" and "externality," belong—in the view we are examining— exclusively to the domain of the real *Ego*.   It would appear, therefore, that the concept of cause has objective reality, no doubt, and is validly applicable to all the realities revealed at any time within the domain of consciousness, *i.e.*

[1] This is a fundamental principle of the Aristotelian and scholastic theory of knowledge.   "*Cognitum est in cognoscente.*"   "*Amina cognoscendo quodammodo fit omnia*" ;   "*quodammodo,*" *i.e. intentionaliter* or *representatively*.   By knowledge the *Ego* is a *microcosm*, a conscious assimilation or apprehension or mirroring of the *cosmos* or *macrocosm*.

within the domain of the real *Ego ;* but since *ex hypothesi* it does not yet appear from inspection of the data of consciousness that there *is* any reality *beyond* the domain of the real *Ego*, it is not clear how the principle of causality can attain to any such reality for us.

Of course it will be pointed out that our intellect, once it has abstracted from the data of consciousness the concept of "something happening," and grasps what this necessarily involves, *viz.* "having a cause," sees immediately and intuitively the necessary and universal applicability of this principle to *all contingent reality as such.* Granted ; but at this stage the mind has, *ex hypothesi,* no knowledge of any reality beyond the *Ego :* since *ex hypothesi* the conscious data characterized by a feeling or sentiment of "otherness" or "externality" are only modes of the real *Ego ;* and the plain man's spontaneous interpretation of them as being *really other* than his *Ego*, or as directly and immediately revealing to him a reality other than his *Ego*, is not at this stage rationally justified,[1] and therefore is not *knowledge* of a *real non-Ego.*

But, it will be promptly urged, we can see by introspection that the whole internal panorama of ever changing, ever appearing and disappearing data, which fill up the conscious domain of the *Ego, cannot be adequately accounted for* by the reality which is the *Ego*, so that we are forced to infer, by the principle of causality, the existence of a reality beyond, and distinct from, and other than, the *Ego.* This *seems* unanswerable. But let us see. The panorama referred to certainly cannot be adequately accounted for by the real *Ego* so far as this real *Ego is revealed in consciousness*, by the real *Ego as consciously apprehended*, or—to put it yet another way—by the *portion* (of the real *Ego*) *revealed in consciousness.* But since, on the hypothesis under examination, we have at this stage neither *knowledge* nor even *sense-awareness* of any *other reality* [2] than the *Ego*, so far from being forced to infer, as a *necessary factor* in the *adequate cause* of our conscious states, a *reality other than the Ego*, we are *actually debarred from making this inference*, and are forced rather to infer that since the consciously apprehended portion of the *Ego* is not the adequate cause of our conscious states, these must be partially caused by the *Ego* acting *unconsciously* and in a manner unknown to us.

And why are we, on the theory, debarred from inferring a *reality other than* the *Ego ?* Because although the data of our consciousness have

[1] Nay, the spontaneous interpretation of these data characterized by "otherness" or "externality," as being *identically* the real *non-Ego* or material universe (thus thought to be immediately and directly given to the *Ego* in external sense perception), is regarded as an *erroneous* conviction by those who reject the theory of immediate sense perception in every form.

[2] It is admitted on the theory that we have sense awareness of *conscious data* characterized by the *feeling* of "externality" or "otherness"; of what we therefore call "appearances" or "representations". But it is held that these are modes of the *Ego*, that sense awareness does not extend beyond them, and that the judgment whereby (without invoking the principle of causality or having recourse to inference from effect to cause) we spontaneously interpret them as revealing to the *Ego* a *reality other than* the *Ego*, does not of itself give us direct and self-evidently justified intellectual knowledge of the existence of a reality other than and distinct from the *Ego.*

furnished us with abstract concepts of unity and plurality, permanence and change, identity and distinction or otherness, etc., and although these concepts are therefore validly applicable to the real *Ego* in its conscious states, at the same time if the conscious data from which they are derived are all *modes of the Ego*, it is impossible to see how the concept of *real otherness* in the sense of *distinction from the Ego*[1] can be obtained from such data ; and yet, *unless we already have such a concept* (*i.e.* of *real* otherness or distinction from *the Ego*, or, of *real non-selfness*), and know it to be objectively and really valid, it is obvious that the principle of causality cannot avail us to infer a cause *really other than the self*.

It may be urged against this that the concept of *real distinction* or *real otherness*, which we undoubtedly derive by abstraction from the real diversity and real changes in the conscious states of the real *Ego*, is seen to be applicable to *all* reality, and therefore to the relation between "the real *Ego* of which we are conscious," as one term, and "some reality other than this," as the other term. We reply that this is so, *provided we already have this latter concept*—of "some reality other than the self,"—and *know this concept to be objectively and really valid*. But on the theory we are examining it seems impossible not merely to know this concept to be valid, but *even to have it at all*. And why ? Because on this theory the only concept of *distinction* or *otherness* which we can derive from the data of our direct consciousness or awareness is the concept of distinction or otherness *among the data, and within the domain, of the real Ego*. For on this theory the *sense-feeling* of "externality" or "otherness" or "*non-selfness*," attaching to some of those data, does not enable us to judge, or justify us in interpreting intellectually, those data to *be really other* than the self. How could we, therefore, on this theory, ever obtain or form the conscious intellectual concept of the *non-Ego* at all,—seeing that the theory denies that there is among the data of our direct consciousness or awareness any counterpart or foundation for it ? In other words, unless *reality other than the self* is immediately given to the self among the data, and in the states, of the latter's direct consciousness or awareness, it seems impossible for us to attain *intellectually*,—by any reflex thought processes of interpreting and reasoning from such data,—to *reality other than the self*. For the concept really requisite for such a transition, *viz.* the objectively and really valid concept of "non-self reality" would not be in our possession.

If, finally, those who think that the *reality* of the *non-Ego* or material universe is not immediately revealed in direct external sense awareness, but only a "product," an "appearance," a "representation" of this universe,— a conscious datum which, though characterized by its feeling of externality, is yet a mode or state of the real *Ego*,—if such philosophers say that in this same sense-feeling of externality attaching to such data we have the veritable and sufficient sense-counterpart and foundation whence to derive by intellectual abstraction the concept of "reality other than the *Ego*,"—then they account, indeed, for the existence of this intellectual concept and for our conscious possession of it, but how do they vindicate its objective and real validity ?

---

[1] And not merely in the sense of distinction or otherness *of one conscious datum from another* within the *Ego*.

If the sense-feeling of "externality" (and "extensity") attaching to certain conscious data of external sense perception cannot be itself interpreted by intellect as manifesting those data to be themselves direct and immediate revelations to the Ego, of a *real non-Ego*, or a reality other than the *Ego*,—if, in other words, notwithstanding this remarkable characteristic of such data, we must on reflection intellectually pronounce such data to be in themselves and in their reality only modes of the real *Ego*,—then does it not follow that the abstract intellectual concept of "reality other than the *Ego*,"—grounded as it is on a feeling which is after all subjective and not significant (to intellect) of *real externality* or *real non-selfness*,—cannot be itself *objectively and really valid?* If the concept be derived from data which, whatever be their external reference, are really modes of the *Ego*,—or rather from a *sense* feature of these data which has itself for intellect no significance of external or non-self *reality*, how can that concept itself enable *thought* to attain to an *external reality*,—seeing that the content or object of the concept is merely the *intellectual abstract* of the *concrete* "sense-feeling of externality," a content which we might describe as "external *appearance*," or "*apparent* externality," or "*ultra-conscious* reference of the *Ego*-reality"? Or how can recourse to the principle of causality serve to give the concept, as its content or object, that which we are looking for, namely, "external or non-self *reality*"? For this principle, as we saw, can itself merely assure us that the total *conscious* content of the *Ego* is not self-explaining. It is at this point precisely that the collateral concept of *distinction* or *otherness* must come in to give definite, positive content to the causal or explaining factor to which the principle of causality refers us.[1] It is not the principle of causality that gives

---

[1] Hence the importance of investigating carefully the origin and grounds of our concept of the *absolute or major real distinction*, understood as the distinction between one really existing being and another, and the tests for the objectively and really valid application of this concept. The whole question is discussed in our *Ontology*, §§ 23, 35-9. *Cf.* especially, § 38, p. 148, where it is pointed out that the relation of efficient causality is not of itself sufficient to establish between the terms of the relation (cause and effect) a real distinction in the sense of a distinction between one existing being (the *Ego*, for instance) and any second really existing being (*e.g.* the *non-Ego*). Of course the relation of efficient causality is sufficient to justify our concept of a real distinction in the sense of a distinction between real states (especially successive states) in the really changing contents of the *Ego* as a self-conscious reality. But if we reflect, in the light of the principle of causality, on the fact that we find in our consciousness states or data which, although they are contingent and therefore caused, we nevertheless do not know to be caused by the self so far as we are conscious of the latter, this reflection alone cannot possibly reveal to thought a *reality other than the self* : it merely identifies the cause (referred to by the principle) with this reality, *provided we have already* what we know to be an *objective and really valid concept of non-self reality*. The question then is, can *thought* (meaning intellectual abstraction, generalization, conception, judgment, and reasoning) reach a *non-self reality* if no such reality be directly and immediately given to the *Ego* in any of its mental processes of direct conscious cognition or awareness? It does not seem possible. We know it is contended by some that even though direct *sense* awareness reveals merely the *Ego*,—variously impressed or affected by conscious states, some of which have an appearance of, or reference to, externality or non-selfness,—nevertheless *thought* can validly conceive and attain to non-self *reality*. But it cannot do so, as we have seen, by the principle of causality,

a positive content to the concept of *otherness-from-the-self.* The objective and real validity of this concept must stand or fall on its own merits. If the direct conscious data on which it is based, and from which it is derived, reveal *only* the *Ego,* it is objectively and really valid only in its application to these conscious data within the real *Ego.* If it is based on, and derived from the direct *sense-feeling* of *externality* in certain of those data, then (1) if this feeling of externality has no significance of *real* externality for intellect, this concept of otherness, together with the principle of causality, can refer us only to an ultra-conscious domain of the real *Ego,* but not to a *reality other than* the *Ego;* while (2) if this sense-feeling of externality reveals the data characterized by it as *really other than,* though directly and immediately manifested to, the real *Ego,* and if intellect can and does interpret as really valid the external significance of this consciously apprehended characteristic of the data of our external sense awareness or sense perception, then indeed the abstract intellectual concept of *otherness,* in the requisite sense of "otherness-*from-the-self,*" is itself objectively and really valid,—and gives definite and positive content to the ultra-conscious causal factor to which the principle of causality refers us. But in this case *we do not really need the principle of causality* to give us reasoned intellectual certitude of the existence of a real world distinct from the *Ego.* For by virtue of the objective and real validity of the concept of "reality-other-than-the-*Ego,*"—a validity which it derives from the conscious data of our external sense awareness, from the fact that a non-self reality is directly given to the *Ego* in these data, as evidenced by their characteristic of "externality,"—we *already possess reasoned intellectual certitude* for the judgment, "That which I apprehend in external sense perception, and the nature of which I interpret intellectually by judgment and inference, I know to be a real universe really existing distinct from, and independently of, myself the perceiver and knower".

unless it has already the valid concept of such reality. And how the concept can be valid if the feeling of externality or non-selfness in the conscious data of external perception,—the feeling from which alone such a concept can be derived,—cannot be itself intellectually interpreted as a direct manifestation of a *real non-Ego* to the real *Ego,*—how in such an hypothesis the concept can be regarded as really valid, we fail to see.

In the context referred to (*ibid.,* § 37, p. 147; p. 146 n.; pp. 151-3), the conclusion is reached that *abstract thought alone* cannot attain to, or identify, the distinction which is the most real of all distinctions, *viz.* that between one individual existing real being and another: of which distinction the most profoundly important instance is the distinction between the real *Ego* and *reality other than the Ego.* It is shown there that for the vindication of the objective and real validity of this distinction abstract thought must appeal to direct conscious awareness of reality in the concrete. But if in the domain of the mind's *direct and intuitive* awareness (whether sentient or intellectual) of reality, there is given *only* the *self-reality,* it is not easy to see how intellectual reflection (through abstract concepts) can ever effect a valid transition from such real *self-*data to a *non-self-reality* (and not merely to an unconscious or subconscious or ultra-conscious domain of the *Ego,* as the intellectual analogue of the "externality"—and "extensity"—of certain of these conscious self-data).

105. (*B*) SPONTANEOUS CONVICTION OF THE EXISTENCE OF AN EXTERNAL MATERIAL UNIVERSE RATIONALLY JUSTIFIED BY INTELLECTUAL REFLECTION ON THE NATURE AND CHARACTERISTICS OF EXTERNAL SENSE DATA.—This brings us to the second of the above-mentioned (103) alternative methods of vindicating a reasoned certitude for men's spontaneous conviction that they can and do know the existence, and something of the nature, of a real material universe independent of their own minds.   According to this view a real external universe, a reality other than the *Ego*, is *given* or *presented* to the latter in the data which we are made directly aware of in external sense perception.   The *Ego* has from the beginning conscious data characterized by the feelings of what we intellectually conceive and describe as "voluminousness" or "extensity," and "externality".   The data so characterized are the foundation and source of our abstract concepts of "extension," "impenetrability," "matter" or "body," "non-self,"[1]—concepts which we compare and contrast with the concepts of "conscious apprehension," "conscious unity of the manifold," "conscious being," "mind," "self" or "*Ego*," concepts simultaneously formed by intellectual activity, direct and reflex, from *all* the data of our direct awareness.   Now we *spontaneously* judge or interpret the data which furnish us with the former set of concepts,—especially the data accompanied and marked by the feeling of "externality"[2]—to be *a reality other than the perceiving and thinking self*.   And reflecting on this spontaneous judgment, and on the concepts whereby we formed it, we can and do see the judgment to be true and the concepts to be objectively and really valid. That is to say, external sense perception, by revealing to us "external" data, reveals to us what we, by interpreting them, rightly judge to be *a reality other than the self*.   In other words, the characteristics of extensity and externality, in certain conscious data, which made these latter *appear* as external to the

---

[1] The concept of "object-of-awareness" is also derived *de facto* from such data, though it can be derived even from the most purely subjective data of consciousness; for intellect sees involved in all possible awareness duality of "conscious subject" and "apprehended object".

[2] The feelings of "extensity" and "voluminousness," which yield the concepts of "extended or spatial reality," "matter" or "body," we do not at first, but only later, detect as characterizing some data which do not appear as "external" but as "internal" or "self" data; and thus we come to realize that the "self" is not merely a "thinking subject," but likewise "a sense-perceiving subject," and is as such *corporeal* as well as conscious or mental. *Cf. infra*, § 116.

Ego when directly aware of them, are now regarded, and rightly regarded, by intellect reflecting on them, as furnishing to intellect direct and immediate evidence, objective and real evidence, for the reasoned judgment that "those data *are really* an actually existing material universe distinct from the reality of the self or *Ego*".

According to this view of the matter, therefore, the real *non-Ego* is just as directly and immediately given in cognition as the *Ego* (100). It is *given* in our direct conscious awareness of data marked by "extensity" and "externality". In our *spontaneous* interpretations of these data of external sense perception it is *cognized* as *really other than the Ego*. And rational *reflection* on the direct data from which we form the concept of a "*real non-Ego*" justifies the objective validity of this concept, and the truth of the judgment wherein we predicate it of these data.

It is true, indeed, that the reality of the *Ego* is the reality about whose actual existence reflection shows our spontaneous conviction to be most unshakeable (31, 35). But do I know my "self" or *Ego* as a permanent being, abiding self-identical amid change of conscious states,—as a being which persists in existence independently of my awareness of it, and whose "*esse*" is not mere "*percipi*,"—have I *this* sort of knowledge of the *Ego antecedently to*, and *as a prerequisite condition for*, my *reasoned conviction* [1] that there also exists, besides myself, a real *non-Ego* which is also a being or domain of being that persists independently of my awareness of it? The former conviction is *not* a prerequisite of the latter. For the very concepts, by the application of which to *some* of the conscious data of the *Ego* as a self-conscious subject, I reach the *former* conviction,—*viz.* the concepts of "actually existing being" (objective to a subject aware of it, and involved in this awareness), "substance," "states," "change," "permanence" or "duration," "identity," etc.,—these very same concepts I *simultaneously and independently* apply to *other* of these data (those affected by "externality"), and I do so with a consciousness *that the application is valid;* and I thus reach the *latter* conviction (*viz.* that there is a *real non-Ego*, which also permanently persists throughout change and independently of my awareness of it) *concomitantly with* my reaching the former.

I see, of course, that this *real non-Ego* must be *cognitively related* to my real self, must be "made one" with me "cognitively" or "*intentionaliter,*" in order that I become aware of it or know it at all, and that this holds good even for my direct sentient awareness, no less than for my thought and reflection. But just as I do not see that a *real identity* of that which I know or become aware of, with myself knowing or aware of it, is *essential* to my knowing or being aware of it, or how such supposition can in the least *help*

---

[1] It is obvious that such a knowledge of the self is not a prerequisite condition for (*a*) my awareness of "externality," or awareness of a distinction between conscious data of external perception ("strong" or "vivid" data) and conscious data of imagination, conception, etc. ("weak" or "dim" data); or (*b*) for my *spontaneous* intellectual *conviction* or *judgment* that the data which thus *appear* as external *are really* external to myself who am aware of them.

me to realize *how* I even know or become aware of my *self* (17, 19, 35, 75, 101) ; so, too, I do not see how I can attain to a reasoned conviction of the separate existence of the *real non-Ego* by *thought*, *i.e.* by way of *inferring*[1] such existence from my own self-known real existence, or even by the use of *concepts* in *judgment* to *interpret* certain data as revealing a *real non-Ego*, *unless these concepts are really and validly applicable to these data, and are already known by me to be thus applicable :* but they cannot be, and be known to be, thus applicable, unless the concrete data of my direct *sentient* awareness— the data from which the concepts are derived—reveal to me, and put me into direct and immediate cognitive relation with, a *real non-Ego* (and not merely with an " externally appearing " phase or aspect of the reality which is my self). The fact is, therefore, that a *real non-Ego* is revealed to me in the data of my direct external sense awareness or perception, and *because it is*, the concepts which I use in judging spontaneously that they reveal a really existing *non-Ego* or external universe are objectively and really valid ; and because reflection shows the fact and the reason of their validity, our spontaneous conviction of the actual existence of an external material universe independent of conscious perception, and distinct from the *Ego*, is *eo ipso* transformed into a reasoned philosophical certitude.

Not only, therefore, does it appear superfluous to appeal to the principle of causality as a means of vindicating philosophical certitude for the spontaneous conviction that the perceived external material universe exists independently of our perception and thought ; but such an appeal would even appear *to be futile in the very hypothesis in which it is deemed essential*, and *to be useful*—as a corroborative vindication—*only in the hypothesis in which it is not really essential*, for this purpose. For if we hold that the *Ego* can and does directly apprehend a *real non-Ego* in the data of external sense perception, and that therefore the concepts whereby we spontaneously judge these data to *be* a *real non-Ego* are validly applied, then by mere reflection on these percepts, concepts, and judgments, and without any appeal to the principle of causality, we have transformed our spontaneous conviction into a reflex certitude.[2] While if we hold that the *Ego* can directly and immediately apprehend, in and through the concrete data of its *direct sense* consciousness or awareness, *only itself* (however variously impressed or affected), how can *thought*, by means of *concepts* derived from such data, *interpret* these or any of them to *be* a *real non-Ego*, or *infer* that any of them involve *real otherness* or a *real non-Ego* ?

At the same time it is conceivable that reflection on the difficulties which may be urged against the possibility of a *direct sense awareness* of anything *really other* than *states of the conscious Ego* would destroy a person's spontanoeus belief that he has in fact such a direct *sense* awareness of a *real non-self world or universe*. And such a person might nevertheless not only rationally justify his conviction that he knows his own self as a real existence ; but also convince himself that the concepts abstracted by his *thought* activity

---

[1] By the principle of causality.

[2] Of course the argument from causality will then confirm this certitude (111) by making us realize that without the already discovered *real non-Ego* as partial cause of our conscious cognitive states, the succession of these in the *Ego* would be inexplicable and unintelligible.

from the concrete data of his direct awareness, and the necessary principles apprehended by thought in the domain of such concepts, are *objectively* and *universally* valid in their application to *all* reality, whether in the domain of *thought* or of *sense.* The exercise of *thought* (thus admittedly valid) in inferring the actual existence and nature of a *real non-Ego* by virtue of the principle of causality, might then effect for such a person the transcending of the self, or the transition to a *real non-Ego*, even though he had persuaded himself that such transcendence or transition was a feat that lay beyond the power of the mind's direct " external " sense awareness.[1]

But it is not likely that many of those who deny that there is any rational justification in the conscious data of external sense perception for the spontaneous judgment that " a reality other than the self exists," will admit that the argument from causality rationally justifies this judgment (vol. i., p. 134).

Moreover, the inference from the *real Ego* to a *real non-Ego* by way of the principle of causality, seems to us to labour under the drawback already indicated : [2] that the principle of causality obliges us to infer *merely* that there *is and must be* an *adequate* cause of our conscious states, that if the *Ego* as consciously apprehended is not adequate cause of them there must be some partial real cause of them *beyond consciousness ;* but it does not assure us that this something beyond consciousness is a reality *other than* the permanently subsisting real *Ego* itself. In other words, the argument does not seem effectively to exclude *monism* of some form or other. The falsity of monism can be effectively established only by vindicating the validity of the *major real distinction* in its application to the objects of our concepts of the *real Ego* and the *real non-Ego.*[3] Of course our concept of " real distinction " or " real otherness," applied to the *non-Ego* as compared with the *Ego*, will be shown to be valid if we can show that it has a real foundation in the concrete data from which we abstract the concepts of " self," " non-self," and " otherness " or " distinction," in the domain of our direct consciousness or awareness. Now if we divide this latter domain into immediate data of *intellectual thought* (" intellectual " consciousness) and immediate data of *sense awareness* (" sense " consciousness), and hold that intellect or thought proper (as well as sense) has direct intuitions of individual concrete existences or happenings, it will not be contended that any of *these* intuitions reveal, or furnish data for the abstract concept of, a *real non-Ego.* For such intellectual intuitions are generally understood to apprehend exclusively the *Ego* consciously thinking, conceiving, judging, reasoning, willing, etc. ;—the view of William of Occam, that *intellect* has direct and immediate intuition of external or non-self reality (82), being regarded as singular and erroneous. The concepts *abstracted* from such intuitions, therefore, cannot reveal a *real non-Ego* to us, for although they are of course *indirectly* applicable to *all* the conscious data we can think of (even those characterized by " externality "), by being *directly* applicable to *our processes of thinking* of these latter, nevertheless, since our consciousness of this " externality " is *ex hypothesi* not recognized to be a *valid cognition* or awareness of an *external* or *non-self reality*, the application of such concepts to " external seeming " data of consciousness cannot trans-

---

[1] *Cf.* JEANNIÈRE, *op. cit.,* p. 224 n.   [2] *Supra,* § 104.
[3] *Ibid.,* p. 29, n. 1.

form these latter into a *non-self reality*. Moreover, as was pointed out above (100) the intuitions and concepts of this intellectual or thought-domain of consciousness are dependent for their existence or occurrence on the direct conscious activities whereby we become aware of what are known as *concrete sense data: nihil est in intellectu quod prius non fuerit in sensu:* the original data of all cognitive activity are given in direct sense awareness.

In these latter, therefore, we must finally seek a valid foundation for our abstract concepts of a "*real non-Ego*," and "*real otherness or distinction from the Ego*". Now, if reflection were to pronounce these sense data, *including their felt characteristic of "externality*," to be really modes or phases or manifestations of the *reality of the Ego*, how would the abstract concepts (of "extension," "matter," "otherness" or "distinction," etc.) *abstracted from* such data by *conception* and *validly applied to them again* in *judgment*, transcend the real *Ego* in such application? They could not transcend it. Or if we applied such concepts in such a way as to make them transcend the real *Ego*, *i.e.* by assuming them to reveal to us a *real non-Ego*, would such application be really valid? It would not; for such concepts would, *ex hypothesi*, not have been derived from any *real non-self data;* they would have had, *ex hypothesi*, no foundation in any *real non-self data ;* since the seeming or felt "externality" of sense data would have been, *ex hypothesi*, not an evidence of *real* externality or non-selfness, but only after all a peculiar and unexplained feature of certain conscious states of the *Ego* itself.

Of course, if our intellectual concepts were innate, *i.e.* obtained by us independently of sense data and sense activities, and if in addition it could be proved·that intellectual cognition revealed to us, through such concepts, and therefore also independently of sense, a domain of real being that would be "objective" not merely in the sense in which every cognition as an act of awareness has an "object," but in the sense of "non-self" or "really distinct from and other than the knowing subject," then indeed it could be intelligibly maintained that even though *sense* did not attain in perception to the *real non-self*, but only to a consciously apprehended mode of the self, nevertheless *intellect* could attain to the real non-self (namely, by the concept of "cause" and the principle of causality) and could prove the "consciously apprehended mode of the self," present in perception, to be at once a *product* and a *representation* of the non-self in the perceiving and knowing subject.[1] But our concepts are not innate ; they are not formed independently of sense-data ; our vindication of their real validity (*i.e.* of Moderate Realism, *cf.* 76-8) has consisted in showing that the objects or contents revealed by them in the abstract to consciousness are the identical objects or contents revealed to consciousness in the concrete in our acts of internal and external sense perception—on the assumption, which we then promised (72) to prove at a later stage, that these latter objects or contents are realities. Now the concept of *real externality* or *real-otherness-from-the-self* is a concept of supreme importance in its bearing on the problem of the knowing subject's capability of transcending self in the process of cognition ; and upon the validity of its appli-

---

[1] *Cf.* PRICHARD'S analogous view that our intellectual knowledge of space and spatial relations is independent of sense perception,—*infra*, §§ 125, 128.

cation to the whole domain of reality which we spontaneously believe to be external the validity of this belief depends. If, therefore, the concrete sense datum (of "felt externality ") from which this concept is formed, cannot be shown, by direct intellectual reflection upon it, to be *real, i.e.* if the data which *are felt* (or *appear*) to be external in normal external sense perception cannot be seen by intellect reflecting on them *to be* eo ipso *really* external, how can we hope to vindicate such real externality for those data, and such real validity for the concept of externality, by appealing to any evidence that can be furnished by *another* concept, namely, that of *causality*, if this concept too be derived, as it is, from immediate data of conscious, concrete (internal) intuition and (external) perception, while as yet none of these immediate data have been shown to be themselves externally real ?

But the contention that intellect, contemplating the direct and immediate data of conscious external sense perception, finds these to constitute an external, material universe distinct from the *Ego*, is not without its difficulties. These we shall examine in the course of the exposition of facts and theories in the paragraphs that follow. The facts are not very numerous ; but the theories,—from absolute subjectivism, idealism, or scepticism, to the most "ingenuous" or "naïf" realism,—are even bewildering in their abundance.

CHAPTER XV.

VALIDITY OF SENSE PERCEPTION: REAL EXISTENCE OF AN EXTERNAL, MATERIAL UNIVERSE.

106. THE FACTS OF SENSE PERCEPTION.—I. All men have an invincible persuasion that certain objects *appear* to them, and *are perceived* by them, as distinct from, and outside of, themselves, and as endowed with certain features such as extension, impenetrability, shape, colour, etc. This *feeling of externality*[1] of such objects has never been denied by even the most extreme sceptics.

II. Hence, men spontaneously judge that outside themselves, and independently of their conscious perceptions, there actually exist real things endowed with such features and qualities. This we may call the *spontaneous judgment of externality or otherness*. It involves two sorts of judgment, the judgment of *existence*,— that a "reality or realities external to the perceiver exist,"—and the judgment of *nature*,—that "this reality is such and such," *e.g.* soft, spherical, cold, yellow, sweet, etc.; that "this is an orange," "that is an oak," "that is a horse," etc., etc. That men spontaneously make and believe such judgments is likewise universally admitted.

III. Antecedently to philosophical reflection men spontaneously believe that the existence of a real, external, material universe, existing independently of their perception of it, is as indubitably evident to them as their own individual existence. Nay, when we want to express the strongest intellectual certi-

[1] Some authors say that on reflection this feeling of externality can be indubitably detected only in the data of *sight*; others only in the data of *touch*; others only in these *two* domains of data; others in the data of *hearing* as well; others even in the data of *taste* and *smell*. *Cf.* JEANNIÈRE, *op. cit.*, p. 385 n. All sensations reveal *objectivity* of course (§ 19). But not all reveal *externality*, *e.g.* the organic sensations whereby we become aware of the internal states and conditions of our bodies. Similarly, the feeling of *voluminousness* or *extensity*, which is held by some psychologists to characterize the data of *touch* alone, is held by most to affect the data of *sight* as well, and by many to affect in some measure the data of all the senses. *Cf.* JEANNIÈRE, *op. cit.*, p. 401, n. 2.

tude of the truth of any judgment we describe it in terms
borrowed from sense perception, we say that such a truth is
manifest, as clear as noonday, palpable, that we *see* it, etc., etc.
It is admitted that so irresistibly does this persuasion of the
independent existence of an external universe force itself upon
men that even those cannot eradicate it, but continue to act on
it, who come to regard it as theoretically indefensible (37).

IV. We classify the conscious data or objects of sense perception into certain broad, clearly distinct and mutually irreducible domains: into colours, sounds, tastes, smells, organic
states (of bodily pleasure, pain, etc.), pressure, resistance to
muscular effort, heat and cold, size and shape, rest and motion,
position, location, number, etc. It is admitted by all that we
have such diversely qualified data or objects of sense awareness.

V. Even a moderate measure of reflection on the various
qualities which we thus apprehend in the "external" data of
sense awareness, and which we ascribe to things spontaneously
judged to exist outside us and independently of our perception,
will convince us that some of those qualities seem to be more
dependent than others, for what they appear to be, on the actual
condition of the bodily sense organs,[1] to be more *relative* than
others to the self as sentient subject. When, for instance, we
say that this stone is *hard*, this orange is *round*, this grass is
green, these clouds are *moving;* and then that this water is
warm, this wine is *mellow*, this perfume is *pleasing*,—we realize
that the former group of qualities belong to the subjects to which
we attribute them, more absolutely and independently of ourselves, than the latter group do to theirs: that what feels warm
to one hand may feel cold to the other, that the same "thing"
may not "taste" or "smell" the same to different people, or to
ourselves at different times, etc. This broad fact is undisputed;
not so, however, its significance, or its application in detail.

VI. Reflection also reveals, among the qualities of sense data
or objects, another broad distinction which has been recognized
in one form or other at all times by students of sense perception:

---

[1] Or, of the self as a *corporeal, organic,* conscious subject. The body, with its
sense organs, is apprehended by us in two distinct ways : (a) by our external senses
in the same way as we apprehend the "external" universe, and as similar to the
latter (corporeal, or material, extended, etc.) ; (b) by the internal, muscular, organic
senses, the functioning of which accompanies that of the external senses and concomitantly reveals the bodily organism as the sentient-conscious self or subject.
The former apprehension may be described as objective, the latter as subjective.

the distinction between what scholastics have called the "proper sensibles" (*sensibilia propria*) and the "common sensibles" (*sensibilia communia*). The former are the concrete qualities, or "qualified" data or objects, of *each separate sense:* colours, sounds, tastes, odours, pressures or resistances, temperatures, organic states. The latter are concrete, "qualified" data or objects, apprehended *in common* or *by more than one sense channel:* shape (*forma vel figura*), size or volume (*magnitudo*), number (*multitudo*),[1] rest, motion. The former are also called the "secondary" sense qualities, and the latter the "primary" sense qualities, of matter (or of "corporeal" or "sense" data).

This division of sense data into "primary" or "common," and "secondary" or "proper," is recognized as grounded in consciously apprehended differences between the two sets of data respectively. But its significance and implications are much disputed. The former or "common" sensibles are clearly all concrete modes of "extensity" or "voluminousness," and appear to be data of sight[2] as well as of *touch*. *Superficial extension* (or *coloured* surface) certainly appears to be a direct datum of *sight*.[3] The *three* dimensions of extension (length, breadth, and depth)— not separately and in the abstract, but together, as "concrete voluminousness"—are a direct datum of *touch* (*i.e.* of the passive sense of pressure, and the active or muscular sense of motion and resistance, combined) ; but whether the third dimension of space is a direct datum of sight, *i.e.* whether, independently of tactual, muscular, and motor sensations, the sense of binocular vision can or does reveal to us *depth* or *distance* from the perceiver, or objects *in relief*,—is a question to which psychologists usually reply in the negative.[4] But, even so, the appellation, "*common* sensibles," is a justifiable description of the concrete modes of extensity which have been so designated.

107. THEIR PSYCHOLOGICAL EXPLANATION AND THEIR SIGNIFICANCE FOR EPISTEMOLOGY.—Now, psychologists are concerned with explaining the origin or genesis, and the growth or

---

[1] *I.e. concrete* multitude apprehended through awareness of *discontinuity* or *interruption* in our feelings of *magnitude* or voluminousn:ss.

[2] All the senses apprehend *change in intensity* of their respective data. The sense of *hearing* can thus, at least indirectly and by association, make us aware of *local motion*. Sensations of taste, being inseparable from accompanying sensations of touch, have a distinctly "voluminous" character ; those of smell also yield a vague feeling of extensity.

[3] *Cf.* MAHER, *op. cit.*, p. 87.   [4] *Ibid.*, *cf.* pp. 129, 135-144.

development, of the various phenomena just enumerated : of the conscious feelings of extensity and externality in certain data of our awareness ; of our spontaneous judgment that an external, material universe exists independently of our awareness ; of our spontaneous conviction that the existence of such a universe is self-evident ; of our spontaneous belief that we know something of the nature and qualities of this material universe ; of our spontaneous discrimination between our minds, our own bodies, and external bodies ; etc., etc. They are not concerned with the *validity* of these spontaneous judgments and beliefs, but only with the mode of their genesis and development from the primitive content of consciousness with its vague characteristics of "extensity" and "externality". Starting from these primitive data, they differ in their accounts of the way in which we come to form the spontaneous judgment and conviction that there exists a *non-Ego* or external universe really distinct from, and other than, and independent of, the *Ego.*

I. Some maintain that the reality of the *non-Ego* is *given* in external sense perception just as early and just as immediately as the reality of the *Ego* is given in all conscious cognition ; and that therefore the spontaneous conviction of the reality of a *non-Ego* or external universe is an immediate interpretation of this originally presented distinction. This position is described as *Perceptionism,* or *Intuitionism,* or the *Theory of Immediate or Presentative Sense Perception.*[1]

II. Others maintain that the *non-Ego,* as distinct from the *Ego,* is *not* a primitive datum of conscious awareness ; that only the *Ego* is apprehended first and immediately ; that from its data there is evolved and mediated a conscious discrimination or distinction between a *non-Ego* and the *Ego,* and a spontaneous belief in the distinct reality of the former. This position is variously described as *Representationism,*[2] or the *Theory of Mediate or Representative or Inferential Sense Perception.* But its supporters differ in regard to the nature of the process by which apprehension of the *non-Ego,* and belief in its distinct and independent reality, are " mediated " : some holding that in the early stages of the conscious life of the individual *all* the conscious data are " internal " or " self " data, and that the individual gradually " ex-

---

[1] *Cf.* MAHER, *op. cit.,* pp. 101 *sqq.* ; JEANNIÈRE, *op. cit.,* pp. 379, 382.
[2] Or " Conceptionism " (*cf. ibid.,* pp. 223-4, 379),—a designation to be avoided as fostering a misleading use of a term proper to the domain of intellect.

ternalizes" or "projects outward" certain of these data, thus building up an "external" domain opposed to, and distinguished from, the "subjective" or "self" domain of reality ; others holding, on the contrary, that the actual process is quite the reverse, that it is a process of "subjectivation" or "internalization," that at first all conscious data appear to the individual as a confused and undifferentiated ocean of "objects," that most of them are gradually apprehended as "external" through a process by which others are "subjectivated" to form a conscious, sentient, organic self or *Ego*, and thus opposed to, and distinguished from, the main group as "objective," "external," or *non-Ego*.[1]

Whichever of these accounts of the genesis of our perception of, and spontaneous belief in, an external universe be adopted, the epistemological problem—the question of *the validity* of this belief—still remains. If men spontaneously judge that what is "given" in consciousness, as an "external," "extended" datum, is a reality other than the *Ego*,—are they *right* in judging so? Is the judgment justifiable before the bar of reason reflecting on the grounds of it? Or, if from the original data, in which that alone which is the real *Ego* is "presented," there is evolved by some process a mediate awareness wherein a "*non-Ego*" is "represented," what rational justification have we for the spontaneous judgment which, in asserting the independent existence of this "*non-Ego*" or external universe, *assumes the validity* of the "representative" or quasi-" inferential " process?

108. THE PROBLEMS AND THE THEORIES.—Can we, reflecting on the data of sense perception, have reasoned or philosophical certitude for the spontaneous judgment and belief that these data reveal (*a*) the existence, and (*b*) something as to the nature, of an external, material universe distinct from the perceiving subject or *Ego*? The answers of philosophers to these questions have varied from the most extreme subjective idealism to an equally extreme affirmation of the naïf realism of the credulous and unreflecting mind. Broadly speaking, the two alternative attitudes—of those who doubt or deny, and of those who affirm and maintain, that we can have such certitude—may be described as *Idealism* and *Realism* respectively. But there are many different phases and degrees of both.

I. *Idealism* doubts or denies that anything beyond the *Ego*, the psychic facts of the self, can be objects of knowledge,

---

[1] *Cf.* JEANNIÈRE, *op. cit.*, pp. 380-1.

can be known really to exist. Hence it is also called *Subjectivism: sceptical* if it *doubts, dogmatic* if it *denies* the possibility
of such (reasoned) knowledge of a universe beyond the *Ego*.
This is the logical issue of the Idealist Postulate, that the
mind cannot transcend itself to know anything beyond its
own states : a postulate insinuated by Locke, partially applied
by Berkeley to deny the reality of matter, fully applied by
Hume to reduce *all* knowledge to awareness of mental "appearances" or "phenomena," and by Mill in his reduction of all
reality to " sensations *plus* permanent possibilities of sensations ".[1]
Idealism is *absolute* or *total* if it holds the sole knowable reality,
the sole object of knowledge, to be the subject's own conscious
states or "representations": the position of Fichte, Schelling,
Hegel, Schopenhauer, Renouvier,[2] etc. Akin to this is what
Leibniz first called "Solipsism" : the view that the conscious self
is the sole reality—with the unverifiable possibility of other similar but really distinct conscious "selves". Idealism is *relative*
or *partial* if it admits philosophical certitude as to the existence
of *something,* some *reality,* other than the *Ego,* but interprets
too narrowly the nature, scope, and object of this certitude.
Thus, Berkeley's *Immaterialism* is subjectivist in so far as it
denies the existence of a material universe as a mind-independent reality, but is "realist" or "objectivist"[3] in so far as it
accords to this universe the reality which consists in its being
a system of perceived, mind-dependent ideas,[4] produced in finite
spirits or human minds by the Infinite Spirit, the Deity. Again,
Kant's *Transcendental Idealism* is a partial or relative idealism
inasmuch as, while it denies that a real *non-Ego* or mind-independent reality can ever become an object of *knowledge,* or
be *known,* it admits that this ("unknowable") reality must be
thought or *postulated* as really existing, and that belief in the
validity of this postulate is justifiable. So, too, the agnostic
position of positivism and phenomenism,—in recognizing the
rational necessity of postulating a reality beyond the domain
of the conscious self, and at the same time denying that we can
know anything about this reality,—is a partial or relative ideal-

---

[1] *Cf. Ontology,* §§ 61, 63, 75.

[2] *Cf.* JEANNIÈRE, *op. cit.,* pp. 381, 438.

[3] Hence it has been described as "objective idealism". *Cf. I.E. Record,* vol.
xxiv., pp. 280-2 ; *infra,* § 123.

[4] Entities the *esse* of which is identically their *percipi* (*cf.* § 102).

ism : a position for which Spencer lays claim to the title of *Transfigured Realism.*[1]

II. *Realism* maintains that we have adequate intellectual justification for (*a*) the spontaneous judgment that a real, external, material universe exists independently of our perception of it ; and for (*b*) many of the spontaneous judgments we form as to its nature and qualities ; while (*c*) reflection can correct the errors of other spontaneous judgments too hastily formed by misinterpretation of our sense perceptions. But between the naïf, ingenuous, unreflecting realism which, by overlooking the part which the sentient self or subject has in determining how external things "appear" in sense perception, often erroneously attributes to these external things qualities or natures which they do not really possess in themselves,— between this extreme form of realism on the one hand and certain other extreme or *hypercritical* forms of realism on the other hand,—forms which almost merge into idealism by declaring all our qualitatively differentiated sense data to be subjective, conscious products, which are merely *symbolically* indicative of the real nature and qualities of the external or non-self universe,[2]—there are many intermediate shades of what is known as *moderate* or *critical realism.* Naturally, too, as regards the *manner* in which we come to know the independent reality of an external universe, the advocates of naïf realism hold the theory of *immediate* or *presentative* or *intuitional* sense perception ; the advocates of hypercritical realism, that of *mediate* or *representative* or *inferential* sense perception ; while among the supporters of moderate or critical realism some hold that sense perception is immediate or presentative or intuitional, others that it is mediate or representative or inferential.[3]

---

[1] *Cf.* JEANNIÈRE, *op. cit.*, p. 437. For different kinds of idealism, historical sketch of its development, and bibliography, *cf. ibid.*, pp. 430-40.

[2] *Ibid.*, p. 425, n. 2.

[3] It may be well to note that the term "inferential" in this general context is ambiguous. What it can mean as descriptive of the process of sense perception itself we shall inquire later. Here we need only call attention to the fact that even if the process of sense perception itself be held to be an *immediate intuition* of a *presented* external sense datum, and even if the spontaneous intellectual processes whereby we *conceive* this presented datum and *judge* it to be really external to us be held to be not "inferential," but motived by immediately apprehended intellectual, objective grounds or evidence, we can also, by *intellectual reflection* on these direct sensuous and intellectual processes, *infer* from the data of sense, by means of the principle of causality (105), that *there is* a reality external to us, or that *it is really* such or such, and that our direct, spontaneous judgment *was justifiable and correct :*

109. DIRECT VINDICATION OF BELIEF IN THE REAL EX-
ISTENCE OF A MIND-INDEPENDENT, EXTERNAL, EXTENDED,
MATERIAL UNIVERSE.—We have already shown that reflection
on the facts of consciousness and memory (97-9) justifies our
spontaneous conviction that the *Ego* is a real substance which
persists self-identically in existence throughout its intermittent
conscious states, and is not the mere series or stream or current
of these states. Will rational reflection also justify our spontaneous conviction that of these data the whole domain marked
by the features of "extensity" and "externality," and therefore
designated as "material," is likewise a domain of substantive
realities which persist in their existence independently of their
intermittent presence in consciousness, or of our actual intermittent perceptions of them?—that the "*external*," "extended,"
or "material" data are really distinct from the percipient subject
or *Ego?* and that the "extended" but "*internal*" material
datum which we call "our body" and which we include in the
total, composite reality of the self or *Ego*, also persists in existence independently of our intermittent mental awareness of
it? The answer is that rational reflection *will* justify these
spontaneous convictions and transform them into reasoned or
philosophical certitudes.

If we can justify our conviction that an extended, *external*
domain of material reality exists independently of, and really
other than, the *Ego* and its perceptive processes, we shall have
no difficulty in recognizing as also rationally justified the conviction that the extended, *internal* material datum which we call
"our body," and which we regard as united with the conscious,
mental principle of our being to form the composite individual
self, also persists in existence independently of its intermittent
presence in consciousness (116).

How, then, are we to vindicate a reasoned, philosophic
certitude for the former spontaneous judgment?

In the first place by a deliberate intellectual scrutiny of the
character of those concrete conscious data which we have called
"common" and "proper" sensibles. It is an absolutely undeniable and universally admitted fact of introspection that some
at least of those data appear or present themselves to conscious-

---

so that even the perceptionist's *fully reasoned conviction or certitude*,—that the
directly perceived external reality is indeed external to him,—can be legitimately
described as being, unlike his sense perception, an *inferential* process.

ness endowed with the concrete character of "externality" or "otherness," that they appear or present themselves as external to, and other than, the conscious, sentient self or *Ego :* coloured external surface extension, resistance or impenetrability, size or volume, shape, spatial continuity or unity, or discontinuity or multitude, spatial motion or rest,—these undoubtedly appear or present themselves as external to and other than the percipient subject. Now if they were not *really* external to and other than the *Ego*, we must ask not only *why* and *how* do they *appear* so, but also *whence* could we derive, or *how* could we possess, the abstract *intellectual concept* of "externality" or "otherness-from-the-*Ego*," at all (104). At some stage or other in the development of the individual's *perception*-processes certain data are concretely felt or apprehended as being of such a kind or so characterized that the individual's *intellect* derives this concept from them and interprets them to be really what this concept represents them to be, *viz.* external to and other than the self. But if those consciously apprehended sense data were really only the self appearing in various phases to the self, and if the felt concrete character of externality or otherness were merely the result of subjective processes of the self opposing and externating certain phases of the self to the self, then the *concept* of "externality" or "otherness" (or "real distinction" in the sense of "otherness-from-the-self") would be objectively and really a groundless and invalid concept; and, furthermore, the appearance of the concrete feature of externality in certain sense data would, as a fact of consciousness, be absolutely unexplained and unaccounted for, nay, would be inexplicable and unaccountable.

For if the data *felt* to be external or other than the self were not *really* external to and other than the self, why should they be *felt so ?* Or what intelligible ground is there for an assumed unconscious sense process whereby the self is supposed to "externate" certain phases of itself, and thus to mediate and lead to what would be the *illusive and deceptive intellectual* processes of spontaneously conceiving and judging this "externality" or "otherness" of such data to be real? There is no rational ground for the gratuitous supposition of such a process,—a process which, if real, would involve in our very nature as cognitive beings a radical and incurable self-deception.

But if, on the contrary, such data are really external to and other than the self, there *is every reason* why they should *be felt to be so,*—and as we shall see presently, there is *no reason* why they should not. Their character of concrete, felt externality, then stands explained. The abstract intellectual concept of externality or otherness is grounded on and derived from an objectively real datum. And the spontaneous judgment which, by means of this concept, pronounces such data of sense perception to constitute an external material universe existing independently of the perceiving subject, is seen to be rationally justified. Moreover, just as conscious states, processes, activities, etc., and the conscious data of memory, involve the reality of the *self* as a permanent *substance*, an abiding, self-identical, substantial subject and agent of these processes (97, 99), so the concrete sense apprehension of the "external," "extended" sense data in question involves the judgment that size, shape, three-dimensional spatial extension, etc., are qualities of a persisting *material substance*. Thus, the "*sense* evidence" or "appearance-to-sense" of extended externality, is adequate "*intellectual* evidence" for the reasoned judgment: "There exists, distinct from and independently of the *Ego* and its conscious perceptive processes, a reality which has the *substance*-mode of being, *i.e.* which exists *in itself*, and which is *material*, *i.e.* endowed at least with the attribute or quality of spatial extension".

110. SOLUTION OF THE GENERAL A PRIORI DIFFICULTY OF IDEALISM AGAINST THIS BELIEF.—Before confirming this conclusion by appeal to the principle of causality (103), or attempting other conclusions which will raise certain difficulties in detail, we may here examine briefly one broad difficulty against the argument by which we have reached the conclusion just formulated.

How can a datum of conscious perception or awareness be really external to or really other than the conscious self or subject? If there be such a reality, a reality which has an existence or *esse* beyond, outside, independent of, and apart from perception, apart from what has *presence* or *esse* in consciousness, is it not clearly impossible for the conscious, sentient self to perceive, or become conscious or aware of, such independent *esse* or *existence?* All that we become aware of must be present in consciousness, and we can become aware of it only in so far as it is present in consciousness. To speak, therefore, of perceiving or becoming aware of any existence, or thing existing, outside and beyond and independently of consciousness, is a contradiction in terms. Whether or not the *only* "*esse*" of "things" is their "*percipi*," at all events their only *perceivable* or *knowable* "*esse*" is their *perceived* "esse," *i.e.* the "*esse*" which they have in and for the consciousness of the perceiver: and whatever this "perceived being" is, it certainly appertains to the perceiver; it is certainly something in and of and for the perceiver; and it certainly is not a "being" or "*esse*" beyond and distinct from and independent of the perceiver. This latter sort of being, if there be such, must be by its very terms unperceivable and unknowable. Therefore the concretely felt feature of "externality" or "otherness" in certain sense data must be itself something *in* the perceiver, and cannot prove those data to be really other than, and independent of, the perceiver.

Idealists, both "subjective" and "objective," ring the changes on this objection indefinitely.[1] It is at the root of the idealist theory of the relativity of all knowledge, according to which the object of knowledge is necessarily *immanent* in the knowing subject, and the latter cannot possibly become aware or cognizant of any reality *transcending* the conscious self or subject. We have met it more than once already (17, 19, 35, 75, 101). It rests partly on a confusion and partly on a gratuitous assumption.

When we say that we perceive a datum which is really external to and other than the self, we do not mean that this datum, when being perceived, stands out of all relation to the perceiver. To say so would indeed be a contradiction in terms.[2] The datum must be cognitively related to, or cognitively one with, the perceiver (20). If there be a reality external to, and independent of, the perceiver, then in order to be perceived it must become cognitively present to, or one with, the perceiver. It is therefore a misconception of the realist's position to represent this as involving the contention that a thing can be perceived out of all relation to the perceiver, or known out of all relation to the knower, or, in other words, that we can *perceive* an *unperceived* thing or know an *unknown* thing. This would indeed be a contradiction; "but there is no contradiction or absurdity in the proposition 'A material world of three dimensions has existed for a time unperceived and unthought of by

---

[1] *Cf. infra,* § 123; MAHER, *op. cit.,* pp. 111, 157-9; PRICHARD, *op. cit.,* pp. 115-18, 125; JEANNIÈRE, *op. cit.,* pp. 444-6.
[2] *Cf.* MAHER, *op. cit.,* p. 158, n. 26.

any created being, and then revealed itself to human minds'".[1]
And this is the veritable attitude of the realist.

The condition that the external or non-self reality, in order
to be perceived, must become cognitively present to, or one with,
the perceiving self, obviously renders not *the reality* itself, but *the
perception* of the reality, dependent on and relative to the perceiver.   That such an external, non-self reality can reveal itself,
or become present, to the perceiving self, has never yet been
disproved : and we hope to indicate later how we may conceive
this revelation to take place (*cf.* § 75).   But we do not hope to
show thereby *how* the fact of conscious cognition takes place.
For the fact of any conscious being becoming aware of anything,
or perceiving or knowing anything, whether this perceived or
known thing be the reality of the perceiver or a reality other
than the perceiver, is an absolutely ultimate and unanalysable
fact which must be simply accepted as such and which cannot
possibly be " explained," or resolved into any terms or stated
in any terms which do not themselves involve and assume the
fact which they are purporting to explain.[2]

This brings us to the gratuitous assumption which, in addition to the misconception of the realist's position, is involved in
the objection we are considering : the assumption, namely, that
whatever is an object of awareness or cognition[3] must be immanent in the conscious subject in the sense of being a determination of the latter as conscious, in the sense that its reality must
be mind-dependent or a manifestation of the conscious subject,
and cannot be anything transcending, or existing beyond and
independently of, the latter.   Thus understood, the assumption
appears to be a misconception of the true principle that whatever
is perceived or known in any way, whatever is an object of awareness, must be *in cognitive relation or union* with the perceiver or
knower,—as an apprehended object of the conscious, cognitive
subject.   This is universally true : and it is just as true of the
reality of the knower (as *object* of *self-cognition*) as it is of reality

---

[1] MAHER, *op. cit.*, p. 111, n. 7.   Cf. MERCIER, *op. cit.*, § 148, p. 405.

[2] Cf. PRICHARD, *op. cit.*, p. 124.

[3] To hold that the *direct and immediate* objects or data of conscious *sense* awareness or cognition are *entitatively* immanent in the *Ego* as *percipient* subject, but that
they *represent* realities other than the *Ego*, so that the latter can *mediately* or *inferentially* perceive the *non-Ego* (106, 108), and can through objectively and really
valid *concepts* attain to a *reasoned intellectual knowledge* of a real, external universe
(103-5),—this position is of course not idealism, but a form of critical realism.

other than the knower (19, 20). But to say that a reality, in order to be known, must be relative to, or dependent on, the know ing subject in this sense, is to say not that the reality itself, but its *becoming known*, its *becoming present* to the knower, its *actual cognition* by the knower, is dependent on the knower: that in order to be known the reality must be actually related to the knower by becoming cognitively present to and cognitively one with the latter. Now this is very different from saying that a reality, in order to be known, must be relative to the knower in the sense that the reality itself, and not merely its presence to the knower or its cognition by the knower, must be immanent in, and dependent on, and determined by,—and therefore in ultimate analysis be partially identical with, and be a partial phase or mani-festation of,—the identical reality which is the knower. This latter is the position of the subjective idealist. As we have pointed out already (101) it seems to spring from the latent assumption that there is some special and peculiar difficulty in conceiving how any being can become aware of reality *other than* itself, which is not encountered when we contemplate the possi-bility of a being becoming aware of the reality which *is* itself. But reflection will show this latent assumption to be groundless; for after all, the identity of a being with itself throws no light on the ultimate *how* and *why* of the fact of conscious cognition or awareness. The question, *How* can a being become aware of *the reality which is itself*, or become the known object of itself as conscious subject? is just as unanswerable as the question, *How* can a being become aware of *reality other than itself?* (19). For the general question, How can a being become aware of *anything?* brings us up against a fact which we must simply accept as ultimate and unanalysable.

To the observation that a stick or a stone or a tree or a plant is identical with itself, and yet not therefore aware of itself, so that *identity* throws no light on the fact of *cognition* (19), the subjective idealist would probably reply (a) that perhaps these things are, for all we know, aware of themselves ; and (b) that from our present (epistemological) standpoint, inquiring as we are into the conditions of the possibility of knowledge, we must start with the conscious events of the individual mind, and therefore do not yet know whether such things as a stick, or a stone, etc., are substantive and indepen-dent realities, and consequently cannot put them on the same level as the conscious *Ego*, or reason about them as we may about the latter, when exploring the conditions involved in awareness : wherefore it is idle to take such things as these, which are supposed to be exclusively *objects* of awareness, as helping us in any way to determine the conditions of the possibility of this peculiar phenomenon or fact of awareness in a reality (such as the conscious *Ego*) which is known to be *subject* as well as object of awareness.

In reply to (*a*), which the idealist urges merely as a defensive tactic, we need only observe that at least until such philosophical theories as panlogism or idealistic monism,—which maintain consciousness or cognition to be *essential* to *all* reality,—are proved, it is certainly the more reasonable course to accept as true the spontaneous conviction of mankind that such things as sticks and stones, trees and plants, are not endowed with consciousness or awareness.

It is, however, the second line of reasoning, (*b*), that reveals the real position of the idealist, and it is interesting to see whither it leads him. For if the idealist really starts, as he professes to start, merely with the conscious current or series of objects of awareness, and with no assumption whatsoever, except, perhaps, that of a *hypothetical* subject aware of such objects, then we have a right to ask him with what sort of "being" or "*esse*" he conceives this hypothetical subject to be endowed. If he says that the only "being" or "*esse*" he can legitimately ascribe to anything is the "being" or "*esse*" which consists in "*percipi*," in "being perceived" in "being object of awareness," then he cannot endow his hypothetical conscious subject or *Ego* with any being other than this, *i.e.* the "perceived being" of the intermittent current of objects of awareness ; and so he has not yet gained any legitimate knowledge of the conscious subject or *Ego* as a real, substantial, permanent, abiding being, with an "*esse*" or existence that is real in the sense of being other than and independent of the "perceived being" or "*percipi*" of objects of awareness : the only "conscious subject" or *Ego* to which he has attained is the ever-changing, intermittent flow of "perceived" or "percept"-entities ; and this does not help him. Such is the nihilistic *impasse* of the "logical idealism" of Remacle and Weber, to which Kant's subjectivism, and indeed all subjectivisms, ultimately lead.[1]

If, on the other hand, our idealist ascribes to his hypothetical "conscious subject" or *Ego* a being which as to its own reality is beyond and independent of the intermittent modes of "perceived being" which he supposes it to assume as object of its own awareness, then after all he is recognizing the possibility of a being having real existence independent of the "presence" or "perceived being" which it may also acquire by becoming an object of awareness. And if he accords such an absolute or mind-independent mode of existence to the reality which he thinks of as the conscious subject or *Ego*, is he not *eo ipso* claiming for himself the power of "transcending" the "conscious presence" or "perceived being," and attaining to the "absolute" or "mind-independent" being, of a reality, *viz.* the reality which is the *Ego*, no less than the realist does when he claims for the mind the power of "transcending" the "conscious presence" and attaining to the "absolute" or "mind-independent" being of a reality, *viz.* the reality which is the *non-Ego?*

---

[1] *Cf.* Jeannière, *op. cit.*, p. 447; Mercier, *op. cit.*, §§ 147-8; *Origines de la Psychologie contemporaine*, chap. v.

Nevertheless idealists cling to their postulate that the mind can know only what is " relative " to it in the sense of being mind-dependent, as if this were a self-evident axiom ; and they try to make it plausible by confounding it with the really self-evident truth that whatever is known by the mind must be "in " the mind or "relative " to the mind in the sense of being *cognitively related* or *present* to the mind. It is only in virtue of such a confusion that they can confront realism with the specious difficulty we have been examining. The worthlessness of such a line of argument is clearly exposed by Prichard in the following passage :—[1]

"At first sight it seems a refutation of the plain man's view to argue thus : 'The plain man believes the spatial world to exist whether any one knows it or not. Consequently, he allows the world is outside the mind. But to be known a reality must be inside the mind. Therefore the plain man's view renders knowledge impossible.' But as soon as it is realized that 'inside the mind' and 'outside the mind' are metaphors, and, therefore, must take their meaning from the context, it is easy to see that the argument either rests on an equivocation or assumes the point at issue. The assertion that the world is outside the mind, being only a metaphorical expression of the plain man's view, should only mean that the world is something independent of the mind, as opposed to something inside the mind, in the sense of dependent upon it, or mental. But the assertion that to be known, a reality must be inside the mind, if it is to be incontestably true, should only mean that a reality, to be apprehended, must really be object of apprehension. And in this case 'being inside the mind,' since it only means 'being object of apprehension,' is not the opposite of 'being outside the mind' in the previous assertion. Hence, on this interpretation the second assertion is connected with the first only apparently and by an equivocation ; there is really no argument at all. If, however, the equivocation is to be avoided, 'inside the mind' in the second assertion must be the opposite of 'outside the mind' in the first, and consequently the second must mean that a reality, to be known, must be dependent on the mind, or mental. But in this case the objection to the plain man's view is a *petitio principii*, and not an argument."

111. INDIRECT CONFIRMATION OF THIS BELIEF BY APPEAL TO THE PRINCIPLE OF CAUSALITY.—In the second last section (109) we vindicated a reasoned or philosophic certitude for the belief that "there exists, distinct from the *Ego*, an external domain of reality which appears as extended or material ". The argument was based on the evidence furnished by direct intellectual scrutiny of the data of conscious external sense perception. We have likewise shown that our *intellectual concept* of "other-

[1] *Op. cit.*, pp. 124-5.

4 *

ness-from-the *Ego*," or "externality," derived from those data, is objectively and really valid (105). We are therefore now in a position to corroborate the conclusion of our argument by considering our spontaneous interpretation of sense perception in the light of a principle, the universal validity of which has likewise been already established (65, 66, 93)—the principle of causality.

Those supporters of realism [1] who in the present general context rely mainly or exclusively on the argument from causality to establish the philosophical certitude of our knowledge of an external world, emphasize the universal real validity of the concept of cause ; and consider the argument peculiarly efficacious as against idealists.[2]   But even though the concept is universally applicable to contingent reality, and even if the idealist admits this, the latter has still to be convinced that there is contingent reality *beyond the domain of the subject's consciousness*,[3]—or beyond the reality of the *Ego* if he recognizes a real *Ego* as subject and cause of conscious states.   And of this we can hope to convince him, if at all, only by proving to him that the concept of "reality-other-than-the *Ego*," which he possesses in common with us, is an objectively and really valid concept.   But how can we prove that it is ?   Only by pointing out that the sensuously felt character of "extended externality " in certain of our sense data can be seen by intellect to be the source from which the concept is derived, and to be therefore for intellect adequate objective evidence of the real validity of the concept (104, 105). In other words, by the same line of reasoning, by the same sort of direct intellectual appeal to the characteristics of conscious sense data, as we have employed in our main argument for the mind-independent existence of a real non-self universe (109).   It is because we believe that if realism cannot be effectively vindicated, as against idealism, by that class of consideration, neither can it be effectively vindicated, apart from such consideration, by the principle of causality alone (*cf.* 105-6),—it is for that reason we now' bring forward the argument from causality merely as corroborative, and not in the first place.

[1] *Cf.* Jeannière, *op. cit.*, pp. 224-7, 382-92 ; Mercier, *op. cit.*, § 140, pp. 384-9.
[2] *Cf.* vol. i., § 35, p. 134.
[3] Kant, for instance, and English phenomenists, admit the validity of causality (as understood by them in the sense of a provisionally, or an absolutely, necessary sequence, respectively) as applied within the whole domain of empirical consciousness.   And even when we have proved against Kant that it is validly applied in inferring an ultra-conscious cause of this whole domain, the principle *itself* will not enable us to determine whether this latter cause is *one* or *manifold*.   We prove it to be manifold,—to be in part *the real Ego*, and in part a whole *pluralistic system* of realities *external to* and *other than* the real *Ego* (all alike themselves contingent, and therefore implying a Supreme Uncaused First Cause),—not by the principle of causality *alone*, but only by the collateral use of another and distinct intellectual concept, namely, that of *real distinction* or *real otherness*, a concept whose real validity, as marking off the "*Ego-* or *self*-reality" from "*non-self*-realities" (and these latter from one another), must be independently established.   We have shown this concept, as applied to the distinction between the *Ego* and the *non-Ego*, to be really valid because grounded in characteristics of the conscious sense data from which it is derived (104-105).

We have already proved, as against Kant,[1] that the *Ego*, through its conscious activities, apprehends itself *as a reality ;* that Descartes, in emphasizing the absolutely indisputable character of our knowledge of the real self in his principle, *Cogito, ergo sum*, was only re-echoing the traditional teaching of scholasticism from the days of St. Augustine (29, 34). Now this self reveals itself as consciously affected by what we may call an ever-changing panorama of apprehended data or objects, namely, the proper and common sensibles. Our conscious perceptions of these data are *contingent events.* Therefore, by virtue of the principles of sufficient reason and causality (64, 65,) these conscious perceptions of data or objects have an adequate cause. But such adequate cause cannot be the self, or anything in the self or really constituting or appertaining to the self. Therefore there must be, beyond and really distinct from the self, a mind-independent reality which, co-operating with the consciously percipient self, will adequately account for the perceptions *de facto* experienced by the latter. Hence there exists, distinct from the self, and independent of perception, a reality—which we call the external, material universe.[2]

Let us consider the steps in this argument. That the *Ego* has conscious perceptions whereby data or objects "externally-appearing," "extended," "coloured," "moving," "resisting," "sounding," etc., are presented in consciousness, is a fact admitted by even the most extreme sceptics and subjectivists : as also is the fact that these perceptions are contingent events, in the sense that they are not self-explaining, that they come and go, appear and disappear, begin to be and cease to be, and so call for explanation or demand a cause. And the objective, real validity of the principle of causality has been already established. Next, the adequate cause of them cannot be the self. Why ? This needs a little reflection.

The main reason is that *we feel ourselves passive* in experiencing such perceptions. Hence Kant recognizes that the empirical content of perception *is given to us from without*, that to account for our perceptions there is and must be a reality beyond and independent of them, and of the self as empirically revealed

---

[1] *Cf.* vol. i., §§ 97, 99, 100. *Cf. infra*, § 134.

[2] Berkeley's alternative inference—" Therefore there exists, distinct from and independent of our minds, a cause of these conscious states, which cause is the Divine Spirit "—will be examined later, § 123. *Cf.* JEANNIÈRE, *op. cit.*, pp. 401-4.

in consciousness (50, 51, 74). Hence, too, Fichte claims that epistemology must take as starting-point *the fact* that in the content of consciousness there is, besides the mobile, subjectively determined portion, another portion independent of subjective contingencies and inseparable from what he describes as the *feeling of necessity.*[1] We *feel ourselves passive, impressed, undergoing impressions, in sense perception.* That is, though the perceptions are *ours,* though it is *we* that *elicit* or *exercise* the conscious, perceptive acts, still we feel them as not being wholly determined by ourselves *in regard to what they reveal to us.* As to the specific character of the various data or objects revealed to us in perception (*i.e.* "*quoad specificationem*"), they appear to arise or take place in us or to present this specific character to us, independently of ourselves ; and therefore to have, as partial cause of their concrete happening, some reality other than the self. Reflection will confirm this spontaneous belief.

(1) It is not merely my *will* that determines these perceptions. I cannot have them by merely willing to have them. And as to what they are, when they happen, they are independent of my will. I cannot have the perceptions which consist in "seeing Rome," or "hearing music," or "carrying a weight," or "tasting sugar," or "inhaling the perfume of violets" by merely wishing to have such perceptions. And on the other hand, when I am in the condition in which I do actually experience any such perception I cannot cease to experience it merely by wishing it to cease.

(2) Nor is it my *imagination* that determines such perceptions. There is the most marked and indisputable conscious difference between the panorama of data or objects brought into consciousness by the play of the imagination in fancies, daydreams, reveries, etc.,—between what are called " mental images " or "*phantasmata,*"—on the one hand, and the data or objects of sense perception,[2] or what are rightly called *percepts,* on the other. Psychologists and philosophers have minutely analysed and abundantly illustrated these differences.[3] The former class of data are largely under the control of the will : we can direct, con-

---

[1] *Fichte's Werke,* i., 419,—*apud* MERCIER, *op. cit.,* p. 385. To this "feeling of necessity " belong the feelings of " extensity " and " externality ".

[2] Including the perception of *organic* states, organic pleasure or pain, etc., in the perceiver's own body.

[3] *Cf.* BALMES, *Fundamental Philosophy,* Book II., chap. iv.

trol, modify the order in which such images present themselves ; we can separate, combine, rearrange the images as we please ; we can thus "produce" or "construct" new data or objects from the remembered materials of perception ; and the power of the "productive imagination" is only limited by the range of those materials and its own finiteness. The latter class,—the percepts, —are, as we saw, beyond the control of the will : the order in which they succeed each other is not consciously determined by us, but is felt to be determined by something other than the self. Moreover, the two classes of data have been distinguished as "faint" or "weak," and "strong" or "vivid" states, or (as Hume named them) "ideas" and "impressions," on account of the superior definiteness, clarity and solidity of the percepts as compared with the images. Finally, in experiencing the latter we are conscious that we ourselves, by our own *active* exercise of imagination, are *producing* (not *ex inhilo*, but from the remembered data of perception) the flow or current of mental objects ; while in experiencing the former we are rather conscious of *passively undergoing* impressions made on us by something independent of the conscious *Ego*.

(3) Nor is it my *thought* that determines such perceptions or originates such data or objects. By thought the individual self or *Ego* elaborates logical relations, judgments, systems of knowledge, sciences, concerning the domain of perceived data ; but it certainly does not produce or construct this domain.

(4) But perhaps the same *Ego*, which *consciously perceives* these data, itself *constructs* or *produces* them by an internal, instinctive, unconsciously operating influence of its own nature? Well, if it did, such influence would have no other claim than its blind, unconscious character, to be described as an "instinct". For the forms of energy we describe as "instincts" in sentient beings follow fixed laws and are uniform and circumscribed in their results. But there is nothing of this in the ever-changing panorama of percepts which constitute the world of any individual perceiver's sense experience. Psychologists can with some success explore and formulate the laws according to which "instincts" operate ; but who has ever dreamt of seeking or formulating laws according to which the world of each individual's sense experience unfolds itself in the order, and with the qualities, which actually characterize it?

(5) But, dismissing the term "instinctive," may it not finally

be urged that, for all we know, it may be the real *Ego* itself that in some unconscious way, and by some unknown and unknowable laws, produces this whole panorama of sense percepts which we —spontaneously and inevitably, but so far as reflecting reason goes, unwarrantably—believe to be a domain of reality other than, and external to, the self,—unwarrantably, since on this possible hypothesis it would be but a phase or manifestation of the real self? Perhaps,—to use the picturesque words of Huxley,[1] —"For any demonstration that can be given to the contrary effect, the collection of perceptions which makes up our consciousness may be an orderly phantasmagoria, generated by the *Ego* unfolding its successive scenes on the background of the abyss of nothingness; as a firework, which is but cunningly arranged combustibles, grows from a spark into a corruscation, and from a corruscation into figures and words and cascades of devouring flames, and then vanishes into the darkness of night".

The concession Huxley had just made to realism was that "there may be a real something which is the cause of our experience".[2] And this something he now declares to be a hypothetical and unknowable real *Ego*,—in the sceptical spirit of Hume. Kant, as we have seen, so far from refuting this scepticism —which was the avowed object of his *Critique* (46, 48)—once more declared the *real Ego* to be unknowable ; and straightway illogically asserted a real distinction between the unknowable *real Ego* and the equally unknowable *real non-Ego*.

But, assuming that the idealist admits at least a real *Ego*, how are we to meet his assertion that *perhaps* the whole domain of data or objects of sense perception, *i.e.* the *seemingly external* material universe, is after all a creation of this real *Ego*, and therefore not really distinct from, and external to, the latter? Let us see what the supposition entails as a possible interpretation of experience. A simple example will help us.[3] Standing at the door and looking into the street, I consciously perceive a succession of data or objects : men, horses, trams, cyclists, etc., passing. Closing and opening my eyes alternately I apprehend different objects after each interval. My action is certainly the cause of my seeing or not seeing (*i.e.* the cause *quoad exercitium actus*). But my action of opening my eyes and seeing is not the cause of the order and diversity and variety of the perceived data

[1] HUXLEY'S *Hume*, chap. iii., p. 81,—*apud* RICKABY, *First Principles*, p. 273.
[2] *Ibid.*   [3] *Cf.* JEANNIÈRE, *op. cit.*, p. 391.

(*i.e.* the cause *quoad specificationem actus*). But perhaps the operation of some unconscious and unknown principle of my own being, of my own real self, is the cause of the specifically diversified successive data? If so, then, why is it that throughout the same total experience, with no apparent change in my whole self other than the successive closing and opening of my eyes, while some data constantly change, *viz.* the passing men, horses, vehicles, etc., *other data reappear as self-identical* each time I open my eyes, *viz.*, the pathway, the pavement, the houses and windows opposite, etc.? Because, the idealist will answer,—not, perhaps, without some sense of uneasiness,—there may be some unconscious, unknowable factor of the *Ego* so operating as to make certain data merely occur, without recurring, and to make others recur repeatedly. So this is the final assertion of the idealist who regards the cognitive transcendence of the self, in the process of cognition, as an impossibility: and indeed if he holds it to be an impossibility his only alternative is that there *must be* such an unconscious or subconscious factor of the real *Ego* as he refers to.

Now, if the idealist were to interpret this, his own final assertion, as necessarily implying literal *solipsism*,—the doctrine that himself, the individual perceiver, is the only reality, and that the whole universe is merely a manifestation of himself to himself,—we might feel in charity bound to warn his friends of his mental condition. But the idealists we have to meet in real life are those who give a quite sane interpretation of their position. Such a one will say to the realist: " The whole 'external' universe (including yourself) is *for me* simply *my representation*, just as the whole universe (including myself), 'external' to you, is *for you* simply *your representation*. But because you are *for me* simply part of my representation I am not so unreasonable, or unreasoning, or discourteous, as to regard you as being on that account one whit less real than myself. What I do contend for is that all reality *so far as it is knowable by me* is simply *a representation in me* of I-know-not-what, a something, which I necessarily think to lie beyond or below *my consciousness*, but which I cannot think to be a reality distinct from myself in so far as I think my conscious self to be a representation of it. And since I regard you and other men as having a mental constitution similar to my own, I am forced to conclude that each of us must finally regard his own conscious self, *i.e.* the sum-total of his conscious representations, and all other similar 'selves,' as

partial self-revelations or self-manifestations of One, Sole, Ultimate and Unknowable Reality, the Absolute."[1]

As against this attitude, how can it be shown that the *ultra-
conscious partial cause* of my perceptions, the cause which accounts
for their specific contents and diversity, for the element of orderliness in their sequence, for the persistence with which certain
groups recur, for *the character of mutual affinity* which Kant had
to recognize in them and illogically referred to the *unknowable
Ego*-cause rather than to the *unknowable non-Ego*-cause (vol. i.,
p. 214, n. 2 ; pp. 347-52),—how can it be shown that this *ultra-
conscious partial cause* is really distinct from, and external to, the
real *Ego ?* Not otherwise than by such an appeal as Jeannière
makes in the example given above to what consciousness testifies
as actually happening in sense perception. But if in such an
appeal we merely emphasize the *total absence of any evidence for
identifying* this *ultra-conscious specifying cause* of our perceptions
with the real Ego, the appeal is not conclusive. For the idealist,
as we saw, can still urge the *possibility* of such identity. To
meet this final position we must go farther and show, by such an
appeal, the *presence of adequate evidence* in conscious sense perception for the judgment whereby we assert *a real distinction*, a
relation of *real otherness*, between the *real Ego* and the *other real
determining factor or factors* of our perceptions. In other words
we must show, as has been shown above (109), by a direct appeal
to sense consciousness, that our intellectual concept of "real-
distinction-from-the-Ego," or "real-otherness-from-the-Ego " is
objectively and validly grounded in the *feeling of externality*
attaching to the data of external sense perception.

The authors who rely principally on the argument from causality to
vindicate a reasoned certitude for our knowledge of a really external universe

---

[1] The whole universe, then, in so far as men can know it,—including men themselves,—is a universe of mental phenomena, appearances, representations, of an
Unknowable Reality in individual minds. It may be recognized as such to be
orderly, to be a cosmos, to reveal purpose, intelligence, design ; and may be therefore
interpreted as indicating that the Reality of which it is a self-evolution or manifestation is Intelligence, Mind, Spirit. This is not far removed from the Hegelian
form of Monism. In so far as subjective idealism identifies " *esse* " (or, at least,
knowable being) with "*percipi*," the only difference between it and Berkeley's " immaterialism " is that the panorama of data consciously apprehended by the individual
mind is regarded by the former as subjectively produced by the one ultra-conscious
" Absolute Reality " (*Monism*), whereas in the latter it is regarded as a system of
" ideas " placed or produced by the Divine Spirit in really distinct created human
spirits or minds (*Pluralism, Theism*). Cf. *infra*, §§ 123, 155.

would, we presume, admit that the proved validity of the concept of "real otherness" is essential to their conclusion. They hold, of course, the real validity of this concept. And if faced, for instance, with Kant's contention that all so-called real distinctions are merely phenomenal, *i.e.* mental, and therefore validly applicable only within the domain of consciously apprehended data, they would have to show in the domain of direct consciousness real grounds for the validity of this concept, just as for the concepts of substance and cause. Now it is easy to show that the concepts of substance and cause are necessarily apprehended by intellect considering the data of direct consciousness, and that these data necessarily imply the *real Ego* as *real substance* and *real cause*. But in order to show that they imply *other* real substances and real causes, the concept of *real-otherness-from-the-Ego* must be likewise shown to be validly grounded in these data. Now we can show that it is so grounded only by pointing to its obvious basis in direct sense consciousness, *viz. the felt concrete character of "extended externality"* in those data, as *adequate intellectual evidence* of its real validity, and of its valid application in the spontaneous judgment whereby we affirm those data or objects to constitute a domain of reality other than the real (perceiving) *Ego*. But we thereby justify philosophically this latter judgment without appealing to causality at all : and that is why we have put this line of argument, rather than the argument from causality, in the first place (109).

Our position is that the spontaneous judgment whereby we affirm the external existence of extended material realities is a direct interpretation of the concrete, intuitively apprehended character of extended externality in certain sense data ; that we can rationally justify our certitude as to the truth of this spontaneous judgment by intellectual reflection on that concrete feature of the sense data, inasmuch as such reflection reveals to us the validity of the concept of "real-otherness-from-the-*Ego*," which concept we have already spontaneously utilized in that judgment ; that, granted the validity of this concept, we can also *infer* as a *conclusion*, by reasoning from the conceived character of these data as contingent, in the light of the principle of causality, the judgment which we have already *spontaneously formed*, and already *justified by direct rational reflection* on the immediately and intuitively perceived concrete character of felt externality in those same data,—thus corroborating, by such inference, our already reasoned conviction ; —that, finally, our conviction that this domain of external reality persists in existence when we are not actually perceiving it, is on a level with our conviction that the self or *Ego* persists in existence when—as during dreamless sleep or periods of unconsciousness—we are not actually aware of the self or *Ego, i.e.* both convictions have the same title to be called inferences from the direct data of consciousness, and, both being equally immediate or equally mediate, neither is strictly an inference from the other (97, 100, 105).[1]

[1] JEANNIÈRE (*op. cit.*, p. 391 n.) quotes the following extract from PIAT (*Un revenant éternel*, in the *Correspondant*, Oct. 25, 1895, pp. 357-8) : "When I place my hand against the wall of my room I establish conscious commerce with an object which is not myself, whose existence is independent of my own. . . . If after a time I again place my hand against the wall I experience once more the same phenomenon of resistance. The same a third time, and as often as I repeat the experiment. Whence I infer that there is beyond my sensation a reality which

"There are many," writes Mercier,[1] "who refuse to admit the necessity of an appeal to causality for certitude of the existence of an external world. They believe that we have a direct intuition of such existence. We are convinced that in this they are mistaken. We perceive immediately in our acts the existence of an *internal* [*i.e.* 'self,'] reality. We have *direct sense intuition of external things*,[2] and, without intermediary, we form the abstract *notion* of what they are ['de ce qu'elles sont,'—apparently the notion of them as 'external,' 'extended,' 'material,' etc. ; and, he should add, the spontaneous judgment that they are such as this (complex) notion represents them to be, with the spontaneous conviction that this judgment is true]. But it is impossible for us to *affirm with certitude the existence* of one or of many *extramental* realities without employing the principle of causality. In the ordinary course of life we do not advert to this inferential procedure, it has become so familiar to us ; habit diminishes the effort of attention and, by consequence, the consciousness of our [discursive or inferential] activity."

From all that we have said, the reader will see that we cannot agree with this view of the matter. Just as we "perceive immediately in our acts the existence of an *internal* reality," so we perceive immediately in the data or objects of these perceptive acts an *external* reality : as, indeed, the author himself asserts in the same context. Then, as to the existence of "extramental" realities, such existence can be affirmed with certitude "without employing the principle of causality," provided the extramental realities are cognitively related, or given, or presented, to the consciously perceiving, conceiving and judging mind, as they are in its concretely felt "external," "extended" percepts, and in the concepts of "extended externality" or "otherness" abstracted from those percepts : just as "without employing the principle of causality" the existence of the reality which is the *Ego*, the existence of the *real Ego*,[2] can be affirmed with certitude provided, and because, this *real Ego* is related, or given, or presented, to the mind in the intuitively

persists in its absence, a reality endowed with a principle of permanence. The astronomer who measures the earth's orbit apprehends the planet only at certain points in its course ; and these points he links up with lines which he has not experienced. It is by an analogous procedure that the psychologist works up his proof of an external universe."

It is quite true that such a process of inference enters, perhaps half unconsciously, into the formation of our conviction that the external world persists when we are not perceiving it. But it plays precisely the same rôle in forming our conviction that the *real Ego* persists in existence when we are not aware of it. This, however, does not alter the fact that without recourse to such a process in either case we can in actual direct consciousness apprehend both the *real Ego* and the *real non-Ego ;* and spontaneously judge both of them to be real, and really distinct ; and by immediate reflection on the characters of the actually apprehended conscious data convince ourselves that there is in these data adequate intellectual evidence to justify both judgments alike.

[1] *Op. cit.*, § 140, p. 386.   [2] Italics ours.

[3] *I.e.* the real *Ego* which is not merely the sum-total or current or series of all conscious data, but which is the substantial unifying principle of all of them; and which, be it remarked, is partly "extramental" in the sense that it includes the felt, extended, material organism or body, and is therefore as such partly "extramental" to consciousness in the same sense as the rest of the material universe is.

apprehended "internal-seeming" data of direct consciousness, both sensuous and intellectual. We can of course infer, by the principle of causality, the reality of the *non-Ego* which we have already both spontaneously and reflectively asserted to exist,[1] just as we can infer the reality of the *Ego* by the principle that perceptions imply a real perceiver. But the ordinary *judgments* by which men assert with certitude that this, that, or the other material thing is external to them, are not conclusions of an inference which has become sub-conscious through custom and familiarity. Whether the process of perception itself is not a sort of "inference" we shall see later.

But after all, it may be urged, is not the real existence of the *Ego* known prior to that of the *non-Ego ?—Proximus sum mihimetipsi*. Have we not emphasized the truth of the positive element in Descartes' principle, *Cogito, ergo sum ?* (100). Is not *it* indubitable even to one who doubts the reality of the *non-Ego ?* And therefore, is not knowledge of the latter somehow dependent on, and mediated by, knowledge of the former? Let us see.

It is quite true that since knowing is a function of the *Ego*, knowledge of reality other than the *Ego* must imply that such reality is related, presented, given to, and made cognitively one with the *Ego*. But so must the *Ego* itself be presented to itself in order to be known. Now let us take the *only* fact which has never been doubted by any sceptic, *viz.* the existence of a "stream," or "series," or "panorama" of "perceptions," "presentations," "representations," "conscious states," "objects or data of awareness "—call them what you will. If we limit the term "mental" to these "perceived entities," and call *them* "the *Ego*," then of course the most extreme sceptic will admit that the existence of the *Ego* is indubitably known. But was this what Descartes meant by the *Ego*, or what we mean by it? No ; but the real perceiver, thinker, knower (30, 31). And when he claimed certitude for the judgment that such a reality really exists, he was assuming (and rightly) the validity of certain intellectual concepts,—those, namely, of substance and cause or agent. But was such a judgment really indubitable? Well, Kant, for one, held it to be groundless,—pointing out that the only *Ego* of which we are certain is the "mental," "phenomenal" *Ego*, which consists in the panorama of representations, and that the *Ego*-substance, the *Ego*-cause or agent (which he of course recognized to be what people ordinarily mean by the "real" *Ego*), being "extramental" or "noumenal," *i.e.* not being any or all of the "phenomena," is necessary unknowable. And prior to Kant, the pan-phenomenism of Hume had likewise doubted the knowableness of the real *Ego* which Descartes declared to be indubitably known because indubitably given in and with the "representations". And so it is given ; only that the reasoned intellectual assertion of it implies the real validity of the concepts of substance and cause or agent. Reasoned intellectual certitude of the existence of the real *Ego* is, therefore, not wholly beyond the possibility of at least an unreasonable and *de facto* unwarranted doubt.

Now let us look at the relation of our certitude of a real *non-Ego* to the really indubitable stream of representations. And let us ask ourselves is doubt about *this* certitude really more possible or plausible, really less arbitrary and unwarranted, than the corresponding doubt about our certitude

---

[1] On the ground of the proved validity of our concept of real externality or real otherness.

in regard to the real *Ego*. It is hard to see how it can be so. We will not ask is the ordinary man really one whit less certain of the existence of an external universe than he is of his own existence. For of course he is not, but this is spontaneous certitude. Let us rather ask does the stream of conscious data furnish *equally valid* and *equally immediate* ground for the reasoned assertion that a real *non-Ego* exists, as it does for the reasoned assertion that a real *Ego* exists? The reader must answer this for himself. To us it seems that the answer must be in the affirmative. The spontaneous judgment that a real *Ego* exists, employs as valid the concepts of *substance* and *cause;* and reflection justifies the assumption of their validity by seeing them to be grounded in, and implied by, the stream of events called perceptions, representations, etc. So, too, the spontaneous judgment that a real *non-Ego* exists, employs as valid the concepts of *substance* [1] and *real otherness* or *real externality*, and reflection likewise justifies the assumption of their validity,—that of the concept of *real externality* by seeing this concept to be grounded in and implied by the concrete, felt feature of externality in certain of the contents of the stream or panorama of perceptions, and that of the concept of substance as in the former case.

It seems to us, therefore, that the rationally indubitable character of our spontaneous judgment that "there exists a *real Ego* (which is not merely the stream of representations but the living subject or substance that has or experiences them)," does not warrant us in pronouncing as any less indubitable, or more liable to rational doubt, the spontaneous judgment that "there exists

---

[1] And also the concept of *extension*, if the spontaneous judgment be taken to be —as it really is—" An *extended non-Ego* or external reality exists". Does this spontaneous judgment also imply as valid the concept of *cause?* We think that *de facto* it does not. If you ask the ordinary man why he is certain that you yourself are really external to him, his answer will not be, " Because I have certain sense impressions of which not I myself, but you, must be the cause"; rather his answer will be, " Because I see you ", We think, moreover, that the spontaneous judgment can be rationally justified by the reflection which will show the concept of " real externality " to be a valid concept. No doubt the consciously apprehended character of external sense perception as a process in which we feel ourselves *passive, impressed, influenced, acted on*, is one of the sources of the concept of cause ; and this concept may be, and perhaps often is, unconsciously operative in our spontaneous interpretations of the data of external sense perception. But nevertheless it is not the concept of causality, but the concept of real otherness or real externality, that gives the spontaneous judgment its specific meaning as an assertion that " *External* reality exists "; and moreover the proved validity of this concept is so essential to the justification of the spontaneous judgment that without it the concept of causality would, as we have seen, be unable to justify this judgment. The two concretely felt characteristics of the whole conscious content of external sense perceptions, *viz.* the feeling of *subjective passivity*, or of their being specifically determined independently of the self as conscious, *i.e.* of the self as concomitantly revealed in the perceiving acts, and secondly the feeling of *extended externality* of the perceived objects,—are themselves consciously distinct data. The former feeling is present even in conscious states identified with the *Ego* or subject as sentient, *e.g.* in perceptions of organic conditions, organic pleasures and pains. It is, therefore, not on the intellectual evidence furnished by *that* feature of our conscious percepts, but rather on the intellectual evidence furnished by the sense feature of *externality*, that our spontaneous judgment of real externality must primarily rely for its rational justification.

a *real non-Ego* (which is not identical with this stream of conscious perception-processes but has a *real being* that is independent of its *being perceived* in these processes)" ; nor does it warrant us in denying that the latter judgment can be rationally justified by the same sort of immediate appeal to the direct data of consciousness whereby we justify the former judgment, or in contending that it can be justified *only mediately* by an appeal to the principle of causality.

CHAPTER XVI.

PERCEPTION OF SENSE QUALITIES.

112. TWO REALIST THEORIES OF SENSE PERCEPTION.—
Having justified the conviction that a real, external, extended
universe *exists*, we have next to inquire what degrees or orders
of knowledge as to *its qualities and nature* can be seen by reflection to lie within the scope of our cognitive faculties; or, in
other words, what information can the proper and common
sensibles convey to us about its qualities and nature. We can
best approach this question by considering how a reality such as
the external universe, now proved to be distinct from and other
than the individual knower, can come at all within the scope of
the latter's awareness.[1]

Here scholastic psychologists are up to a certain point
unanimous. All alike teach that the process of sense perception
must be conditioned by the *cognitive union* of the external reality
with the individual perceiver,[2] and that this union is effected by
the action of the former on the latter. The perceiver is not always
in the act of perceiving. To pass from the condition of mere
capability to perceive, into the condition of *actually* perceiving
this, that, or the other datum or object, he must be determined by
the active influence of the external reality upon him. This influence by way of efficient activity takes the forms of various
material energies (light, heat, sound, mechanical motion or impulse, etc.) in the universe external to the sentient self or *Ego*,

---

[1] The scholastic theory of cognition, whether sensuous or intellectual, of external
reality through the medium of *species intentionales*, is obviously not intended as an
attempt to prove *that* we can know an external reality; but, presupposing as already
established the truth that we do know such reality, it is an attempt to show *how* we
come to know it.

[2] " Cognitum est in cognoscente " ; " perceptum est in percipiente " ; " sensibile
in actu et sensus in actu unum sunt " ; " anima cognoscendo quodammodo fit omnia ".
But this *immanence* of the known in the knower, this *identity* of the known with the
knower, is not necessarily *real*; it is only " cognitive," " *intentionalis*," " *in ordine
cognitionis*," not " *in ordine reali* ". *Cf.* §§ 110, 129.

and the form of nerve energy in the sense organs, nervous system, and brain. These organs being animated by the mind or conscious principle, the nerve impulse produces in the mind a *cognitional determinant* which the scholastics called the "*species sensibilis impressa*". To this the conscious subject reacts by a process whereby it *becomes aware of something*. This conscious reaction or process or condition of actual awareness is what the scholastics called the *species sensibilis expressa*. By describing this process of conscious awareness, whether in its initiation ("species *impressa*") or in its full actuality ("species *expressa*"), as a "*species*" ("*forma*," εἶδος), the scholastics simply meant to convey that by means of the cognitive process the conscious subject or mind is *conformed* or *assimilated* to the apprehended or known reality. And by describing the *species* as "*intentionalis*" they meant to guard against the crude conception of cognition as taking place by anything like a physical reproduction of the object in the subject, or a physical, material, photographic image of the former in the latter. If they called the process of perception, or the mind as perceiving, a *likeness* ("*similitudo*") or *image* ("*imago*") of the perceived external reality, they added that this likeness or image was *sui generis*, a something which mirrored, in terms of vital, cognitive consciousness, the external reality.

In this theory, on which there is no need to enlarge in the present context,[1] we must now fix our attention on one main question. Is the whole mental modification or "impression" or "determination," whereby the sentient subject is aroused into the condition of awareness,—or the whole subjective, psychic process, including the psychic state or condition which is the product or term of this process,—the *object which the conscious perceiver becomes directly and immediately aware of*? Or, to put it in the technical language of scholasticism: Is the *species sensibilis expressa* "id *quod* percipitur"? Is it the mental impression or state or condition itself that is the direct and immediate object of the mind's awareness? The result of the perceptive process is conceived to be the production, in the perceiver, of a state of conformity or assimilation of the latter with the external reality. Does this mean that there is constructed or produced in the perceiver a mental image or representation of the extramental reality, and that it is this mental image or

---

[1] For the psychology of the process, see MAHER, *op. cit.*, pp. 51-4. *Cf.* also vol. i., §§ 75, 76.

representation which is *immediately present* in consciousness to the perceiver, so that it is of this mental image *as object* that the perceiver is directly and immediately aware? If these questions be answered in the affirmative, then it will be further pointed out that, this mental object of awareness being specifically determined by the influence of the external reality, and being the natural "cognitive" or "intentional" representation of the reality, the perceiver by becoming directly and immediately aware of the former, *perceives, i.e.* apprehends *through* it ("*per- capere*"), and *in* it and *from* it, the external reality.[1] The *species sensibilis expressa* would thus be—not only as a psychic, per- ceptive process, a *means by which*[2] the perceiver apprehends the external reality, but also—a *direct object* of awareness,[3] and at the same time a medium *in* which[4] he perceives the external reality mirrored or represented, and a sort of mental datum *from* which,[5] by a process analogous to inference, he would attain to conscious sense knowledge of the external reality.

The view just suggested expresses the theory of mediate or representative sense perception. But there is the alternative theory of immediate or intuitional or presentative perception, referred to above (107). According to this view the *species sensibilis expressa*, the whole mental modification and process, with its resulting state or condition, is only the means by which[6] the external thing is directly presented to and consciously appre- hended by the perceiver: the process is not constructive of a mental object which would be itself first apprehended, and in and through which, as an image or representation, the represented external reality would be mediately apprehended. The mental or psychic effect of the action of the external reality on the mind, and of the mental reaction thereto, on the one hand does not itself come into consciousness or become an object of direct awareness; nor on the other hand does it wholly pass away with the cessation of the conscious, perceptive act. The fact that the mind can remember—can recall, in their absence, and recognize —"external" data previously perceived, proves that the psychic

---

[1] *Cf.* vol. i., § 75, p. 265, n. 3 ; *infra*, chap. xix.

[2] " Medium *quo*."   [3] " Objectum *quod* percipitur."

[4] " Medium *in* quo " or " *per* quod ".   [5] " Medium *ex* quo."

[6] " Medium *quo*."—Perception is of course *mediate* in the sense that it is medi- ated or brought about by a mental process ; but in the view of perceptionists it is immediate in the sense that no apprehended mental object intervenes between the perceiver and the presented extramental reality.

effect of perception must have persisted, though unconsciously, in the sentient subject. Now in the act of remembering,—and also in the act of imagining,—what the mind directly contemplates, what is immediately present to it, is not the external reality, but a mental substitute of the latter, a *mental image* or *phantasma* constructed by the mind in virtue of some permanent or persisting dispositions wrought in it by its previous act or acts of sense perception. But in the bare act of perception itself,—apart from mental imagery that may accompany it,—it is the external reality itself (*i.e.* some phase or aspect of it) that is, according to the perceptionist theory, immediately present to, and apprehended by, the perceiver.

Between those two views scholastics are divided.[1] Few have defended the theory that the perceptive functions of *all* the external senses are intuitive or immediate,—that the *immediate data* of *all five* senses are, as perceived, extramentally real. Those who do defend perceptionism for the most part contend merely that the immediate data of touch (resistance or impenetrability, surface extensity),—many add those of sight (*coloured* surface),—and some those of hearing (sounds),—are as such extramentally real.[2]

The medieval scholastics generally regarded external sense perception as a process *directly intuitive* of *reality external to and other than the perceiver.*[3] Nor does the fact that they spoke of the *species* as a likeness (*similitudo*) or image (*imago*) or representation (*representatio*) of the reality militate against this interpretation, for they are emphatic in asserting that the *species* is not *that which is perceived* (objectum *quod* percipitur), but only

---

[1] JEANNIÈRE remarks that *outside* Scholasticism the perceptionist theory has practically no support: "Praeter Scholasticos vero, fere nemo Perceptionismum tenet" (*op. cit.*, p. 224). And he adopts the statement of VALENSIN (*Dictionnaire de théol. cath., Art. Criticisme Kantien*, col. 750) that the non-scholastic philosopher who rejects perceptionism is not *eo ipso* a subjectivist but merely contends that *there is* an epistemological problem in sense perception (*l.c.*, n. 1).

[2] *Ibid.*, pp. 224, 426.

[3] St. Thomas, following Aristotle, teaches that the *sensibilia propria*, when not being actually perceived, are still *really* in the things which constitute the external material universe,—not however *actually*, but only *potentially*, as real potencies of the latter to reveal itself to us as it actually does in our specifically different external perceptions. This, however, as we hope to show, is consistent with perceptionism. JEANNIÈRE thinks that it is open to doubt whether St. Thomas was really a propounder of the theory of immediate sense perception, and quotes (*op. cit.*, pp. 409-10) a passage from the *De Veritate* (i., 11; *cf.* i., 17, 2 ad 1; iii., 75, 5; 76, 8) which seems to imply the theory of mediate or representative perception.

the means by which (medium *quo*) *the external reality is perceived :* but conceiving all knowledge as an *assimilation* or *conformity* of the knowing subject with the known object, and so, as a sort of reproduction of the latter in the former, they regarded the *species*, *i.e.* the determination of the cognitive process by the external reality, as the principle whereby this mental assimilation or conformity is effected.

It is a mistake, therefore, to represent scholastics generally as teaching that in sense perception there is question of two sets of sense qualities,—a set of extramental external qualities in the things, and a set of internal qualities in the consciousness of the perceiver.[1]   In distinguishing (with Aristotle) between the "potential" condition of sense qualities when *unperceived*, and their "actual" condition when *being perceived*,[2] the medieval scholastics had not at all in contemplation the modern distinction between "states of consciousness" and their "extramental correlates," or the consequent problem of the similarity of the latter to the former and the inferribility of the latter from the former.   It is this modern distinction which Jeannière,[3] for instance, presupposes when he inquires "whether or not it is certain that there exist formally in things qualities corresponding to the sense qualities regarded subjectively, whether, *e.g.*, colours exist in things " ; and when he replies, "Such existence must be admitted if it can be shown that the [conscious] impression of colours cannot be explained unless colours exist, as such, in things, or that colours cannot exist causally in things unless they exist formally also in things ".   Then he goes on to contrast the "common scholastic view " (especially of the medieval scholastics) with the view of "most modern philosophers " (including many scholastics whom he cites [4]), in the following terms : " The scholastics commonly considered the sense qualities *in us* to be altogether similar to the qualities which exist *outside us in bodies*.   Nowadays, however, most philosophers teach that sense qualities consist causally [*i.e.* as 'outside us in bodies '] not in any *quality* of things but in a *quantitative* element, *i.e.* in certain vibratory motions of the air or the aether.   Such motions undoubtedly exist ; but who will prove that they exist without any *qualitative* elements ? "[5]   The modern "representationist" attitude is here properly indicated ; and we shall duly examine its tendency to regard the extramental material universe as a system of merely *quantitative*, *i.e.* space-filling and moving realities.   But the first sentence, in which the author describes the common view of scholastics, scarcely does justice to these philosophers, and for the reason already stated, *viz.* that they did not contemplate *two* sets of known or knowable qualities at all, but rather one set of extramental *qualities* and another set of mental or cognitive *processes* or *perceptions*, of which these extramental qualities were the directly apprehended terms or objects.[6]

---

[1] *Cf. infra*, § 129.   [2] *Infra*, §§ 121-3.   [3] *Op. cit.*, p. 426.
[4] *Cf. infra*, p. 69, n. 1.   [5] *Op. cit.*, *ibid.* (italics ours).
[6] *Cf. infra*, §§ 121, 125.

Modern scholastics lean perhaps rather to the side of mediate or representative sense perception.[1] This is mainly owing to the difficulties which modern scientific discoveries in the domains of physics and physiology are supposed to have raised against the view that the "sense qualities" of which we are directly and immediately aware in conscious sense perception are in the external reality independently of our perception of the latter. No doubt the physical sciences have taught us much that was unknown in the Middle Ages regarding the energies of matter and the laws and modes of their operation; the physiology of the sense organs, the brain and the nervous system, has shed much new light on the physiological basis of sense consciousness; and experimental or physiological psychology has investigated very closely the connexion between the conscious phenomena of sense perception and their organic conditions and correlates in the brain and the nervous system. But whether the information brought to light by such researches can help us in any way to determine whether or how far the *data* or *objects* of which the conscious perceiving subject *becomes directly and immediately aware* in sense perception are in the external material universe in the absence of all perception of them; or are "extramental" indeed, but *dependent on the perceiver's organism* for what they are, when he is actually perceiving them; or are purely mental or conscious effects of external, material energies,—this is a larger question on which these sciences have not thrown much light,[2] and which will be decided gradually in the sections to follow.

113. THEIR BEARING ON THE PROBLEM OF ITS VALIDITY.— Before proceeding let us here glance at the bearing of these two theories respectively on the epistemological problem of the validity of our intellectual concepts and judgments concerning external material reality. When in previous chapters (ix.-xii.) we were engaged in establishing the objective and real validity

---

[1] This of course is the view of those who hold that the *sense qualities* do not exist in the extramental reality *formally*, as they are perceive[d], but only *virtually* or *causally* (*cf. infra*, §§ 121, 125). Of these JEANNIÈRE gives a long list, *op. cit.*, pp. 426-7, including such names as FRÖBES, S.J.; BALZER, S.J.; DE LA TAILLE; R. DE SINÉTY; GRÜNDER, S.J.; BALMES; DOMET DE VORGES; PIAT; PALMIERI, S.J.; MAHER, S.J.; LAHR; SORTAIS; MATTIUSSI; DE MUNNYNCK, O.P.; GUTBERLET; SCHMIDT; HAGEMAN; DE BROGLIE; MERCIER and the Louvain School. *Cf.*, however, *infra*, § 113, p. 70, n. 2.

[2] *Cf. infra*, § 124.

of intellectual concepts, we pointed out repeatedly that there are two steps in the process of vindication : *firstly*, that of showing that the concepts are derived from, and grounded in, and validly applicable to, the concrete individual data of the domain of sense consciousness ; and *secondly*, that of showing that these latter are themselves *real*, *i.e.* revelations or manifestations of reality to the knowing mind. The first step was accomplished in the chapters just referred to. With the second we are concerned in the chapters of Part IV.

Now those who hold the theory of mediate or representative sense perception realize that since in their view the data or objects directly and immediately attained by perception are *not* extramental *external reality*, but only intramental or intra-conscious objects of the individual's awareness, they have still to explain, and to justify before the bar of reflecting reason, the process whereby the conscious subject transcends those internal objects of awareness to know external reality. So far as we can ascertain, the transition is held by many to be *virtually* effected in the purely sense process itself. *Perception* would be a sense process of cognitively *apprehending* something *through* something else (*percipere = per-capere*), *i.e.* extended, external reality through the internal data or objects of direct awareness,—presumably because of the felt features of extended externality in these latter. And it is held to be *formally* effected in the spontaneous judgment of external existence, which accompanies such perceptions and whereby the perceiver interprets the latter as revealing to him an external domain of reality.[1] But this judgment has to be rationally justified ; and, as we have seen, they justify it mainly if not exclusively by an appeal to the principle of causality.[2]

But our perceptions are accompanied not merely by spontaneous judgments of *existence*, but also by spontaneous judgments about the *qualities* and *nature* of the externally existing reality. For we spontaneously judge that the latter has all those qualities which we have called the primary and secondary qualities of matter, or the common and proper sensibles : that it is a real manifold of corporeal substances or bodies ("*multitudo*"), which

---

[1] *Cf.* Jeannière, *op. cit.*, p. 398 (6).

[2] This mode of justification is employed not by representationists alone. For instance, Mercier, who employs it, holds that " we have a direct sense intuition of external things, and, without intermediary, form the abstract *notion* of what they are " (*op. cit.*, p. 386 ; *cf. supra*, p. 60).

have real size and shape ("*magnitudo,*" "*forma,*" "*figura*"), rest
and motion ("*quies,*" "*motus*"), colour, sound, taste, smell,
temperature, impenetrability, etc. But now, if the senses, sever-
ally or collectively, reveal to the perceiver *directly and immediately*
only mental objects or data, internal to the perceiver, what can
the latter know by means of these, or how can he know anything
by means of them, about the real qualities and nature of the
extramental, external universe? The reply is that whatever he
can know he does know by inference through the principle of
causality, and the principle of similarity of effect to cause.[1] The
internal objects or data are *representations* of qualities in the external reality; they are specifically determined in the perceiver
by the influence of the external reality; as effects they must have
an adequate cause; therefore, corresponding to the specific and
mutually irreducible differences in the conscious representations,
he can infer that there must be *analogous,* mutually irreducible,
real, and really distinct qualities in the extramental or external
material universe.[2] The real qualities which are in matter in the
absence of perception, and independently of the latter, and which
are the causes of the directly apprehended data which we call
smells, tastes, colours, sounds, heat or cold, hardness or softness or
roughness or smoothness of texture, pressures and resistances,
are not indeed *univocal* with their effects in the conscious perceiver;
—how could a quality of inert, inanimate matter be *univocally the
same* as the effect wrought by it or the datum produced by it in
a vital, conscious, perceptive mind?—but they must, withal, be
analogous to the latter, for the latter are *cognitive* reproductions
or representations produced in the mind by the external material
qualities: they are mental effects which cognitively assimilate
the perceiving mind to the perceived external reality which is
their cause, perception as a cognitive process consisting precisely
in this assimilation. We are clearly warranted, therefore, by the
principle of causality, in inferring not merely that there *is* or
exists, corresponding to the conscious sense representations, an
external reality (whose real qualities and nature must remain unknowable,—which is Kant's position,—or of whose real qualities
the conscious representations are *mere symbols* and can give us
no positive information,—which is Spencer's equally agnostic
theory of "symbolic" or "transfigured" realism[3]), but also in

---

[1] *Cf. infra,* chap. xix.   [2] *Cf.* JEANNIÈRE, *op. cit.,* pp. 425-6; *infra,* § 125.
[3] *Cf.* MAHER, *op. cit.,* pp. 123-4; *infra,* § 125.

inferring that this reality is a manifold of corporeal substances endowed with qualities, of the ontological constitution of which, as
they are in themselves, we have not indeed such *univocal* knowledge as would be afforded by direct and immediate conscious
intuition of them, but an *analogical* knowledge based on direct
intuition of their effects in consciousness, and which knowledge,
so far as it goes, conveys real and genuine information about the
material universe.

Such is the main contention of *moderate* or *critical* realism as
propounded especially by scholastic supporters of the theory of
mediate or representative sense perception,[1] and as distinguished
from the so-called "natural," "naïf," "ingenuous" realism of
perceptionists. It recognizes the existence of a serious epistemological problem,[2] that, namely, of justifying the realistic interpretation of sense perception as a process through which we are
enabled to reach a certainly valid knowledge of the existence,

[1] *Cf.* JEANNIÈRE (*op. cit.*, p. 229, and n. 1), where he meets this difficulty, urged
from such an agnostic standpoint as that of Kantism : "A thing cannot be known by the
[consciously, directly apprehended] impression it produces ; for (*a*) the impression is
not the thing ; (*b*) nor is it an effect that faithfully expresses [or represents or mirrors]
the thing ; for (*c*) it is an effect received by [or wrought in] the [conscious] subject
and received conformably with the mode of being of the latter [secundum modum
recipientis].   Wherefore there is no relation of resemblance between the impression
and the thing."   In reply to (*b*) and (*c*) he points out that there are in sense consciousness concrete sense-complexes which, compared with one another, are seen to
be totally heterogeneous and absolutely and ultimately irreducible to one another,—
complexes, for instance, which intellect conceives as a *horse*-complex, or an *apple-tree*-
complex, etc. (*cf.* vol. i., § 91, p. 351) ; and that these demand in the extramental reality
which is the cause of them,—on the principle *operari sequitur esse*, and as a *sufficient
reason* of their irreducible diversities,—a corresponding irreducible diversity of efficient energies or real qualities : inasmuch as such *wholly heterogeneous* effects could
not be rationally accounted for by attributing them to one and the same *supposed
homogeneous* cause (or " causa *equivoca*," *cf. Ontology*, § 98, *c, d, g, h ;* § 104).   And
concluding, thus, that metaphysical agnosticism is refuted by the proved necessity of
recognizing a " specific heterogeneity " in the extramental reality, he supposes this
final question to be addressed to him : What is it, in the extramental reality, that
constitutes ontologically or really the sufficient reason of such or such a sensation
(" onion," " honey," " cheese," etc.) ?   To which question he replies : " *Je n'en
sais rien.* Et si le perceptioniste le sait, qu'il le dise.—*I don't know.* And if the
perceptionist knows let him inform us."   *Cf. op. cit.*, pp. 392-400 ; 411-24 ; and
especially 425-8.

[2] *Cf.* JEANNIÈRE, *op. cit.*, p. 395 n. : " If the external world is given to us in a
subjective representation, it is clear that both *de facto* and *de jure* the problem arises :
What is the value of this representation ?   Does it present the world as it is, or does
it transform the message entrusted to it ?   If sense data be purely subjective states,
that is to say wholly unrelated to the non-subjective, then the mind is irremediably
shut up within itself. Hence subjectivism, agnosticism, solipsism, idealism ; hence
also modernism, which looks like a hopeless effort to escape from the ' black hole '
with its doom of mental suffocation."

qualities, and nature of an external material universe ; and in their chosen line of defence its advocates claim that they cannot fairly be charged with betraying the realist position by granting too much to idealism.[1]

What, now, is the epistemological problem for the perceptionist? If "the *object perceived* by the senses is identically the *external object*,"[2] if we apprehend the real *non-Ego* "in the same way, *i.e.* just as immediately"[3] as the real *Ego*, it is obvious that the problem of justifying the validity of sense perception will "assume a wholly different form"[4] from that in which it presents itself to the representationist. It will not now be the problem of discovering whether and how the external world can be, and be known to be, "conformable to its sense representation":[5] the perceptionist will meet the problem, thus stated, "by a *nego suppositum*,"[6]—since he holds that world to be immediately given in perception.

The problem for him will be *firstly*, to show that even though the real *non-Ego* or external universe "be as immediately and identically given"[7] in consciousness as the *real Ego*, nevertheless *error is possible* in regard to it, or in other words that we may and sometimes do judge it to be otherwise than it really is. This, indeed, will not be difficult to show. For although error is equally impossible in regard to the "internal data"[8] wherein the real self is supposed to be given, and the "external data"[9] wherein the real non-self is supposed to be given,—*i.e.* considering those data *as mere facts or objects of awareness* (96-100),—nevertheless just as error is possible and notoriously prevalent in regard to the real nature of the *Ego*, which "is given by identity and not in a [mental or representative] substitute," so it is possible—and actually prevalent—in regard to the real nature of the "identically given" external universe. How it is possible in both cases alike will appear later. Briefly it is because *knowledge* does not consist in a mere passive awareness of a continuous flow of ultimate fractional elements of objective reality (whether self or non-self reality) presented simultaneously and successively in an ever-changing panorama to the conscious subject ; but is a mental

---

[1] *Cf.* GRÜNDER, S.J., *De Qualitatibus Sensibilibus* (Herder, 1911), pp. 12-20 ; JEANNIÈRE, *op. cit.*, p. 427, who after citing a long array of names in support of representationism says, "Quare non amplius decet hanc sententiam tanquam fidei ruinosam damnare".

[2] JEANNIÈRE, *op. cit.*, p. 394 n.   [3] *Ibid.*   [4] *Ibid.*
[5] *Ibid.*   [6] *Ibid.*   [7] *Ibid.*   [8] *Ibid.*   [9] *Ibid.*

interpretation of all this, a process of comparing and relating the
ultimate fractional elements directly given to the knower, a process of giving meaning and restoring unity and order to the
apprehended data, of piecing them out and reconstructing them
as it were, so that by the possession of this intellectually elaborated and inter-related and systematized product, called *science*,
the mind of the knower is *pro tanto* conformed or assimilated to
reality.   And this being so, the fact that *each of the ultimate
elements* immediately given to us, whether in our *percepts* or in
our *concepts*, is " given necessarily as it is," [1] and is, as such,
objectively real,—does not at all involve that our *judgments* are
always and necessarily *true*, or that " we can never be deceived " [2]
(22, 75).

Secondly and principally, the perceptionist will have (*a*) to
show, as against idealists, that the arguments on which these
rely as proving that the mind can know nothing about extramental
reality, are inconclusive ; and (*b*) to show that the difficulties
urged against perceptionism from the fact that *things often appear
to the senses otherwise than they really are*, do not really conflict
with perceptionism rightly understood ; or, in other words, to
show that the apparent discrepancy between the way in which
external things *appear* in sense perception and the way in which
they *really are*—together with the consequent error of the unreflecting, spontaneous interpretations of sense evidence—arises
from want of advertence to the fact that the manner in which
such things appear to sense must be in a certain measure dependent on, and influenced by, and relative to, the *organic conditions*
of the sentient, perceptive self or subject (106).   If it can be
shown that the discrepancy is compatible with the direct sense
intuition of data that are really external, and that the inadvertence
can be rectified by reflection on the conditions required for a
right interpretation of these data, then the reasons for abandoning
perceptionism and falling back on the theory of mediate or representative perception will have been shown to be insufficient.
Whether the perceptionist theory will stand the test of the difficulties remains to be seen. [3]

With a view to approaching the question as to what we can
know of the *qualities and nature* of the external universe we
must next examine the distinction referred to above (106) between " proper" and " common" sensibles, the relation of these

---

[1] JEANNIÈRE, *op. cit.*, p. 394 n.   [2] *Ibid.*   [3] *Cf. infra*, chaps. xix., xx.

to intellect, and to certain thought-objects which are in themselves or *per se* attainable only by intellect in and through the
data of sense and cannot be described as "sensible" or "objects
of sense" except "per accidens" ("sensibilia *per accidens*").

114. RELATION OF "PROPER" AND "COMMON" SENSIBLES,
OF "SENSIBILIA *PER SE*" AND "SENSIBILIA *PER ACCIDENS*" TO
INTELLECT.—The scholastic analysis of sense data into "proper"
and "common" sensibles may possibly mislead by reason of its
incompleteness: especially in view of the fact that the "primary
qualities" or "*common* sensibles" are claimed on the one hand
to be themselves *percepts* and on the other hand to be (as to what
they really are) less relative to, and more independent of, the
nature and conditions of the self as percipient subject, than the
"*proper* sensibles" are; and to furnish to the abstractive faculty
of *thought* more distinctively "external" or "non-self" data than
the proper sensibles do for our intellectual knowledge of a real,
external, three-dimensional, spatial universe.[1]

The fact that the sensible features of "externality," and
"extensity" or "voluminousness," are furnished simultaneously
in *different qualities of conscious data* (*e.g.* in visual and tactual
sensations),—and not only as unified in a subjective unity of
consciousness, but also as unified in one spatial and external
continuum having colour, resistance, volume, shape, motion, etc.,
—this fact undoubtedly presents to intellect, reflecting intro-
spectively on sense perception, the strongest evidence in justification of the spontaneously assumed objective and real validity of
our concepts of "extension" and "space". In other words the
"*sense* evidence," or "*appearance* to *sense*," of extensity and externality attaching to concrete data,—apprehended by sense as
voluminous or space-filling (*size*), as continuous or discontinuous
(*unity, number*), as having definite limits (*shape*), as at *rest* or in
motion,—is also "*intellectual* evidence," or "*appearance* to *intellect*," of these same data intellectually conceived as an external

---

[1] "The perfect identity of ratios subsisting between parts of space, *e.g.* the relation of the side to the diagonal of the square, known through visual and tactual
sensations, the mathematical power of the blind, the recognition of circular and
square figures by those just receiving sight for the first time, present an irresistible
testimony to the reality of what is affirmed by such diverse witnesses. In addition
to this the manifestation of extension in the two different experiences of colour and
pressure enables us to detach in a singularly perfect manner the common element,
and so to form an abstract idea of extension, far surpassing in clearness those derived
from any single sensuous channel."—MAHER, *op. cit.*, p. 157; *cf. ibid.*, pp. 101,
159 62.

universe of spatially extended real bodies. That is a fact which we have already emphasized (105). But here we want to scrutinize the "perceptual" character of those primary qualities or common sensibles in relation to the various "concepts" which thought abstracts from sense data.

Whatever can be perceived in the concrete by sense can be conceived in the abstract by intellect. Whatever is "sensible" is likewise "intelligible".[1] Of every single concrete sense datum and of every concrete complex of such data,—of every "sensibile proprium" and of every unified or composite datum (or "sensibile commune") presented by the joint action of different external senses, and of the inner or "common" sense or faculty of association (the "sensus communis" of the scholastics),—we have or can have an abstract intellectual concept. But the functions of these various external and internal senses, whether in isolation or in conjunction with one another, are confined merely to *reporting* or *registering* or *presenting* some concrete (simple or complex) datum in consciousness. So far as the senses go, these data are all, so to speak, *inarticulate, uninterpreted*, without *meaning* :[2] each is simply a "something there," a "something present". It is intellect that must give each a meaning by conceiving it as some mode or other of *reality*, as a colour, taste, sound, etc.; as size, shape, motion, rest, etc. ; as a quality, relation, action, cause, substance, etc.[3]

---

[1] Is whatever is intelligible (or an object of thought) also sensible (or an object of sense) ? To say that whatever is intelligible must be also *itself* an object of sense (a "sensibile *per se*") would be sensism. And Kant's position,—that although we can *think* or *conceive* the suprasensible we cannot *know* it to be *real*,—is near to this. The truth is that whatever is intelligible (to the human mind), although it need not be *itself* an object of sense (a "sensibile *per se*"), must nevertheless be cognitively conjoined with something that is itself an object of sense. That is, it must be either a "sensibile *per accidens*," like the *essences, substances, causes, relations*, etc., apprehended in our direct (sensuous and intellectual) experience, or something the reality of which we can prove to be necessarily implied by this experience, and which we can conceive only *analogically*, or by concepts which have their *proper* application to realities that are *themselves* directly sensible. *Cf.* vol. i., §§ 65, 66, 74, 77.

[2] "Meaning" is something essentially *rational, intellectual, conceptual*.

[3] *Cf.* art. *Appearance and Reality*, by the present writer, in the *Irish Ecclesiastical Record*, vol. xxiv. (September, 1908), pp. 275-80. The article is the second of a series of three in the same volume ; and these are a continuation of an earlier series under the title, *Subject and Object in Knowledge and Consciousness*, in the preceding volume (xxiii., April, May, and June, 1908) of the same periodical. As the articles discuss in some detail many points in connexion with consciousness, knowledge, perception, conception, phenomenism, Kantism, etc., it may not be amiss to give this reference to them.

When we think and speak even of a "proper sensible," such as *red, redness,* and say that "*redness* is a proper object of the sense of *vision,*" we must remember that this sense does not apprehend "redness" *in the abstract,* but merely that it apprehends an individual, concrete datum which intellect simultaneously conceives in the abstract, and to which intellect gives the name *red, redness :* conceiving it also at the same time as a *thing* or *reality,* an *accident* or *quality,* a *colour,* of some *substance.* And so of the other proper sensibles.

But by the simultaneous functioning of the separate external senses, and of the unifying and associating faculty of the internal sense or *sensus communis,* we have also presented in sense consciousness complex or composite *concrete data* in which intellect apprehends or conceives such thought-objects as *unity* or *continuity ; plurality* or *multitude ; volume, magnitude,* or *three-dimensional extension ; form, figure,* or *shape ; rest* or *motion.* Now when these are called "*common* sensibles" it is not meant that each of them is apprehended *in the abstract* (and known and named as such) by any joint action *of the senses.* It is only meant that the individual, concrete data, from which intellect abstracts these thought-objects, are complex or composite data for the presence of which in sense-consciousness the functioning of *more than one* external sense is needed. Nor is it implied that any such composite sense-datum has in it any sense element beyond the *sensibilia propria* contributed by the separate senses (external and internal) which co-operated in presenting it to consciousness.

Of course the *perception* of such a composite datum as a "sensibile *commune*" involves the conscious discrimination, association, and co-ordination or unification of the proper objects of sight, passive contact, active touch or muscular and motor sensations : their unification not only in a subjective unity of consciousness but in an objective unity of composite datum or content. Now, there are of course *intellectual* functions of discriminating, associating, co-ordinating, unifying, etc.—functions which enter into the process of comparing, judging, interpreting. But, subserving these, there are analogous *sense* functions which belong to the internal sense or "sensus *communis,*" the faculty of sensuous association :[1] an organic or sense faculty of the sentient conscious being, having in the brain and nervous system partly the same physiological basis as the external senses, and

[1] *Cf.* Maher, *op. cit.,* pp. 92-6, 197-9.

possessed not only by man but by animals generally. By means
of this internal sense the sentient-conscious being can apprehend
in the concrete relations [1] of co-existence and sequence, permanence and change, similarity and diversity, among its sense data ;
and can have feelings of "recalled" or "remembered" or "past"
data, and "anticipations" of future similar data. But these are
all *concrete percepts*, not *abstract concepts*. They do not involve
the essentially rational or intellectual process whereby we apprehend "relation," "difference," "similarity," "duration,"
"sequence," etc., *as such* or *in the abstract: i.e.* by which we
apprehend the *essence* (or "*quidditas*") of the presented datum,
or *what the concrete datum is.*

When, therefore, we speak of three-dimensional extension
or size or volume, of shape or form, of multitude or number, of
rest or motion, as "primary (*sense*) qualities" or as "common
sensibles," we must distinguish between the *concrete* condition in
which alone they can be *percepts* or *sense* data, and the *abstract*
condition in which they are *conceived* by *intellect* as *objects of
thought.* If in the former condition we claim them to be *percepts*,
"common" percepts, but nevertheless real percepts or objects
of *sense* awareness, "sensibilia *per se*," we must remember that
we have called in the aid of the internal or "common" sense,
or faculty of sensuous association, unification, etc., to make
them so.

But intellect conceives in the abstract not only those "common" sense data, but also each of the "sensibilia *propria*" or
proper sense data: the function of abstract thought is closely
allied with *every* conscious sense cognition. Hence in their *abstract* condition the *proper sensibles* are objects of *intellect*, of
thought or conception ; and conversely it is only in their concrete
condition that the so-called *common sensibles* are indeed really
objects of sense.

But intellect furthermore apprehends in the abstract, in and
through the (proper and common) data of sense,—*i.e.* by reflecting

---

[1] Sense can apprehend a concrete individual relation between two or more concrete individual sense terms, though it cannot apprehend *relation in the abstract*, or
what a relation is. Cf. vol. i., § 91, iii. ; PRICHARD, *op. cit.*, pp. 228-9. The scholastics
sometimes spoke of this sensuous apprehension of relations between associated sense
terms as sensuous "judgment " after the analogy of intellectual comparison or judgment proper. Apart from instinct, these sensuous apprehensions of concrete relations explain animal "memories," "anticipations," "inferences," etc., and constitute
portion of the domain of what is commonly called "animal intelligence".

on, and interpreting, and reasoning from, these latter,[1]—certain thought-objects, of which it is assumed that the senses alone could not make us cognizant even in the concrete: and these are described as being objects of sense only "*per accidens*," *i.e.* by being really conjoined with data which are themselves (proper or common) objects of sense. The "common sensibles" no less than the "proper sensibles" are claimed by scholastics to be direct data of *sense* perception, to be *percepts*, not concepts. This they express by saying that both the "proper" and the "common" sensibles are "sensibilia *per se*," *i.e.* that they are *themselves* objects of the *senses*, as distinct from certain other data or objects of knowledge which cannot be designated "objects of *sense*" except "*per accidens*". These other objects of knowledge are themselves data of *intellect*, and can be only described as being "accidentally or concomitantly sensible" ("sensibilia *per accidens*"): because they are *objectively* conjoined with the data that are "sensibilia *per se*," or objects of sense perception proper, and are apprehended by the intellectual faculty which is *subjectively* a faculty of the same conscious self that possesses the sense faculties. Thus, *substance* is not itself a datum of any sense. Substance, and the various kinds of substances, simple and composite, spiritual and material,—and *cause*, and *relation*, and their various kinds,—are themselves objects of intellect, *conceived* objects, "intelligibilia" *per se*.[2] Yet, although we *see* only *coloured surface*, and *taste* only such a sense quality as *sweet*, and *touch* only a *hard, cold, resisting* surface, we nevertheless say, "I see a *man*," "I taste *honey*," "I feel *ice*," etc.[3] But "man," "honey," "ice," etc., are substances, and, as such, are objects only of thought or conception, not of perception. Hence, as such, they can be said to be perceptible or sensible only *per accidens*, inasmuch as the concrete data which are directly

---

[1] Has intellect any concrete intuitions of its own, independently of sense activity, from which also to derive abstract thought-objects? " Nihil est in intellectu quod prius non fuerit [*aliquo modo*—saltem *per accidens*] in sensu ? " *Cf.* vol. i., §§ 74, 77 ; *supra*, §§ 100, 105.

[2] *Cf. Ontology*, § 62, p. 218.

[3] Similarly I may say "I *see* the *sweet honey* ". But I do not really *see* the *sweetness*. Sweetness is *itself* ("*per se*") an object only of taste. What I see is the *coloured surface* of that which I otherwise know to be also sweet. Thus sweetness is indirectly or concomitantly an object of vision : it is "visibile *per accidens*". To be thus an object *per accidens* of any faculty, a datum must be (1) itself an object *per se* of some other faculty, and (2) objectively conjoined with what is an object *per se* of the former faculty. *Cf.* JEANNIÈRE, *op. cit.*, pp. 386-7.

attained by sense really and objectively embody these other objects which are apprehended only by intellect, *viz.*, substance, cause, matter, spirit, intellect, will, thought, volition, etc.

Now it might, perhaps, be maintained that sense *does* make us aware of all these objects *in the concrete :* that it makes us aware of *material* substance in the concrete, and therefore of substance and all its accidents, of being or reality and all its modes, *in the concrete :* and that therefore all knowable modes of reality are *themselves (per se)* objects of sense *in the concrete* as well as of intellect *in the abstract :* so that all *intelligibilia per se* (as *abstract*) would be *sensibilia per accidens*, just as all *sensibilia per se* (as *concrete*) would be *intelligibilia per accidens*.[1]

If this latter assertion were understood in the sense which we have explained as the *true* meaning of the aphorism, *Nihil est in intellectu quod prius non fuerit in sensu, i.e.* if it were understood to mean that all modes of reality which become intelligible to the human intellect become objects of the latter only through concepts which, being derived from sense data, are *properly* applicable only to the *per se* sensible or material modes of reality, the modes that are made " immaterial " or " intelligible " only " negatively " or " by abstraction " (71, 74, 76),—it might be allowed to pass as admissible. But if it (and the assertion immediately preceding it) were understood to mean that only such modes of reality as are *themselves, per se*, sensible, are intelligible and knowable by the human mind, these assertions would then be expressions of the erroneous doctrine of *Sensism*.[2]

As a matter of fact sense does *not* make us aware of substance, or of material substance, or of cause, spirit, intellect, volition, etc., *even in the concrete*. We may, no doubt, say that it makes us aware of *materiality* in the concrete ; for materiality in the concrete means just all those concrete qualities, proper and common, which are *themselves, per se*, objects of sense. But if we were *merely* sentient beings, like the lower animals, and had no higher or rational cognitive faculty, we could never attain to *any* awareness of substance, cause, spirit, intellect, will, etc., even though we sensuously apprehended beings which were really substances and causes, which really had a spiritual nature and spiritual faculties such as intellect and will. To say that such modes of being are for us " sensibilia *per accidens* " is really another way of saying that we do not sensuously perceive them at all, but that intellect conceives or apprehends them in and with the data which we do sensuously perceive.

Now all the positive content of our concepts of substance, cause, attribute

---

[1] Are *space* and *time* "*per se* intelligible " or "*per se* sensible " ?   Are they *per se* " concepts," objects of *intellect*, or *per se* " percepts " objects of *sense*.   *Per se* they are concepts, objects of *intellect* ; for the terms *space* and *time* express *abstract* objects.   They are sensible, or objects of sense, only *per accidens*.   They are *per se* neither proper nor common sensibles.   No one sense and no combination of senses can perceive them.   They are objects elaborated by thought through the addition of *rational relations (entia rationis)* to our concepts of the "*common* sensibles," *extension* and *motion* respectively.   *Cf. Ontology*, §§ 84, 85.

[2] *Cf. supra*, p. 76, n. 1.

or accident, quality, power, faculty, relation, action, etc., is derived from the " material " data of sense consciousness, together with the data furnished by reflection on the immediate intuitions we have of our own higher (intellectual and volitional) activities (71, 100, 105). But intellect, reflecting on those concepts, and on *all* the data of our conscious experience, can see that those concepts or thought-objects, considered apart from the sense-data in which they were originally apprehended, are applicable to modes of reality *that are not themselves*, or *per se, sensible;* can see the *possibility* of such *positively immaterial* modes of reality ; and can infer the *actual existence* of such modes of being—the rational, intelligent, spiritual, human soul with its spiritual faculties ; and the Divine, Infinite, Necessary Being or First Cause—as necessarily involved in, and implied by, the direct data of conscious human experience (71). And it can see at the same time that such concepts, though they can be applied to such positively suprasensible or immaterial realities only by emptying them of their sensible or material content (*via negationis*), can give us a knowledge which, though negative and analogical, is nevertheless, so far as it goes, an objectively and really valid knowledge of such suprasensible or spiritual domains of being (66, 74, 100).

115. EXTRAMENTAL REALITY OF THE "COMMON" SEN-SIBLES, OR "PRIMARY" SENSE QUALITIES VINDICATED.—We are now in a position to answer the questions : What can we know with reasoned or philosophic certitude about the *qualities and nature* of the domain of reality which has already (109-11) been proved to be really external to and distinct from the conscious perceiving mind?[1]

I. We can know that this domain of reality is *substantial*, or endowed with the *substance*-mode of being. For we have proved it to be really distinct from, and not a mere phenomenon in, the perceiving subject. Therefore it must *exist in itself.*[2]

II. We can know (*a*) that it has *volume* or *three-dimensional extension*,[3] *i.e.* the fundamental quality or property on account of which we call a reality *corporeal* or *material ;* (*b*) that it consists of a *multitude* of really and numerically distinct corporeal entities or bodies, and specifically distinct collections of such bodies, each individual body being endowed with *shape or figure, rest or motion,*

---

[1] From the conscious, perceiving *mind :* we put it in that way so as to include in the domain in question the self *as corporeal and organic.* Our conviction of the unity of this latter in a concrete individuality with the mind, and of its real distinction from the extra-organic or non-self universe, will be examined presently.

[2] *Cf. Ontology*, §§ 62, 63.

[3] Not merely in the improper sense of something that can *cause* or produce in us data endowed with " extensity,"—as the Divine Spirit does according to Berkeley's theory,—but in the proper sense of something that is itself extended, that is an integral whole of parts outside parts (continuous or contiguous) in space. *Cf. Ontology,* § 83. JEANNIÈRE, *op. cit.,* p. 400.

local or spatial relations and interactions ; (c) that each individual perceiver's body is really distinct from the rest of the material universe ; (d) that the " secondary " sensible qualities or " proper " sensibles,—resistance or impenetrability, heat and cold, light and colours, sounds, tastes and smells,—are *qualities of the material or corporeal substances*, and therefore really exist, independently of our perception of them, in these corporeal substances, no less than these latter themselves and the " primary " qualities or " common " sensibles referred to in (a) and (b).

(a) That the external domain of reality has three-dimensional extension is made manifest by rational reflection on the features of concrete surface extensity, texture, pressure, resistance, voluminousness, which characterize this domain of reality as immediately and directly given in concrete tactual, muscular, and visual sensation-complexes : in other words by the same sort of reflection as we have employed to vindicate the *real externality* of the domain of external sense perception (109).

(b) Extensional or spatial *discontinuity* in simultaneously apprehended concrete, complex sense data or objects, is itself (in the concrete) a direct datum of sense awareness. Spatially or extensionally distinct individual sense data, marked by constant, stable, persistent, and mutually irreducible complexes of sense qualities (colour, size, shape, texture, taste, etc.) are constantly appearing and re-appearing in sense consciousness. If these directly and immediately apprehended sense data are themselves real so is their multiplicity real. But we have proved that they are themselves real ; therefore their multiplicity is real.

We have already shown that our complex specific or class-concepts—*e.g.* " gold," " apple," " eagle," " man," etc.,—are determined as to their respective contents by *objective affinities* in the constitutive notes of each [1] (89, 91). The obvious ground of those affinities lies in our simultaneous and successive sense awareness of perceptually distinct and mutually irreducible sense data embodying those distinct complexes of conceptual notes or factors. We have established the general thesis that our abstract and universal concepts are objectively real, that they are applicable to, and have their concrete counterpart in, the data of sense.

---

[1] *Specific diversity*, or *difference in nature*, among sense-data is *per se* an object of intellect ; it is " sensibile *per accidens*," being grounded in the irreducible, stable, constantly recurring, qualitatively diversified sense data. *Cf.* JEANNIÈRE, *op. cit.*, p. 406.

This is true, therefore, of our concepts of unity and plurality, continuity and discontinuity, identity and distinction, " selfness " and " otherness ". Since these abstract concepts are applicable to the concrete data of sense,—to " this gold," " this apple," " this eagle," " this man," simultaneously presented in sense perception,—it follows that if these separate sense data are themselves real, so must the concretely perceived " separateness," or " oneness " and " otherness," or " distinction," be real. And similarly, if the concretely perceived datum be a simultaneous spatial plurality of " golds," or " apples," or " eagles," or " men " : if each complex sense percept,—*e.g.* the " gold "-percept, the " apple "-percept, etc.,—be real, so must the perceived plurality in each such percept be real.

Sense plurality, therefore, reveals the material universe as a *real, numerical* multiplicity of beings. These beings we arrange intellectually in collections or classes by means of our specific and generic class-concepts. These concepts, grounded as they are in such stable, mutually irreducible, constantly recurring, and qualitatively differentiated sense data as *e.g.* " man," " horse," "apple," "gold," "water," etc., obviously give us a genuine intellectual insight into the *real natures* of these material beings. For the concepts are abstract representatives of the concrete percepts. And while sense reveals the stable, irreducible, concrete complex of perceived qualities, intellect apprehends it as a real substance having a specific essence or nature as determined by the perceived qualities. It is *through the qualities* revealed to sense that we apprehend intellectually *the specific natures* of material realities and arrive at their " essential " definitions. The substances, essences, specific natures, and specific distinctions, of things are *per se* objects of intellect, and *per accidens* objects of sense (114). Moreover we can apprehend intellectually the natures or essences of material things only in so far as these are revealed to us through sense qualities. This is the import of the scholastic aphorism, *Operatio sequitur esse; Qualis est operatio talis est natura*. We have no direct, intuitive, intellectual insight into their natures or essences.[1] Hence our " essential " definitions of

---

[1] *Cf. Ontology,* §§ 61-3. " How do we reach a knowledge of the *specific natures* of substances? . . . We know just precisely what their accidents reveal to us—that and nothing more. We have no intuitive insight into their natures ; all our knowledge here is abstractive and discursive. As are their properties—their activities, energies, qualities, and all their accidents—so is their nature. We know of the latter

the natures of things are really formulated in terms of properties
or qualities of those natures, and not in terms of the essences
themselves.[1] This abstractive and discursive knowledge of the
real natures of the things of sense is, of course, an intellectual interpretation, an "induction" from perceived data. The correct-
ness of such interpretations must depend on accuracy of sense
observation, and is perfected by the "education of the senses"
through experience. Spontaneous interpretations are always
hasty and often erroneous. It is the aim of physical and natural
scientists, each in his own department, by careful employment of
the Inductive Method of research, to extend the sphere of our
knowledge of the natures of things, and of the laws of their
behaviour.

The conclusions we have reached concerning the real plurality
of the domain of sense depend on the proved validity of our intellectual concept of the "real distinction,"—especially the "*major*
real distinction*" (as between individual and individual), and
"distinction or otherness *from-the-self*" (104, 109, 111). Nor
are they any less dependent on the validity of this concept if
they be established as realist supporters of the theory of *mediate*
sense perception establish them (113), by appeal to the principle
of causality.[2] Furthermore, the present thesis merely asserts the
possibility of a reasoned or philosophical certitude for the judgment that *some* of our concrete, complex perceptual unities, *e.g.*
"this man," "that man," "this apple," "that apple," etc., are
each a real unity, a real individual being, really distinct from
other such beings. It does not assert that whatever is a perceptual unity is *eo ipso* a real unity. While it asserts, for instance,
that I can know the piece of gold in my right hand to be really
distinct from the piece of gold in my left, it does not assert that
the *perceptual* unity, the unity *for sense*, of either piece, is the
unity of one individual being : each piece may be a multitude
of really distinct individual entities. But it does assert that

just what we can infer from the former. *Operatio sequitur esse ;* we have no other
key than this to knowledge of their specific natures."—*Ibid.*, pp. 218-19.

[1] *Cf.* ARISTOTLE, *De Anima*, L. i., c. i., § 8. St. Thomas, *De Ente et Es-
sentia*, c. v. : "In rebus enim sensibilibus ipsae differentiae essentiales nobis
ignotae sunt : unde significantur per differentias accidentales quae ex essentialibus
oriuntur, sicut causa significatur per effectum suum,"—*apud* JEANNIÈRE, *op. cit.*, p.
422 n. So, for instance, when we define "man" as a "*rational* animal," the *differentia* "rational" really indicates what is a property of the nature rather than a con-
stituent of the nature itself.

[2] *Cf.* JEANNIÈRE, *ibid.*, pp 406, 423-4.

although the *proper application* of our intellectual concepts of
" real unity or individuality," " real plurality," " real distinction,"
"real otherness," etc., is in some cases doubtful and difficult,[1]
there is nevertheless in our concretely perceived distinctions of
" internal, " " external," " spatially extended " sense data, not only
adequate ground for the formation of such concepts, but also evidence which is seen on reflection to be adequate for some of our
spontaneous applications of those concepts, as, for example, in
the judgments that individual men, animals, birds, fishes, etc.,
are each one individual real being, and each really distinct from
the others. Similarly, although it recognizes that we may be
mistaken in judging successively repeated perceptions to be (because of their objective similarity) perceptions of the same reality
(*e.g.* of the same individual man), or *vice versa*, to be (because of
their dissimilarity) of different realities (*e.g.* of different individual
men),—as happens in cases of mistaken identity,[2]—it asserts that
nevertheless the concretely perceived objective similarities and
dissimilarities between successive perceptions of complex data
that are conceptually and specifically the same ("men" for instance), furnish adequate intellectual evidence for reasoned certitude as to the truth of some,—indeed most,—of our judgments
of individual identification and discrimination.[3] And the reason
of all this is simply that the concrete perceptual grounds for the
concepts used in such judgments are just as clear and cogent for
intellect reflecting on their significance as is the concretely perceived " externality " whereby we conceive and judge this whole
domain of data to be " external " to, and " other than," the perceiver (109) : so that it would be irrational and inconsistent to
accept the intellectual verdict that this domain is an "external
reality" and to reject the intellectual verdict that it is a domain
of "external *realities*".

The difficulties urged against the thesis that the external
universe is *pluralistic, i.e.* a plurality of really distinct beings, may
be reduced to a few broad classes. First, there are the difficulties

---

[1] *Cf. Ontology,* §§ 29 (p. 121); 31 (p. 124) ; 37 (p. 147); 38 (p. 151).

[2] Treated in Inductive Logic as the fallacy of " mal-observation ". *Cf.* JEAN-
NIÈRE, *op. cit.*, p. 423.

[3] *Ibid.* The modern " Bertillon system " of identifying human individuals by
their finger-marks is an invaluable scientific improvement on the old-time signs of
human individual identity as embodied in the couplet :—

    " Forma, figura, locus, tempus, stirps, patria, nomen :
    Haec ea sunt septem quae non habet unus et alter ".

urged from the standpoint of intellectualist monism: by the Eleatics in ancient Greece and in modern times by Hegelians. Such, for instance, is one of Zeno's well-known puzzles: "If there were really different beings any two of them would differ from each other only by some third reality, and this again from each of the former by a fourth and a fifth reality, and so on *ad infinitum*: which would involve the absurdities of infinite number and infinite regress.[1] Therefore all plurality must be apparent, not real." Or again, "That in which 'things' would differ must be *reality* or *being*. But reality or being is self-identical and common to all 'things'. Therefore plurality is an illusion." Such sophisms arise from assuming the abstract intellectual view of reality to be adequate, from an erroneous interpretation of the significance of the universal concept, from gratuitously assuming the conceptual unity of the object of our abstract notion of "being in general" to be as such a real unity.

A similar difficulty, arising from the realistic pantheism of Spinoza, is based on a gratuitously assumed definition of substance, a definition which identifies the latter with Necessary, Self-Existent Being.[2]

Then there is the difficulty arising from the anti-intellectualist intuitionism of Bergson and his school in our own time (86). If sense alone reveals reality as it is, and if in ultimate analysis the data of sense are not *data*, but *a datum*,—one dynamic, evolving continuum,—into which intellect alone introduces distinctions to meet practical needs, and if all distinctions are thus subjective and unreal, then of course, plurality is an illusion. But those "ifs" are too directly opposed to the verdict both of senses and of intellect to call for serious consideration here.

Finally, in Kant's theory, all plurality, in so far as it is knowable, is merely mental or phenomenal. We have already examined this general attitude in regard to intellect. We shall return to it later in regard to the data of sense.

116. DISTINCTION OF PERCEIVER'S ORGANISM OR BODY FROM THE "EXTERNAL" UNIVERSE.—(*c*)[3] The individual perceiver can have reasoned certitude that his own body is really distinct from the rest of the material universe. This has been virtually proved by establishing the reasoned certitude of the perceiver's judgment that a real universe external to himself

---

[1] *Cf. Ontology*, § 31, p. 125 n.　　　　[2] *Ibid.*, § 64, pp. 229-32.
　　　　　　　[3] *Cf.* § 115, p. 82.

exists (109). As sense perception and intellectual reflection develop, the individual perceiver gradually interprets his organic, tactual, muscular, visual and auditory sensations as revealing to him two separate domains of data, the one not only objective to consciousness but external, the other objective indeed to consciousness but internal or identical with the perceiver himself. For instance, sensations of double touch, experienced when the perceiver touches his own body, are consciously and psychologically different from those experienced when he touches a door or table or other external object. When he pushes with his hand against the wall he is conscious of a force or energy opposing his own, an energy which he cannot identify with his conscious self. When he pushes his right hand against his left he is also conscious of a force or energy opposing his own, but which other energy he also identifies as his own. So also the complex muscular and auditory sensations experienced in hearing one's own voice are different from those experienced in hearing another's voice. From such concrete sense data he abstracts the intellectual concepts of "self" and "not-self" and applies them in the spontaneous judgment whereby he pronounces the "externally felt " world to be really other than and distinct from his own "feeling and felt " organism. And reflection justifies the spontaneously assumed validity of the concept of real otherness (105, 109).

We have established the various theses formulated above (115) under I, and II (*a*), (*b*), (*c*), on the assumption of perceptionism, that reality is directly given in the data or objects of sense awareness (113). Realist supporters of the theory of mediate perception establish those same theses by an appeal to the principle of causality, on the lines already indicated [1] (113). The theses under II (*a*) and (*b*) assert in general terms the validity of our belief in the real extramental existence of the "primary" sense qualities or "common" sensibles. But since these are complexes of the " secondary" qualities or "proper" sensibles, the character of their extramental reality is obviously at least in some measure dependent on that of the latter. We have now to explain and establish the character of the extramental reality of these latter as formulated in the thesis under II (*d*) above (115), and especially to examine that feature of them referred to in a preceding section (106, V) as their greater or less *relativity* to the organic condition of the conscious, sen-

[1] *Cf.* JEANNIÈRE, *op. cit.*, pp. 400 *sqq.*

tient subject.   In doing so we must bear in mind the conclusion just established under II (c); for the fact that the conscious, sentient subject or perceiver is not merely a *mind* or *conscious principle*, but a conscious, animated *organism*, endowed with the extended, material or corporeal mode of being which also characterizes the "external" domain of reality,—this fact must have its influence on the qualities of the "external" data apprehended through the instrumentality of the bodily organism.

CHAPTER XVII.

RELATIVITY OF SENSE QUALITIES TO PERCEIVER.

117. RÔLE OF PERCEIVER'S ORGANISM AS PARTIAL DETER-
MINANT OF "EXTERNAL" SENSE QUALITIES.—When we have
justified our certitude regarding the real existence of an external,
extended, material universe ; and of an extended, material organism or body which, though an object of perception, is felt and
known to be subjectively allied with the conscious principle, and
identical with the perceiving subject; and when, finally, it is
realized that the perception of qualitatively distinct and mutually
irreducible sense data or objects is inseparably allied with, and
absolutely dependent on, the functioning of the distinct bodily
organs called "sense organs,"—the important bearing of these
latter on the character of our insight into the qualities and nature
of the external material universe, and the peculiar rôle of the
individual perceiver's *body* as the medium and connecting link
between the individual *mind* or consciousness on the one hand
and the "external" universe on the other, ought to be at once
apparent. For on the one hand since the universe perceived as
external is really external to and other than the perceiver, and
since the latter is not always actually perceiving it, his perceptions of it must be determined in him by the *active influence* of
this external universe on his mind or consciousness (112). But
on the other hand, the medium through which this influence is
conveyed to the perceiver's mind or consciousness,—*viz.* his own
body, with its brain and nervous system and definitely differentiated "external" sense organs,—is itself an extended, material
reality, and is therefore itself endowed with whatever sense
qualities we may find ourselves justified in attributing to matter
as existing in the external universe independently of our actual
perception of them. And furthermore, the specifically distinct
and mutually irreducible qualities which we consciously apprehend through the functioning of the various "external" sense

organs present themselves as they do in consciousness dependently on the specific structure and functioning of those sense organs. That is to say, if our consciously apprehended sense data are not determined as to their qualities, or *quoad specificationem*, by the self as conscious, or by the mind or conscious principle of the perceiver, or by any subconscious factors of the perceiver's mind,—and all this we take as already duly established ;—if these qualitative differences, therefore, are in the presented data or objects, and are therefore determined, not *by* consciousness, but *for* consciousness,—it is nevertheless clear on the other hand that these qualities and qualitative differences are not in the external universe, and determined by the latter, *to the total exclusion of the perceiver's sense organs*, or *in total independence* of these. For, manifestly, whatever *e.g.* " redness " may be in the external universe, it can be what it actually is as present to sense consciousness only because it is presented to sense consciousness by the sense organ we call the eye ; nor could the sentient subject become aware of it at all in the total absence of this organ and its functioning. Nor, whatever "sound" may be as a real property of the external material universe, could he ever become aware of sound, or have this datum or object presented to consciousness, without the organ and function of hearing. And even if "sound" and "colour" are different, as they exist in the external universe independently of his actual perception of them, at all events the proximate reason why he apprehends them as different, and a *conditio sine qua non* for his perception of them as different, is that they are brought into cognitive union with his consciousness through differently constructed and differently functioning bodily sense organs, *viz.* the ears and the eyes. And the same is true of the other "proper sensibles," or proper objects of the other external senses,—those of taste, smell, temperature, passive touch, impenetrability or resistance to muscular effort, and organic states or conditions.

Furthermore, since the perceived qualities of extended, material, *external* things are perceived dependently on the functioning of the *perceiver's own* extended, material, or bodily sense organs,—since their perception is conditioned by the latter, —these qualities will be determined to be what they are as presented in the concrete to the perceiver, not alone by the actual material conditions of the "external things" themselves, but also by the actual material conditions of the sense organs

through which the external data are made present to the conscious perceiver. Thus, to take a few familiar examples, if the
perceiver's own hand is cold he will experience the water into
which he plunges it as "warm," whereas if his hand be hot he
will experience the same water as "cold". If his palate be in
its normal physiological condition he will experience the taste of
sugar as "sweet," whereas if through illness it be in an abnormal
or diseased condition he may experience the taste of sugar as
"bitter". If his eyes be in a normal condition he will see the
colour of a field of poppies as "red," whereas if his eyes happen
to be affected with that not very uncommon condition known as
"colour-blindness" or "Daltonism," he will see it as "grey" or
"green"; or, if he press the corner of one eye with the finger,
he will see *two* objects where normally he would see only *one*.
Again, in certain conditions of the brain and nervous system and
sense organs, conditions which occur very commonly during
sleep, or during feverish illness, he may apprehend what he spontaneously judges to be external things, but what as a matter
of fact are mere mental images resulting from the activity of
the imagination: such erroneous interpretations of imagination-
images as real (external) percepts,—occurring in dreams, fevers,
delirium tremens, and all conditions of insanity,—being known
as *hallucinations*. Or he may think that what he perceives in
the fog is a policeman when it is only a lamp-post: such erroneous interpretations of real (external) perceptions being known as
illusions.[1]

118. RELATIVITY OF EXTERNAL SENSE QUALITIES TO
PERCEIVER'S ORGANISM. SENSE ILLUSIONS AND DECEPTIONS.
"INFALLIBILITY" OF PERCEPTION.—Now from such facts a few
inferences are fairly obvious. The *first* is that the sense quality
with which the datum or object presents itself to the consciousness of the perceiver is not *exclusively external*, in the sense of
belonging to the external reality *altogether independently* of the
actual condition of the sense organ through which the datum is
presented.

A *second* is that we must carefully distinguish between the
actually presented datum or object itself (or its mere *presentation*
to the perceiver), and the spontaneous judgment whereby the
latter interprets it (or *represents* it to himself as being such or
such).

---

[1] *Cf.* MAHER, *op. cit.*, pp. 171-8; JEANNIÈRE, *op. cit.*, p. 388 n.

A *third* is that not only is intellect thus spontaneously co-operating with external sense, but that also the imagination—with its stock of images acquired in past perceptions and stored up through memory and mental association—is constantly supplementing, subjectively moulding and filling in, the presented and perceived external datum or fraction of external reality : so that the spontaneous intellectual interpretation is never of the bare percept itself but rather of the percept in its whole concrete, sensuous, psychic context.

A *fourth* is that since the actual organic condition of the sentient subject,—*i.e.* of the perceiver's brain, nervous system, sense organs,—is a partial determinant of the concretely "qualified" datum or presented object, if this condition be abnormal it may cause a datum or object to be presented as external which has no reality at all outside the perceiver's own organism ; or whose reality outside and independently of the perceiver's organism is presented to the perceiver (owing to the abnormal and disturbing co-operation of the latter's organism) *otherwise* than it would be presented to the normal perceiver : in which case the spontaneous judgment of the abnormal perceiver will make him the victim of an hallucination or an illusion until such time as intellectual advertence to his own abnormal condition will enable him to rectify this judgment. And this is true whether the abnormal organic condition be congenital or supervening, permanent or transitory, curable or incurable.

A *fifth* inference is that, distinguishing between the whole concrete datum or object presented to consciousness by the co-operation of (*a*) the external reality, (*b*) the external sense organ (with the brain and nervous system) subserving perception, and (*c*) the brain and nervous system subserving the internal senses (the faculties of association, imagination, and memory),—distinguishing between this whole concrete datum on the one hand, and the perceiver's spontaneous interpretation of it on the other, the former is in every case necessarily what it is and as it is, and the latter alone can be erroneous. In the concrete conditions, objective and subjective,—whether normal or abnormal,—in which the datum is presented to consciousness, that datum could not be other than it is. The man plunging his heated hand into lukewarm water does really feel a "concrete cold" datum, and plunging his cold hand into the same water he does really feel a "concrete hot" datum. The person to whose diseased palate sugar tastes bitter is really aware of the concrete sense datum, "bitter". The colour-blind perceiver, looking on the field of poppies has really present to consciousness a datum which he rightly designates "grey" or "green". The person who presses the corner of one of his eyes is really aware of a twofold datum or object. In dreams, hallucinations and illusions he really has presented in consciousness the data or objects which he thinks to be external things, or to be such or such external things. In other words, the *senses themselves neither err nor deceive.* They do not err because they do not judge or interpret, but merely present, register, report a "something," a "datum," an "object" to the conscious perceiver. They do not *themselves* deceive because they always present or register or report that precisely which under the circumstances they must : they simply could not present a datum other or otherwise than they actually do : according to the organic condition in which they are, and according to the condition in which the external influence impresses them, so must the presented datum be, nor can it be otherwise : nor can the perceiver be deceived in judging that he has this datum consciously present to him.[1]

But the presentation of a sense datum can be *an occasion* of deception to the perceiver, inasmuch as the latter may judge that the datum is external, or how it is externally, without adverting to the fact that the presented datum is partially determined by the condition of his own organism, and that this condition is, perhaps, abnormal. And just as the subjective, organic condition of the perceiver may be an occasion of error in his spontaneous judgment, so may the abnormal condition of the external thing itself, or of the physical medium spatially intervening between the latter and the sense organ of the perceiver.[2] A trite and telling example of this source of error is the familiar fact that a *straight* stick partially immersed in water and seen obliquely appears *bent.* Or again, to a person sitting in a moving

---

[1] As St. Thomas expresses it (*Summa Theol.*, I., Q. xvii., a. 2) : "Per hoc quod sensus ita nuntiant sicut afficiuntur, sequitur quod non decipiamur in judicio quo judicamus nos sentire aliquid ; sed ex eo quod sensus *aliter afficitur interdum quam res sit,* sequitur quod nuntiet nobis aliquando rem aliter quam sit, et ex hoc fallimur per sensum *circa rem,* non circa ipsum sentire". (Italics ours : "aliter afficitur . . . quam res sit," *i.e.* otherwise than the normal sense is affected by the thing in normal external conditions ; for it is the normal sense, perceiving the external thing in normal external conditions, that enables us to discover *how the thing really is,*— "*quomodo res sit* ").

[2] *Cf.* preceding note.

train which is passing another train that is stationary, the latter appears to be moving and the former at rest : a double or compound illusion. Or, an object seen through the microscope appears much larger than "it really is". Or, two plane images placed side by side and seen through the stereoscope appear as one object in relief. Or, we still see in the heavens stars which ages ago ceased to emit light. Or, the setting sun appears as visible above the horizon when it is really below the horizon. Or, certain atmospheric conditions at sea or in the desert produce the optical illusion,—known as the *mirage*,—of ships, trees, etc., seen inverted in the heavens.

Now such "illusions of the senses," though puzzling to the plain man, have never shaken his spontaneous belief in the trustworthiness of his senses under normal conditions. But philosophers, who have tried to think out the bearing of these illusions on our spontaneous beliefs regarding the existence, qualities, and nature of an external domain of reality, have been more than puzzled by such illusions : many have been driven by them into the position of theoretical scepticism, subjectivism or idealism.[1] This, however, is an unjustifiable conclusion if it can be shown, as we hope to show, that such errors and illusions can be both explained and corrected by reflection.

For the realist, however, who holds that sense data reveal to us not only the existence, but in some measure the qualities and nature, of an external domain of reality, they do raise a serious question as to whether or how far this external domain of reality has, apart from sense perception, the ("secondary" and "primary") sense qualities of which we become aware in the actual process of perception. Following up, therefore, in the light of those "illusions," the inferences set forth above,—inferences which already partly explain the illusions,—we may ask this general question : If the presented "external" sense data *partly* depend,—as regards the concrete qualities with which they present themselves to the conscious perceiver,—on organic conditions of the perceiving self or subject, can we determine whether or how far those qualities are really in the external domain of reality independently of the perceiving self or subject ? Well, if we include the perceiver's own organism in the domain of material reality which has been proved to exist independently of actual perception, independently of the perceiver's conscious-

[1] *Cf. infra*, § 128.

ness, and which is in this sense extramental as opposed to what is essentially dependent on mind or consciousness,—there seems to be no valid reason for denying or doubting that those sense qualities, secondary and primary, are qualities of—at any rate—*extramental or material reality*. To this we shall return presently for the purpose of examining the distinction drawn between the *potential* and the *actual* reality which some of those qualities are supposed to have in the material domain, apart from perception, and in perception, respectively.

If, however, we ask whether or how we are justified in locating those qualities in the *external* domain of material things, apart from and independently of the rôle played in perception by the *material sense organs of the perceiver's body*, we shall find it necessary to recognize explicitly the import of a distinction which in practice we are always making implicitly, spontaneously, and unreflectingly, in our ordinary processes of external sense perception : namely the distinction between concrete, "qualified" data or objects apprehended by the perceiver *in normal conditions*, organic or subjective or internal, and physical or objective or external, and other such data perceived *in abnormal conditions*.

119. CONDITIONS OF "NORMAL" AND "ABNORMAL" SENSE PERCEPTION.—Reflection on the facts of sense experience, on our spontaneous judgments regarding the immediate data of sense, and particularly on the occasional illusions or deceptions or erroneous interpretations of which we are the victims, convinces us that we can rely on these spontaneous judgments only when the whole conscious process takes place under normal conditions, and that we can, by attending to the actual conditions, either at the time or at least by reflection after the fact, either forestall or correct erroneous spontaneous interpretations. These conditions are partly on the side of the perceiver and partly on the side of the perceived datum or object.

The perceiver himself must be mentally and physically in a sane and healthy condition. That is to say, he must be awake and in such normal condition of mental and organic health as to be capable of discriminating between a datum which is a *percept* and a datum which is presented by *imagination* through the abnormal functioning of the brain and nervous system.[1] And secondly, in the case of a percept, the sense

---

[1] *Cf.* JEANNIÈRE, *op. cit.*, p. 419: "postulatur ... sanitas psychica subjecti, saltem talis qua possit discernere sensationes proprie dictas a sensationibus imaginatis".

organ or organs concerned in presenting it must be free from
any such disturbing and abnormal condition, whether congenital
or acquired, as would involve the presentation of this datum
otherwise than it would be presented by a sense organ or organs
in a normal condition.   Hence a person affected by " colour
blindness " must correct his spontaneous interpretations of colour-
data so as to bring these judgments into conformity with those
of normal people.[1]

Then, on the side of the external datum : the spatial and
physical conditions of the object under perception, and of the
medium between the object and the perceiver, must also be normal in order to secure that the perceiver's spontaneous judgments
as to the qualities of the external datum or object be accurate.
Many, perhaps most, of those judgments are rather inferences
from what we directly perceive, but inferences so natural, prompt,
and automatic that they are for the most part semi-conscious
or sub-conscious : a consequence of which is that unreflecting
people think they *perceive*,—*i.e.* see, or hear, or touch—what
they really only *infer* from that which is directly perceived.[2]

In our perceptions of the " primary " or " common " sensible
qualities especially, the intellectual processes of judgment and
inference predominate.   No doubt we *perceive* data endowed
with volume or *three-dimensional extension*, with *shape* or *figure*,
with spatial continuity and *unity*, or discontinuity and *plurality*,
with *rest* and *motion*.   But the *relative* size of objects, their
relative positions in space, their distance from one another and
from the perceiver, their state of motion or rest *relatively* to
one another and to the perceiver,—these are not percepts at
all, but *estimates, i.e. interpretations* and *inferences*, based on the
concrete percepts.

Now it is, of course, only experience that enables us to
determine in perception the physical, external conditions, which

---

[1] The *exact location* of the data of the " organic sense " or " common sensibility,"
as it is called (*cf.* MAHER, *op. cit.*, p. 69),—*i.e.* organic processes and conditions,
aches and pains, etc.,—involves interpretation of these data, and is an endowment
gradually acquired by experience.   It is in virtue of this acquired "sense habit "
that a person who has had a portion of a limb amputated continues to feel, *i.e.* to
locate spontaneously, pains, aches, etc., *in the amputated portion* of the limb.

[2] *Cf. Science of Logic*, ii., § 238, pp. 162-4.   And, moreover, as we have already
remarked (118), apart from judgment and inference altogether, it requires close
introspective analysis to isolate the naked percept itself from the subjective
contribution made by the imagination and the faculty of association to the whole
conscious content in any individual process or act of external perception.

are normal, and those that are abnormal : the conditions in which we may as a rule rely on our spontaneous judgments of perception, and those in which such judgments will need correction. It is, for instance, by experience we know the external conditions in which a straight stick looks bent, in which an object at rest appears to be moving or *vice versa*, in which two objects unequal in size appear to be equal in size. It is by experience we know, and allow for, the effects of coloured spectacles, of the stereoscope, the microscope, the telescope, etc. By experience, too, we know and allow for the effects of distance and perspective on the size and shape of visible things.

120. EPISTEMOLOGICAL IMPORT OF THE DISTINCTION.—It needs no further illustration to make us realize that in our spontaneous interpretations of the immediate data presented in sense perception, we distinguish between normal and abnormal conditions, and between natural and artificial conditions, of the actual perception process. But the important question is, What does the distinction between normal and abnormal conditions imply in regard to the spontaneous judgments which attribute externality, extensity, size, shape, rest, motion, colour, and other sense qualities, to our immediately perceived sense data ?

It implies this at all events : that when we realize the conditions of any actual external sense perception,—whether conditions of the perceiver's own sense organs, or conditions of the " external " or " extra-organic " domain of reality,—to be *abnormal*, we regard the perceived external reality as being externally *otherwise* than it is reported or presented by the sense organs to consciousness, and spontaneously judged by the intellect interpreting this presentation without advertence to the abnormal conditions. In other words, we recognize that in such a case the rôle played by the abnormal conditions, whether organic or extra-organic, in presenting the external reality to consciousness, and in that presentation partially determining the quality or character of the presented datum, precludes us from judging (if we are to judge rightly) that the external reality is really and externally as it is presented to the conscious perceiver. Or, to put it in another way, we recognize that if the abnormal conditions are organic, the *relativity* of the presented datum to the perceiver's organism, the *dependence* of the presented datum on the sense organ, is *special and exceptional ;* and that if the abnormal conditions are extra-organic, the presented datum is likewise specially and exceptionally influenced by its relativity to or dependence on these : so that in neither alternative can we rightly judge that the presented external or extra-organic reality has really and externally the character or quality with which it is presented, but must in both alternatives make allowance for the influence of the abnormal conditions in discerning how much (so to speak) of the presented datum or quality is really extra-organic or external.

Secondly, the distinction implies that when all the conditions of an actual external perception are normal, the qualities of the presented sense datum can be rightly affirmed of *the perceived external reality*, inasmuch as those qualities are qualities of this reality as normally presented to consciousness. It *does not imply* that those qualities, presented to consciousness, are *wholly independent of the determining influence of the sense organs.* It recognizes that in *all* perception the qualities of the presented sense datum are partially determined to be what they are by the organic nature or structure and conditions of the perceiver's own material or corporeal sense organs, through the instrumental functions of which the external reality is presented to the individual perceiver's consciousness. But when these organic determining factors, on the subjective or "self" side of the process, are normal, and, being normal, are the same for all normal individual perceivers, their determining influence on the qualities of the external reality presented through their operation is not indeed denied, for it is undeniable, but is *tacitly and rightly ignored* as being something essentially involved in the subjective, organic side of the presentation of external reality to the perceiver's mind or consciousness. Hence the individual perceiver abstracts from this presupposed, uniform influence of his own organic nature as a sentient being, on the reality which he perceives, when he (both spontaneously and reflectively) judges this reality to *be* as it *is presented,*[1] *viz.* to be external, extended or three-dimensional, one or manifold, at rest or in motion, to have shape, resistance, colour, sound, temperature, taste, smell, etc.

121. THE NATURE OF EXTERNAL SENSE PERCEPTION INVOLVES RELATIVITY OF ALL EXTERNAL SENSE QUALITIES (INCLUDING CONCRETE EXTERNALITY ITSELF) TO PERCEIVER'S

---

[1] *I.e.*, on the assumption that the extra-organic conditions of perception also are normal.

ORGANISM.—The same intellectual reflection which brings out explicitly the partial *dependence* of all presented sense data and their qualities on the nature, structure, and conditions of the perceiver's own sense organs, and their consequent *relativity* to the latter, also brings out explicitly the fact that when this total subjective factor or determinant of sense data and their qualities is normal, and therefore uniform for all normal perceivers, its influence may be and must be ignored as something which, though essentially involved in the very nature of sense perception, and therefore entering into the very meaning of those sense data and qualities, does not falsify the judgments by which we pronounce those data to be perceived *realities*, and ascribe the qualities of those data ("externality," "extension" and the rest of the "common" and "proper" sense qualities) to these perceived realities. Let us now examine and illustrate this position in detail.

The "externality" of the immediate data of external sense perception,—the externality perceived or felt in the concrete and conceived in the abstract,—is not independent of, or unrelated to, the internal or subjective organic medium through which it is apprehended. What sort of knowledge of "externality" or "otherness" a purely spiritual or purely intelligent, non-sentient being would have, we can only conjecture through analogy with our own sort of knowledge (100). But the perceived and conceived externality or otherness is none the less real because our knowledge of it involves its presentation to consciousness *in the manner demanded by our nature as organic, sentient beings*, or in other words, because its cognitive union with us as conscious perceivers must be effected *conformably with our nature as perceptive, i.e.* dependently on the nature and structure of our sense organs : *cognitum est in cognoscente ;* and *quidquid recipitur, secundum modum recipientis recipitur.*

There is indeed one sense in which it would be absurd to say that the externality—*or any other sense quality*—which we attribute to the externally perceived domain of reality is in this domain, or characterizes this domain, *apart from perception or conception,* "in the same way" as it is in this domain *as actually perceived or conceived.* It would be absurd, namely, to say that the *feeling* of concrete externality, or the *conception* of abstract externality,—or *perceived* or *conceived* externality,—is in the domain of external reality *when this domain is not being actually perceived*

7 *

or conceived. The "externality" (or any other sense quality) as perceived or conceived, is *the term of a vital, conscious act,* cognitively one with the conscious perceiver or conceiver. The same externality (or other sense quality), as it is in the unperceived or unconceived external reality, is not an actual percept or concept, is not the actual term of a vital, conscious act, is not affected with feeling or awareness, with conscious perception or conception, by being cognitively one with a conscious perceiver or conceiver : but none the less the externality (or other sense quality) is a real characteristic of the reality which is perceived or conceived, and affects this reality whether or not the latter is being actually perceived or conceived.

It ought to be fairly obvious that when any sense quality,—such as "externality," "extension," "resistance," "motion," "colour," "heat," etc.,—is claimed to be in the reality which is perceived, and to be in this reality independently of our actual perception of the latter, this claim does not at all involve any such puerile contention as that there is in the *unperceived* reality a conscious state, or the term of a conscious process, or a perception or percept (73) of the sense quality, or a perceived sense quality.[1] Yet some writers appear to think that those who hold sense qualities to be *formally* in the perceived external universe apart from our perception of the latter are committed to a curious contention of that sort. The impression appears to be due partly to a failure to distinguish between the conscious perceiver or subject of perception, the conscious process or state or condition

---

[1] *Cf.* Jeannière, *op. cit.*, p. 425: "Saepe vitio vertitur Scholasticis quod ex. gr. dulcedinem subjectivam seu formalem attribuant rebus, vg. saccharo. Quod tamen est maxime falsum." But the author's explanation seems to attribute the theory of mediate sense perception to scholastics in general : "Scilicet distinctio est facienda inter *esse physicum* quod res habet in se et *esse intentionale* quod habet in cognoscente. Hinc dulcedo non habet idem esse in gustante et in saccharo. In gustante est affectio quaedam *sui generis,* qua sentiens cognoscit id quod hujus affectionis est causa, et cui tribuit non affectionem sui, sed id ratione cujus haec affectio, ut talis, producitur. Idem dicatur de colore et de ceteris sensibilibus." This would seem to imply that there are *two* "sweetnesses," one in the perceiver's consciousness and the other in the sugar ; that the former, which is an "affectio quaedam *sui generis,*" is what the perceiver *first and directly* becomes aware of ; and that the latter is inferred from this as its cause. But there *are not two* "sweetnesses " : the "affectio which is in the perceiver's consciousness is not a perceived (mental or subjective) "sweetness" but a *perception of* the external, sugar sweetness. The entire perceptive process is the "esse intentionale" of this external quality. Looked at from the side of the perceiver it is the latter's "perception "; looked at from the side of perceived external quality it is the "presentation" or "presence" of this quality to the conscious perceiver. *Cf. infra,* § 125 ; *supra,* § 112.

of perception, and the reality which is the object of perception and which in actual perception becomes the term which the perceiver is made aware of through the process ; and partly to an unfortunate, though perhaps not wholly avoidable, ambiguity of meaning in the names of the sense qualities : an ambiguity noted by Aristotle and St. Thomas, and to which we shall return presently.

Again, take the common sensibles,—superficial and three-dimensional extension or magnitude, shape and multitude, and rest or motion,—as revealed in the concrete through the co-operation of the internal or " common " sense, or faculty of unification, with the external senses of touch and sight.[1] These characteristics of immediate sense data are presented with the perceiver's own organism, no less than with extra-organic or external reality, as objects of perception. They are all partly dependent for what they are on the organic medium through which they are presented to consciousness. When, therefore, they are presented in the concrete as qualities of " external " data, and are spontaneously attributed to the perceived external realities as being really in these latter, it is not denied that those qualities as perceived by us in the external realities are nevertheless relative to the nature, structure, and conditions of the perceiving organism. A partial reason why they are presented to us and apprehended by us, as they are, in all their actual specific and irreducible varieties, is because the various sense organs through which they are presented to us are differently constructed. But this is a partial reason only : because in the first place diversity of sense organs implies *diversity in the qualities of the external realities* apprehended through those organs : if *external* material reality were homogeneous there would be no sufficient reason for heterogeneity or diversity of structure in the sense organs through which that reality is presented to consciousness. And secondly, *different* external qualities,—*e.g.* different colours, different resistances, different magnitudes, different rates and directions of motion, different tastes, smells, temperatures,—are presented through *each* separate sense organ. This partial dependence of the sense qualities (*quoad specificationem*) on diversity of sense organ, and their consequent relativity to the perceiving subject

---

[1] And possibly with the other external senses in so far as these present a vague voluminousness or extensity in their respective data. *Cf. supra,* § 106, p. 37, n. ; p. 39, n. 2.

as organic, is of course primarily true of the proper sensibles. But if the common sensibles are objectively unified concrete complexes of the proper sensibles (114), the dependence of those also on the perceiver's organism, and their relativity to him as an organic subject, must likewise be admitted. This dependence and relativity are indeed involved in the very nature of sense perception and are presupposed by intellect in its conception of the sense qualities in the abstract. But when such dependence and relativity are normal, the intellect properly abstracts from them in its attribution of the sense qualities and their differences to the extra-organic domain of material reality.

Finally, if we examine the secondary or "proper" sense qualities—colours, sounds, tastes, smells, qualities of contact, pressure, resistance, temperature,—we shall find that they are distinctly relative to and dependent on subjective, internal, organic conditions of the perceiver, for the specific characters with which they present themselves to consciousness in actual perception. Hence there has been much doubt and controversy even among realists as to whether or how far or in what way these secondary sense qualities are in the external universe independently of our actual perception. Can an external material thing or object be said to have *colour* or *taste* or *smell* apart from all sense perception of it? Is there *sound* in rushing winds, the falling waters, the waves crashing on the breakers, if there be no sentient being present to hear it? Is ice *cold* and *smooth* and *impenetrable* when there is no sentient being actually touching it? Everyone is perfectly familiar with each of these sense qualities *as it presents itself to his consciousness* in actual external sense perception. But because every such sense quality is partially determined to be what it is for the perceiver (in actual perception) by the nature, structure, and actual condition of the internal or subjective factor which is his own organism, are we to conclude that the sense quality which he is immediately and directly aware of is not in the domain of *external* reality at all, as the idealist contends? Or is it that, being itself a mental impression or representation produced in his consciousness by the influence of the external reality on his mind through the medium of a bodily sense organ, the sense quality is not in the external reality *formally, i.e.* as it is consciously represented or apprehended, but is only in the external reality *virtually* or *causally*, so that there is in the external reality a quality which is the "analogical" cause of the immediately apprehended conscious impression,—as the realist supporter of mediate or representative sense perception contends?[1] Or perhaps, even though it is partially determined by and relative to the perceiver's own nature as an organic being, nevertheless the sense quality as immediately present to and consciously apprehended by him, if it is perceived *in normal organic* (and external) *conditions*, is really, actually, and *formally* in the external domain of reality,—as the perceptionist contends?

Before setting forth in detail some at least of the very many solutions offered by philosophers, and which may be brought under one or other of the three broad alternatives just suggested, we may say that the first or idealist position must be rejected as erroneous, and that as between the two realist positions the second ought not to be adopted without sufficient reason for abandoning the third.

[1] *Cf.* JEANNIÈRE, *op. cit.*, pp. 425-8.

CHAPTER XVIII.

EXTERNAL REALITY OF ALL SENSE QUALITIES VINDICATED. "HYPERPHYSICAL IDEALISM" AND "PHYSICAL REALISM".

122. IN NORMAL CONDITIONS OF PERCEPTION THIS RELA-TIVITY IS COMPATIBLE WITH EXTERNAL REALITY OF SENSE QUALITIES.—That all the sense qualities alike are *extramental*, that the proper sensibles no less than the common sensibles (115) are real characteristics of a domain of reality which exists inde-pendently of the perceiver's mind, a domain which he apprehends as "material reality" and distinguishes into two parts, *viz.* the "external universe" and "his own body or material organism," we consider to be as certain as the already established extra-mental existence of this material domain itself. Of this domain he becomes aware by becoming aware of the sense qualities. If these are not really in it and do not really characterize it, how can he be certain even of its extramental existence? And if they are not extramentally real how can they be in an extra-mental reality or characterize it or reveal it to him?

But when they appear to him in actual perception as affect-ing the *external* or *extra-organic* or *non-self* domain of reality, can he be sure that they are really in this domain notwithstanding the fact that for the specific determinations with which they are presented to his consciousness they are *partially* dependent on the subjective or self factor which is his own organism? The answer is that he can, provided that this organic, subjective or self factor is normal: and this he can determine with certitude by experience. He attributes the particular taste, or smell, or colour, or sound, or temperature, or texture and resistance, to the datum which he apprehends as external. He is right in doing so provided he knows, as he can know by comparison of his ex-periences with those of other perceivers, that the sense organ through the function of which the particular quality is reported to him is normal. For then he knows that the determining in-fluence of the sense organ on the presented sense quality is a normal, uniform influence essentially involved in all perception, affecting in the same way for all normal perceivers the externality of the external sense quality in its presentation to consciousness, and therefore in no way falsifying the judgments by which he pronounces the various normally perceived sense qualities and their differences to be in the external domain of reality, to be real determinations of this domain, and to be properly and formally predicable of it. When, for instance, the normal perceiver apprehends snow as white, and spontaneously asserts that " snow is white," he means not that the colour-quality in question is wholly independent of the nature, structure, and conditions of his visual sense organs for its specific character as present to his consciousness ; nor that the external or extra-organic element of the whole presented datum, considered apart from actual perception, is the same as this element *plus* the organic element in the whole concrete datum as presented *per modum unius* in actual perception ; but that, abstracting from the normal and uniform subjective or organic element, the external or extra-organic element *which he calls " whiteness,"* and which is *what he means by " whiteness,"* is really in the snow whether he perceives it or not, is immediately apprehended by him in actual perception, and, being external to and independent of him, is in no way altered by his actual perception of it. He understands " whiteness," therefore, to be a quality, not of the actual perception as a psychic or conscious process ; nor of the perception as an organic, brain and nerve process ; nor of the psychic or conscious modification, or the organic, brain and nerve modification, resulting from either process ; nor of the specific element contributed by the brain, nerves, and visual organs to the total presented datum ; [1]

[1] There is a school of writers who, with MÜLLER (1801-58), make *all* qualitative differences in sense data depend exclusively on the different " specific energies " resulting from variety of nature and structure in the sense organs (*cf.* JEANNIÈRE, *op. cit.*, pp. 415, 427-8). According to these the *external* reality, in itself homogeneous, is *subjectively* discriminated by virtue of its being apprehended through differently constructed and differently functioning sense organs : it is apprehended by the eye as colour, by the ear as sound, by the sense of temperature as heat, etc. No doubt, the proximate and partial reason why the data, *e.g.* of the eye and the ear, are consciously different, is because these sense organs differ in structure and function. But this is only a partial reason, and, in so far as it operates uniformly, should be taken for granted, and should be understood to leave unaltered and unaffected the specifying influence of the external, extra-organic elements of the presented data. It is these that *ultimately* determine the consciously perceived variety in our sense data ; it is these that are denoted by the names of the various sense qualities, and not any condition or energy of the sense organs ; without these the

but *of the external or extra-organic element* specifically determined by the nature of the external reality itself and immediately presented to consciousness in actual perception.

And what thus applies to "whiteness" applies in its proper measure to all the sense qualities. The names of the various proper or secondary sense qualities,—of colours, sounds, tastes, smells, tactual and temperature qualities,—are not names of *mental states*, or of *organic states*, conditions or qualities, *of the perceiver*: they are names of qualities of external or extra-organic bodies.[1]   But Aristotle, St. Thomas, and the scholastics generally, while holding that these qualities are really in external bodies independently of our actual perception of them, realized the necessity of distinguishing between the *unperceived* reality of these qualities, and the characters which their reality assumes in our actual perception of them : between these qualities *in actu* (ἐν ἐνεργείᾳ) and *in potentia* (ἐν δυνάμει).[2]   In the untasted sugar there is real *sweetness* but not the sensation or perception or taste of sweetness, or actually perceived sweetness ; in the unseen snow there is real *whiteness* but not the *vision* of whiteness, or actually perceived whiteness ; in the unheard tempest there is real *sound*,[3] but not the *hearing*[4] or actual sensation or perception of sound ; in the unsmelt violet there is real perfume but not the actual smell or perception of the perfume ; and so on.   In other words, if we understand the name of the sense quality to denote this quality *as actually perceived*, and thereby to connote as part of its meaning the actual conscious perception process or state itself, then of course the quality so named cannot be in the *unperceived* external domain *actually* (inasmuch as the sensation or perception process is absent from the unperceived domain) ; but nevertheless the *unperceived* quality is *really* there, and we can say it is there *potentially* or *virtually*, meaning thereby, not that the

specific structures and energies of the latter would be unintelligible ; nor can any useful purpose be served by transferring the spontaneously judged "external " sense qualities to the perceiver's own organism, and wresting the recognized meaning of the names of the various sense qualities so as to make these names signify states or conditions of the perceiver's organism : any more than by making them signify conscious or mental "ideas" or "representations".   *Cf. supra*, § 121, p. 101 ; *infra*, § 124.

    [1] And, of course, of the organism itself *as an object of sense perception.*

    [2] *Cf.* Maher, *op. cit.*, pp. 153, 159-61.

    [3] " *sonus*," " *sonatio* "—Aristotle, *De Anima*, L. III., lect. 2 ; St. Thomas, *Comm. de Anima, in loc.—apud* Maher, *op. cit.*, p. 160, n.

    [4] " *auditus*," " *auditio*,"—*ibid.*

quality is any less really there when unperceived than when perceived, but that as unperceived it is a *potential* or *virtual percept or term of a conscious perceptive process ;* in other words, that it is a reality capable of being perceived though not actually perceived. This is the perfectly intelligible sense in which, as explained above (121), we can say that sense qualities are not in external bodies "formally" or "in the way in which they are perceived": apart from actual perception they are in those bodies "as unperceived," or "virtually" or "potentially," not as *actual* but as *potential* "percepts" or terms of conscious perception.

However, although the ambiguity which prevails as to the proper application of the names of the secondary sense qualities calls for this distinction in the interests of clearness, it is nevertheless true that in ordinary usage these names are understood to denote qualities *really in external bodies independently of actual perception ;* and even when reflection has convinced us that the external qualities are partially influenced in their actual presentation, by the structure and condition of the perceiver's sense organs, to appear as they do, we see no sufficient reason in this for including the subjective, organic element (when normal and uniform) in the meaning of the names whereby we designate the external or extra-organic qualities.

123. SECONDARY QUALITIES ARE NO LESS EXTERNALLY REAL, AND NO MORE DEPENDENT ON PERCEIVER FOR WHAT THEY ARE PERCEIVED TO BE, THAN PRIMARY QUALITIES. BERKELEY'S IMMATERIALISM.—If, however, the distinction between the "potential" and the "actual" reality of sense qualities in the external domain be understood to mean that in this domain, and apart from actual perception, some sense qualities, *viz.* the proper sensibles, existing only potentially, *have a less degree of external reality,* so to speak, than others, *viz.* the common sensibles, as existing actually and with a fuller degree of external reality,—the distinction does not seem to have any real ground in the facts. For if the proper sensibles are partially relative to or dependent on a subjective, organic factor, for the specific characteristics wherewith they are presented in consciousness, so too are the common sensibles which are unified complexes of those: and this relativity or dependence can, when normal, be ignored in the common no less than in the proper sensibles.

If, as perceptionists hold, the specific data of which we be-

come directly aware in normal external perception are external
qualities presented through the functioning of the sense organs,
then these qualities, whether primary or secondary, exist in the
same way in this domain independently of actual perception :
if we say that the primary qualities exist "formally" or
"actually" in the external domain apart from perception, so do
the secondary qualities.

If, on the other hand, as representationists hold, the immediate data of external sense awareness are in *all* cases conscious
impressions or representations produced in us by corresponding
external causes, then if such immediate data be said to exist in
the external domain apart from perception only "causally,"
"virtually," "potentially," when they are secondary qualities, the
immediate data which are primary qualities must also exist in this
way only, and not "formally" or "actually," apart from actual
perception.   Jeannière, for instance, defends the representationist
theory, that the senses do not attain to reality as it is, but only
to its appearances,[1] and that nevertheless we can know things as
they are in themselves so that we can attribute to them predicates
that are really intrinsic to them.[2]   But he also holds, and rightly,
as we think, that *no distinction should in this respect be made* between *primary* and *secondary* qualities.   And the reasons he gives
are sound : (*a*) because the grounds for admitting or rejecting
(the external reality of) both classes of qualities are the same ;
(*b*) because philosophers who reject the secondary qualities generally proceed to reject the primary also ;[3] (*c*) because (even on
the representationist theory) "impressions" of colour, sound,
taste, smell, etc., demand corresponding external "causes" just
as much as extension, or the "primary" or "common" sense
percepts.   The author adds that it is the duty of the *epistemologist* merely to show that the *secondary* qualities are *real* characteristics of external bodies independently of perception ; that *what*
these qualities are externally is a question between the *cosmologist* and the physical scientist.   The same, however, is true of
the primary qualities.

[1] "Sensibus attingi res non in se, sed in suis apparentiis "—*op. cit.*, p. 417.
[2] "Posse cognosci res ut sunt in se, ita sc. ut eis tribuere liceat praedicata quae
eis vere sint intrinseca "—*ibid.*   Query : How ? if the predicates are abstract concepts of concrete sense *appearances*, and if these appearances, being intramental
impressions or representations, are obviously not intrinsic to the external realities ?
Cf. infra, § 127.
[3] *Ibid.*, § 125.

Berkeley's[1] *Immaterialism,* or *Objective* (or "*Acosmic*," or *Hyperphysical*) *Idealism,* is an apt illustration of the tendency to deny the external reality of the *primary* qualities when that of the *secondary* qualities has once been rejected. His theory, to which we have already referred incidentally (*cf.* 102, 111), has never failed to win adherents ; but perhaps none of these have rivalled their master in the ingenuity with which he himself defended his position and gave it such a peculiar fascination for reflecting minds. It will be convenient to examine the theory briefly in the present context.

The qualities perceived by our senses are only mental states or " ideas". Sight does not reveal extension to us, but only colours mentally associated with the extension revealed by the sense of touch. But extensional qualities are, like those of the other senses, only mental states. All the sense qualities, primary and secondary alike, are only mental states. In fact all the ob-jects of our direct awareness must be mental states, and only mental states : partly imagination images, partly internal feelings and emotions, and partly " sensations " or " perceptions " or " ideas of the senses ". Their *esse* is *percipi :* they are essentially mind-dependent entities : it is impossible to prove, and irrational to believe, that they have or can have any extramental reality, any being beyond the consciousness of the perceiver. If, then, the sense qualities or " ideas of the senses " appear in stable, uni-form, clearly differentiated groups or aggregates, to each of which we give a name such as " apple," " oak," " rain," " horse," " house," " human body," etc., and all of which make up the domain of reality which we call the " sensible " or " material " universe, the principle which groups these qualities into definite wholes or sense-objects cannot possibly be the supposed extra-mental, inert, lifeless, unconscious, and unperceiving thing which philosophers have called " matter " or " material substance " :[2]

[1] Berkeley was born in Co. Kilkenny, Ireland, in 1685, and was educated in Trinity College, Dublin, where he studied the works of Locke and Descartes. He travelled in Italy and France, visiting Père Malebranche (in Paris, 1711) with whose philosophical views he had strong sympathies. The memorable Bermuda project (1723-31) of converting the American Indians is typical of his deeply philanthropic character. Later he became Protestant Bishop of Cloyne, where he combined the study of Plato with practical work for the amelioration of the hard lot of an oppressed people. He died in 1752. His principal works are the *New Theory of Vision* (1709), the *Principles of Knowledge* (1710), *Three Dialogues between Hylas and Philonous* (1713), and *Alciphron, or the Minute Philosopher* (1731).

[2] The influence of the perverted notions of substance expounded by Locke and Descartes are here plainly noticeable. *Cf. Ontology,* §§ 61-4.

for sense qualities, being mind-dependent ideas, can exist only in a conscious, perceiving substance, *i.e.* in a mind or spirit. The concept of matter is the concept of a mere abstraction ; and to think of matter as a real, extramental substance or subject of sense qualities is to think a contradiction in terms. Matter, in the meaning of an extramental or mind-independent reality or substance, is a mere figment of the mind's abstraction : no such reality exists. What is called matter, or the material universe (including, of course, our own bodies) is simply the system of sense qualities or phenomena or ideas in individual, conscious, perceiving minds or spirits : and each of these human minds or spirits knows of the real existence of other similar minds or spirits, really distinct from and independent of itself, by inference from the presence in itself of other idea-aggregates similar to the idea-aggregate which it has learned to designate as its own " human body ". But the whole system of ideas in each human mind, and which each one calls the external world or universe, *is* a *system*, a *cosmos*, obviously permeated by law, order, regularity, uniformity. It clearly demands an explanation, and must have an adequate cause. But, just as clearly, it is not caused by the individual perceiving human mind or spirit ;[1] and to suppose it to be caused by an extramental something called " matter," which is a mere figment and not a reality at all, is manifestly absurd ; therefore it must be caused or produced or placed in each human mind or created spirit by the Self-Existent, Divine, Uncreated Spirit, God. Just as the mental idea-aggregates which we call " human bodies " are mental symbols which reveal to us the real existence of other human minds or spirits, so the whole constant, regular, orderly panorama of ideas which each human mind apprehends as " the universe " is for each such mind a symbol revealing the real existence of the Divine Spirit. Matter, therefore, does not exist. Only three orders of reality exist : (1) created spirits or human minds, (2) the Uncreated Spirit, and (3) ideas caused or created in human spirits by the Divine Spirit. The system of ideas, moreover, which constitutes "the universe" for and in each created spirit is a system of entities which are mere symbols : their sole function is to teach us all we can infer from them about our own nature as created spirits, and about God the Uncreated Spirit. They are not themselves in any way active or operative ;

[1] *Cf.* reasons given in § 111 above.

they are not causes ; causality is an attribute of spirit only, not of the " ideas " which constitute the " world of sense ".

Such are the broad outlines of Berkeley's philosophy. We shall offer a brief criticism of the main points.

In the *first* place, he fails utterly to give a rational vindication of his knowledge of, and belief in, the existence of his own mind, the human mind, as a substance, a spiritual substance : and his own principles make such vindication impossible, and such belief inconsistent, and therefore irrational. For if the " material substance " which men suppose to be the subject characterized by sense qualities be an unreal figment of thought because it is not an object of direct awareness, and having no *percipi* has therefore no *esse* or reality, so *a pari* the " spiritual substance " or substantial " mind " or " soul " or " spirit " which men suppose to be the conscious subject of mental images, emotions, feelings, sensations, perceptions, thoughts, and mental states of all sorts, is likewise only an unreal figment of thought inasmuch as it also is not an " idea " [1] or object of direct awareness, and therefore, having no *percipi*, it has no *esse* or reality. Hence, so far as we can know, the mind is not a substantial reality, but simply " a heap or collection of different perceptions united together by certain relations, and supposed, though falsely, to be endowed with simplicity and identity".[2] Thus, in the pan-phenomenism of Hume, Berkeley's principles logically lead to an extreme scepticism which is the very antithesis of Berkeley's own beliefs and intentions.[3]

Secondly, this issue cannot be avoided by the plea that the sense qualities imply a subject, no doubt, but, being "ideas " or " mental " states, require a spiritual or mental substance,[4] though not a material substance : for on Berkeley's principle that *esse* is *percipi* it can be argued that the supposed "spiritual " substance is just as *extramental* as the supposed material substance—in the

---

[1] *Cf. Principles of Human Knowledge* (*Philosoph. Classics*, Kegan Paul, 1907), p. 116 n.

[2] HUME, *Works*, i., 534,—*apud* TURNER, *History of Philosophy*, p. 520.

[3] *Cf. Three Dialogues*, etc. (*Philosoph. Classics*, Kegan Paul, 1906), p. 96 : " *Hylas* : . . . in consequence of your own principles it should follow that *you* are only a system of floating ideas, without any substance to support them " : to which Berkeley can only reply, in the person of *Philonous* : " I know or am conscious of my own being ; and that *I myself* am not my ideas, but somewhat else, a thinking, active principle, etc." : which is incompatible with the principle that knowledge is only of " ideas," that all " *esse* is *percipi* ".

[4] *Cf. Principles*, etc., § 91, p. 83.

sense that the former is *no more an object of direct awareness*, or has no more "*percipi*," than the latter. And this brings us to inquire what Berkeley can have meant by the contention that *esse* is *percipi*.[1] It is capable of at least two meanings : (1) that all the objects *of our direct conscious awareness* are necessarily mind-dependent entities or " ideas " [2]; or (2) that *all knowable* realities, —howsoever knowable, whether intuitively or inferentially, and whether by sense or by intellect,—are mind-dependent entities or " ideas ". Moreover we may ask, in regard to both alternatives, (*a*) of *what* mind is there question? and (*b*) do they imply that the *only* reality of the objects in question consists in their being perceived or known by the mind in question, so that by ceasing to be thus perceived or known they would simply cease to be?

Now if understood in the sense of the first alternative, the principle, " *esse* is *percipi*," is recognized as limited, as not being universal, and as admitting the possibility of our " knowing," and therefore " becoming aware of" realities which are *not* mind-dependent, whose *esse* does not consist in their *percipi*, in their " being known". Berkeley seems to have held that the individual mind can and does know the existence of *itself* [3] and of *other human minds* [4] and of the *Divine Mind*, and yet that these

---

[1] *Cf supra*, §§ 101, 102.

[2] *I.e.* understanding " ideas " in the wide sense in which they include the mental content of external and internal perceptions or sensations, images of the imagination, emotions, etc.

[3] *Cf. supra*, p. 111, n. 3.

[4] *Cf. Principles*, etc., § 90, p. 82 : " We comprehend our own existence by inward feeling or reflexion, and that of other spirits by reason. We may be said to have some knowledge or notion of our own minds, of spirits and active beings, whereof in a strict sense we have not ideas." (For Berkeley an " idea," in the strict sense, does not represent anything beyond itself: " ideas " are merely mental objects : from which, however, interpreted as symbols and effects, we can infer the reality of the Divine Spirit.) Again he writes (*ibid.*, 140, p. 116) : " In a large sense, indeed we may be said to have an idea ('or rather a notion,' 2nd edit.) of *spirit*; that is, we understand the meaning of the word, otherwise we could not affirm or deny anything of it. Moreover, as we conceive the ideas that are in the minds of other spirits by means of our own, which we suppose to be resemblances of them [*i.e.* of the ideas in other spirits] ; so we know other spirits by means of our own soul— which in that sense is the image or idea of them; it having a like respect to other spirits that blueness or heat by me perceived has to those ideas perceived by others." And again (*ibid.*, 142, p. 118) : " *Spirits* and *ideas* are things so wholly different, that when we say ' they exist,' ' they are known,' or the like, these words must not be thought to signify anything common to both natures. There is nothing alike or common in them." *Cf.* also *Three Dialogues*, etc., p. 92 *sqq.* (Third Dialogue). So, then, we have some notion or knowledge of created spirits and the Divine Spirit, as well as of " ideas ". But it is hard to see, on Berkeley's principles, how we can have any notion or knowledge of the former unless in so far as they are

realities are not mind-dependent, not mere ideas in the individual mind "knowing" them, that their *esse* is not merely *percipi*. There are, then, it would appear, besides things (*viz.* "ideas ") whose *esse* or reality is *percipi*, other things (*viz.* "spirits," human and Divine) whose *esse* or reality is not *percipi* but rather *percipere*, *i.e.* realities which are essentially conscious or cognitive, or, as Berkeley would say, "spiritual ". If this is so, the principle "*esse* is *percipi*," is accepted not in the universal sense of the second alternative given above,—which would lead to something like Kant's phenomenism,—but in the limited sense in which it applies only to *some* knowable objects. But in that case the question whether the sole reality of any given kind of perceived or known object,—for example, a sense quality,—consists in its being perceived or known, *i.e.* the question whether it is essentially a mind-dependent entity or "idea," cannot be decided by appealing to the principle, "*esse* is *percipi*," as of *universal* application, but must be decided by consideration of the special kind of object in question, to determine whether the principle applies to it or not.[1]

And this in fact is the line taken by Berkeley. With a rare ingenuity and wealth of subtle reasoning he endeavours to show [2] that the sense qualities are essentially mind-dependent entities or "ideas," and that the concept of an extramental "material substance," in which they would be supposed to inhere is self-contradictory. But he does not succeed. If there are other realities, *viz.* "spirits" or "minds," whose being does not consist in their being actually perceived, but which are extramental or independent of mind in the sense that their reality persists unaffected by my knowledge or perception of them, and which can

objects of conscious awareness or cognition, *i.e.* unless in so far as they are "mental phenomena" or "ideas": any knowledge of what they are beyond this, and in themselves, seems impossible.

[1] *Cf.* PRICHARD, *op. cit.*, pp. 121-2: "We can only decide that a particular reality depends upon the mind by appeal to its special character. We cannot treat it as a reality the relation of which to the mind is solely that of knowledge. And we can only decide that all reality is dependent upon mind by appeal to the special character of all the kinds of reality of which we are aware. Hence, Kant in the *Aesthetic*, and Berkeley before him, were essentially right in their procedure. They both ignored consideration of the world simply as a reality, and appealed exclusively to its special character, the one arguing that in its special character as spatial and temporal it presupposed a percipient, and the other endeavouring to show that the primary qualities are as relative to perception as the secondary. . . . In order to think of the world as dependent on mind, we have to think of it as consisting only of a succession of appearances, and in fact, Berkeley, and, at certain times, Kant did think of it in this way."

[2] *Cf. Principles*, etc., *passim*.

and do exist whether I know or perceive them or not, it is at
least not *prima facie* impossible that sense qualities may exist
extramentally in an extramental material substance whether I
perceive the qualities or know the substance or not.   Berkeley
contends that the extramental existence of " matter " or " material
substance," a thing which would be neither a perceiving or knowing reality on the one hand, but an " unthinking,"[1] " unperceiving,"[2] " senseless substance,"[3] nor a mind-dependent,
" perceived " or " known " mental reality[4] on the other hand,
is impossible and self-contradictory.[5]   But in the end all his
arguments in support of the contention come to this, that sense
qualities are ideas, that ideas can exist only in a mind, that
they cannot be produced in our minds by an inert, extramental
substance such as matter is supposed to be : " In the very notion
or definition of *material substance* there is included a manifest
repugnance and inconsistency. . . . That ideas should exist in
what doth not perceive, or be produced by what doth not act,
is repugnant." [6]   But if sense qualities are *not* ideas, and if matter
is *not* inert but *active*, the repugnance disappears.   Now, Berkeley
simply took over from Descartes and Locke the *erroneous* notion
of matter as an *inert, inactive* substance.   Such a notion of matter
cannot be defended as objectively valid : matter is active and does
produce in us perceptions of its sense qualities.   And furthermore,
Berkeley has nowhere *proved* that sense qualities can be only
ideas.   Of course, if he could prove that, then indeed it would be
contradictory to conceive them as existing in an *unperceiving*
substance such as matter.   What he really does is to identify
and confound *perceptions* of sense qualities with sense qualities
themselves.[7]   We have already referred (121) to the absurdity
of supposing that *perceptions* of the sense qualities exist in
extramental material things ; or that the sense qualities exist
in the same way in material things, *when unperceived* by us, as

---

[1] *Principles*, etc., §§ 24, 86.   [2] *Three Dialogues*, etc., p. 94.
[3] *Ibid.*, § 67.
[4] The sense qualities being " ideas " in the perceiving mind, the concept of
matter has nothing real corresponding to it : it is nothing extramental ; and intra-
mentally it is not an " idea " distinct from the " ideas " which are the sense qualities.
[5] " The absolute [*i.e.* mind-independent or extramental] existence of unthinking
things [other than " ideas " in a thinking or perceiving mind] are words without a
meaning, or which imply a contradiction."—*Principles*, etc., § 24, p. 43.
[6] *Three Dialogues*, etc., p. 94.
[7] For this common idealist confusion of the cognition, or cognitive act or process, with the thing known, *cf.* PRICHARD, *op. cit.*, pp. 133-4 ; *supra*, §§ 121, 122.

they appear in the conscious act of perception, if we mean by this latter expression that when being actually perceived they are the objects or terms of vital, conscious, cognitive acts of a perceiving mind : for of course when unperceived they are not objects or terms of any conscious act. Sense qualities, however, are not *acts* of perception but *objects* of perception. They are not *processes* or *states* of consciousness or awareness, but *terms* of awareness, *i.e.* objects in which these processes or states *cognitively* " terminate ". Berkeley has failed to bring forward any *a posteriori* or experiential ground for the view that these qualities, which become *objects* or " intentional " *terms* of our perceptive acts, are essentially, and in their own proper reality, mind-dependent entities or " ideas " ; and the only *a priori* ground of the view that they must be so, that their *esse* is *percipi*, consists simply in the gratuitous idealist postulate that the mind cannot " transcend " itself to become directly aware of anything which has reality independently of mind. But we have already repeatedly shown that such an assumption is unwarrantable. The position, then, is this : Berkeley contends that the *esse* of sense qualities is their *percipi ;* and there are only two conceivable ways of defending this contention,—(1) on the ground that they are *realities simply,* and that all reality is essentially *percipi ;* or (2) on the ground that they are realities *of a special kind,* to which actual perception is essential. But the first line of defence inevitably frustrates all knowledge of anything beyond the flow of conscious states in the individual mind, and leads to subjective phenomenism and agnosticism ; and the second line of defence can be sustained only by gratuitously confounding *objects of cognition* with *cognitions of objects.* If *all* " esse " is " percipi," pan-phenomenism is the unavoidable consequence ; if all " esse " is *either* " percipi " (" ideas ") *or* " percipere " (real " minds " or " spirits "), Berkeley fails to show how we can attain to a genuine knowledge of these latter as they really are, and not merely of " perceptions," " appearances," " representations " of them ; and between these two positions he is constantly wavering.

Thirdly, some of Berkeley's critics have rightly pointed out that his theory involves the erroneous doctrine of Occasionalism, at least in its less extreme form : the doctrine, namely, that there is no *efficient causality* in the material universe ; [1] for on his

---

[1] For analysis of Occasionalism, *cf. Ontology,* § 105.

8 *

theory this universe is only a system of "ideas" which are but "symbols" and "occasions" of the activities of created spirits and the Divine Spirit.

But some of his critics think that his theory cannot be successfully refuted by any line of argument directly based on analysis of the data of our experience: that it can be effectively disproved only by an *argumentum ad hominem* showing that the theory is incompatible with the attributes of Wisdom and Veracity which Berkeley, as a Theist, admits and defends in the Deity. Thus Maher writes[1] : "We have never seen any experiential argument which, strictly speaking, disproves the hypothesis of hyperphysical Idealism. God, without the intervention of a material world, could *potentia absoluta* immediately produce in men's minds states like those which they experience in the present order. The only demonstrative argument against the Theistic Immaterialist is, that such a hypothesis is in conflict with the attribute of veracity which he must ascribe to the Deity. God could not be the author of such a fraud." And we find, among many scholastic writers, Jeannière, for instance, relying on an appeal to the Divine Wisdom and Veracity against Berkeley.[2]

Now, of course God could *potentia absoluta* produce our actual experience without a material universe ; and of course, also, He could not be the author of such a fraud. But Berkeley's contention is that there is no fraud ; that the plain man's belief in the *absolute* existence of a *material* universe *apart from all perception* (if indeed the plain man really entertains such a belief : for Berkeley contends that it is the imperfect reflection of philosophers, mistaking mental abstractions and figments for realities, that is responsible for such belief) can be seen by mature reflection to have been groundless. And he can, moreover, point out that realist *defenders of the theory of mediate perception* themselves hold the plain man to be wrong, mistaken, deceived, if he believes (as he does) that the *immediate object* of his awareness is *external material reality* (since on their theory it is a mental state) ; and that they do not see in this anything inconsistent with the Divine Wisdom or Veracity. If then, he might urge, a little further and deeper reflection can convince us (as he himself contends that it can and ought to convince us) that the proper inference from these consciously perceived states or objects, which we call sense qualities, is not to the existence of a (superfluous and self-contradictory) material reality existing independently of mind, but directly to the existence of an Eternal, Intelligent, Divine Being, how can this conclusion,—which does not run so much more counter to the supposed common belief of the plain man than does the position of the representationist,—be fairly accused of derogating from the Divine Wisdom and Veracity, or of making the Divine Being the author of a fraud,—since the illusion of the supposed common belief is, at all events, in neither case an *invincible* illusion ? To meet this retort the realist defenders of mediate perception must show (a) that on this theory the plain man is not deceived as to *what* he perceives, but only as to

[1] *Psychology*, p. 109, n. 6.
[2] *Op. cit.*, pp. 104-3 : "Causa impressionum extensionis non est Deus". *Cf. supra*, § 111.

how he perceives, and this not invincibly ; and (*b*) that on Berkeley's theory he would be *invincibly* deceived in regard to the very nature of *what* he perceives. It is only by *analysis of the experienced facts of perception* he can hope to establish the former point ; and he really cannot establish the latter—except indeed by showing, *on other grounds revealed by a similar analysis*, that Berkeley's theory is *false*. For if the only possible refutation of the theory lay in the contention that it makes God the author of a deception, in other words, if no exception can be taken to, or no defect found in, *the theory itself,—i.e.* in its *interpretation of experienced facts*, in its *principles*, and its *deduction from these principles*,—then this admitted intrinsic soundness of the theory would *eo ipso* prove the plain man's illusion to be *not invincible*, and would thereby show that the Divine Veracity is not really touched by the theory. We prefer, therefore, not to rely on the argument from the Divine Attributes, but rather to test Berkeley's theory by facing it with the ultimate facts of consciousness, by examining its interpretation of these, and analysing its assumptions in the light of them.

Fourthly, Berkeley's attempt to reach rational certitude of the existence of an Eternal, Divine Spirit, from the supposed essentially mind-dependent nature of the sense qualities, is a failure; and thus, despite his intentions, his theory points towards agnosticism and subjectivism. Beyond the aspects of it we have just examined there lies this larger issue, which we can best approach by asking the question : If the material universe is for each individual perceiving mind simply a system of ideas in this mind, what becomes of the universe when it is not being actually perceived by this individual mind ? Here Berkeley has not, perhaps, made his position as clear as one might desire. Either there are as many " material " or " sensible " universes as there are minds, or there is only one " material " universe apprehended in common, more or less fully from case to case, by all minds. The first alternative would follow if the *esse* of a sense quality consisted in its perception by the *individual mind :* there would be as many similar sense qualities, and similar systems or " universes " of sense qualities, as distinct individual minds ; and the reality of each such universe would be measured by, and dependent on, and co-extensive with, the ever-changing actual content of the individual's consciousness : the general similarity of the conscious sense experiences of all human minds being the result of a Divinely established harmony between these minds, and of the similarity of the " ideas " placed in them by the Divine agency. In the second alternative the one universe or system of " ideas " or sense qualities would be contemplated in

varying degrees by all created minds,[1] so that when any one
individual mind ceases to be actually and consciously perceptive
the system ceases to exist *relatively to it*, but not *absolutely*, for
it is still being perceived by other created minds. In that case
the *esse* of a sense quality does not consist in its *being perceived*
by *any particular mind:* it has, after all, an *esse* or reality which
is independent of its being perceived by this or that particular
mind. But whether we adopt the alternative of one sense universe, or as many as there are created minds, the question still
remains: If there were no human mind, or if all human minds
were conceived to be non-existent, to cease to exist, would there
be still a " material " or "sense " universe?

Berkeley says of "all the choir of heaven and furniture of
earth" that "so long as they are not actually perceived by me,
or do not exist in my mind or that of any other created spirit,
they must either have no existence at all, or subsist in the mind
of some Eternal Spirit ".[2]   And again, "I conclude, not that
they have no real existence, but that, seeing they depend not on
my thought, and have an existence distinct from being perceived
by me, *there must be some other mind wherein they exist* ".[3]
Hence he proves the existence of God to his own satisfaction,
"from the bare *existence* of the sensible world," in this wise:
"*Sensible things do really exist ; and, if they really exist, they are
necessarily perceived by an infinite mind: therefore there is an infinite mind, or God*".[4]   Now these passages seem to imply the
Ontologism of Malebranche, that "we see all things in God".
Berkeley, however, distinguishing between "ideas " and " archetypes " of ideas,[5] repudiates this ontologistic interpretation of
his position.[6] If, therefore, we accept his disclaimer, he must
mean that the "ideas" which we see are *creations* according to

[1] Does this involve a real difficulty against the distinct individual reality of each
created mind ?   When the " ideas " or sense qualities are said to be " in " each, or
" present to " each, these phrases have, of course, no spatial signification : space is,
for Berkeley, one of the " ideas " or sense qualities. But how *one and the same*
system of " ideas " could be dependent for its reali y on its being perceived by
distinct minds is not very clear.

[2] *Principles*, etc., § 6, p. 32.   [3] *Second Dialogue*, etc., p. 64.
[4] *Ibid.*, p. 65.
[5] " No idea or archetype of an idea can exist otherwise than in a mind."—
Second Dialogue, etc., p. 66. " These ideas or things perceived by me, either themselves or their archetypes, exist independently of my mind."—*Ibid.*, p. 68.
[6] " Mark it well ; I do not say, I see things by perceiving that which represents
them in the intelligible Substance of God."—*Ibid.*, p. 69.

the Divine Archetypes, that they are created by God, but are by their nature dependent for their reality on their perception by created minds. While created minds exist, God, of course, sees in these minds the created "ideas" which constitute the "material" or "sensible" universe. Therefore, were created minds non-existent, or did they cease to exist, this universe must likewise be non-existent or cease to exist: there would remain only the *possibility* of them in the Archetype Ideas in the Divine Mind,—*if such a Mind could be proved to exist.*

But "from the bare *existence* of the sensible world," or system of perceived sense qualities, we cannot infer the existence of a Divine, Eternal Spirit merely on the ground that if no finite, human mind existed, the system of sense qualities would continue to exist (and require a Divine Mind in which to exist): for if these are dependent on human minds they cease to exist with the cessation of such minds,—and we can neither know of, nor speculate about, any "archetypes" whatsoever, *until we have proved otherwise the existence of God.*[1]

But perhaps the desired inference can be made on another and distinct ground, on the ground, namely, that the system of perceived sense qualities demands an adequate cause, and that the only adequate cause of them is the Divine, Eternal, Self-Existent Being? Undoubtedly ; but such inference cannot proceed "from the bare *existence* of the sensible world" directly to the Divine Being, in the way in which Berkeley has it. From a consideration of the *nature* of the "sensible world," and also of our perceiving and thinking minds, as *contingent, caused, mutable, finite realities,* we can infer the existence of a Necessary, Eternal, Self-Existent First Cause. But Berkeley's direct inference, by way of causality, "from the bare *existence* of the sensible world" to the Divine Being, assumes (1) that the sensible world is merely a system of ideas or phenomena in our human minds, and (2) that this system of ideas or phenomena cannot be caused by a universe of extramental, material substances endowed with material qualities, forces, and energies. But the perceptionist repudiates the former assumption (so that for him the latter does not arise) ; and the representationist repudiates at least the latter assumption ; and Berkeley's attempt to vindicate both assumptions amounts ultimately to this, that the notion of a reality which is neither a *knowing, perceiving* reality (" Mind," " Spirit," essentially "conscious," "perceptive," "cognitive ") or a *known, perceived* reality (" Idea," "essentially mind-dependent," whose very *esse* or *reality* is being *in,* or *present to,* and apprehended by, Mind or Spirit) *is self-contradictory.*[2] Now

---

[1] *Cf. Ontology,* §§ 18, 19.
[2] This idealist principle is sometimes called " the principle of *immanence* ". *Cf.* JEANNIÈRE, *op. cit.,* pp. 444-6.

this contention, which is at the very basis of *all* idealism, whether monistic or theistic, *will not stand the test of analysis.*

Its plausibility lies in the fact that it is a misconception of a very profound truth, the truth, namely, that the whole knowable or intelligible universe which falls within human cognitive experience can be proved to be *de facto* dependent, for its reality, and therefore also for its intelligibility, on an Eternal, Divine Mind. Not that there is anything self-contradictory in thinking of an unconscious, inanimate, material universe having a real, extra-mental existence independently of our cognition of it : we can without any self-contradiction think of such an extramentally real material universe, just as we can likewise think of our own minds and other minds really existing even when they are neither consciously thinking nor being thought of by any human mind. But, when we reflect on the *nature* of our minds, and of the universe of their direct experience, we can prove from the character of these, as *caused* and *contingent* realities, the existence of a Necessary, Self-Existing Divine Being. Then we can understand not only that their *actual reality* depends on Him as *Creator and Conserver*, but also that their *intelligibility* depends on Him as their *Intelligent Exemplar* or *Prototype.* Thus we see that if there are realities which can and do exist independently of their being actually perceived or known by human minds,—as, for instance, the material universe, and indeed human minds themselves,—and which therefore do not depend on human minds either for their reality or for their intelligibility, these realities must have their being from an Intelligent First Cause, in Whose Mind, therefore, all material (and all created) reality is ideally represented in Eternal Divine Exemplars. It is only, however, *when we have thus proved* that their *contingent actuality* implies and *depends on* the existence of a Divine *Creating* Intelligence, that we can see it to be—not, indeed, self-contradictory, but—*erroneous* to conceive material reality as existing and as *not being known* by *any* mind : for we then know that whether it is actually perceived or not by human minds it is eternally known by the Divine Mind ; and, further, that its intelligibility for human minds lies in the fact that both the material universe and human minds are creatures which, according to the measure of their finite natures, are intelligible expressions of the Divine Essence as Exemplar and Prototype of all created or finite reality.

Now idealism may be said to have stumbled accidentally on this truth ; for the idealist, while grasping the substance of it, wholly misconceives the way in which the human mind can legitimately attain to it. For the idealist's contention is that all reality, essentially and as such, involves its *being actually known* by some mind, its being an *object apprehended* by some mind, its being thus *dependent* by way of knowledge on some mind : [1] so that if it be not considered essential to material reality to be known by, and essentially dependent on, *individual human* minds, then there *must* be *some* Mind co-existent with it, which knows it : whether we conceive this Mind as *immanent* in our minds and their objects, *i.e.* pantheistically, with Fichte, Schelling, Hegel, etc., and human minds and material nature as manifestations of it ; or as *transcendent*, *i.e.* theistically, with Berkeley, and finite minds and their

[1] " Knower and known form an inseparable unity, and . . . therefore, any reality which is not itself a knower, or the knowing of a knower, presupposes a mind which knows it."—PRICHARD, *op. cit.*, p. 116, interpreting Kant's position.

objects as creations of this Transcendent Divine Mind. In other words, idealists contend that *being real* essentially implies *being known;* and that this is self-evident : so that if the material universe has a reality independent of finite human minds, and could have existed before there were any human minds to perceive it, then there must *evidently* be a Universal, or All-embracing, Eternal Mind, Whose knowledge of it is essential to its reality.

The simple reply to all this is that *being real* is not evidently synonymous with *being known;* that it is not at all self-evident that the former implies the latter. Rather what is evident in regard to the knowledge which the *human* mind has of reality is that this knowledge *presupposes the independent reality of its object, i.e.* presupposes that the reality which is known is not dependent for its reality on *our knowing* it. Even realities which are dependent for their being on our minds are not dependent for this being on our minds *as knowing them.*[1] Next, if there be a Mind other than human minds, we must conceive Its knowing after the analogy of our own knowing ; and if it be contended that reality as such is essentially dependent on It, the essential dependence must be other than that of *being known*, for the knowing of such a Mind must likewise, if considered *merely as knowing*, presuppose the known reality as being real independently of its being known ; nor can the existence of such a Mind be inferred from the not merely gratuitous but erroneous assumption that reality, essentially and as such, evidently involves *being known.* The existence of such a Mind must, therefore, be proved in some other and legitimate way, if at all.

Individual human minds are obviously finite, and the existence of each,— at least, its individual self-conscious existence,—has had a beginning. Considering, therefore, the relation of the perceived and known material universe to those minds, we can see that if the reality of this material universe does not essentially involve its being known by them, this assertion of science is quite intelligible : that there was a time when the material universe really existed, and when human beings or human minds did not as yet exist to perceive or know it. But the idealist cannot so easily give an intelligible interpretation of the assertion. Can *he* intelligibly " talk of a time a long way back in the process of evolution, when consciousness as yet was not"?[2] " Mr. Spencer thinks the idealist has no right so to speak, Mr. Sully thinks he has."[3] Mr. Balfour also agrees with Spencer in subscribing to "the assertion, that 'if idealism is true, then evolution is a dream'. For evolution [and physical science, apart from any theory of evolution] supposes a . . . period during which there was no consciousness in the universe. Such a universe, as an existence, cannot have been ideal, and cannot be affirmed now by the idealist : for it would once have been a universe out of all human thought, which Mr.

[1] *Cf. supra*, §§ 101, 102. PRICHARD, *op. cit.*, p. 119 : " We should say that an act of thinking presupposes a mind which thinks. We should, however, naturally deny that an act of thinking or knowing, in order to be, presupposes that it is known either by the thinker whose act it is, or by any other mind. In other words, we should say that knowing presupposes a mind, not as something which *knows* the knowing, but as something which *does* the knowing."

[2] RICKABY, *First Principles*, p. 269. [3] *Ibid.*

Bain, on his principles, rightly concludes to be a 'manifest contradiction'."[1]
Such hesitations and uncertainties at least show it to be very far indeed from
self-evident that the existence of a reality, as such, essentially implies either
its being known by *human* minds, or by *some other* Mind. The existence
of a material universe antecedently to the existence of human minds, cannot,
of course, be consistently asserted by the idealist unless he holds that besides
human minds there exists some other Mind by which it was then known.[2]
But, as we saw, he cannot infer the existence of any other Mind "from the
bare *existence* of the sensible world" through the unproven assumption that,
since it is manifestly not produced by and dependent on individual human
minds, its mere reality implies its being essentially an object of the thought
or knowledge of some other Mind.

Hence he is still face to face merely with the two sets of data, namely,
(1) human minds, and (2) their immediate objects, the material universe. If
he is to infer the existence of an Eternal Mind from them, it is not by considering the mere existence of the material universe as a reality and claiming
that as such it essentially implies *being known* by such a Mind. It is, rather,
by considering the *nature* of human minds and material things that we can
prove the existence of a Necessary, Intelligent First Cause. We can, for
instance, argue on the following lines : If the material universe existed antecedently to human minds, and if these originated in it, they cannot have
originated *from* it. Nor can they have been always in it in a potential or
unconscious condition, and have been gradually evolved from it. For they
are realities of a higher order than matter. Hence they must have been
"introduced at some time or other into" the material universe, which is "of
a wholly different order"[3] from them. Human minds and material things

---

[1] RICKABY, *First Principles*, p. 282.

[2] For the individual idealist, *time* is, of course, like space and the sense qualities,
a mind-dependent entity, or, as Berkeley would describe it, an "idea". But if *time*
is only an idea placed in human minds by the Divine Spirit, and having its eternal
Exemplar in the Divine Spirit, another problem for Berkeley must be this,—Is time
also a *real* mode of the *real existence* of human spirits, or does it only affect the
"notion" or "knowledge" we have of them ? And if the latter be the case,—as
Berkeley's principles demand,—does it not turn out after all that we know minds or
spirits (including our own mind) only as they *appear*, and not as they *really are* ?

[3] PRICHARD, *op. cit.*, p. 127. The author rejects such "introduction" as impossible. Observing that realism implies " not that the existence of the physical
world is prior to the existence of a mind, but only that it is prior to a mind's actual
knowledge of the world " (*ibid.*, p. 128), he himself adopts the view that there must
always have pre-existed, with the physical universe, "a mind or minds" capable of
becoming actually "conscious" or "knowing". "A mind cannot be the product
of anything or, at any rate, of anything but a mind. . . . In other words, knowing
implies the ultimate and unoriginated existence of beings possessed of the capacity
to know " (*ibid.*, pp. 127, 128). But the view to which he thus briefly suggests his
adherence is not only less preferable than the doctrine of creation, which he refuses
to consider, but is rationally indefensible and metaphysically impossible. For it
assumes human minds to be *uncaused*, to have an " ultimate or unoriginated existence," or at least to have been produced by, or evolved from, such uncaused beings
endowed with a "capacity to know"; and this involves the self-contradictory
notions of (a) beings that would be *necessarily* existent and uncaused and eternal,
yet finite and imperfect, of (b) a *plurality* of such beings, and of (c) the universe

being, moreover, both alike *contingent* realities, imply the existence of a Necessary First Cause, capable of producing them from nothingness, *i.e.* an Intelligent, Eternal, Infinite Creator. Thus we see that the universe of mind and matter, the universe of direct human experience, implies an Eternal Mind, not formally as *knowing*, but formally as *causing* or *creating*, and *conserving* this universe.

Having reached this conclusion, scholastics then see that the universe *as actual* has an essential relation of dependence on the Divine Mind *as Creative;* and that *as intelligible, as possible*, it has likewise an essential relation of dependence on the Divine Mind as *Intelligent, i.e.* that its being *knowable* and *actually known*, its relation to Mind *as knowing*, its *ontological truth*, is an essential or transcendental attribute of all reality : *Omne Ens est Verum : Ens et Verum convertuntur*.[1] Hence we find scholastic writers, as for instance, Cardinal Zigliara, recognizing, in their criticisms of the monistic idealism of Fichte and Schelling, that these authors are right in maintaining the essential priority of Mind, though wrong both in the method whereby they think we attain to knowledge of such a mind and in their interpretation of the relation of this Mind to the universe of direct human experience.[2]

itself as a collection of such beings. But there is a more obvious metaphysical impossibility in the contention that the grade of *actual being* or *perfection* represented by *actually conscious, perceiving* and *knowing* minds, can have been produced by, or evolved from, and is *adequately accounted for by*, the *lower* and *less perfect* grade of reality represented by beings supposed to be only *capable of*, or endowed with the *capacity of*, knowing. For the *actual* is more perfect than the *merely potential :* it cannot be adequately explained by the potential : the potential as such cannot actualize itself : in the real or ontological order the actual must, by metaphysical necessity, precede the potential. *Cf. Ontology*, chap. ii., especially §§ 9 and 10.

[1] *Cf. Ontology*, §§ 41-2 ; 18-20. The scholastic thesis that "ontological truth," —or relation, as object, to the Divine Intellect as knowing,—is essential to all reality, presupposes as proved the existence of an Eternal Omniscient Intellect. It is not directly derivable from the mere consideration of reality as such. " Reality " is not one of those relative terms which essentially involve in their import and definition a relation to something else. *Cf.* PRICHARD, *op. cit.*, pp. 132-3 : " If we consider what we mean by 'a reality,' we find that we mean by it something that is not correlative to a mind knowing it. It does not mean something the thought of which disappears with the thought of a mind actually knowing it, but something which, though it can be known by a mind, need not be actually known by a mind."

[2] *Cf.* ZIGLIARA, *Summa Philosophica*, ii., *Psychologia* (27), vii. : " Si quis recte animadverterit, in exposita doctrina Fichtii latet implicite sed aperte hoc principium : Omnia quae sunt aut esse possunt in rerum natura continentur necessario in subjecto cogitante, seu intellectu intelligente, qui proinde non se habet ad intelligibile in tota sua latitudine ut patiens, sed ut forma omnium in ordine intelligibili, ut principium efficiens in ordine reali entium quae ab ipso sunt diversa. Et hoc principium est verissimum et concedendum est. Non enim concipi possunt objecta quaecunque realia, ut distincta ab intellectu, nisi antea ponantur existentia in ordine intelligibili seu ut *ideae;* nihil autem potest existere in ordine intelligibili nisi in intellectu.—In quo ergo fallitur Fichte ? In designatione subjecti cogitantis, seu intellectus praecontinentis et efficientis intelligibilia ; nam ponit illum intellectum esse τὸ *ego* humanum, cum quo simul identificat *non-ego*, atque proinde pantheismum psycho-egoisticum concludit. In hoc errat vehementer. . . ."

Similarly, criticizing Schelling's theory, he writes (*ibid.*, ix.) : " Videre ex se lector potest Schellingii principium esse illud ipsum quod in doctrina Fichtii latere

We see, then, that Berkeley fails to establish a reasoned human certitude of the existence of a Divine, Eternal Spirit from consideration of the sense qualities as *a special kind of reality*, inasmuch as he fails to prove his contention that their extra-mental existence in a material universe is self-contradictory. Secondly, we see that the attempt to establish such certitude by the contention that reality essentially and as such implies a knower, that *all* reality is or implies "*percipi*," likewise fails, inasmuch as this also is an unproven postulate so long as the existence of a Divine, Eternal Mind is not independently established; though, of course, when we know otherwise that such a Mind exists we can see that all finite, created reality is *de facto* essentially dependent on that Mind,—dependent for its *actuality* on that Mind *as Creative*, and for its *intelligibility* on that Mind as *Knowing* or *Intelligent*. Finally, when Berkeley contends that every reality must be either a " Mind " ("knowing," "*percipere*") or an " Idea " ("*percipi*," " mind-dependent "), we see that his explanation of our knowledge of " minds " is no less unsatisfactory than his explanation of the nature of what he calls " ideas ". For if he were consistent he should hold that our *real and genuine* knowledge of "minds," even of our own mind, reaches not to these minds as they really are in themselves, but only to " notions " which, as objects of individual awareness, are at most symbols of unknowable realities lying beyond consciousness: which is subjective or phenomenist idealism.

124. PHYSICAL SCIENCE AND THE SENSE QUALITIES. PRESUPPOSITIONS OF SCIENTIFIC THEORIES. PHYSICAL REALISM.— We have seen (121, 123) that while the primary qualities are no less relative to the perceiver than the secondary, it is impossible to regard either class of qualities as mere states of consciousness, mere phases or modes of the individual perceiving mind. Now some have thought to find a *via media* between the idealist position on the one hand, and that of intuitive or perceptionist realism on the other, by defending the view that the sense qualities are neither conscious states nor modes of the external universe, but

diximus, nempe: Necesse est ut *ideale* et *reale* ad unum principium revocentur, quod utrumque explicet et utriusque sit ultima ratio. Hoc principium repeto esse verissimum, imo fundamentum, quo tota nititur, quo tota niti debet philosophia; quia necesse omnino est ut reale (natura finita) praecedatur ab ideali; ideale autem non potest ultimatim esse nisi in intellectu improducto, per se existente et aeterno, qui solus sit realitas praecedens meram idealitatem, atque ideo non solum cognoscat sed efficiat intelligibile ipsum seu ideale."

modes or states of *the perceiver's organism.*[1] This theory is known as *Physical Realism.* Owing to its unquestioning acceptance of external reality *as conceived and interpreted by scientists in modern physical theories*, it is favoured by many scientists who, while rejecting intuitive realism, do not care to commit themselves to idealism. As a peculiar form of representationism it deserves attention both for its application of the principle of "inference by similarity," and for the opportunity it offers of examining the presuppositions and assumptions common to itself and to the current conceptions and theories of Physical Science. Its line of reasoning is somewhat like this : Science, which is "knowledge at its best," [2] assures us of the real nature of external qualities or objects. Since nothing external can be immediately apprehended, but only inferred (by the principle of similarity) from data that are internal, we can ascertain the real nature of these latter data only by asking ourselves from what kind of data can we have inferred the objects which science assures us to be externally real. Such data must, on the one hand, be *internal* (for the internal alone can be immediately apprehended) ; but they must, on the other hand, be physical, *i.e.* of the same order as the objects inferred by science and indicated by it as externally real : they cannot be merely *psychic* states, for psychic states could not be like external physical objects. Therefore the data in question must be really states of the perceiver's brain, nervous system, and sense organs. But the only objects which science assures us to be externally real are the (inferentially perceptible) extension, volume, shape, motion, etc., which are like their internal sensible correlates, and such transcendentally inferred imperceptible modes of the former as *e.g.* corpuscles, undulations of æther, etc. : [3] which imperceptible modes correspond externally to the internal secondary qualities. And the reason why the former externals are like their internal correlates, and the latter unlike theirs, must be because the perceiver's sense organon is so constituted that it is capable of assuming in itself, and presenting to consciousness, states *similar* to the primary externals under

---

[1] " For example, the hot felt and the white seen are produced by external objects and are apprehended by internal sensations of touch and vision, but are themselves respectively the tactile and the optic nerves sensibly affected in the manner apprehended as hot and white."—CASE, *Physical Realism* (London, Longmans, 1888), p. 25. " The hot felt is the tactile nerves heated, the white seen is the optic nerves so coloured."—*Ibid.*, p. 24.

[2] *Op. cit.*, p. 37.   [3] *Ibid.*, pp. 34-5.

the influence of the latter, whereas it can assume and present to consciousness under the influence of the secondary externals only states dissimilar to these.[1]

Unfortunately, however, for this theory, there are no really sufficient grounds for holding that the external causes of the internal organic states called "primary qualities" are *like* these qualities, while the external causes of the internal organic states called "secondary qualities" are *not like* these latter : that "for instance, external motion is like sensible motion, but external heat is an imperceptible mode of motion while sensible heat is not sensibly a motion at all ".[2]

For if the immediate datum or object of sense awareness is always only an internal organic condition of the perceiver's own sense organon (*i.e.* the *sensorium* or external sense organ, the brain, and the nervous system), and if what is external is known only by being inferred from this, then when we see a moving train or feel a shower of hailstones the only reason we have for inferring that the real "external motion" of the train or of the hailstones is like the "sensible motion,"—*i.e.* the motion which is the direct object of our awareness and which on this theory is always a nerve motion (though it appears to consciousness certainly not as a nerve motion but as a train or hailstone motion),—is the reason contained in the principle that the effect must resemble its cause. In other words, the inferred external cause must resemble the internal, sensible appearance which is its effect. But the internal, sensible appearance is an immediately apprehended nerve motion or organic condition appearing as an external train or hailstone motion. Therefore the *real* external train or hailstone motion must resemble the internally *apparent* train or hailstone motion which is really the nerve motion or organic condition immediately apprehended.

But whatever force there is in this presentation of the matter, it applies equally to the secondary qualities such as heat. According to the theory, "sensible heat is not sensibly a motion at all " : that is, what we are immediately aware of in perceiving heat, and what is therefore an organic condition of our own nerves, is a conscious datum in no way resembling the conscious datum which is present in *e.g.* our vision of a *moving* train or our tactual perception of the *moving* razor in shaving : the immediate data of our awareness in these two cases being likewise

[1] *Op. cit.*, pp. 23, 26.   [2] *Ibid.*, p. 26.

organic conditions of our own nerves.   But if we infer from these
latter organic conditions (about the real nature of which scientists
know comparatively little; but about which we all know that
they reveal, or appear as, train motions and razor motions respectively), that their external causes are real motions similar
to the internal appearances assumed by the. organic conditions
themselves, surely we can and must infer from the *consciously
different* organic condition which is " sensible heat " that its external cause and counterpart, *viz.* " external heat " as a quality of
the external world, is *something different* from the " external
motion " which is the supposed cause of the " sensible motion,"
rather than that " external heat is *an imperceptible mode* cf [ex-
ternal] motion ".

The author's reason for the latter inference is " because, though
at first sight sensible heat would demand a similar external object, *when all the facts of sensible heat are accumulated they are
found to be the kind of facts that are only produced by motion*".[1]
So " sensible heat," which is admitted to be " not sensibly a
motion at all," can be shown by " corpuscular science "[2] to be
producible only by the influence exerted on our organism by an
insensible mode of insensible external motion,[3]—*i.e.* by a something about the nature and modes of which we can know only
what we infer, by the law of similarity, from " sensible motion,"
which sensible motion, whatever it really be,[4] is admittedly wholly
unlike " sensible heat "?   *But no Science, corpuscular or otherwise,
has achieved any such feat.*[5]

Nor is the reason alleged for the contention (attributed to
Science[6]) that " external, insensible objects " resemble internal
sensible objects in " primary qualities " but not in " secondary
qualities," and that, " as they are in external nature,"[7] the latter
are " insensible modes "[8] of the former,—as sound as it is plausible.   It runs as follows :[9] The " sensible effect," *i.e.* that of which
we are directly aware in perception, is the result of two causes,
the " external world " and the " nervous system," the latter receiving the influence of the former " according to its susceptibility": a principle which we have already recognized (121);

---

[1] *Op. cit.*, p. 26,—italics ours.
[2] *Cf. ibid.*, p. 23.   [3] *Ibid.*, pp. 23, 31-2.
[4] On the author's hypothesis it is *really* an internal nerve motion, *appearing* as
an external spatial motion of bodies.
[5] *Cf. supra*, § 112.   [6] *Ibid.*, p. 23.   [7] *Ibid.*
[8] *Ibid.*   [9] *Ibid.*, p. 30.

though we should say rather that the whole external perception process is the result of two causes, (*a*) the external world, and (*b*) the complex self-cause, at once conscious and organic.   But mark the author's application of the principle, *Quidquid recipitur, ad modum recipientis recipitur:* "The nervous system is far more susceptible of similar effects from primary than from secondary qualities.   It is more capable of reflecting the waves of the sea than the undulations of the æther."[1]   Hence "sense sometimes presents motion as motion, but cannot help presenting the hot, the red, etc., as heterogeneous to motion, because of the structure of the sensory nerves; [but] science, by comparing sensible motion with the sensible facts of the hot, the red, etc., infers that the external cause of the latter is really a mode of motion ".[2] Now this claim on behalf of Science, to have established a similarity of external primary qualities to their supposed internal sense correlates, and a dissimilarity of external secondary qualities to theirs, is no better than a *petitio principii*.   For Science must start from what we are directly aware of.[3]   If, therefore, what we are directly aware of when perceiving "the waves of the sea " be a physical motion or condition of our nervous system, and if science assumes the right of inferring that because this sensible, nervous motion or condition *appears* as motion of " the waves of the sea," therefore the real and external (and, on this theory, "insensible" though "inferentially perceptible") motion of "the waves of the sea " is *like* the appearance assumed by the nervous motion or condition, how can it consistently refuse to infer that the real, external, "insensible " correlate of the internal, "sensible" nerve motion or condition which *appears* as heat is also *like* this latter appearance?   As a matter of fact there is no ground for supposing that the perceiver's nervous system (in *Physical Realism*), or the perceiver's mind or consciousness (in ordinary *Representationist Realism*), "mirrors" or "reflects" or "represents" the *inferred* external qualities of the external

---

[1] *Op. cit.*, p. 30.   The "knowledge " which we have of the nervous system is of the same order as the knowledge we have of extra-organic matter : its validity, therefore, is part of the general problem.

[2] *Ibid.*, p. 31.

[3] And Epistemology likewise : not from what *scientists conclude* to be externally real (the " physical objects of science," or " present objects of scientific knowledge "— Case, *op. cit.*, p. 36), nor from the forgotten and unknown " original data of sense " in childhood (*ibid.*, pp. 25, 35, 36), which is not the only alternative, but from the " sensible data "—and all other conscious data (10)—of mature life.   *Cf. infra*, pp. 132, 137.

universe more similarly,[1] so to speak, when these are primary
or "quantitative" qualities (extension, shape, motion, unity,
multitude, etc.) than when they are secondary qualities (heat,
colour, taste, smell, and tactile qualities).

Physical Realism, therefore, though commendable for its
assertion, as against Idealism, that the direct objects of our sense
awareness are physical realities and not ideas or psychic states,
nevertheless labours under very serious defects, some of which
are needless concessions to Idealism, while others are peculiar
to itself.

The obvious truth that whatever is known in any way, whether
sensuously or intellectually, must be consciously or cognitively
("*intentionaliter*") present to, or one and continuous with, the
knower, it interprets as implying not indeed that the direct and
immediate object of awareness must be an idea or psychic state
of the knower, but that it must be really internal to and really
one with the knower: that therefore in perception it must be an
organic condition of the perceiver, since nothing "external" can
be "immediately perceived".[2]   But it is neither self-evident
that nothing external can be immediately perceived, nor can we
admit the assertion that "scientific analysis" has proved the immediate perception of the external to be impossible.[3]   If external
reality, by acting on the perceiver's sense organs, can efficiently
influence the conscious, perceptive mind or principle which
animates those sense organs, to elicit a consciously perceptive
act, we see no reason for denying that the external cause or
stimulus can be also the directly apprehended term of this
perceptive act.

Of course if the efficient causal influence of the external
factor be conceived, or rather imagined, as being productive only
of internal organic or nerve qualities which are imperceptible
modes of motion in the perceiver's material organism, then indeed direct conscious or cognitive continuity of the external
factor with the perceiver's consciousness would be impossible.
But in the first place such a narrow and one-sided conception of
the nature and scope of efficient causal influence is unwarranted
and erroneous.[4]   And in the second place, even if accepted, it
would not in the least enable us to see why or how we become

[1] That we should rather expect the reverse has not escaped the notice of Idealists.
Cf. *infra*, § 125.

[2] *Ibid.*, p. 28.   [3] *Ibid.*   [4] *Cf. Ontology*, § 104, pp. 392-6.

consciously aware of our internal nerve conditions or qualities as taste, smell, heat, colour, tactual texture or resistance ; or as extension, volume, magnitude, shape, motion, spatial discontinuity, or number.

This, therefore, is another defect in physical realism. The perceiver's organism is material. The effects supposed to be wrought in it by the action of the external world must therefore be on this theory the same as the effects wrought on external bodies themselves by their own interaction, *viz.* primary qualities (supposed to be all reducible to modes of motion of a virtually or formally extended, atomic or discontinuous, or spatially continuous, matter or æther substrate), and secondary qualities (supposed to be varieties of this motion), in the internal and organic, no less than in the external and extra-organic, domain. It does not in the least explain how we come to know any qualities of the *external* material universe to say that we become directly aware of what must be really the same classes of qualities in the *internal* material universe which is our own material organism, and infer the former from the latter. For the latter qualities, though subjective or internal in the sense of being qualities of our organism, are still physical or *extramental*, or beyond and independent of consciousness.[1]   To say that we immediately apprehend one (extramental) *nerve state or condition* as hot, another as red, another as bitter, another as surface extension, another as solidity or volume or shape, another as motion, and so on, is to make an ultimate assertion of something just as mysterious and incapable of further analysis, and certainly no more credible, than the assertion that what we immediately apprehend in those various ways are states, conditions, or qualities of the external material universe itself.

If the concretely qualified data or objects of which we become directly aware in normal external sense perception are not really external, as they are spontaneously judged to be, if they are really internal (whether psychic and intramental, or organic and physical and extramental), and if "everything external is inferred"[2] from such internal (psychic or organic, immediately

---

[1] The idealist escapes this difficulty by holding that no sense qualities are physical, that all are purely mental or psychic. The supporter of ordinary representationist realism escapes it by holding that the internal effects from which he infers the external qualities are not merely organic, but are psychic, mental, conscious impressions or representations.

[2] *Op. cit.*, p. 28.

apprehended objects of awareness), then there is certainly one procedure which we are *not at liberty to adopt* without valid justifying reasons, and that is to take *one* set of those internal "sensible objects" or "data of awareness," *viz.* the so-called primary qualities, size and shape, rest and motion, spatial continuity and discontinuity or plurality; to infer from these the existence of *similar* qualities in the external domain; to interpret the external correlates of *the other set* of direct objects of awareness, *viz.* the so-called secondary qualities, heat, colour, sound, taste, smell, and tactile data, as modes or varieties of the external correlates of the former set, *i.e.* as modes of externally moving, voluminous or space-filling realities (whether these be atoms, electrons, dynamic monads, æther, or what not); and thence to conclude that the second set of external correlates, the secondary qualities as they are externally, being like the first set because interpreted as modes or varieties of these, are *unlike* their own sensible or directly apprehended internal correlates, *viz.* sensibly apprehended heat, colour,[1] taste, smell, etc.

[1] "It is assumed that there is not even plausibility in the supposition of continuity or identity between colour proper [*i.e.* what is present to consciousness in perception of colour] and its physical conditions in the way of light vibrations." —PRICHARD, *op. cit.*, p. 87 n. If that which we *sensibly* apprehend as colour be *intellectually* conceived and interpreted to be merely vibrations or undulations of æther in the extramental domain,—and we neither affirm nor deny that extramental colour is or involves this: we leave that question to the physicist and the cosmologist; but if it is so, if extramental colour is rightly conceived and interpreted intellectually to be or to involve undulations of æther,—where is the difficulty in holding that this same self-identical extramental reality which is *intellectually conceived* as æther undulations is *sensibly perceived* as the object of awareness which we call colour? At all events (assuming the truth of some form of realism) this much at least we know about the extramental reality in question, that it is in the *extramental* domain something real which we *perceive* or *apprehend sensibly* as a colour, as red, or blue, or yellow, etc.; and if perceptionism be true we know that if the organic conditions of perception be normal the extramental reality is an *external* or *extra-organic* reality sensibly apprehended as red, or blue, or yellow, etc. *How* we are to *conceive and interpret intellectually* the nature of this external reality the physicist may undertake to discover, while *the epistemologist has to scrutinize the presuppositions of the physicist's hypotheses and methods of induction.* Cf. Art. "*Appearance and Reality*" in the *Irish Ecclesiastical Record*, vol. xxiv. (Sept. 1908), p. 278, n. 2: "It is sometimes contended . . . that the material energy or property which we call 'redness' cannot in its own external reality (being an undulation of the ether) be in any way l ke 'our sensation of redness'. This shows a deplorable confusion of *sense perception* with *intellectual conception*. The *same reality* which we call 'redness' on account of the definite state of *sense-consciousness* aroused in us by the vision of it, we call 'a property of matter,' an 'active quality,' an 'energy,' a 'wave-motion' on account of the concepts, judgments, inferences, theories, formed by our *intellects*, reflecting on the data which that

Yet this is undoubtedly the procedure which has led many physical scientists in recent times to build on their perfectly legitimate scientific hypotheses regarding the nature of light and heat and sound and other physical realities, such as chemical, electric and magnetic energies, in the external domain, the distinctly philosophical and epistemological theory that this domain consists *solely* of a reality (æther) or realities (atoms, electrons, ions, etc.) endowed with the *primary qualities*, motion, volume, continuity or discontinuity, dimensional limits or figures, etc., and that the *secondary sense qualities* are subjective, internal, consciously apprehended effects produced by the primary qualities and their insensible modes in the perceiver.

Advocates of this theory must obviously have started by assuming either that the primary sense qualities themselves, *i.e.* consciously apprehended size, shape, figure, motion, rest, unity and number, or else *inferred similar correlates* [1] of these, are real and actual characteristics of the external domain of reality. Else what value could their hypotheses have as explanations of the external domain, since their hypotheses are conceived in terms of those primary qualities. But if we immediately apprehend these as external so do we immediately apprehend the secondary qualities as external. And if we know the external primary qualities only by inferring them as similar to internal directly apprehended correlates, then in the first place it cannot be said that *we know them better* than we know these latter; and in the second place we not only can infer, but if we are consistent we ought to infer, that the external correlates of the directly apprehended secondary qualities are likewise similar to these.

It is useless to appeal, with physical realism, to a supposed different degree of susceptibility of the perceiver's sense organism,

reality furnishes to those intellects through the medium of sense-consciousness."
—*Cf. ibid.*, pp. 278-80.

[1] The physical scientist as such usually commences (without troubling himself with any theory of external perception) by taking for granted, like the plain man, the external reality of the physical universe and *all* its sensibly perceived qualities. Then, with a view to exploring what some or all of the secondary qualities are externally, *e.g.* what sound, or light, or heat is externally, he proceeds to assume that they are (insensible) modes of the primary qualities (*e.g.* that they are vibratory or undulatory motions of space-filling atoms or æther, etc.), and to see how his hypotheses will "work" or "explain the facts,"—continuing to assume all the time that these primary qualities are really and externally, and for *intellect* reflecting on them, the same as they appear, or similar to what they appear, internally or consciously to *sense*.

or a difference in the rôle played by the brain and nervous system, in affecting the transition from the sensibly conscious data to their external correlates, in the two sets of qualities. For since the whole sense organon is an extramental, material factor, we cannot say that it presents to consciousness *one* set of qualities *as they are*—whether in itself or in the extra-organic domain, or partly in the one and partly in the other, but in both cases— *beyond or independently of consciousness*, and *another* set *otherwise than they are beyond or independently of consciousness*. Obviously we cannot say this *without begging the whole question*. And moreover, granting the reality of the rôle played by the perceiver's sense organon in perception, and the consequent relativity of what is perceived through its functioning, this relativity must necessarily apply to the primary as well as to the secondary qualities, for the primary qualities are also *sense* qualities, and are apprehended only through the functioning of the various sense organs.

That the external domain of material reality is characterized only by the primary qualities, that these are like the correlates of which the perceiver is directly conscious, that the secondary qualities are really and externally *only* modes of the primary qualities, and that as such they are unlike the correlates which the perceiver directly apprehends as sensible taste, smell, colour, sound, etc.—these assertions are not proved, and *cannot be proved*, by any scientific research in the external, physical domain: they are partly assumptions, and partly inferences from certain ways of using the assumptions. If the scientist assumes that the primary qualities are really and externally that which he is directly aware of, or similar to that which he is directly aware of, and if he then proceeds to interpret the secondary qualities, as external, in terms of the primary, and supposes them to be insensible modes of the primary, he will of course have nothing left in the external domain but the primary and their insensible modes. But he can accept this position only by gratuitously ignoring the fact that he had the same right, and in consistency the same duty, to assume that the secondary qualities as objects of direct awareness are either themselves external or have similar external correlates, or else by assigning a justifying reason for assuming (cognitive) identity or similarity of the external with the consciously apprehended data in the case of the primary qualities and not in the case of the secondary qualities : and this difference of procedure cannot be justified by any scientific consideration *which presupposes and is dependent on his having made the assumption in the one case and not in the other.*[1] Furthermore, if he accepts the position, he has to

---

[1] And it is exclusively considerations of this kind that are urged from the standpoint of physical science in favour of the view that only the primary qualities of matter are really and externally as they are perceived. Every such consideration is a *petitio principii.*

accept a conclusion in regard to the secondary qualities which is the direct reverse of his assumption in regard to the primary qualities, namely, that what corresponds really and externally to the directly apprehended internal secondary sense qualities is *unlike* these latter : a conclusion which no consideration that is based on his actual assumption can justify.

The secondary qualities, as they exist externally, are qualities of a reality which has also the primary qualities of extension and motion. Those secondary qualities have therefore externally a quantitative side. And it is perfectly legitimate for the physical scientist to conceive and interpret this aspect of them in terms of the primary qualities, *e.g.* of extension and motion. But this does not justify either the scientist or the philosopher in concluding that, externally, they are *merely* extension and motion, or that they have not, externally, the qualitative differences which sense consciousness detects between visual, auditory, gustatory, olfactory, and tactual data. When it is said that for science heat, colour, sound, etc., are motions of extended or space-filling media (*i.e.* insensible motions of insensible media, but *conceived after the analogy of sensible motions of sensible media*) ; that therefore they are really such and cannot be as they are perceived by sense to be ; that as perceived by sense they must be only (organic or mental) states of the perceiver,—these inferences far outrun their premisses. For if the scientist abstracts from the manner in which the secondary qualities appear to sense and conceives them after the analogy of the primary qualities (assuming that these *really are* as they *appear* to sense),—if in other words he conceives only their quantitative or extension-and-motion aspects,—then even if his interpretation of their external reality or nature be right as far as it goes, even if they are really as he conceives them intellectually after the analogy of extension-and-motion, it by no means follows that *such intellectual conception of them is adequate*, that they have not also externally the secondary or qualitative aspect which they are apprehended by sense as having, or that these secondary, qualitative aspects are only internal states produced in the perceiver by heterogeneous moving and space-filling realities.[1] On the contrary, if the scientist's assumption that the external primary qualities are intellectually and really, by identity or similarity, what they are sensibly apprehended to be, consistency with this assumption would demand the same for the external secondary qualities.

We may be right *e.g.* in intellectually conceiving "red" as an insensible external æther undulating 482,000,000,000 times per second. But since our concepts of æther and undulations are derived from the data directly present to sense consciousness in our perceptions of sensibly extended or space-filling and sensibly moving matter, or in other words from primary sense qualities assumed to be either themselves externally real or to represent *similar* external realities, and since these concepts are externally valid only on the assumption that our perception of extension and motion validly presents or represents these external primary qualities, it is clear that these concepts, when they are used to interpret the external correlate of the " red " which is present to consciousness, even though they be proved to be validly applicable to this "external red " (or external correlate of what is present to consciousness as " red)," cannot *adequately* represent the external reality of "redness," but only

[1] *Cf. Science of Logic*, ii., § 228, pp. 127-35 ; *Ontology*, § 11, pp. 70-1.

the quantitative, æther-and-undulation (or insensible extension-and-motion) aspect of it. There is another intellectually conceived aspect of it which we have an equal right to regard as externally real, namely, that which is presented or represented in the concrete percept, "red," which is present to our visual sense consciousness. For if we hold that sensibly perceived extension and motion (from which we derive our concepts of external æther and external undulations) are externally real, or have externally real correlates similar to themselves, we have an equal right to hold that sensibly perceived redness (from which we derive our concept of redness as an external quality) is itself externally real or has an externally real correlate similar to itself. To say, therefore, that because external redness is validly conceived by "quantitative" concepts as externally undulating æther, it cannot be also validly conceived by the "qualitative" concept which represents it as a something external sensibly apprehended as red, is not only to confound abstraction with negation, but also to *accept* the external validity of *derivative* concepts (æther and undulations),[1] and the propriety of their *application* to explain the real nature of the external reality sensibly apprehended as "red," and at the same time to *deny* the external validity of the *direct* intellectual concept for which the derivative concepts were *substituted*, namely, the intellectual concept of "redness," although this concept has precisely the same claim to external validity as the direct concepts of extension and motion from which the concepts of æther and undulations were derived. For all three concepts, "extension," "motion," and "redness," are abstracted from specific concrete sense data immediately present to sense consciousness with the common characteristic of felt externality.

It may, perhaps, be true that the external reality of "redness" *involves* insensible æther undulating at a certain rate, and we may perhaps be said to *know* this ; but we cannot be said to know that the external reality of redness is *this alone*, or to know the external reality of insensible æther and undulations *better* than we know *e.g.* a field of poppies to be really external to us and to have a characteristic or quality the reality of which consists partly at least (whatever be its total reality) in appearing to our sense consciousness in external perception as "redness". Yet it is a common procedure with many modern writers on sense perception to start from the nature of external physical realities *as conceived by scientists* through such quantitative concepts as those of atoms, electrons, æther, undulations, etc., concepts *formed from the primary sense qualities as present to consciousness*, and to infer that because the external correlates of the *secondary sense qualities present to consciousness* have been interpreted by scientists through such concepts, and when so interpreted are of course unlike these secondary or proper sensibles, therefore these latter, as perceived, cannot be in the external domain at all, but must be merely organic or psychic states of the perceiver. Such writers attribute to physical science an achievement of which it is innocent : they seem to think that it has made us more certain of the external reality of atoms, electrons, æther, undulations, etc., than we are of the external reality of sensibly perceived motion, extension, shape, number, etc., *from the (primary sense) percepts of which those concepts have been formed ;* and more certain

---

[1] *I.e.* derived from the concepts of *extension* and *motion*, which latter concepts were in turn abstracted from concrete sensibly apprehended extension and motion.

that those concepts, applied to the external correlates of our *secondary sense percepts*, represent to us faithfully (or even adequately) the nature of the external correlates of these secondary sense percepts, than we are that those external correlates are externally as they are presented in our secondary sense percepts and represented by the concepts formed from these. But physical science has thrown, and can throw, no such light on the problem of sense perception (112). And if by abstracting from what we may call the *qualitative* aspects of external physical realities, the aspects revealed in the proper or secondary sense qualities, and fixing its attention on their *quantitative* aspects, the aspects revealed in the common or primary sense qualities,—because these are found more amenable to its exact, quantitative calculations, hypotheses, and methods of experiment and verification,[1]—science has thus achieved notable triumphs of discovery which give us ever-increasing power over the manipulation of physical forces, it is nevertheless the duty of the epistemologist to explore the epistemological presuppositions of physical science. It is his duty to examine the grounds of the validity of the concepts used by it ; to look into its application of these concepts ; to point out especially that its procedure of *accepting* the externality of the common sensibles (and the external validity of direct and derivative concepts based on them) and *abstracting from* the externality of the proper sensibles (and from the external validity of the concepts based on these), does not at all imply *negation* of the external validity of these latter percepts and concepts, or involve the contention that secondary sense qualities and qualitative differences are merely internal states of the sentient perceptive subject. It is his duty to show that the transference of secondary qualities from the external to the internal domain is by no means a proof that these are merely internal, but only a conclusion from the procedure of applying "inference by similarity" to the primary qualities alone and not to the secondary, and at the same time mistaking *abstraction from* what this inference would yield concerning the secondary qualities, for *negation* of a similar external counterpart of these latter ; and to note, finally, that since physical science can never hope to show why or how *e.g.* 482,000,000,000 vibrations of æther per second produces the internal sensation of "red," it merely hands over this and similar data unexplained to the physiologist or the psychologist.[2]

If the secondary sense qualities, as they are conceived to be externally

[1] *Cf. Science of Logic*, ii., §§ 243, 246, 224 (pp. 110-12).

[2] The sense perception of "redness," or of any other sense quality, is, of course, like the fact of knowledge itself, an ultimate, unanalysable fact which cannot be "explained" in terms of anything simpler than itself. Yet some writers seem to think that they are called upon to "explain" such facts; and some physical scientists seem to think that they have "explained" "redness" by stating that it is externally a certain rate of undulations of æther, and that it is internally a (psychic or organic) state of a certain conscious tone or quality which we feel and name as "redness," and which is the only internal state that the external rate of æther-undulation can produce. No scientist has of course ever "explained" why just this undulation-rate produces just this definite sort of internal state ; nor is any scientist called upon to explain what, if it be a fact, is an ultimate fact. Yet some scientists appear to think that it is "explainable," and that their theories cannot be held as verified so long as they fail to explain it. *Cf.* passage quoted from Sir John Herschel's *Discourse on Natural Philosophy, apud* CASE, *op. cit.,* p. 12.

by the physical scientist, are unlike what they appear internally, this is merely because the scientist has conceived them after the analogy of primary internal sense data and their supposed similar external correlates, to which the internal secondary qualities consciously bear no resemblance. He has not *proved* but *assumed* that there is similarity between the "internal" and the "external," or the "apparent" and the "real," in the one case, and dissimilarity in the other. If what is external can be known only by inference (on the principle of similarity) from the internal, then it is surely an inversion of the facts to assume, as Professor Case seems to assume, that we know the external better than the internal : that we know what the secondary qualities are externally, or as "physical objects of science," better than we know what they are internally or as "data of sense ".[1]

For the reasons already given this line of thought is unconvincing. (1) It is not proved that the external cannot be immediately perceived. (2) Not only for the child [2] but for the man, not only for the physical scientist but for the psychologist and the epistemologist, "sensible data are the *causa cognoscendi*" of whatever can be known about the whole *material* domain, whether internal or external. (3) The author nowhere proves those sensible data to be states of the nervous system,—and even if he did that would not *explain* our awareness of them, for the possibility of awareness of a state of the self is no less mysterious than the possibility of awareness of a state of the non-self. (4) Seeing that scientists are supposed on this theory to infer "the physical objects of science" from *one section* of our sensible data by the law of "similarity," it cannot be maintained that the external reality of these objects is "better known" than the sensible data from which they are inferred, or that we should start from the former in investigating the validity of sense perception. In modern times many "scientific" theories have been propounded concerning the existence and nature of the æther, molecules, atoms, etc. ; concerning light, colour, heat, as modes of motion of these entities ; concerning the interpretation of secondary qualities in the *external* domain as specific varieties of the primary qualities [3] ; concerning the reducibility of all *qualitative* differences in this domain to *quantitative* differences, *i.e.* to different modes of *motion* of a *quantitative, voluminous, extended* material substrate, whether atomic (*discontinuous*) or *continuous*, or in other words to differences of primary qualities ; concerning the consequent and necessary banishment of the *secondary* qualities as such to the internal domain of the perceiving subject. But surely, when we approach the epistemological problem—What is the nature of those data of sense awareness? Are they internal or external? Are they self or non-self? Are they extramental, physical realities, or mind-dependent, psychic states ?—it is an inversion of right method to seek the solution of this problem by assuming as certain the external reality of those qualities, and those alone, which scientists regard as externally real, without inquiring into the validity of the presuppositions and processes whereby scientists have come to regard them, and them alone, as externally real. Some of Professor Case's criticisms of Idealism are unexceptional, and indeed unanswerable. But his own position misconceives the rôle of the perceiver's organism in the perceptive process, while his adoption of representationism

[1] *Cf. op. cit.*, pp. 27-8, 35-9.   [2] *Ibid.*, p. 36.   [3] *Ibid.*, pp. 23, 29.

and inference by similarity leaves that position exposed to some of the main difficulties against Idealism itself. It has not been proved, but assumed, by representationists that the internal effect of the external quality is the production, in the perceiver, of a directly apprehended *datum* (organic or psychic) *similar* to itself. May not the effect produced internally by the external quality be rather *the conscious perception of this latter itself*, as perceptionists contend? At all events if the principle of inference by similarity be applied at all, it should be applied to perception of secondary no less than of primary qualities, unless valid reason be shown for not applying it to the former. And so far from such reason having been shown, idealists have not been slow to point out that if such inference be not applicable to secondary qualities neither can it yield certitude about the external nature of primary qualities, and that we should therefore consistently adopt the transfigured or symbolic realism of Spencer, or the cosmothetic, hypothetical realism of Kant, or else candidly confess with Idealism itself that extramental reality is wholly problematic and therefore unknowable.

Before indicating this historical line of speculation we may here observe that if we have dwelt at such length, in the present section, on Physical Realism, and on the bearing of current physical theories regarding the external, material domain, upon the general problem of sense perception, our object has been to counteract the widely prevalent impression that because physical theories have wrought such unparalleled achievements in the external domain, they have also yielded, in regard to the nature and objects, and the scope and limits, of sense perception, certain revolutionary inferences which must be accepted without exploring the presuppositions, in regard to perception, on which these inferences are based. It is throwing no discredit on physical science to say that such an impression is erroneous and mischievous : physical science is not accountable for it : it is not entertained by really scientific minds : reflecting scientists are aware of the epistemological assumptions underlying their theories, and of the dependence (for validity) of the latter upon the former ; and they would be the last to deny to the inquirer into the knowledge-value of sense perception the right to explore these presuppositions and thereby to appraise the real knowledge-value of the theories based upon them.

CHAPTER XIX

125. IDEALISM AND THE SENSE QUALITIES. ABUSE OF
"INFERENCE BY SIMILARITY" FROM "REPRESENTATIONS".—
The general conclusion to be drawn from the two preceding
sections (123, 124) is that the Aristotelian and scholastic distinction between two conditions of sense qualities in the external
domain, namely, their *actual* condition when being actually perceived, and their *potential* condition apart from perception (122),
must not be understood as implying that one set of these
qualities, the common sensibles, are less relative to the perceiver
and externally more real apart from perception, than the other
set, the proper sensibles (123); and much less as implying the
theory of mediate perception, and this other assertion which is
intelligible only on this theory, namely, that the external primary qualities are *like*, while the external secondary qualities are
unlike, our conscious representations of them.

If we look for the origin, in modern philosophy, of this distinction between the primary or quantitative characteristics and
the secondary or qualitative characteristics of the domain of our
sense experience; of the notion that externally the former are
like and the latter unlike our internal representations of them;
and of the consequent tendency to regard the secondary or
qualitative characteristics as belonging exclusively to the
internal domain of the perceiver,—we shall have to go back
to Descartes (1596-1650) and his contemporaries.[1] Without
dwelling on the devious and doubtful method whereby Descartes
attained to certitude about *any external* reality by invoking the
Divine veracity (100), it will suffice to say that because he had
"clear and distinct ideas" of extension and motion and their
modes, and "obscure and confused" ideas of colour, taste, sound,
smell, temperature, and tactile qualities, he held the former to

---

[1] *Cf.* JEANNIÈRE, *op. cit.*, pp. 436-7.

be extramentally real,[1] and the latter to be *extramentally something or other*, vaguely apprehended as the cause of these obscure conscious representations. Meanwhile, in England, Francis Bacon (1561-1626) had fixed attention on the inductive study of the external universe, and Thomas Hobbes (1588-1679) re-echoed the view of Descartes by teaching that "All the qualities called sensible are, in the object which causeth them, but so many motions of the matter, by which it presseth on our organs diversely".[2] He even went farther than Descartes by continuing: "Neither in us that are pressed are they anything else but divers motions; for motion produceth nothing but motion".[3] Such assertions, leaving consciously apprehended qualitative differences unexplained, would not have been so confidently made if it had occurred to their author to ask himself on what sort of assumptions regarding the scope of conscious perception he knew "matter" and "motion" and "organs" to be not mere conscious states, and yet to cause conscious states so entirely unlike them. But Locke (1632-1704), like Descartes, did concern himself with the problem of sense perception; and like the latter too, he assumed both that the immediate objects of all our knowledge must be ideas, or psychic, conscious states of the knowing subject,[4] and that externally the primary qualities are like, and the secondary qualities unlike, our ideas of them. Berkeley (1685-1752) pointed out that if we are immediately aware only of our own ideas, or psychic or conscious states, and that if the nature of what is extramental is known only by inference, through similarity, from these ideas, we should in consistency hold that both the primary and the secondary extramental correlates are equally like our ideas of them.[5] Finally Hume

[1] And abstract, three-dimensional *extension* to be *the essence of matter*: externally these primary qualities were *assumed to resemble* the "clear and distinct ideas" which they produced in us, and which were regarded as the immediate objects of our awareness.

[2] *Leviathan*, I., c. 1.

[3] *Ibid.*

[4] Professor CASE thus pithily outlines the persistent progress of this assumption in modern philosophy: "Psychological idealism began with the supposition of Descartes that all the immediate objects of knowledge are ideas. From Descartes it passed to Locke and Berkeley. But with Hume it changed its terms from ideas to impressions. Kant preferred phenomena, Mill sensations. The most usual terms of the present day are sensations, feelings, psychical phenomena, and states of consciousness. But the hypothesis has not changed its essence, though the idealists have changed their terms,—*Verbum, non animum, mutant.* They at least agree that all sensible data are psychical objects of some kind or other."—*Op. cit.*, p. 15.

[5] Unfortunately, instead of repudiating the gratuitous postulate of Idealism, and investigating the merits of the alternative assumption,—that what we are immedi-

observed that if the so-called primary qualities are apprehended only by the co-operation of two or more external senses with the internal faculty of association, co-ordination, and unification (114, 123), while the so-called secondary qualities are apprehended each as the proper datum of some one separate external sense, there is certainly more of the subjective or self factor in the elaboration of the former qualities (as present to consciousness) than of the latter; and that therefore the former ought to be *less like* their supposed extramental correlates than the latter.[1]

Thus, under the overshadowing influence of the fundamental gratuitous assumption of Idealism,—that the mind can become directly aware only of its own states,—we find the pendulum of scepticism about the nature of the extramental oscillating from the one-sided inference that the primary but not the secondary qualities of extramental reality may be inferred to be similar to our ideas of them, to the opposite and equally one-sided inference that if we are to infer similarity of the extramental at all we should infer it in regard to the secondary rather than the primary qualities.

And so the reflection is once more (104) forced upon us : If we allow that in *sense perception* we are never directly *aware* of the extramental, but always only of an intramental or psychic object, can we *know intellectually* that this object is an "appearance" or "representation" *produced in the mind by an extramental cause*, and can we have reasoned intellectual certitude of the existence and nature of this extramental cause? In common with realist supporters of the theory of mediate sense perception we hold it for an undoubted fact that the *knowing* subject can *intellectually* transcend self and attain to a *reasoned conviction* of the reality of a non-self domain of being. *Our* reason, however, for holding that fact to be undoubted is because we also hold it an indubitable fact that in normal sense perception *sense* directly reveals *a real non-self* to *intellect*, or in other words that such *normal sense evidence* of what a directly perceived reality *appears*, is identically valid *intellectual evidence* of what this reality *really is* (105).

ately aware of is extramental material reality,—he rejected the latter altogether, and held that our ideas are not representations of realities beyond themselves at all, but are themselves the only realities,—placed in our minds by the Divine Spirit. *Cf. supra*, § 123.

[1] JEANNIÈRE, outlining the progress of Idealism, has this significant observation : " Principio semel introducto participationis subjecti cognoscentis in objecto conficiendo, aperta est via omni licentiae vel potius audaciae".—*Op. cit.*, p. 437. *Cf.* MAHER, *op. cit.*, p. 154. In Kant's philosophy also, as MAHER remarks (*ibid.*), " the objective significance of the two groups is similarly reversed ". The primary qualities, extension and motion, are products of the *a priori* forms of perception, *space* and *time*, while the secondary qualities are somehow in the material that is supposed to be " given from without ". *Cf. infra*, § 130.

If, on the other hand, all the immediately apprehended conscious data from which we abstract our concept of cause were phases of the self-reality, it is difficult to see how inference from effect to cause would attain to the existence of non-self reality for us (104).[1] Furthermore, the validity of the logical process whereby we infer from the nature of an effect *similarity in the nature of the cause*, is not self-evident or universal. It is experience alone that can tell us,—experience of causes producing effects similar in nature to themselves,—how far we can safely use such inference, or what degree of similarity,—univocal or analogical,—we may infer in a particular case.[2] For we have also experience of causes producing effects dissimilar in nature to themselves. All that is self-evident is that the *adequate* cause of any effect must pre-contain *equivalently* or *eminently* the perfections of its effect.[3] But this gives us no certain guidance as to the *kind or degree of similarity* we are justified in attributing to the extramental factor in perception, if we can know this latter only by inferring it as partial cause of the " conscious appearance " or " psychic representation " which alone we are supposed to be capable of apprehending directly and immediately.

---

[1] Kant himself in his " Refutation of Idealism " (*Critique*, tr. MÜLLER, pp. 779-80), arguing that " consciousness of [one's] own existence is, at the same time, consciousness of the existence of objects in space outside [one's self]," and remarking that in his proof " the trick played by idealism has been turned against it," has this observation : " Idealism assumed that the only immediate experience is the internal, and that from it we can no more than *infer* external things, though in an untrustworthy manner, as always happens if from given effects we infer *definite* causes : it being quite possible that the cause of the representations, which are ascribed by us, it may be wrongly, to external things, may lie within ourselves ". The observation is just ; but, unfortunately, Kant's own improvement on the idealism he sought to refute is not appreciable, inasmuch as in his own theory " space " and " outside " are mere domains of the mind. *Cf.* vol. i., §§ 61, 97 ; *supra*, § 100; *infra*, chap. xxii.

[2] The aphorism *Omne agens agit simile sibi*, is a rough inductive generalization from our observation of the propagation of species in the domain of living organisms. —*Cf. Ontology*, § 98, p. 372 (*f*). Nevertheless it is the principle upon which representationists must rely in vindicating a knowledge of extramental reality. Thus JEANNIÈRE, in answer to the difficulty, " How can we, from an internal representative state, come to know an external reality, especially a heterogeneous reality? "—replies, " We can do so quite intelligibly by the principle of causality : there exists a proportion between effect and cause, so that the effect bears some resemblance to the cause : *agens agit sibi simile* ".—*Op. cit.*, p. 446. In the same context he refers to the view of some authors, that " by the apprehension of this resemblance the external thing itself is immediately apprehended " ; and he rightly observes that this is only confusing the issue, inasmuch as the " resemblance " is not *really identical* with the " thing ". But the view referred to cannot be perceptionism, for the perceptionist repudiates the view that what we apprehend is the " resemblance," " image," or " mental state ".

[3] " Whatever be the nature of efficient causality, *actio* and *passio*, or of the dependence of the produced actuality upon the active power of its adequate efficient cause, the reality of this dependence forbids us to think that in the natural order of efficient causation a higher grade of reality can be actualized than the agent is capable of actualizing, or that the agent can naturally actualize a higher or more perfect grade of reality than is actually its own."—*Ibid.*, p. 371. Is the truth of this latter statement self-evident ? It has been questioned by a scholastic writer, Professor Laminne of Louvain, in the *Revue neo-Scolastique*, Feb. 1904—*ibid.*, n.

Hence the "transfigured" or "symbolic" realism of Spencer, that our conscious states are mere symbols of an extramental but unknowable reality : a realism almost attenuated to idealism. And hence, also, the phenomenism of Kant, that we can know only mental appearances, but are forced to postulate the reality of an unknowable extramental or noumenal cause of them. Those idealisms are rejected by realist advocates of the theory of mediate sense perception : but since according to these latter the domain of being which is directly presented in sense perception and represented in intellectual conception is a "self" domain of mental states, their refutation of such idealisms will appear unconvincing to many. For instance, the difference between their own form of critical realism and the "symbolic" or "transfigured" realism of Spencer is not great. Distinguishing between the being ("*esse intentionale*") which the sense object has in the perceiver, and the being ("*esse physicum*") which it has outside the perceiver, Jeannière says : [1] " It must at least be held that the former resembles the latter,—not indeed in the manner in which *e.g.* the colour of one rose resembles the colour of another, but by *some analogy of proportion* [2] founded in the fact that the one is cause of the other (113). Hence we have a *proper* concept of formal or subjective colour or sweetness, but not, if we speak strictly, of extra-subjective colour or sweetness." Explaining this he continues : [3] "There is a certain proportion or resemblance (analogy) between the *non-Ego* and the impressions produced in the *Ego* by the *non-Ego*. Therefore the knowledge I have of the things that cause my impressions is not purely *symbolic*, such, for instance, as the light of the semaphore signalling a ship. Things are in themselves what they must be in order to produce in the human organs all that we are conscious of experiencing." On this we may remark (1) that Spencer would distinguish between *artificial* and *natural* symbolism, and would hold the percept to be a *natural* symbol of the extramental ; (2) that it is not the effect produced in the sense *organs* by the *external* reality, but the effect produced in *consciousness* by the *extramental* (organic and extra-organic) reality that representationists hold to be the immediate object of awareness ; (3) that while the perceptionist regards *the whole perception process* to be, in scholastic terms, an *imago, similitudo, reproductio intentionalis*, of the extramental reality, he repudiates altogether the view that the *esse intentionale* or *esse mentale* (20, 102) which the latter (the *esse reale* or *physicum*) thus obtains in the perceiver,—whether as *species impressa* or *species expressa* (112),—is itself an object of direct awareness, a *prius cognitum*, from which the knower would infer the reality of a similar extramental correlate. [4] The scholastic aphorism, "Cognitum est in cognoscente secundum aliquam sui similitudinem," [5] simply means that the mind, by virtue of the whole cognitive process, becomes a *similitudo* of the known reality, or is "assimilated or conformed" to the latter ; it does not mean that this mental state, this "similitudo intentionalis," is *first* known, and its extramental cause inferred from it (112). "Of, what, then [the author continues], it will be asked, have we *proper* concepts ?—(*a*) We have *proper* concepts of the facts of consciousness ; of toothache, etc. ; of green, red, sweet, bitter, resisting, etc. (*b*)

---

[1] *Op. cit.*, p. 425. [2] On the subject of *analogy*, *cf. Ontology*, § 2, pp. 36-42.
[3] *Ibid.*, n. 2. [4] *Cf. infra*, § 129. [5] JEANNIÈRE, *op. cit.*, *ibid.*

Of all else we have only *analogical* concepts : of the soul, God, substance, cause, etc. (*c*) At the same time things in themselves are said to be known by *proper* concepts when they are known by their *natural* (*per se*) effects on our organs, effects of which we have proper concepts. For example, I have a proper notion of the cherry because of the proper notion I have of its sensible effect. On the other hand when the thing in itself is not known to me by its proper or natural sensible effects I have only analogical notions of it." The perceptionist holds that we have proper concepts of all extramental (organic and external) *material* qualities, causes, and natures or substances ; because he holds that these are all directly given either to sense (*sensibilia per se*) or to intellect with the data of sense (*sensibilia per accidens*). For the representationist, however, the concepts under (*c*) cannot really be " proper," but only " analogical " .

The progress of Idealism also forces upon us the reflection that if we once admit the secondary qualities to be mere mental or psychic states or " sensations," produced in us by external reality, we shall find it difficult to maintain, as against the Kantian form of Idealism, that the primary qualities,—extensional or spatial determinations,—are externally real. Of this we have an interesting illustration in Prichard's otherwise very excellent criticism of Kant's speculative philosophy.

Examining Kant's view that we are aware only of "appearances" *produced* in us *by* things, he says, " To speak of appearances produced by things is to imply that the object of perception is merely something mental, *viz.* an appearance. Consequently access to a non-mental reality is excluded ; for a perception of which the object is something belonging to the mind's own being *cannot justify an inference to something beyond the mind*, and the result is inevitably solipsism."[1] The principle here is that because an appearance is "something mental," "belonging to the mind's own being," we are not justified in inferring to the extramental. But he goes on immediately to allow that the secondary qualities of bodies are not in the bodies, are not extramental, but are " sensations "[2] produced in us by the extramental. Being therefore only "sensations," or "something mental," neither can they "justify an inference to something extramental " or give us any information as to the real nature of the latter. What, therefore, can we know about the real nature of the extramental, material universe ? Well, we have the primary qualities, or " spatial relations" of this universe to fall back upon. These, Prichard contends (against Kant), we can and do know to be extramentally real. So the material universe is, then, (really and extramentally) merely a system of homogeneous,[3] space-filling, three-dimensional, spatially moving and interacting realities ? And how can we know even such a system of space-filling and moving realities to be extramental ? Because the primary qualities which reveal it are not sensations or sense-percepts, dependent on a perceiver, but are conceived or intellectually apprehended thought-objects ; and being intellectu-

[1] *Op. cit.*, chap. iv., p. 76 (italics ours).   [2] *Ibid.*, p. 86.
[3] Or, from the *heterogeneous* "sensations" or "mental realities" which the secondary qualities are held to be, may we infer heterogeneity (and, if so, what sort of heterogeneity ?) in the extramental causes of them ? Prichard holds, of course, that the " sensations" are produced in us by extramental realities. Knowledge of the latter he does not, however, seem to regard as inferred or inferrible from the former, but as attained independently of these.

ally judged to be extramentally real they must therefore *be* extramentally real, —inasmuch as "it is a presupposition of thinking that things are in themselves what we think them to be ".[1]

It will be instructive to examine somewhat more in detail the line of thought by which the author reaches these not very satisfactory conclusions.

He says we must allow the secondary qualities,—even colour, which presents special difficulties,—to be merely facts of the mental or psychic order, "sensations," [2] produced in us by external reality. They are not even appearances of external bodies: "when once the issue is raised it is difficult and, in the end, impossible to use the word 'appear' in connexion with these qualities. Thus it is difficult and, in the end, impossible to say that a bell *appears* noisy, or that sugar *appears* sweet. We say, rather, that the bell and the sugar produce certain sensations (*not* 'appearances') in us." [3] The case of colour he then proceeds to examine, and concludes that it too is a mental state or sensation, that in respect of colour " things look what they never are " ; [4] but that the fact of their " looking " or " appearing " coloured implies that they *are* (1) real, and (2) extended or spatial.[5] He then faces the Kantian difficulty " that just as things may only *look* coloured, so things may only *look* spatial ".[6] This he meets by the contention that as a matter of fact what things *look* or *appear* to be spatially they never *are* spatially ; that their *real* (*i.e. three-dimensional*) spatial determinations are always *other than*, and are in no limiting cases coincident with, what they *appear* spatially to be ; that what they *appear* in point of spatial extension always implies " correlation to a percipient," [7] whereas what they *really are* in point of spatial extension always is, nay means, what they are "independently of a percipient " ; [8] that, therefore, " it is so far from being true that we only know what things look and not what they are, that in the case of spatial relations we actually know what things are, even though they never look what they are ".[9] But if we have to admit " that we perceive things as they look, and not as they are," [10] or that we perceive only what things *look* spatially, how, he asks (1) can we have ever come to believe that things *are really* spatial, and (2) how can we know that this belief is not illusory? His reply is that this belief is implied in our knowledge of what things *look* spatially, and that we know this belief not to be illusory because in regard to spatial relations there is no transition *in principle*, but only *in respect of details*, in passing " from knowledge of what things look to knowledge of what things are " : [11] in other words, since it is undeniable " that we can and do state what things appear " [12] in respect of spatial relations, and since the possibility of knowing what things look or appear spatially implies throughout the " consciousness " [13] or " belief " [14] that things really are spatial, it must follow that things really are spatial.

---

[1] *Op. cit.*, p. 100.　　　　　[2] *Ibid.*, pp. 85 *sqq.*

[3] *Ibid.*, p. 86. *Cf.*, however, *infra*, § 128. We agree with the author's refusal to regard such produced mental states (if we admitted the secondary qualities to be such) as " appearances ".

[4] P. 87.　　　　　[5] P. 88.

[6] P. 89. *All* the *primary* qualities, being spatial determinations, are involved in this charge.

[7] P. 91.　　　　[8] *Ibid.*　　　　[9] P. 91.　　　　[10] *Ibid.*

[11] P. 92.　　　　[12] P. 93.　　　　[13] P. 92.　　　　[14] P. 91.

We must confess we are not convinced by this line of defending the external reality of spatial determinations against Kantism.

(1) In the first place the author urges, against Kant's position, that "an 'appearance,' being necessarily something mental, cannot possibly be said to be extended " ;[1] that we cannot predicate of an "appearance" spatial determinations such as "convergent,"[2] or divergent, etc. ; that "an appearance cannot be spatial".[3] Very well ; but "sensations" are also "something mental," and yet, on the author's view (that the secondary qualities are sensations), we can predicate of these "mental" facts or states that they are "red " or "hot " or "bitter " :[4] but if so, then, after all, why not predicate of "appearances" that they are spatial? It may, however, be urged that there is, after all, a difference ; but then what about this other fact : Is not "extensity " or "voluminousness" a *spatial* "sensuous element "[5] or datum of the *tactual* and *organic* senses, whose data, being secondary qualities, are presumably regarded by the author as "sensations"? When arguing that the primary qualities, *i.e.* spatial determinations, are separable from colour, he says, by way of confirmation,[6] " moreover, if the possibility of the separation of the primary qualities from colour is still doubted, it is only necessary to appeal to the blind man's ability to apprehend the primary qualities though he may not even know what the word 'colour' means ". But can the blind man become conscious of "the primary qualities," or "spatial relations," apart from his tactual, organic, and motor perceptions? And the data of these latter are presumably secondary qualities, and therefore "sensations". "Of course," the author continues, " it must be admitted that some sensuous elements [*i.e.* 'sensations,' 'mental' facts] are involved in the apprehension of the primary qualities,[7] but the case of the blind man shows that these may relate to sight instead of to touch ". Yes, it shows that some of them may ; but are there no "sensuous elements" in the blind man's tactual data? Surely there are ; and the point is, can *he* apprehend "spatial relations" apart from these? Nay, are not the vaguely felt "extensity " and "voluminousness " of our visual, tactual, organic, gustatory (and possibly auditory and olfactory) sense data, themselves "sensuous elements " or at least inseparable from the "sensuous elements" in these perceptions,—if by "sensuous elements " the author means the mental facts or data which he takes the secondary qualities to be? So far as introspection can discover, the "spatial determinations" which we call primary qualities—the felt "externality," "extensity," "voluminousness,"—are inseparable from the secondary qualities which the author calls "sensuous elements," in our conscious sense data. The author seems to realize this, for he adds : "Moreover, it, of course, does not follow from the fact that sensuous elements are inseparable from our perception of bodies that they belong to, and are therefore inseparable from, the bodies perceived ".[8] Nevertheless, if we separate them we must show cause for separating them.

---

[1] *Op. cit.*, p. 76.   [2] P. 81.   [3] P. 93.

[4] For these must be *real* predicates of *something* : if not of extramental realities, then of mental states.

[5] *Cf.* p. 91 n.   [6] P. 91 n.

[7] So "primary qualities," or "spatial determinations " are "apprehended ". By sense or by intellect ? If by sense, then they "appear " to, and are "perceived by " sense. If by intellect, *cf. infra*, p. 147.

[8] *Ibid.*

Now, if they are separate or separable, and if we ask how do we apprehend or become conscious of these spatial determinations at all, there seem to be only two alternative answers possible. Either they too are sense data and therefore "relative to perception,"[1] and dependent on the percipient just in the same way as the secondary qualities or "sensuous elements" are. This we believe to be the case. But if, this being the case, the secondary qualities were also held to be mere sensations or mental facts it could no longer be consistently argued against Kant's view that "an appearance cannot be spatial". Hence the author, holding that the secondary qualities are only mental facts or sensations, adopts the second possible alternative answer to the question suggested, *viz.* that the primary qualities, or "spatial determinations," are *not sense data at all*, that they "cannot of their very nature be relative to perception";[2] that they are exclusively *concepts*, objects of *thought*, that they belong to what things are really, *i.e.* to what things are for thought, for conception and judgment, and not to what things appear to perception.[3]

(2) Now this view is not supported by introspection.[4] It is, we believe, an illustration of the dangerous tendency to which we have already called attention (114), the tendency to lose sight of the primary qualities as *concrete*, directly presented and felt sense *percepts*, and so to regard them exclusively as *abstract*, intellectually represented *concepts* or *thought-objects*,—a danger increased by the fact that we can think and reason about sense data only through concepts, *i.e.* by intellectually apprehending "what they are," so that it requires a special effort of abstraction on our part to avoid reading into *sense* data as such what belongs to them only as *conceived* (114). Moreover, the view that real (three-dimensional) spatial characteristics must belong only to what things are, and not at all to what they appear, (*a*) is based on the mistaken assumption that what things really are must be wholly independent of what they appear ; and (*b*) by leaving unexplained how we come to know intellectually what things really are, it can yield no convincing refutation of Kantism.

(*a*) If what things appear to sense is relative to the perceiver, nevertheless, if at the same time we can by reflection discover the way in which they are relative,—*viz.* to the perceiver *as organic*, and not as mental and consciously perceptive (126),—and if we can allow for such relativity in judging what the perceived things are really and externally, then we can know what they are really and externally even though we know that what they appear to sense is partly relative to, and dependent on, the organic constitution of

---

[1] *Op. cit.*　　　　[2] P. 91 n.　　　　[3] *Ibid.*, pp. 99, 100.

[4] Reflection on the data of sense consciousness fails to discover any difference as to mode of presence or presentation, between directly apprehended "extensity," "externality," "solidity," "voluminousness,"—*i.e.* spatial characteristics,—and colour, sound, temperature, etc. That we become aware of the former *with* the latter is undeniable. For consciousness they are inseparable. If it be contended that, notwithstanding this apparent inseparability, the former are not sensuously apprehended at all, that they are known by intellect but do not appear to sense, the contention can be supported only by showing that real spatial characteristics can be proved to be of their very nature unperceivable. This the author tries to do, but, as we think, unsuccessfully.

the perceiver. Of course, " our apprehension of what things¹ *are* is essentially a matter of thought or judgment " ; ² but we are by no means at liberty to add, " and not of perception ".³ For if our thought or judgment is not an interpretation of what things appear to sense, or is not at least based upon and motived by, what they appear to sense, what is it an interpretation of? Moreover, it is implied, and rightly, that what things really *are* is what they are for thought or judgment (*i.e.* for *true* judgment). But things cannot be thought, conceived, judged, except in so far as they are " related " or " relative " to intellect, or in other words in so far as they " appear " to intellect.⁴ What things really *are* (*i.e.* something at least of what they really are) is what they are conceived, interpreted, represented, to be, by intellect (judging *truly*). When, therefore, we contend that intellect can know things as they really are, absolutely, this cannot mean that what they are when they are known, or what they are known to be, is independent of their " appearing " to intellect, but only that what they really are is not *altered* by this " appearing," and that this " appearing " itself is a function of their reality.⁵ This is what must be established as against Kant. It is not established by asserting (what is quite true) that " it is a presupposition of thinking that things are in themselves what we think them to be " ; ⁶ and (what is true only in a certain sense) that " from the nature of the case a presupposition of thinking not only cannot be rightly questioned, but cannot be questioned at all ".⁷ It cannot, of course, be really doubted, but it can be provisionally questioned and explored ; and since, among others, Kant has explored it, he must be met by showing ⁸ that the relation of reality to intellect interpreting it does not shut reality off from all possibility of its being known as it is. But this cannot be effectually shown, in regard to the spatial characteristics of material reality, by declaring that these must really be as intellect conceives or apprehends them, so long as no account is given of the way in which such characteristics become cognitively related to, and are apprehended by, intellect.

(*b*) Prichard says " it is the view that what a thing really is it is, independently of a percipient, that forms the real starting-point of Kant's thought ".⁹ But it is also an essential part of Kant's thought that what a thing really is it

---

¹ This is true of *all* things, but it is only " material " or " spatial " things that are under discussion here.

² *Op. cit.*, p. 99.   ³ *Ibid.*   ⁴ *Cf. infra*, §§ 127, 128.

⁵ Prichard says " an appearance, as being *ex hypothesi* and appearance to someone, *i.e.* to a percipient, must be relative to perception " (p. 93). But if perception implies an appearance of something to a perceiver does not thought imply an appearance of something to a thinker? Knowledge is an interpretation or representation of something. But the " something " must appear to the knower : he must be aware of it. Is not therefore this " appearance," or " something appearing " likewise relative to the knower? *Cf. infra*, §§ 127, 128.

⁶ P. 100.   ⁷ *Ibid.*

⁸ The fact that in this process of testing the capacity of intellect to know reality as it is, we are *supposing* its capacity to *reach true conclusions* in the testing process itself (*i.e.* its capacity to apprehend reality at least thus far) militates just as much or as little, neither more nor less, against Kant's critics than against himself. The fact, inevitable as it is, has not deterred men from undertaking the delicate and difficult task of using thought to explore the springs of thought.

⁹ P. 91.

is, independently of a *conceiver*, independently of *thought, judgment, know-ledge*. Moreover, both statements, as to what a thing really is, are true in the sense that "what a thing really is" cannot be influenced or altered either by perception or by thought ; but Kant defended the statements interpreted in the sense that "what a thing really is" it can never "appear" either to sense *or to intellect*. When, therefore, Prichard admits this in regard to sense, and then tries to show, against Kant, that spatial relations really are as we *think* them, or as they appear *to thought*, every step in his argument can be countered by the contention that spatial relations are apprehended (whether by sense or by intellect) in the same way as the secondary qualities are apprehended (*i.e.* perceived and conceived), and that since he admits the secondary qualities, whether in the concrete or in the abstract, whether perceived or conceived, to be only mental facts, so must spatial relations be only mental facts.

For instance, answering the objection that our belief in the reality of space (however it has arisen) may be after all an illusion, Prichard writes : " If assertions concerning the apparent shape, etc., of things presuppose the consciousness that things *are* spatial, to say that this consciousness is illusory is to say that all statements concerning what things *appear*, in respect of spatial relations, are equally illusory. But since it is wholly impossible to deny that we can and do state what things appear in this respect, the difficulty must fall to the ground."[1] Admitting that "we can and do state what things appear" in respect of spatial relations, Kant would simply reply that such statements are illusory, and the consciousness implied by them is illusory, *only if* the "things" to which they are understood to apply be regarded as extramental things, not if the "things" be regarded as "mental facts".[2] This implies, of course, that it is possible to distinguish between the true or real[3] and the false or apparent[4] *within the domain of mental* facts or "phenomena,"[5] a possibility which Kant proceeds to defend.

Again, in attacking Kant's defence Prichard writes : "We presuppose that that quality is really, and not only apparently, a quality of a body, which we and every one, judging from what it looks under various conditions (*i.e.* 'in universal experience'),[6] must believe it to possess in itself and independently of all perception".[7] But how can a judgment formed "from what [the body] looks under various conditions " tell us what or how the body really is, if the body never under any conditions looks what it really is ? What right have we to form such a judgment, or to entertain such a belief, if all the body's *appearing* or *perceptible* qualities ("what it *looks* under various conditions ") are, by being relative to a percipient, *not real* (because not "independent of

---

[1] *Op. cit.*, pp. 92-3.
[2] We might also argue that the statement that a thing *appears* red implies the consciousness that it *is* coloured. Yet Prichard holds this consciousness to be illusory unless "thing" be understood to mean a "sensation" or "mental fact". Hence he must either hold that all statements based on it are illusory, or else recognize the possibility of distinguishing between "real" or "true" appearances and "deceptive" or "false" appearances within the domain of mental facts or sensations,—precisely what Kant does regarding spatial relations.
[3] *Erscheinung.* [4] *Schein.* [5] *Cf. ibid.*, p. 79.
[6] *Critique* (MÜLLER), p. 37. [7] P. 99.

perception "), and if its *real* qualities (*i.e.* real three-dimensional extension, real shape, real position, real motion, etc.) *never appear*, or are *never perceived?* How does intellect apprehend these latter, if not in the data of sense? "We do not *perceive* but *think* a thing as it is."[1] But how or whence does intellect apprehend the predicates whereby it thinks the thing, if not in the data of sense? Prichard, however, has admitted that the data of sense, or "what things appear," are relative to the perceiver in the sense of being themselves mental facts ;[2] and he sees that predicates or *thought*-objects, derived from data which are relative in that way could not yield knowledge of what things other than mental facts can really be. The only alternative is that intellect can apprehend what things really are, *directly* and *of itself*, and *apparently without any aid from sense.* Of course what a thing really is in respect of spatial relations is directly "correlated with thought,"[3] because it is thought, not sense, that interprets what anything really is ; but even if its correlation with thought did not involve its correlation with sense also, we should have not merely to assert, but to show, as against Kant, that the former correlation did not alter or transform the reality : and we should therefore have to show *how* thought apprehends the extramentally real,—a point to which Prichard does not appear to have directed his attention. Correlation of reality with thought *does*, however, *involve correlation of reality with sense.* Nor does this necessarily involve the confounding of thought with sense,— however Kant may stand in relation to this charge.[4] For our intellectual knowledge of what material, spatial things are really and extramentally, is certainly derived from what they appear to sense. And the only proper way of showing, as against Kant, that nevertheless we can know intellectually what things are really and extramentally, is by exploring the nature of the relation in *both* cases, and showing that, when rightly understood, it does not screen off the extramental reality either from intellect or from sense.

We shall have more to say later in criticism of the general position that what we become directly aware of, whether in sense cognition or in intellectual cognition, is and must be only a "representation " or "appearance," "produced " in us by a something which this mental product is supposed to represent.[5] But before doing so we have next to examine the difficulties which may be urged against the form of Intuitive or Perceptive Realism so far outlined in our inquiry.

Before passing from Idealism we may here note an objection which is sometimes unthinkingly urged by idealists against realism in general. Vibrations of the air or the æther, they argue, are quite unlike our sensations of sound and colour : therefore

---

[1] *Op. cit.*, p. 99.

[2] He admits that spatial characteristics which are *de facto* real and external *appear* to *sight* and to *touch* (*cf.* p. 91 n.) ; but holds that they appear *otherwise* than they really are : " in the case of spatial relations . . . things . . . never look what they are ". Hence predicates derived from " what they look " could never inform us as to what they really are,—any more than if " what they look " as regards spatial relations were merely mental facts or " sensations," which he considers the secondary qualities to be.

[3] P. 100.   [4] P. 99.   [5] *Cf.* also vol. i., §§ 92, ii. ; 93.

our sensations in general cannot give us any information about the nature of external reality. Such an objection, coming from an idealist, is suicidal, for, as Rickaby points out,[1] "he forgets that it has been by the senses that the vibrations have been discovered, and that if the scientific result is worth anything, it proves the ability of the senses to give us information about the facts as they are in external nature". In other words the objection is based on an assumption which is the very negation of idealism, *viz.* the assumption, common to physical science, that at least motion and extension are really and externally identical with, or similar or analogous to, that which we internally perceive them to be.

126. GENERAL DIFFICULTIES AGAINST CRITICAL PERCEP-TIONISM.—Our general contention has been that external sense perception puts us into direct and immediate cognitive contact with external or non-self reality. But we have not denied that the specific qualities with which this reality is presented to con-sciousness are partially dependent on and relative to the subjec-tive or self factor which is the perceiver's own organism.[2] On the contrary, we have contended that such dependence and relativity must be recognized in every datum or quality or object, including externality itself, presented to the conscious perceiver (120, 121). But, distinguishing between normal and abnormal (organic and external) conditions of perception (119), we have asserted that *in the case of normal sense perception* the *dependence* of the external, perceived reality on the subjective, organic factor, and the conse-quent *relativity* of its perceived specific quality to the perceiver, *may be ignored, i.e.* that *we may abstract from them* in attributing the specific quality to the external reality,—not as if the relativity and dependence were not there, for they are always there, in-volved in the very nature of the perceptive process whether this be normal or abnormal,—and not as if the specific quality as perceived and attributed to the external reality were understood

---

[1] *First Principles*, p. 284.

[2] We accept MERCIER'S summing up of the psychology of external sense per-ception : " The natural *specific dispositions* of the sense faculties and the *nature of the external excitants* constitute the ultimate reason of *qualitative* diversity of our sensations. This statement, commonplace as it may appear, is the last word of the psychology of sensation."—*Psychologie* (6th edit.), vol. i., § 75, p. 167. For the re-spective rôles of the sense organs and the external reality, in perception, *cf. ibid.*, pp. 159-67 ; *Origines de la psychologie contemporaine*, p. 365 ; also NYS, *Cosmologie*, § 226, pp. 334-7.

to be in the latter irrespectively of the determining influence of the structure and condition of the perceiver's organism upon it, —but because in normal perception this ever-present influence of the internal, organic factor, in partially determining what the external reality is perceived to be, is itself *constant and uniform for all perceivers*, and while tacitly understood to be always present, is also tacitly and rightly understood to be incapable of unconsciously misleading or falsifying the judgments in which we attribute the perceived qualities and qualitative differences to the external reality.[1]

It may perhaps occur to the reader to doubt if the view we are advocating is really a form of *perceptionism* or *intuitionism*,— to doubt whether it really admits after all a direct and immediate awareness of external sense qualities *as they are externally*. It *is* a form of perceptionism. As distinguished from every form of the theory which holds the direct object of sense awareness to be an internal, conscious (organic or psychic) " reproduction " or " representation " or " appearance," and the external to be inferred (whether consciously or sub-consciously) from this " representation," the theory here advocated holds the external reality to be directly presented to the perceiver's consciousness, and the perceiver to be directly aware of it. It holds the internal effect of the external factor in sense perception not to be the production of a *consciously apprehended* datum imaging or representing the external in consciousness, but rather to be the production of *the conscious perception process itself* by means of an *unconsciously wrought psychic modification* (the " *species impressa* ") : this whole process being an " assimilation " of the perceiver to the external factor which is the term of the process as consciously perceptive.

---

[1] For instance, we know that sound is a something external, of which we could not become aware unless through the organ of hearing, and colour a something external, of which we could not become aware unless through the organ of vision : that the perceived difference between colour and sound is *partly* due to a known difference (from which, as constant, we abstract) in the specific structure and constitution of these two kinds of sense organ, but is also itself externally a perceived difference in qualities of the external perceived reality ; that the difference between a high and a low sound perceived in the same conditions of the perceiver, or between red and blue perceived in unchanged conditions of the perceiver, is in each case a difference in real modes or characters or qualities of the perceived external reality : though in each of these cases, likewise, it is functions of *different parts* of the auditory and the visual sense organs respectively that subserve the conscious process of perception, and therefore in their measure determine the qualities perceived,—a determining factor from which we abstract in so far as we know it to be normal, and therefore constant and uniform.

But it realizes that the unconscious psychic modification, which determines the conscious perceptive process both *quoad exercitium* and *quoad specificationem*, is itself wrought not by the sole influence of the external factor on the perceiver's mind or conscious principle, but by this influence as conveyed, and modified or determined in the transmission, by the perceiver's sense organon. Hence it holds that the external is directly perceived indeed, but perceived nevertheless only through the instrumentality of the internal, material organon which presents it to the perceiver's consciousness. ·Moreover, it recognizes this influence of the subjective, organic factor : it points out that only when this influence is normal, and therefore uniform for all perceivers, does its presence cease to count in the qualitative differences which come from the external factor but are presented through the instrumentality of the internal factor ; and that therefore in normal perception, and only in normal perception, can the *presentation* of the qualities and qualitative differences to consciousness, or their *appearance* to consciousness, be *identically* a *part or function* of their *external reality*. And by recognizing these implications of the perceptive process the present view avoids the erroneous implication of *naïf* or *unreflecting* perceptionism, that the presentation or appearance of the external reality to consciousness is not only direct, but uninfluenced by any subjective factor, and that therefore the external *always really is* as it *appears* to the perceiver. Our position rather is that the presentation or appearance of any datum to sense consciousness is indeed always part and parcel, so to speak, of the *extramental* material domain of being, and this whether the perception be normal or abnormal ; but that the presentation or appearance to sense-consciousness of a datum as *extra-organic*, non-self, external, and as being qualitatively such or such, is part and parcel of the *external* reality *only when the organic conditions of perception are normal,* and not otherwise.

I. Now the first consideration arising from this view may appear in the nature of a difficulty. It is this. The distinction between normal and abnormal perception makes truth and certitude about the qualities and nature of the external, material universe dependent on the *common assent or judgment of men.* If, for instance, that only is *really and externally* red which *appears* as red to *normal perceivers* (and not to the colour-blind), it follows that no individual perceiver can declare a colour to be really and externally red merely because it appears so to him, until he knows furthermore that it appears similarly to the general mass of mankind, *i.e.* until he knows that his perception is normal. And so of every other sense quality, primary as well as secondary. Hence the ultimate test of the truth of the individual perceiver's spontaneous interpretations of his own perceptions is not their "sense evidence" *for him*, or "what they appear" *to him*, but this as checked by what they appear to the general mass of mankind.

On reflection, however, it will be found that this conclusion goes somewhat too far. The individual perceiver cannot know that other men exist unless by first believing the evidence of his senses : so that what or how things appear to them cannot underlie or replace the evidential function of what or how things appear to himself. What really happens is that he commences by accepting the latter evidence ; that he gradually finds it corroborated by what he learns of other men's experience ; that if any of his own senses be abnormal he soon discovers the discrepancy between the verdict of this sense in his own case and the corresponding sense verdict of men generally ; or that he may learn of the existence of exceptional individuals who have some sense or senses to which things appear otherwise than they do to men generally. Thus he realizes *not* that the reason why each normal perceiver believes things to be really and externally such or such is because he knows that other normal perceivers cherish a similar belief,—for he knows that to rely on this as an ultimate reason would be to fall into a vicious circle. Rather he realizes the reason of each normal perceiver's belief—that things are really and externally such or such—to be because things *appear* to each individual to be really and externally such or such ; but he sees at the same time that there is in this belief the implicit assumption or convention that "really and externally such or such" means "really and externally such or such, *abstracting from the normal, uniform, subjective influence which the perceiver's organism has on the manner in which the external reality appears, or is presented, to the consciousness of the perceiver*".

When, for instance, I say "This field of poppies is really and externally red," my *reason* for saying so is because it *appears so* to me ; and I know the reason to be valid because I have verified by experience the assumption underlying it, *viz.* that I am a normal perceiver. And what I *mean* by the statement, "This field of poppies is really and externally red," is that the field of poppies has really and externally a quality which appears in the same way to all normal perceivers ; which, however, appears in this way to them not independently of the subjective influence of each one's sense organon ; but which, nevertheless, abstracting from this influence because it is normal and uniform, they rightly regard as being really and externally what it appears to them, and what they designate as " redness ".

What we mean by saying that any sense quality is "really and externally such or such " is that it is really and externally a quality which appears or reveals itself in a certain way to the normal perceiver ; not that its appearance is uninfluenced by the subjective, organic factor, but that this influence, when normal and uniform, does not interfere with our judgment as to what the quality is really and externally : all such judgments being based on the tacit assumption or convention that such qualities *are* "really and externally " what they *appear* to *the normal perceiver.* What is " redness " really and externally ? It is really and externally a quality which is so named because it appears in a certain uniform way to all normal perceivers, but which appears in a different way to certain individuals whose visual organs are abnormal, in the way namely in which " green " appears to normal perceivers. The colour-blind individual, gazing on a field of *red* poppies, sees it as *green*. The cause of the difference is obviously the subjective organic factor. What, therefore, are we to infer ? That the colour-blind individual sees something which does not exist really and externally ? Or that he does not see something which does exist really and externally ? We are to infer both, so far as colour-quality is concerned. For by " real and external " red or green we mean the quality which appears or reveals itself as such *to the normal perceiver.* The extra-organic colour datum, which is the field of poppies, exists really and externally the same, independently of all perceivers, normal and abnormal alike ; by no one of them, however, is it perceived independently of the influence of the perceiver's own subjective, organic factor; but it is understood to be "really and externally " what it appears *when the organic factor is normal, i.e.* in the present case " red ". The colour-blind individual, therefore, has a real perception of a real quality which is "really and externally " what it appears to normal perceivers, *viz.* red, but which, while appearing thus to normal perceivers, appears to

him otherwise than it does to them, *i.e.* otherwise than it is
"really and externally," and this because of his subjective,
organic abnormality,—for which he must learn to allow, by
correcting what it registers, so as to judge in conformity with
normal perceivers.

II. From the relativity just recognized there arises this
general difficulty : If what is consciously apprehended in sense
perception is even partially dependent on the perceiving subject,
then sense perception does not reveal to us extra-subjective or
extramental reality as it is in itself. Hence the realist interpretation of sense perception is unwarranted, and must be
abandoned for idealism. This difficulty we now purpose to
examine explicitly.

There is no getting away from this relativity of all sense
qualities to the structure and conditions of the perceiver's sense
organs. It has to be recognized by the supporter of mediate or
representative sense perception no less than by the perceptionist.
If what we become immediately aware of be a mental appearance
or representation (from which the real and external quality be
inferred), then it becomes necessary to distinguish between normal
or "absolute," and abnormal or "relative" or "subjective"
appearances, and to hold that it is only from the former we
are entitled to infer what the perceived quality is really and
externally : thereby recognizing the implicit convention that
what the quality is "really and externally" is determined for
our *knowledge* by what it "appears" to the normal perceiver,—
the subjective, organic contribution to this "appearance" being
left out of account because it is normal and uniform.[1]

But what the student has to bear in mind is that this inevitable relativity of external reality, as a datum of sense perception, to the constitution of the perceiving subject as organic,
in no way compromises the validity of external sense perception
as a conscious apprehension of external reality. We can apply
both to *sense perception* and to *intellectual knowledge*,—*i.e.* conception, judgment, interpretation,—what Maher has so clearly
expressed concerning the relativity of knowledge in general. In
his *Psychology* [2] he distinguishes between the false sense in which
the *Relativity of Knowledge* is understood by idealists and the

---

[1] *Cf.* JEANNIÈRE, *op. cit.*, pp. 417-18.   [2] Pp. 157-8.

sense in which it can be truly said that all knowledge is relative. After explaining the former sense [1] he continues :—

Another, and what we maintain to be the true expression of the *Relativity of Knowledge*, and one which is in harmony with the theory of immediate or presentative perception, holds—(*a*) that we can only know as much as our faculties, limited in number and range, can reveal to us ; (*b*) that these faculties can inform us of objects only so far, and according as the latter manifest themselves ; (*c*) that accordingly (*a*) there may remain always an indefinite number of qualities which we do not know, and (*β*) what is known must be set in relation to the mind, and can only be known in such relation.

So much relativity is necessarily involved in the very nature of knowledge, but it in no way destroys the worth of that knowledge. If knowledge is defined to imply a relation between the mind and the known object, and if the *noumenon* or *thing-in-itself* is defined to signify some real element of an object which never stands in any relation to our cognitive powers, then a knowledge of *noumena* or *things-in-themselves* is obviously an absurdity.[2]

[1] "All systems of philosophy," he writes, "which reject the doctrine of immediate perception of extended reality must maintain that our knowledge is relative to the mind in the sense that we can never know anything but our own subjective states." This opening statement goes, perhaps, too far, at least if we are to understand by "extended reality" "*external* extended reality"; for, as we have seen, there are many realists who hold that although the object of our "*immediate* perception" is always a state of the self, nevertheless we can infer by the principle of causality an external or non-self reality. "Among these [systems]," he continues, "the most consistent thinkers . . . are the idealists proper. They logically maintain that if we have no knowledge of anything beyond consciousness, it is unphilosophical to suppose that anything else exists. This thoroughgoing view is represented by Hume, and by Mill at times. The great majority of modern philosophers, however, shrinking back from this extreme, have adopted some intermediate position akin to that of Kant or Mr. Spencer. They maintain that while all our knowledge is relative to our own mental states, and in no way represents or reflects reality, yet there is *de facto* some sort of reality outside of our minds. Our imaginary cognitions of space, time, and causality are universal subjective illusions either inherited [Spencer] or elaborated by the mind [Kant] ; consequently since these fictitious elements mould or blend with all our experience, we can have no knowledge of things in themselves, of *noumena*, of the absolute. But notwithstanding this, and in spite of the fact that the principle of causality has no more real validity than a continuous hallucination, these philosophers are curiously found to maintain the existence of a *cause*, and even of an external, non-mental cause, of our sensations. . . . [But] if by *noumena* are understood, as Kant on the one side, and sensationalists like Mr. Spencer on the other seem to mean, hypothetical external causes of our sensations, then we must, in the first place, deny the assumption that we can only know our own conscious states, and, in the second, we must point out the fundamental contradiction common to both schools of disputing the objective or real validity of the principle of causality, whilst in virtue of a surreptitious use of this rejected principle they affirm the reality of an unknowable noumenal cause."

[2] *Op. cit.*, p. 158. *Cf. ibid.*, n. 26, quotation from MARTINEAU, *A Study of Religion*, vol. i., p. 119 : "To speak of 'knowing' 'things in themselves' or 'things as they are,' is to talk of not simply an impossibility, but a contradiction ; for these

It is obvious, of course, that there *may be* in the real world multitudes of qualities of which we can know nothing, through lack of appropriate perceptive faculties; and it is even possible that some of the lower animals may have organic perceptive powers which make them aware of some such qualities, just as we know that in some of those animals the perceptive powers they have in common with us far exceed ours in range and intensity (44). The more important point, however, is that those qualities which we do know we know only in so far as these "manifest themselves to us" and are "set in relation to the mind"; and that they "can only be known in such relation".[1] Applying this to sense perception it means that all the data which make up the whole domain of sense experience, and all the sensible qualities and characteristics of these data, can be consciously perceived, can become objects of sense awareness, only in so far as they are "set in relation," or "appear," or "manifest," or "reveal" themselves, to the perceiver. But we have seen that they depend *partially*, for what they appear, on the subjective, organic factor of the perceiver: that they appear as they do to the perceiver *partly* because the perceiver himself is organically constituted as he is. When, therefore, he judges that they *really are* as they *appear* to the *normal perceiver*, he is not at all denying that in the process of "appearing" or "being presented" to consciousness in sense perception the sense realities (whether organic or extra-organic) are *partially* specified, modified,—we may even say transformed or metamorphosed, to use the very language affected by the more moderate school of

phrases are invented to denote what *is* in the sphere of *being* and *not in the sphere of thought*; and to suppose them *known* is *ipso facto* to take away this character. The relativity of cognition (*i.e.* in the sense defined) imposes on us no forfeiture of privilege, no humiliation of pride; there is not any conceivable form of apprehension from which it excludes us."

[1] Even such material things and qualities as are known without their having been ever perceived by any human being (and all who admit the existence of an external material universe at all will admit that we can have reasoned certitude about the existence of portions of it which have never been perceived) are known only by being related to the mind through other things or qualities directly perceived. "What is given in one or more relations may necessarily implicate other relations, and these may subsist not merely between the mind and other objects, but between the several objects themselves. Still, mediate cognitions of this kind are knowledge only in so far as they are rationally connected with what is immediately given. Our knowledge of *the mutual dynamical influence of two invisible planets*, which faithfully reflects their reciprocal relations, is but an elaborate evolution of what is apprehended by sense and intellect in experiences *where subject and object stand in immediate relations*."—*Ibid.*, n. 25,—italics ours.

idealists,—by the subjective, organic factor. He merely holds that such subjective influence, and such relativity of sense realities to the perceiver's own organic constitution, being inseparable from the very nature of the perceptive process, are tacitly understood to be always there, but are likewise understood *when normal* not to affect the truth of the judgment whereby he interprets those sense realities to be "really" (and "externally" in the case of "externally appearing" data) as they appear *to the normal perceiver.* Furthermore, when he asserts that in sense perception he is directly aware, not of a "conscious state" or "psychic appearance" or "mental representation," but of an *extramental* reality, his interpretation is one which no idealist[1] can disprove until the idealist assumption—that nothing extramental can be in direct cognitive relation to mind, that the mind can know only its own states,—is vindicated. And finally, when he asserts that in external sense perception he is directly aware neither of a mental appearance nor of an organic condition, but of an extra-organic, external, and sometimes spatially distant reality,—and that he is aware of this reality as it is really and externally,[2]—his interpretation cannot be shaken until it be proved that a material reality, spatially distant from a perceiver, cannot become the direct term of the latter's awareness by awakening his conscious perceptive activity through its operative influence on his bodily sense organs.

127. THE MAIN DIFFICULTY.—We must next examine a form of difficulty which is brought against the theory of immediate sense perception and plausibly supported by appeal to a variety of facts commonly described as "sense illusions" (118). It may be stated as follows:—[3]

If that which is present to consciousness in perception, that of which we are directly and immediately aware, be the external reality, then *contradictory predicates would be true of the same reality.* But this is obviously impossible. Therefore what is present to consciousness is not the external reality but a psychic or mental "appearance" or "representation" produced by the

[1] And no supporter of the theory of mediate or representative sense perception.
[2] Knowing that "what it is really and externally" means "what it appears to the normal perceiver": the very real but normal and uniform subjective influence of the perceiver's organism on "what it appears," being an element of difference which is tacitly understood to be really there but to be left out of account in equiparating the meaning of those two phrases.
[3] *Cf.* JEANNIÈRE, *op. cit.,* pp. 398-9.

reality, and from which under due conditions we can infer the
latter.[1]   And that contradictory predicates are affirmed of what
is present to consciousness is abundantly evident from facts like
the following : " Tepid water is cold to the hot hand and hot to
the cold hand (*i.e.* *is* simultaneously cold and not cold); the
same house is larger or smaller, the same tower is square or
round, according to the distance of the observer ; the sun is
two feet in diameter to one person and one foot in diameter to
another, though its real magnitude is great and does not change ;
the same colour is red to one and green to another (*i.e.* to a
Daltonian); the same substance is sweet to one and bitter to
another ; the same insect is tiny or large according as seen with
the naked eye or through a microscope ; things are purple or
yellow according as seen through purple or yellow glasses ; stars
are now visible which have ceased to exist long ages ago ;
sometimes people see two suns in the heavens, while there is
only one *de facto ;* and so of innumerable other examples ".[2]
Now such facts can be easily explained, and all contradiction
avoided, if the contradictory predicates be understood to have for
their subjects not the one self-identical external reality, but the
mental appearances produced by it ; for while it remains the
same these do indeed differ through change in the subjective
and the external or spatial conditions of perception, so that it is
not to *the same* subject that the contradictory predicates refer.
Hence in all such examples as those referred to, the copula "*is*"
means "*appears*" : otherwise error is incurred by an unlawful
transition from the order of appearances to the order of reality.[3]

Now in reply to this difficulty we purpose showing *firstly*,
that the manner it suggests of avoiding self-contradiction is not
the *only* way of doing so, or in other words that perceptionism
as propounded in the preceding sections is in no way self-con-

---

[1] The conclusion, as formulated by JEANNIÈRE (*op. cit.*, pp. 398-9),—" Ergo, *ne
violetur principium contradictionis,* dicendum est realitatem sensibus referri, *non ut est
in seipsa, sed ut apparet sensibus* " : "reality is reported by the senses *not as it is in
itself, but as it appears to the senses,*"—seems to make the (perceived) "appearance "
and the (known) " externality " two aspects or modes or conditions of one and the
same reality (*cf. infra*, §§ 128, 129) ; but he clearly supposes that contradiction can be
avoided only by holding that in every such case the contradictory predicates should
be understood to refer not to the external reality but to the mental appearances,—
which are really different and therefore really susceptible of contradictory predicates,
—while the external reality of which they are appearances remains of course one
and the same unchanged reality.
[2] JEANNIÈRE, *ibid.*   [3] *Ibid.*, p. 399.

tradictory ; and *secondly*, that there are very grave reasons against adopting the suggested distinction between "mental appearances" and "external reality" as a satisfactory explanation of the facts.

First, then, the facts alleged are undeniable. Moreover, it must be admitted that if "what reality appears to the *individual* perceiver in any and every condition, organic and extra-organic, of perception," be judged to be a function of the "reality as it is externally,"—in other words if *naïf* perceptionism, which does not take account of the part played by the actual conditions, organic and extra-organic, of perception, in determining how the external reality appears, be adopted,—then indeed self-contradiction would result: water would be simultaneously hot and not hot, the same colour would be red and not red, etc., etc. But if, on the contrary, our interpretation of "what the thing is really and externally" takes the influence of these conditions into account, and allows for them,—if it is realized that we know "what the thing *is* really and externally" only by "what it *appears* to the *normal* perceiver," so that this latter appearance is always understood to be implied in the very meaning of "what the thing *is* really and externally,"[1]—then, while what we perceive is not a mental appearance but the extramental reality, not a single one of the predications in the examples cited, or in any other examples, is really self-contradictory. For whenever in such a case we make a number of incompatible predications about the perceived reality, they are incompatible because they refer to what the thing appears *under different sets of* (organic or extra-organic) *conditions :* and only *one* predication (in respect to the domain of predication in question), whether it be among the predications actually made or not, can refer to "the thing as it *is* really and externally,"—"what it *is* really and externally" being known to us only through "what it *appears* to the *normal* perceiver," since this mode of appearance is a real function of "what the thing *is* really and externally". It is a question of understanding what we mean by our assertions that material things "are such or such really and externally". This has been explained already, and we may refer the reader again to our

---

[1] *I.e.* the function of *appearing* in a certain way *in normal conditions of perception* is a real function of the external reality, and is precisely the function, and the only function, which makes it possible for us to *know intellectually what the thing is*, in so far as we have (inadequate) intellectual knowledge of this latter.

discussion of one of the examples given above,—that of Daltonism (126). For the sake of illustration let us take another
example. A person in one part of the world sees the sun high
in the heavens " a foot in diameter "; another in a different part
of the world sees it sinking near the horizon " two feet in diameter ". Suppose they judge it accordingly. Both judgments
refer to the same "external reality ". Both predicates are *right*
if they are referred to "what this reality appears " to each in the
two separate sets of spatial conditions ; both predicates are *wrong*
if they are referred to " what this reality *is* externally (in respect
of size or diameter) ". What it *is* externally in this respect is
not what it appears to any one or more individuals, for such
appearances include the influence of different spatial conditions
of distance and perspective : what it *is* really and externally in
point of size, is what its normally appearing size—which differs
in varying spatial conditions—is interpreted to be for a reality
situated at such a distance from normal perceivers.[1]

This, of course, raises again the question, How do we *know
intellectually* what a reality is *really and externally?* And particularly it raises the question—of which more presently—as to
the significance of our concept of space. How can we *know*
(intellectually) *that* a reality is *external*, or *what* it is externally,
otherwise than by seeing, through reflection, that the contents of
our abstract intellectual concepts of extension, externality, space,
etc., *given* in the concretely felt extensity and externality of the
immediate data of sense perception, are *real ;* and that when a
sense datum *appears* to the *normal* perceiver as extended, spatial,
external, it is *therefore* not only *conceived intellectually to be* so,
but *is really* so ? The two people looking at the sun perceive
something real. How do we or they know? How else but because we and they regard sense perception as a process which
makes us aware of *reality ?* They perceive something *extramental* and *external.*[2] Again, how do we or they know? Because we regard the sensuously felt *extramentality* of the immediate
data of consciousness as being *eo ipso* real, and the sensuously felt
externality of such data as being *in normal conditions* of sense per-

---

[1] *Cf.* JEANNIÈRE, *op. cit.*, pp. 413-14 : " Ex eo quod res apparet vg. dulcis aut
amara, quadrata aut rotunda, rubra aut viridis, non est certum illam rem esse talem
qualis apparet, nisi intellectus attenderit ad omnes sensus qui aliquid de ea referunt,
et constiterit ab eis illam rem *modo normali* referri ".

[2] *I.e.* extra-*subjective*, extra-*organic*.

ception *eo ipso* real. But suppose we refuse to regard any immediate data of sense consciousness as being at all extramental,
and insist on regarding them all as *intra-subjective, intramental*
entities, how then are we ever to *know* that there is anything
beyond, anything really extramental or external?

Realist supporters of the theory of mediate sense perception
have recourse to the principle of causality—a procedure which we
need not re-examine here. But let us return to the difficulty set
forth above, and endeavour to show in the *second* place how unsatisfactory it is to account for the apparent contradictions of
sense perception by recourse to the view that in preception we
become immediately aware only of " appearances ".

If in sense perception we become immediately aware only
of what are (intellectually interpreted to be) subjective, psychic,
mental states, and not of anything (interpreted to be) external
(or even extramental), then, since on the one hand intellect conceives, and interprets in judgment, only the content[1] of these
states, and since on the other hand it is not contended that intellect can, independently of sense, come into cognitive relation
with (what is interpreted as) external reality,[2] it would seem to
follow necessarily that all our intellectual knowledge, all our concepts, predicates, and judgments are of the real domain of *mental
states* only,—externality itself, perceived or conceived, concrete
or abstract, being no exception, but just a mental state like all
the others. No doubt, the concept of cause, like that of substance, is derived from these states and is validly applied to them
to bring to light their real implications ; but how can it bring to
light *real externality* as an implication of them if the concept of
externality itself is emptied of real validity by the contention
that the concrete sense correlate—immediately felt externality—
from which the concept is derived, is not real externality at all
but merely a feature of a state of consciousness? (104, 111).
When, therefore, Jeannière asserts that by the senses we attain

[1] Including the real implications of this content.
[2] *I.e.* this contention is not put forward at least by scholastics, who, as defenders
of realism, are contemplated in the text. It is the scholastic view that intellect
directly apprehends the real self in its conscious processes, and rightly interprets
the self as an extramental reality, *i.e.* a reality whose real being (*"esse"*) is independent of its being consciously apprehended (its *"percipi"*), but that even such
conception has for its content only the sense content of the direct conscious processes by which such intellectual apprehension is conditioned (*cf.* § 100) ; but
scholastics do not contend that intellect has any apprehension or conception of
external or *non-self* reality independently of the data furnished by sense (100, 105).

"to things not in themselves but in their appearances,"[1] and that nevertheless "things can be known as they are in themselves, *i.e.* so that we can attribute to them predicates which are really intrinsic to them,"[2] he is equivalently asserting that concepts whose real contents are derived only from conscious states of the self have contents which are really intrinsic to external or non-self reality : for only if they have such contents are they "really intrinsic " (in content) to this reality. But it is only if the latter is given in the concrete, felt externality of the immediate data of " external " sense perception, and if the abstract concept of externality (derived from this concrete) is thus known to be really valid, that our *other* concepts can be known to have contents really intrinsic to external reality.

Furthermore, it is useless to discuss what qualities can or cannot be attributed to " external " things, or "things as they really are " until the real validity of our abstract intellectual concept of externality is first vindicated. In support of the main objection stated above, Jeannière argues that because *e.g.* the external object is a square tower, and the perceived object is not a square tower (but a round tower), therefore the perceived object is not the external object. But this assumes that we know *that* there is a reality *external* to us, and *what* it is really and externally, while *the real difficulty of his own position* (that sense only makes us aware of conscious states of the self, called " appearances ") is to show how he can know *any object whatsoever* to be an *external* reality.

"According to the perceptionist," he writes, "the appearance (perceived object) = external object (that which is outside me). Now, facts prove this to be inadmissible. Let us give these two in syllogistic form : (1) *The external object is a square tower ; but the perceived object (appearance) is not a square tower (but a round tower) ; therefore the perceived object is not the external object.* (2) *The perceived object (the appearance) is actual ; but the external object is not actual (v.g. a star extinct ten thousand years ago) ; therefore the perceived object is not the external object.* To my very great confusion (he continues), I have to confess that the replies to those two common syllogisms (second figure ; mood, *Camestres*) have always appeared to me unintelligible. 'The data of physiology,' says the Abbé COSTE,[3] 're-

---

[1] He refers of course to external things ; and the expression means that by the senses we attain not to the external things but to mental states. The ambiguity of such modes of expression will be examined later (128, 129).

[2] "Praedicata quae eis vere sint intrinseca."—*Op. cit.*, p. 417 ; *supra*, § 123, p. 108, n. 2.

[3] *Rev. du Clergé français*, 1st August, 1903, p. 534.

move all doubt that the direct object of our visual perception is the effect of
the retinal image, as the retinal image itself is the effect of the external
body.' With the same author, I regard the thesis of the Abbé DUBOSC on
The Formal Objectivity of Colours [1] as undoubtedly ingenious, but as not
proven."[2]

Now we doubt if any reflecting perceptionist would allow that his view is
fairly expressed by the formula "*appearance* (perceived object) = external object". We doubt if even the unreflecting plain man would hold that what
an individual perceives ("perceived object") is *always* the "external object".
Bearing in mind that *sense itself* does not pronounce or judge its object to
be internal or external, and that when we speak of the "sense verdict" or
"sense evidence" we always mean our *intellectual interpretation* of what is
given or presented in sense consciousness,—a fact which is sometimes lost
sight of in this connexion,—bearing that in mind, our statement of perceptionism would be rather something like this : "The object perceived *under
normal conditions* is identically the real, external object : not of course adequately the latter, but a real function or aspect of the latter". In the second
place we believe that even the *naif*, unreflecting perceptionist would agree
with us in repudiating the identification of "appearance" and "perceived
object" in the author's description of perceptionism. When an object "appears" or "is presented" to consciousness, whatever be the nature of this
object, whether it be mental or extramental, internal or external, we have a
right to demand justification for the very questionable procedure of setting
up this process of "appearing" or "being presented" as *a new object* supposed to intervene between consciousness and the original object.[3] Of this
more anon (128, 129). Coming now to the syllogisms, we might ask how anyone who holds that sense reveals to him only mental states can *know* that
what he judges to be "a square tower" or to be "not actual" is an "*external object*" at all, as *distinct from a mental state*. But letting even that
pass, the major of the first syllogism means that what appears in sense perception *under normal conditions of distance and perspective* as a square
tower is judged to be therefore really and externally a square tower ; and the
minor means that this same reality appears *under other conditions* as a round
tower, *i.e.* otherwise than it appears under normal conditions, *i.e.* otherwise
as "it really and externally is " : from which the only legitimate conclusion is
that what a thing appears under special conditions is not what it appears under
normal conditions (*i.e.* " what it really and externally is " : the "external object ").—The distinction between what a thing may "look" or "appear"
and what it "is," will be examined below (128, 129).—The major of the
second syllogism means " The object (or reality) here and now perceived or
appearing is judged to be (externally) actual " ; the minor means that what
we know otherwise through inferences from other perceptions of external
reality (and we could know *nothing* of *external* reality were real externality
not presented, and known to be presented, to sense) enables us to judge—
not that the appearing reality (the " perceived object ") has *no* present external actuality, and that our present perception is merely of a mental state or

[1] *Ann. de philos. chrét.*, 1835, t. 130, pp. 449 *sqq.*; 592 *sqq.*
[2] *Op. cit.*, p. 399, n.   [3] *Cf.* PRICHARD, *op. cit.*, p. 133.

"appearance," but—that the perceived object has not *all* the external actuality which we would naturally attribute to it if we interpreted external reality according to *present* perceptions and without taking note of the knowledge gathered from *other perceptions,* and interpretations and inferences from these.[1] In the present instance though the star is itself extinct there is real and external light still travelling from it. The legitimate conclusion from the premisses is simply that the total actual reality of the external object is not identical with, or determined solely by, the portion which at any given moment we can perceive.

As to the Abbé Coste's assertion, we may merely remark that while the physiologist can trace the physiological effects of the retinal image on the optic nerves and on the brain, and while he can say that the concomitant, or immediate consequent, of the cerebral excitation is a *conscious act of visual perception,* no facts brought to light by his order of investigation can help him in the least to make any assertion whatever on a question concerning this wholly new order of phenomenon (*i.e.* the consciously perceptive visual act),—the question, namely, as to what is the direct object apprehended through this perceptive act (112, 124).

[1] *Cf.* JEANNIÈRE, *op. cit.*, pp. 413-14 ; *supra*, p. 162, n. 1.

CHAPTER XX.

IDEALISM AND THE DISTINCTION BETWEEN "APPEARANCE" AND "REALITY".

128. ANALYSIS OF THE DISTINCTION BETWEEN WHAT THINGS "ARE" AND WHAT THEY "APPEAR".—Not only in the preceding section, but time and again from the very commencement of our investigation, we have encountered the distinction between what things *are* and what they *appear*. The distinction, understood in a wide sense, runs through every domain of our cognitive experience,—marking off in a general way the "real" from the "apparent," the "genuine" from the "seeming" or "deceptive," the "true" from the "false". Thus, we are warned that "appearances are deceptive," and "not to judge by appearances".[1] Whatever be the implications of the distinction, and its bearing on the possibility of our knowing what things really are, it is obvious that the distinction has its origin in the domain of *sense perception*, and that it must be closely connected especially with our manner of apprehending *space*. It is perfectly familiar even to the "plain man,"—and fairly perplexing even to the advanced student of epistemology. It issues in puzzling problems. For example, if on the one hand we hold that what appears, or is presented, to consciousness in *sense perception* is *the real*,—that (external) sense perception puts us into direct and immediate cognitive contact with (external) reality ;—and if also what intellect conceives in the abstract is this same concretely presented reality, *i.e.* if the *thought*-objects by which it represents and interprets the given sense concrete are also real,—how can *error* or *deception* be possible, or how can things ever "appear," or "be judged to be," otherwise than they really are?[2] If, on the other hand, it be held that *sense perception* does

---

[1] "The common advice, ' Do not judge by appearances,' would be unmeaning if it were interpreted literally; for, after all, what have we to judge by except appearances ? "—*Science of Logic*, i., § 66, p. 128.

[2] We shall deal later *ex professo* with this aspect of the matter. *Cf. supra*, § 112.

not make us directly aware of, or put us into immediate cognitive relation with, *extramental reality*, but directly reveals to us only mental states provisionally assumed to be "reproductions" or "representations" or "appearances" of extramental reality; and if also (as before) *intellect* gets all its interpreting concepts or thought-objects *from these mental states, i.e.* if the objects of thought are identically the concrete "intramental" objects of sense, only apprehended now in the abstract,—how can *truth* or *genuine knowledge* be possible, *i.e.* how can it transcend what things appear *mentally*, and attain to what they really are *extramentally*?

It will be worth while, therefore, to examine the distinction, with a view to seeing whether or how it is possible, from normal sense perception of how things *appear* spatially, to attain not only to a knowledge *that* things *are really spatial*, but also to a knowledge as to what sort their real spatial attributes and relations are. The inquiry will naturally lead up to an exposition and criticism of Kant's theory on space, time, and sense qualities generally.

When the plain man distinguishes between "appearance" and "reality," between what a thing "appears to be" and what it "really is," he is certainly thinking not of two distinct "things," —one a "mental" thing (an "appearance") and the other an "extramental" thing (a "reality"),—but of one and the same (extramental) thing under two aspects, *viz.* of this thing as (he thinks that) it now appears, and of this same thing as (he thinks that) he otherwise knows it to be. Yet philosophers, reflecting on the distinction, have come to think of two distinct things, *viz.* the extramental thing (the "thing-in-itself" the "noumenon") and a "mental" thing which they call an "appearance" or "phenomenon"; and some philosophers have concluded that we can never get beyond knowledge of the latter, while others have contended that though we can know directly only the latter we can derive from this direct knowledge an inferential knowledge of the former. Since the distinction between what things really are and what they appear "first arises in our ordinary or scientific consciousness (*i.e.* the consciousness for which the problems are those of science as opposed to philosophy),"[1] we must inquire whether the distinction as revealed there justifies

---

[1] PRICHARD, *op. cit.*, p. 79.

such philosophical conclusions.   Let us see how Prichard deals with it in his criticism of Kant.

" In this consciousness [he writes] we are compelled to distinguish between appearance and reality *with respect to the details of a reality which, as a whole, or in principle, we suppose ourselves to know*.   Afterwards in our philosophical consciousness we come to reflect on this distinction and to raise the question *whether it is not applicable to reality as a whole*.   We ask with respect to knowledge in general, and not merely with respect to particular items of knowledge, whether we know or can know reality, and not merely appearance. . . . Consequently, in order to decide whether the distinction will bear the superstructure placed upon it by the philosophical consciousness, it is necessary to examine the distinction as it exists in our ordinary consciousness.

" The distinction is applied in our ordinary consciousness both to the primary and to the secondary qualities of matter. . . . We say, for instance, that the moon looks [1] or appears as large as the sun, though really it is much smaller.   We say that railway lines, though parallel, look convergent, just as we say that the straight stick in water looks bent.   We say that at sunset the sun, though really below the horizon, looks above it.   Again we say that to a person who is colour blind the colour of an object looks different to what it really is, and that water into which we put our hand may be warmer than it appears to our touch.

" The case of the primary qualities may be considered first. . . . [And] it will be sufficient to analyse the simplest, that of the apparent convergence of the railway lines.

" Two points force themselves upon our notice.   In the first place we certainly suppose that we perceive the reality which we wish to know, *i.e.* the reality which, as we suppose, exists independently of our perception, and not an ' appearance ' of it.   It is, as we say, the real lines which we see. Even the term 'convergent,' in the assertion that the lines *look* convergent, conveys this implication. . . . We can say neither that an appearance is convergent nor that the appearance of the lines is convergent.   Only a reality similar to the lines, *e.g.* two roads, can be said to be convergent.   Our ordinary thought, therefore, furnishes no ground for the view that the object of perception is not the thing but merely an appearance of or produced by it. In the second place the assertion that the lines *look* convergent implies considerable knowledge of the real nature of the reality to which the assertion relates.   Both the terms ' lines ' and ' convergent ' imply that the reality *is* spatial.   Further if the context is such that we mean that, while the lines look convergent, we do not know their real relation, we imply that the lines really possess some characteristic which falls within the genus to which convergence belongs, *i.e.* we imply that they are convergent or divergent or parallel.   If on the other hand, the context is such that we mean that the lines only look convergent, we imply that the lines are parallel, and therefore presuppose

---

[1] " Looks " means " appears to sight," and " looks " is throughout used as synonymous with " appear," where the instance under discussion relates to visual perception.

complete knowledge in respect of the very characteristic in regard to which we state what is only appearance. The assertion, then, in respect of a primary quality, that a thing looks so and so implies knowledge of its general character as spatial, and ignorance only of a detail; and the assertion that a thing only looks or appears so and so implies knowledge of the detail in question." [1]

He then draws attention to the general difficulty arising from our use of the terms "looks" and "appears" :—

" If the lines are not convergent, how is it possible even to say that they *look* convergent ? Must it not be implied that at least under *certain* circumstances we should perceive the lines as they are ? Otherwise why should we use the words 'look' or 'appear' at all ? Moreover this implication can be pushed further ; for if we maintain that we perceive the real lines, we may reasonably be asked whether we must not under *all* circumstances perceive them as they are. It seems as though a reality cannot be perceived except as it is." [2]

Such is the difficulty which has given rise to the philosophical view that "the object of perception is not the reality but an appearance". How has the view arisen from it ? In this way :—

" Since we do distinguish between what things look and what they are, it would seem that the object of perception cannot be the thing, but only an appearance produced by it. Moreover the doctrine gains in plausibility from the existence of certain illusions in the case of which the reality to which the illusion relates seems non-existent. For instance, if we look steadily at the flame of a candle, and then press one eye-ball with the finger, we see, as we say, two candles ; but since *ex hypothesi* there is only one candle, it seems that what we see must be, not the candle, but two images or appearances produced by it." [3]

Nevertheless such facts furnish no real ground for the philosophical view that " the object of perception is not a reality, but an appearance," and the distinction between "what a thing looks" and "what it is" can be explained without recourse to such a supposition. The distinction does imply that "at least under *certain* circumstances" we perceive things "as they are"; but it does not imply that therefore "under *all* circumstances" we should "perceive them as they are". For, in so far as we know what external [4] things are really and externally, we know this

[1] PRICHARD, *op. cit.*, pp. 80-2 (italics in first paragraph ours).
[2] *Ibid.*, p. 82.   [3] *Ibid.*, pp. 82-3.
[4] Even in abnormal sense perception it is a real function of *extramental* reality (including the *perceiver's organism*) to appear as it actually does. In the case of sense illusions and hallucinations it is the intellect that is at fault in judging the perceived reality to be exclusively external when it is either partly organic (as in illusions) or wholly organic (as in hallucinations). In both cases a product of

from what they appear in *certain, i.e. normal* circumstances : our intellectual knowledge of " what they are really and externally " is an accumulation of judgments or interpretations of "what they appear " to our various senses *in normal conditions,*—their necessary relativity to the subjective *organic* factor being always understood in these judgments.[1] Hence it does not follow that " what a thing appears " in any individual act or process of perception must be always a part or function of what the thing is really and externally, *i.e.* of what it is known to appear in normal perception ; for the individual act in question may be abnormal, and if it is, what the " external " thing appears in it will be partly due to the abnormal organic factor, and therefore will not reveal " what the thing is really and externally ".

The distinction in question certainly supposes that in some cases at least we perceive things as they are ; for in regard to external things *part of what we mean* by " what they are really and externally " is "what we know them to appear in normal sense perception ". Let us pursue Prichard's analysis. He continues :—[2]

The distinction between the actual and the apparent angle made by two straight lines presupposes a limiting case in which they coincide. If the line of sight along which we observe the point of intersection of two lines is known to be at right angles to both lines, we expect, and rightly expect, to see the angle of intersection as it is. Again if we look at a short portion of two railway lines from a point known to be directly above them, and so distant that the effects of perspective are imperceptible, we can say that the lines look what they are, *viz.* parallel. Thus from the point of view of the difficulty which has been raised, there is this justification in general for saying that two lines *look* parallel or *look* at right angles, that we know that in certain cases what they look is identical with what they are. In the same way assertions that the moon *looks* as large as the sun receive justification from our knowledge that two bodies of equal size and equally distant from the observer *are* what they look, *viz.* of the same size. And in both cases the justification presupposes knowledge of the reality of space and also such insight into its nature as enables us to see that in certain cases there must be an identity between what things look and what they are in respect of certain spatial relations. Again, in such cases we see that so far is it from being necessary to think that a thing must be perceived as it is, that it is not only possible but necessary to distinguish what a thing looks from what it is, and precisely in consequence of the nature of space. The visual perception of spatial relations from its very nature presupposes a particular point of view . . . and is therefore

imagination (a genuine " mental image") is confused in consciousness with the perceived object, or mistaken for a perceived object.

[1] *Cf. supra,* §§ 120-2.   [2] *Op. cit.,* pp. 83-5.

subject to conditions of perspective. This is best realized by considering the supposition that perfect visual powers would enable us to see the whole of a body at once, and that this perception would be possible if we had eyes situated all round the body. The supposition obviously breaks down through the impossibility of combining two or more points of view in one perception. But if visual perception is necessarily subject to conditions of perspective, the spatial relations of bodies can never look what they are except in the limiting case referred to. Moreover, this distinction is perfectly intelligible, as we should expect from the necessity we are under of drawing it. We understand perfectly why it is that bodies must, in respect of their spatial relations, look [*i.e.* to sight] different to what they are. . . . It is, therefore, needless to make the assertion "Two lines appear convergent" intelligible by converting the verb "appears " into a substantive, *viz.* an " appearance," and then making the assertion relate to an " appearance ". For . . . the assertion . . . is perfectly intelligible in itself though not capable of being stated in terms of anything else.[1]   If we generalize this result [he concludes], we may say that the distinction between appearance and reality, drawn with regard to the primary qualities of bodies, throughout presupposes the reality of space,[2] and is made possible, and indeed necessary, by the nature of space itself.

The distinction, therefore, between what the primary qualities or spatial relations of things "look" or "appear" *to sight*, and what these qualities or relations are "really and externally," is

[1] " It is important," the author adds (*ibid.*, p. 85 n.), "to notice that the proper formula to express what is loosely called ' an appearance ' is ' A looks or appears B,' and that this cannot be analysed into anything more simple and, in particular, into a statement about ' appearances '. Even in the case of looking at the candle, there is no need to speak of two 'appearances' or ' images '. Before we discover the truth the proper assertion is ' The body which we perceive looks as if it were two candles,' and, after we discover the truth, the proper assertion is ' The candle looks as if it were in two places '."

The inclination to speak, in such cases, of perceiving " two images " (and to draw the erroneous conclusion that what we *always* perceive is merely a mental " image " or " appearance," and never the " external reality ") is due to the fact that we have, and are constantly exercising, the faculty (imagination) of reproducing " mental images " of perceived objects in the absence of these latter. The case in point is a simple and admirable instance of an " optical illusion ". We " know " that " what appears " is external to us because we interpret the concrete " felt externality " to be real, and are conscious that the actual conditions, abnormal though they are, are not so abnormal as to vitiate this interpretation. But " what it appears " (" two candles ") is not " what it is really and externally " (" one candle "). If we " know " this is the case, how do we know it ? Because we know (1) that " what it is really and externally " *means* (*i.e.* means partially, inadequately : the part of its reality known through interpretation of what it reveals to us through the sense of vision means) what it is known by us *to appear in normal conditions of visual perception ;* and (2) that the conditions of our actual perception are *not normal*, and therefore do not reveal " what the thing is really and externally ".

[2] Rather " presupposes that we know spatial relations to characterize, and appertain to, the extramentally external thing or reality which appears ". But *how* we know or can know this, the author seems to us to leave unexplained. *Cf. supra,* § 125 ; *infra,* pp. 173-5.

quite intelligible without recourse to the assumption that what we see are only mental appearances. It presupposes (1) that we know what things are really and externally in respect of these qualities; and (2) that we know the nature of space and the conditions of visual perception to be such that only in certain cases is "what the thing appears to sight" (as regards spatial relations) identical with what we otherwise know these spatial relations to be "really and externally". But of course we know intellectually what space is and what spatial relations are "really and externally," only from the way in which things *appear* spatially to our senses—especially to sight and touch (active and passive touch, including the muscular sense of motion and resistance to muscular effort)—*in normal sense perception.* Reflection shows us that in the end it is really meaningless to contend that things never reveal to us their primary qualities or spatial relations as these are "really and externally"; for by what these qualities and relations are "really and externally" *we mean* what they appear to us *in normal sense perception, i.e.* what we judge them to be by interpreting them as thus appearing,—through the aid of concepts derived from what they reveal to our consciousness in sense perception.[1]

Hence we are forced to disagree with Prichard when, after pronouncing all the *secondary qualities* to be merely conscious states or "sensations" (and to be by implication incapable of giving us any knowledge about extramental reality) he goes on to contend that our *sense* apprehension even of the primary qualities or spatial relations never reveals these as they are really and externally[2] (and by implication that our intellectual knowledge of what real extension, externality, space, and spatial relations are, is altogether independent of what they appear in sense perception). On the contrary, we *do* perceive (1) not only the primary qualities, but (2) the secondary qualities, as they are really and externally; and moreover (3) if this were not so we could never prove against any form of idealism that the *intellectual knowledge* we have of a world of data characterized by such qualities is knowledge of a really extramental, external, spatial universe, and not merely a knowledge of subjective mental phenomena or conscious states (125).

[1] It must not be forgotten that we accumulate our knowledge of what things are "really and externally" by using concepts derived from *all* the data of the *various* senses. Therefore what an external thing presents in any individual act of perception is usually only a small part of what we already know the total external reality of the thing to be. And this knowledge is always helping us to check, and adjust, and if necessary correct, "what the thing appears" in any individual perceptive act whose object we are interpreting: it is constantly guarding us from erroneous and hasty spontaneous interpretations. *Cf. supra,* § 127, pp. 162, n. 1; 166, n.

[2] *Cf. supra,* § 125, pp. 144 *sqq.*

(1) Prichard's own analysis of the convergence of the railway lines proves that " in limiting cases " we visually apprehend spatial relations as these are " really and externally ". But what they are " really and externally," in respect of spatial relations, we can know only by intellectual interpretation of what they appear in normal perception to *all* the senses which reveal " extensity," " externality," " voluminousness,"—especially to the senses of sight and touch. Prichard, however, holding that our intellectual knowledge of what things are spatially is independent of perception and always represents them otherwise than as they look in perception, goes on to contend that even in the limiting cases referred to " what a thing looks and what it is " are after all not " identical ".[1] The reason he gives is plausible but not convincing : it is that all such limiting cases refer only to *two* dimensions of space, " *e.g.* convergence and bentness,"[2] whereas *real* spatial relations are always *three*-dimensional, so that what a thing *appears* spatially to sight can never be identical with what it *really is* spatially. Now, even if we grant that sight alone can apprehend only two-dimensional extension,[3] it would follow merely that what a spatial thing appears to sight is not *the whole of* what it really is spatially ; but surely it would not follow that what the thing appears spatially to sight cannot be *a real part or function of* its total spatial reality. " It is obvious," says Prichard,[4] " that two dimensions are only an abstraction from three, and that the spatial relations of bodies, considered fully, involve three dimensions." Of course ; but because the two dimensions are only abstractions, are they on that account not real ? Are the two dimensions, perceived by sight in the spatial things, not really in the latter ? They certainly are. " A body may be cylindrical, and we may see a cylindrical body ; but such a body can never, strictly speaking, *look* cylindrical."[5] It can never look cylindrical to sight *alone*, because of the conditions of perspective ; but it can look what our knowledge of the real spatial shape of a cylindrical body tells us that it ought to look in such conditions. And how do we know the real spatial shape of a cylindrical body, or that any body is really and externally cylindrical, unless by interpreting what it appears to *sight* and *touch* in normal conditions ? From the fact that real spatial relations are three-dimensional Prichard infers " that terms which fully state spatial characteristics can never express what things look, but only what they are ".[6] The inference is quite too sweeping. Such terms can never express what things look *to sight* in any individual perception, or what they appear *to touch* in any individual tactile or muscular or motor perception ; but such terms can and do express (our intellectual interpretation of) what things appear to us in *all* our various *normal* visual, tactile and other " extension-revealing " perceptions : for this is precisely what such terms do express to us about things by expressing " what they are ". How otherwise could we know what things are " really and externally " in respect of spatial relations ? It is by " judging from what it looks under various conditions,"[7] and in no other possible way, that we know intellectually whatever we do know about the spatial qualities

---

[1] *Op. cit.*, p. 90.   [2] *Ibid.*
[3] Binocular vision would appear to give us at least a rudimentary *visual* consciousness of *objects in relief*, *i.e.* of the third dimension of space. Possibly, however, such consciousness is not independent of *muscular* sense data.
[4] *Ibid.*   [5] P. 91.   [6] *Ibid.*   [7] P. 99. *Cf. supra*, § 125, p. 149.

and relations which a body has really and externally. And these spatial qualities which we judge to be in the body "really and externally " we judge to be there not only "independently of all perception," [1] but independently of all *conception, thought, judgment*, as well. But to say that they are there independently of perception and thought is very different from saying that we can reach knowledge of them by thought independently of perception ; for their reality cannot be known unless by coming into relation with sense, and through sense with intellect : and that they can be known to be there really and externally and independently of perception and thought, means simply that by reflection on our cognitive processes we can see that their relation to sense and intellect does not transform their presentation to sense or falsify their representation by intellect.

(2) The secondary qualities likewise are perceived in *normal* conditions of perception " as they are really and externally ". The distinction can likewise be drawn between what they "appear " in any individual act of perception, and what they are known to be "really and externally," *i.e.* what they are known to be by "judging from what " they look " under various [normal] conditions ".[2] Of course the distinction between what things *look* or *appear* and what they *are* is of most frequent occurrence in reference to *spatial* qualities as apprehended by *sight*. But it is also drawn in reference to colour. Arguing against the externality of colour, Prichard refers to the difficulty of determining " the right colour of individual bodies " as "insuperable " ; and he concludes that they have no colour, that "colour is not a quality of bodies ".[3] But even if colours were mere " mental facts " or "sensations " we should have to recognize the distinction between " right " and " wrong " colour-sensations ; and if the cause of the distinction be not *extramental* [4] (whether organic or extra-organic), the distinction is inexplicable. Colour is, however, a real quality of external bodies. What a colour *appears* in any individual act of perception depends *partly* on organic conditions : hence the phenomenon of colour blindness. But even in normal organic conditions there is the further consideration that the same body seen from different standpoints " presents " different colours. This, however, only proves that it has these colours simultaneously, that it reflects different "light vibrations " in different directions.

So, too, in regard to the other secondary qualities. It *is* possible to draw a distinction between " what they *appear* " in any individual act of sense perception and " what they *are really* and externally " ;—this latter meaning what they are known to appear in normal conditions of perception.[5] It may indeed be "difficult and, in the end, impossible to say that a bell *appears* noisy " ; [6] but we can and do rightly say, " the pitch of the whistle from the approaching train *appears* to grow higher, but I know it *really* remains the same," [7] or again, " I *seem* to hear a humming noise around me, but I *know*

[1] *Op. cit.*, p. 99.   Cf. *supra*, § 125, p. 149.
[2] P. 99.   [3] P. 87.   [4] *Cf. supra*, § 125.
[5] Relativity to *normal* organic factors being tacitly understood not to falsify the interpretation of what they are extra-organically or "externally ". Cf. *supra*, § 122.
[6] *Op. .it.*, p. 86.
[7] *Cf.* " The railway lines only *appear* convergent, but I know they *are really* parallel ".

there is really no noise but only an organic affection of the ear ". Similarly, it is *not* impossible to say that "sugar *appears* sweet ".[1] No doubt, the usual expression is "sugar *tastes* sweet " ; which is another way of saying that "sugar *appears* sweet to normal perceivers," which again, intellectually interpreted, means " sugar *is* sweet ". But a person whose sense of taste is, from whatsoever cause, abnormal, can and does rightly say, "this sugar only *tastes* or *appears* bitter to me, but I know it *is really* not bitter but sweet ". Similar instances may be discovered in sensations of temperature, touch, and smell. And the implication of the distinction is the same throughout : in no case does it imply that what we perceive is only a "mental state," whether we call this a "sensation " or an "appearance " ; but in all cases it implies (*a*) that what appears in any and every act of sense perception [2] is *extramental* reality ; (*b*) that what this extramental reality *appears* in the individual perception is partly dependent on subjective, organic factors, and on extra-organic or external conditions ; (*c*) that what it *appears* will differ from what it *is* if those factors are abnormal ; inasmuch as (*d*) by what it *is* (in so far as we know what it is) we mean the knowledge we have of it by interpreting what it appears *in normal conditions* of perception.

(3) Finally this latter knowledge is—as far as it goes—knowledge of an *extramental* universe *as it is extramentally,* because cognitive relation of the latter to the mind, whether in perception or in conception, does not transform or alter it by the projection into it of any subjective *mental* factors. Furthermore it is knowledge of an *external,* spatial (and otherwise physically "qualitative ") universe *as it is externally,* because its cognitive relation to the perceiving subject *as organic* can be known by intellect reflecting on the process of perception ; can be discovered to be normal or abnormal as the case may be ; is understood, when known to be normal and uniform, to be included in what we mean by real externality, and, when known to be abnormal, can safeguard us from the error of judging that "what the thing appears " in such circumstances is " what it is really and externally ".

On the other hand, if we held the secondary sense qualities to be "mental states," and the primary qualities or "spatial determinations " never to be *really and extramentally* what they *appear,* or as they *are perceived,* then, since we have no other way of *knowing intellectually* what spatial qualities and things are *really and extramentally* than by *judging from what they appear,* it would inevitably follow that our supposed knowledge of what they *are really and extramentally* is an illusion.

The assumption that we can have intellectual knowledge of an extramental, real, spatial universe, independently of all that appears to consciousness in sense perception, is gratuitous and erroneous. If there is such a universe, intellectual knowledge of it is conditioned by its being cognitively related to intellect ; and it cannot be cognitively related to intellect unless through its cognitive relation to sense. If, then, it always appears to sense otherwise than it is, so consequently must it appear to intellect otherwise than it is : in

[1] *Op. cit.,* p. 86.

[2] Including sense " illusions," *i.e.* misinterpreted perceptions of external things really presented to the perceiver ; but not including hallucinations which, being imagination processes, do not "present " any *external* object, though they have an *extramental, organic,* real cause.

which case all our knowledge would be illusory *if understood to refer to what reality is extramentally;* but if understood to refer to "how it appears" it would still be possible to distinguish between "what it appears" *normally* and "what it appears" *in abnormal, special conditions,* and to designate the former "true knowledge," and the latter "false or illusory knowledge," of "how reality appears". This is Kant's position. It cannot be met by arguing that, in the distinction between what things *appear* (*e.g.* in respect of spatial relations) and what they *are*, (*a*) we know "what they *are*" irrespectively of what they appear, or that (*b*) by "what they *are*" we mean "what they are but never appear"; for neither of these contentions can be sustained. We refute his position rather by recognizing that the distinction between "what things appear" (in regard to spatial and other sense qualities) and "what they are" is a distinction between what they may appear in an individual, abnormal case, and what they are known to appear normally; by admitting also the possibility of confining the distinction between *abnormal* ("*Schein*") and *normal* ("*Erscheinung*") to "what things *appear*"; but by showing that there is no ground whatsoever for supposing either that "what things *appear*" in *normal* perception is anything other or otherwise than "what they are really and extramentally and externally," or for supposing that "what they appear *to intellect*," *i.e.* what they are interpreted or represented to be by intellect, is a metamorphosis or transfiguration of what they really are,—a transformation gratuitously supposed to be effected by subjective, mental factors contributed in the process whereby they are cognitively related to the intellect.

129. How Kant Derives two "Things" from one "Appearing Thing".—From all that has been said in the preceding sections regarding the distinction between what things "are" and what they "appear," the general conclusion emerges that this distinction can be satisfactorily explained without erecting the "appearances" of things into a system of *secondary, subsidiary, mental* "things,"—realities "of the second order," so to speak,—and supposing these to intervene as a *tertium quid* between the knowing mind and the primary, original realities. "Knowing" in any form,—whether by perceiving, conceiving, judging, interpreting, etc.,—is a mental *activity* or *process* which implies that something, some reality, "appears," or "is presented" or "represented," as object to the knower: the "appearing," etc., being identically the cognitive process regarded from the objective side. We are, of course, at liberty to transform these verbs into substantives, and to speak of "perceptions," "appearances," "presentations," "representations," etc.; but even if we do, they still signify processes, and certainly the mere linguistic change from verb to substantive does not transform *processes of cognition* into *objects of cognition.* Yet it has been

a rather too common procedure on the part of philosophers, in their analysis of cognition, to interpret this process as implying a set of intramental objects,—which they variously describe as "appearances," "representations," "phenomena," "images," "symbols," etc.,—intervening between the knowing mind and the reality which is given to it to know.

The scholastics spoke, indeed, of a "*species*" or "*imago, similitudo intentionalis (impressa)*," as *determinant* of the cognitive process, but they took care to make it abundantly clear that they did not regard this "*species*" as a *known object :* " species non est *id quod* cognoscitur, sed *id quo* mens cognoscit rem ". And when they spoke of the achieved cognitive process as terminating in a "*species intentionalis expressa*" of the known reality, they meant just as clearly, not that the mind consciously apprehended any mental image of this reality, but that by virtue of the whole cognitive process the mind became "assimilated" or "conformed" to the known reality (112).

It was with the advent of Idealism that the immediate object of the mind's awareness, in the process of cognition, began to be regarded as being something necessarily immanent in, or really one with, the knowing mind, and not as being the extramental reality itself. To vindicate for the mind the possibility of knowing the latter became henceforth a problem of how to "construct the bridge" from the knowing mind or subject to the extramental reality as object.[1] For, once it is assumed that the mind can come into direct cognitive contact only with its own conscious states a serious doubt arises as to whether or how it can ever know any reality beyond these,—any extra-subjective or extramental reality (112, 113). Naturally, those who believed in the possibility, despite the assumption, regarded those directly known conscious states as "impressions," "ideas," "images," "representations," "appearances," "phenomena," etc., produced by the extramental reality in the mind, and as mentally "reproducing," "mirroring,"" reflecting," "representing" this reality, which would thus be known indirectly and inferentially through the medium of these conscious, mental substitutes. But the question immediately arose : How can we be sure that these conscious states are produced by anything extramental, or that if they are they represent it faithfully? To vindicate certitude on this point Descartes appealed to the Divine Veracity, and Malebranche to Divine

[1] *Cf.* JEANNIÈRE, *op. cit.*, p. 443.

Revelation ; while Berkeley combined the assumption of Idealism with the principle of causality to reason away the material universe and to infer the existence of God from human minds and their "ideas". These attempts to establish reasoned certitude about extramental reality failed,—and could not but fail. Meanwhile, some scholastics came gradually to consider that *so far as the objects of the individual mind's direct and immediate awareness are concerned*, these objects cannot in any circumstances be the *non-self*, but must always be the *self*, variously affected or determined in the ways revealed as conscious states (127); and in regard to sense perception they therefore naturally adopted the representationist theory. But holding, and rightly, that in these states *reality as such* is revealed *to intellect*, and that the intellectual concepts of substance, cause, etc., derived from these states, are objectively and really valid, they have contended that reasoned certitude about the existence and nature of a real non-self or external universe can be mediately attained by the principle of causality. We have pointed out the need there is, in this procedure, to vindicate the objective and real validity of *another* intellectual concept, which is inevitably involved if certitude about a real non-self universe is to be attained, *viz.* the concept of *real externality* or *real otherness from the self-reality*, which latter, on this theory, forms the *total conscious content* from which the individual intellect derives all its concepts (104, 111). Nor do we see how the validity of this concept is to be vindicated if we allow that in our direct cognitive processes non-self reality is never present to consciousness and is never an object of the mind's direct cognitive awareness. Not only, therefore, do we think that there is no sufficient reason for abandoning the perceptionist position, but furthermore, we consider it is by adopting it,—by maintaining that among the conscious data of our direct cognitive awareness the real non-self is revealed with the same directness and immediacy as the real self (105, 111),—that we can most effectively meet all forms of subjectivism and agnosticism, which either by denying the validity of the principle of causality altogether, or— what comes practically to the same thing—limiting its valid application to the conscious domain of mental states or "appearances" or "phenomena," conclude that speculative reason offers no reliable "bridge" from knowledge of these appearances to knowledge of any reality beyond consciousness.

It is Kant, especially, who has made the widest use of those supposed direct objects of awareness called "appearances" or "representations," as interlopers between the mind and reality. His whole system is based on a confusion of the *process* of cognition with the *object* of cognition[1]: for it is only by such confusion that an "appearance" can be set up as a *tertium quid* between the mind and reality. We may, therefore, introduce his doctrine on sense perception by seeing how he involves himself in this confusion.

He asks whether space and time are relations which belong to things as they are in themselves even if these were not perceived, or which belong to things only as these are perceived ;[2] and he concludes that they belong to things only as these are perceived. This can only mean "that things are not in reality spatial [and temporal] but only look or appear spatial [and temporal] to us ".[3] But if so, "space is an illusion, inasmuch as it is not a property of things at all " ;[4] and the same is true of time. This, however,

"is precisely the conclusion which Kant wishes to avoid. He takes infinite trouble to explain that he does not hold space and time to be illusions. Though *transcendentally ideal* (*i.e.* though they do not belong to things in themselves), they are *empirically real*. In other words, space and time are real relations of *something*, though not of things in themselves.

" How, then, does Kant obtain something of which space and time can be regarded as really relations? He reaches it by a transition which at first sight seems harmless. In stating the fact of perception he substitutes for the assertion that things appear so and so to us the assertion that things produce appearances in us. In this way he obtains an assertion which introduces a second reality distinct from the thing, *viz.* an appearance or phenomenon, and thereby he gains something other than the thing, to which space can be attached as a real predicate. He thus gains something in respect of which, with regard to spatial relations, we can be said to have *knowledge* and not illusion. For the position now is that space, though not a property of things in themselves, *is* a property of phenomena or appearances ; in other words, that while things in themselves are not spatial, phenomena and appearances are spatial. . . .[5]

" It may be said, then, that Kant is compelled to end with a different distinction from that with which he begins. He begins with the distinction between things as they are in themselves and things as they appear to us, the distinction relating to one and the same reality regarded from two different points of view. He ends with the distinction between two different realities, things-in-themselves,[6] external to, in the sense of independent of,

[1] *Cf.* vol. i., §§ 92-3.   [2] *Critique* (Müller), p. 18.
[3] PRICHARD, *op. cit.*, p. 73.   [4] *Ibid.*   [5] *Ibid.*
[6] " It should be noticed that ' things-in-themselves' and 'things as they are in themselves ' have a different meaning."

the mind, and phenomena or appearances within it. Yet if his *argument*[1] is to be valid, the two distinctions should be identical, for it is the first distinction to which the argument appeals. In fact we find him expressing what is to him the same distinction now in one way and now in the other as the context requires."[2]

The perception process looked at from the side of the perceiving subject, is *the perceiving of an object by a subject*, and looked at from the side of the object, is *the appearing of an object to a subject*. We now see how Kant erected this event into a *tertium quid* which he interposed as a "phenomenon" or "appearance" or "mental object," or "object of awareness" between the mind and the real object. By this identification of *process* and *object* he succeeded in getting a set of subsidiary, secondary, *mental* entities, of which space and time might be really predicated, and our knowledge of which, as spatial and temporal, might be said to be genuine knowledge and not illusion. This procedure of converting the *perceiving* or *appearing* of objects into *objects perceived* has set an example which has been too easily adopted and too widely followed in philosophies far removed from Kantism. Its legitimacy should not be allowed without full justification. As a matter of fact we shall find Kant attempting to justify it, in other words, attempting to prove that the spatial objects of our empirical perception *must* be *only* mind-dependent or intramental objects, "phenomena," or "appearances," from a consideration of the nature of space as revealed in geometrical judgments,—his contention being that space can be only a mental form of perception and that therefore spatial objects can be only mind-dependent entities.[3] And we hope to show that he fails to make good his contention.

Neither, however, can we assume *a priori*, or as beyond all possibility of at least *provisional* doubt and investigation, that what the mind immediately apprehends in perception is *not* an intramental and somehow mind-dependent object, which would be, perhaps, an "image," "representation," "appearance," etc., produced in consciousness by the extramental reality. What we have rather to show, and what we have so far endeavoured to show, is that in the facts of our cognitive experience there are no sufficient grounds for such a supposition ; and that the supposition itself, whatever about its grounds, so far from

---

[1] For the argument in question, *cf. infra*, § 133.
[2] PRICHARD, *op. cit.*, p. 75.   [3] *Cf. infra*, § 133.

helping us to understand those facts, rather introduces a further perplexing factor into attempts at explaining them. These remarks are prompted by the following passage in which Prichard urges rather forcibly the untenability of Kant's position :—

The final form of Kant's conclusion, then, is that while things in themselves are not, or, at least, cannot be known to be spatial, "phenomena," or appearances produced in us by things in themselves, are spatial. Unfortunately, the conclusion in this form is no more successful than in its former form, that things are spatial only as perceived. Expressed by the formula "phenomena are spatial," it has, no doubt, a certain plausibility ; for the word "phenomena" to some extent conceals the essentially mental character of what is asserted to be spatial. But the plausibility disappears on the substitution of "appearances"—the true equivalent of Kant's *Erscheinungen*—for "phenomena". Just as it is absurd to describe the fact that the stick only looks bent by saying that, while the stick is not bent, the appearance which it produces is bent, so it is, even on the face of it, nonsense to say that while things are not spatial, the appearances which they produce in us are spatial. For an "appearance" being necessarily something mental, cannot possibly be said to be extended.[1] Moreover, it is really an abuse of the term "appearance" to speak of appearances *produced by* things, for this phrase implies a false severance of the appearance from the things which appear. If there are appearances at all, they are appearances *of* things and not appearances *produced by* things. The importance of the distinction lies in the difference of implication. To speak of appearances produced by things is to imply that the object of perception is merely something mental, *viz.* an appearance. Consequently access to a non-mental reality is excluded. . . .[2]

This passage precedes the author's detailed analysis of the distinction between "appearance" and "reality" ; and, admitting its summary character, the author proceeds to vindicate it in the manner already examined (125, 128).

The objection (he writes[3]) will probably be raised that this criticism is much too summary. We do, it will be said, distinguish in ordinary consciousness between appearance and reality. Consequently there must be some form in which Kant's distinction between things in themselves and phenomena and the conclusion based on it are justified. Moreover, Kant's reiterated assertion that his view does not imply that space is an illusion and that the distinction between the real and the illusory is possible within phenomena requires us to consider more closely whether Kant may not after all be entitled to hold that space is not an illusion. The objection of course

---

[1] *Cf.*, however, *supra*, § 125.
[2] PRICHARD, *op. cit.*, pp. 75-6 (*cf. supra*, § 125, p. 144).   [3] *Ibid.*, pp. 76-7.

is reasonable. No one can satisfy himself of the justice of the above criticisms until he has considered the real nature of the distinction between appearance and reality.

But in investigating the nature of the distinction, Prichard unfortunately admits that the *secondary* qualities are mere "mental facts" or "sensations"; and hence "access to a non-mental reality," from *their* presence in consciousness, "is excluded". Moreover the admission is fatal to the accessibility of "a non-mental reality" as the veritable subject of the *primary* qualities or "spatial relations". Nor can the "non-mental" reality of these be vindicated against Kant by the *mere assertion* that their non-mental reality is a necessary presupposition of knowledge; or that the distinction between a "deceptive" ("*Schein*") and a "genuine" ("*Erscheinung*") "mental fact" or "appearance" is unintelligible.

CHAPTER XXI.

KANT'S THEORY OF SENSE PERCEPTION, SPACE AND TIME.

130. GENERAL VIEW OF KANT'S DOCTRINE OF SENSE PERCEPTION.—We have now to examine Kant's teaching on the validity of sense perception, culminating as it does in the view that *space* and *time* are not features or characteristics of *what is given* in sense perception, but are *a priori* mental endowments, pure *forms* of sensibility, which render sense perception possible. If it is true that Kant never relinquished his hold on extramental reality, it is equally true that he kept his hold on it in defiance of the whole theory outlined in the *Critique of Pure Reason*. Many of the positions adopted in the course of the *Critique* are untenable,[1] if not indeed meaningless,[2] unless on the assumption that at least in sense perception the mind is directly aware of extramental reality,—an assumption that is fundamentally opposed to the main assumption underlying the *Critique*.

We do not consider that Kant is to be blamed for not having avowedly presupposed the validity of man's spontaneous conviction that the mind can know reality as it is, and conducted his analysis in the light of this presupposition,—though *de facto* it is really latent in the opening passages of the *Critique*, where he says that "by the sensibility objects are *given* to us,"[3] where he speaks of "objects which affect our senses,"[4] and where he speaks of reality *in the plural* as "things in themselves," seemingly identifying these with real bodies in space.[5] But we do think that he adopted an unjustifiable procedure by introducing tacitly at an early stage of his inquiry the *opposite* assumption, viz. that the mind *cannot* know reality as it is,[6] and by allowing this as-

---

[1] *E.g.* the supposition that only *a priori* judgments, and not *a posteriori* judgments give rise to any "problem of knowledge" (*cf.* § 55; PRICHARD, *op. cit.*, pp. 3, 7, 66-8).

[2] *E.g.* the supposition that the cause of sensation is "a spatial and temporal world" of "physical bodies," and that "this world is what we come to know".— PRICHARD, p. 32.

[3] *Critique*, p. 40.   [4] *Ibid.*, p. 715.
[5] *Cf.* PRICHARD, *op. cit.*, pp. 30, 32.   [6] *Ibid.*, p. 30.

sumption, perhaps unconsciously but none the less effectively, to bias his whole analysis of our cognitive functions and their *a priori* mental conditions, and indeed so to bias this analysis that it inevitably issues in subjectivism.

That in the earlier portion of the *Critique* Kant vacillates between the realist and the idealist views of sense perception will be apparent from a comparison of the opening passages of the *Introduction* (47) and the *Transcendental Aesthetic* (51), with his subsequent treatment of the general problem of knowledge. He commences by asserting that in intuition or perception, and there alone, cognition directly reaches its " objects "; that in perception these act upon our sensibility and produce sensations therein ; that thereby objects are "given to us": " The effect produced by an object upon the faculty of representation, so far as we are affected by it, is called sensation. An intuition of an object by means of a sensation is called empirical " (51). Now here he identifies the " objects " with the " causes " of sensation, and he is manifestly thinking of these as things and events in the physical universe of space and time, for his aim is to explain our sense knowledge of this latter. But as the sensation is in the mind and the supposed cause or causes of it beyond and outside the mind, and as he cannot see *how anything extramental can be presented to the mind* or become an object of the mind's aware-ness,[1] he rejects the view that the causes of our sensations are bodies and events in the physical universe, substituting the as-sumption that they are an unknowable reality ;[2] and he leaves us

---

[1] In other words, how the mind can " transcend itself " (21). In one remarkable passage of the *Prolegomena* Kant admits that it is at all events possible, if not posi-tively intelligible, that a thing present to perception can reveal itself *as it is in itself.* " Were our perception necessarily of such a kind as to represent things *as they are in themselves*, no perception would take place *a priori*, but would always be empiri-cal. For I can only know what is contained in the object in itself, if it is present and given to me. No doubt it is even then unintelligible how the perception of a present thing should make me know it as it is in itself, since its qualities cannot migrate over into my faculty of representation ; but *even granting this possibility* [italics ours], such a perception would not occur *a priori*, *i.e.* before the object was presented to me. . . . " (*Prol.*, §9; *cf*. PRICHARD, *op. cit.*, p. 55). If the " thing " is " present " to " my faculty of representation," why should the " qualities " of the thing have to " migrate over into " the latter, in order that the thing be known as it is in itself ? The notion that such " migration " is necessary reveals a rather crude and mechanical conception of the process of cognition ; nor is it easy to see how the mystery or obscurity of the latter is one whit lessened by supposing any sort of *real* identity of the perceiver and the perceived (*cf*. § 21).

[2] Kant's employment of the principle of causality here, to infer a transcendental reality correlative to our sensations, is manifestly inconsistent with his own theory as to the limits of its valid and legitimate employment.

wondering *what* "objects are given to us by the sensibility". What is given is simply a manifold of sensations, a "raw material of . . . sensuous, impressions"[1] (47), whereby we are to become aware of a physical universe of bodies and events in space and time. How this can be done is now the problem.

"For if [writes Prichard] the contribution of the sensibility to our knowledge of the physical world is limited to a succession of sensations, explanation must be given of the fact that we have succeeded with an experience confined to sensations in acquiring a knowledge of a world which does not consist of sensations. Kant, in fact, in the *Aesthetic* has this problem continually before him, and tries to solve it. He holds that the mind . . . superinduces upon sensations, as data, spatial and other relations in such a way that it acquires knowledge of the spatial world."[2]

In stating the problem Kant appears to have been undoubtedly influenced by his assumption of realism, *i.e.* the spontaneous conviction of mankind that our sensations are caused by (extramental) bodies in space. And even after he had rejected this assumption and ascribed the origin of sensations to extramental, unknowable "things in themselves," he continued to speak of these latter in terms which show that he was really thinking of bodies in space. In corroboration of this, Prichard refers to "certain passages in the *Critique* which definitely mention the 'senses,' a term which refers to bodily organs," and to "others to which meaning can be given only if they are taken to imply that the objects which affect our sensibility are not unknown things in themselves, but things known to be spatial. Even the use of the plural in the term 'things in themselves' implies a tendency to identify the unknowable reality beyond the mind with bodies in space. For the implication that different sensations are due to different things in themselves originates in the view that different sensations are due to the operation of different spatial bodies."[3]

Prichard even contends that the problem of the *Aesthetic*, "How do we, beginning with mere sensation, come to know a spatial and temporal world?" is only a problem "so long as it is supposed that the cause of sensation is a spatial and temporal world or part of it, and that this world is what we come to know. If the cause of sensation, as being beyond the mind, is held to be unknowable and so not known to be spatial or temporal, the

[1] *Critique*, p. 715.   [2] *Op. cit.*, p. 31.   [3] *Ibid.*, p. 32.

problem has disappeared." [1] We would say rather, that the problem is changed. It is now no longer the (insoluble) problem, "How do we, beginning with mere awareness of our own individual mental states, originated by a supposed extramental reality, ever come to know this latter?" It is now the (fictitious) problem, "How do we transform a chaotic stream of isolated sensuous impressions (originated in us by an unknowable reality) into the orderly system of mental appearances which we apprehend as the physical, material universe of space and time,—and which, be it remarked incidentally, uncritical people by a spontaneous illusion believe to be extramental?" His solution of this problem (51) is that, whereas the visual, tactual, auditory, gustatory, and olfactory elements (*i.e.* what are called the "proper sensibles" or the "secondary qualities" of bodies) in our states of sense consciousness constitute the *matter* or *data* or chaotic manifold of sense impressions, the *space* and *time* elements in these states (the "common sensibles" or "primary qualities") are not given empirically, with or in those sensation manifolds, but are pure mental forms of *a priori* intuition ; and that only by the *a priori* synthesis of these with the empirical data is it possible for us to become conscious or aware of anything as a phenomenon of physical nature existing in space and time.[2] We shall now deal separately and in order with his attempts to prove space and time to be *a priori* forms of sense perception.

131. KANT'S ACCOUNT OF "FORMS OF INTUITION" CONFUSED AND AMBIGUOUS.—A first confusion to be noted in Kant's treatment of sense perception is his use of the ambiguous expression "*form* of intuition" in quite distinct meanings. On the

---

[1] *Op. cit.*, p. 32.

[2] Thus, the primary qualities of bodies are, if anything, more subjective than the secondary inasmuch as those belong to the nature of the mind *necessarily* and *a priori*, while these are originated in it *contingently* and *a posteriori* by an unknowable extramental cause (125). *Cf.* MAHER, *Psychology*, 4th edit., p. 121, n. 16 ; p. 154. Of course Kant would claim that space and time, being *a priori*, and thus accounting for the characters of necessity and universality in geometrical and other mathematical judgments, are more "objective" (in his sense of the term) than the secondary qualities revealed in our states of sense consciousness. But since his arguments for this *a priori* character of space and time imply that in the *empirical*, *a posteriori* perception of the *secondary* qualities of bodies, where the data are *present* to the percipient, we apprehend these qualities as they are in reality, it should follow that the former alone are phenomenal, and the latter real. "This conclusion would of course be absurd, for what Kant considers to be the empirically known qualities of objects disappear, if the spatial character of objects is removed."—PRICHARD, p. 67. Kant escapes the absurdity only by withdrawing the initial realist assumption regarding empirical perception.

one hand he clearly means by it a *general mode* or *capacity* or *power*
of perceiving, as distinct from the actual perceptions in which this
power is manifested. But then, again, speaking of space, for instance, as a form of perception,[1] he also speaks of it as an *actual
perception of empty space.* Claiming such a perception to be possible (*de facto* it is not possible), he identifies the supposed actual
perception of empty space with the power of perceiving that
which is spatial, and calls space a pure perception. " The confusion," says Prichard, " is possible because it can be said with
some plausibility that a perception of empty space—if its possibility be allowed—does not inform us about actual things, but
only informs us what must be true of things, *if* there prove to be
any ; such a perception, therefore, can be thought of as a possibility of knowledge "[2] rather than as actual knowledge.

A second and more serious confusion is that while space, as
a form of *intuition*, is opposed, as a way in which we perceive things,
to a way in which things are, Kant nevertheless speaks of space
indifferently as a form of *intuition* and as a form of *phenomena, i.e.*
of that which we perceive.[3] Sensations alone are "given " to us.
By the aid of the spatial form of sense intuition we so arrange
these sensations as to constitute and to know the spatial world of
bodies. Bodies in space are arrangements of sensations. And so
space, a form of *intuition,* " being, as it were, a kind of empty vessel
in which sensations are arranged, is said to be the form of *phenomena,*"[4]—which latter is really only another way of saying that
all bodies are spatial.

When Kant speaks of removing from "the representation of
a body " on the one hand all that belongs to conception and on
the other hand all that belongs to sensation, and says that "there
still remains something of that empirical intuition, *viz.* extension
and form " (51), this residue, "extension and form," obviously
belongs to the perceived body : if it is a " form " of anything it
is a "form " of the latter. Yet in the very next sentence he says
that it belongs to " pure intuition, which *a priori* . . . exists in the
mind as a mere form of sensibility ". But he does not say
whether it belongs to this " pure intuition " as its *form, i.e.* as a

[1] The terms "intuition " and "perception " are used throughout as synonymous.
[2] *Op. cit.,* p. 37.
[3] *Cf.* passage quoted, § 51, vol. i. The confusion is analogous to that of *conception* with *objects conceived*—§ 92.
[4] *Ibid.,* p. 38 (italics ours).

general mode or power of perceiving, or rather as identical with the actual pure *a priori* intuition itself : because he confounds the " form " of pure intuition with the *actual* intuition of empty space. Prichard thus sums up those various confusions : "The form of phenomena is said to be the space in which all sensations are arranged, or in which all bodies are ; space apart from all sensations of bodies, *i.e.* empty, being the object of a pure perception, is treated as identical with a pure perception, *viz.* the perception of empty space ; and the perception of empty space is treated as identical with a capacity of perceiving that which is spatial ".[1]

Now if Kant meant by "*forms* of intuition," consistently and exclusively, mental *capacities* or *powers* of apprehending what we become aware of as being endowed with this, that, or the other quality, then of course it is true that the mind has such " forms," and has them *a priori* :[2] in other words, it is true that the mind, in order to become aware of anything as *e.g.* hard, or cold, or white, or bitter, or loud, or sweet-smelling, or extended, or moving, etc., must have, as a prerequisite condition for such actual perceptions, the corresponding mental capacities or powers of perception. But in that case we should say that there are not merely *two a priori* forms of sense perception, but as many as there are distinct, perceptible sense qualities in physical nature : and the two forms whereby we apprehended the qualities, space and time, we should call not space and time, but *forms of our perception of* space and time. Kant, however, contends that all the other sense qualities, except space and time, belong to the mental *material* of perception, *viz.* to sensations, while space and time alone are mental *forms* of perception ; and he does so because [1] he is thinking of " forms " of perception or intuition not now as capacities of perceiving but as " forms " of *phenomena* or things perceived, "*i.e.* as something in which all bodies or their states are, or, from the point of view of knowledge, as that in which sensuous material is to be arranged ; for [2] there is nothing except space and time in which such arrangement could be plausibly said to be carried out ".[3]

---

[1] *Op. cit.*, p. 40.

[2] Similarly, the only admissible sense in which we can speak of *a priori* " concepts " or " categories " or forms of the understanding, is that of intellectual powers or capacities of conceiving or apprehending intellectually the substances and accidents, causes and effects, etc., which constitute reality.

[3] *Ibid.*

132. Space not an A Priori Perception. Analysis of Kant's Arguments.—We now come to the main arguments by which Kant supports his contention that space is (1) apprehended *a priori* (2) by a process which is not *conception* but *sense intuition ;* and that therefore space is not a quality or relation of things in themselves but only of phenomena or mental appearances.

A. His first argument to prove that space is apprehended *a priori* is stated thus :—

Space is not an empirical concept[1] which has been derived from external[2] experience. For in order that certain sensations should be referred to something outside myself (*i.e.* to something in a different part of space from that where I am) ; again, in order that I may be able to represent them (*vorstellen*) as side by side,[3] that is, not only as different, but as in different places, the representation (" *Vorstellung* ") of space must be already there. Therefore the representation of space cannot be borrowed through experience from relations of external phenomena, but, on the contrary, this external experience becomes possible only by means of the representation of space.[4]

The drift of the argument is plain enough. It is that in order, for example, to apprehend that A is in front of me and to the right of B, I must have first apprehended empty space : I must apprehend empty space before I can apprehend individual spatial relations between things : therefore our apprehension of space is an *a priori* perception. Certain points, however, deserve to be noted. (1) It is *sensations* that assume spatial relations by being placed "side by side," "in different places," but it is bodies in the physical universe that are in space : the physical universe is therefore a system of spatially arranged sensations. (2) The representation of space is here set forth as *a priori* not merely in the sense of a *transcendental mental form* which is itself *independent of experience,* and *renders experience of things in space possible,* but in the sense of *temporal* priority, in the sense that *actual* apprehension of (empty) space must *precede* all conscious perception of things as spatially related.

To the argument itself we may reply, *firstly,* that it is not the supposed apprehension of empty space (which would be

[1] *Begriff,*—the term here does not mean a " concept " in the strict sense, but has the general sense of " representation "—*Vorstellung ; cf.* next sentence.
[2] *äusseren,*—not " external " in the sense of " produced by something extramental," but merely in the sense of " spatial," as the context in the next sentence shows.
[3] *äusser [und neben*—2nd edit.] *einander.*   [4] *Critique,* pp. 18-19.

presumably an individual apprehension of an individual mental object, " empty space ") that has to be proved to be *a priori ;* it is rather the apprehension of *the nature of space* as something *necessarily and universally such for all human minds,* and as thus grounding the necessity and universality of geometrical judgments,—it is such an apprehension as this that has to be proved *a priori ;* and the argument does not prove this.[1]

Secondly, we have no actual sense perception or sense intuition of empty space antecedently to our empirical sense perceptions of individual spatial things and relations, or indeed subsequently either.   We prove this, not by appealing to the fact that we are never conscious of such a perception,—for according to Kant the supposed pure *a priori* perception of empty space is not a conscious process,—but by denying that there is any ground for postulating it.   To account for our empirical sense perception of individual spatial things and relations all we need to postulate on the part of the mind is the *power* or *capacity* for eliciting such an act of perception, and the reduction of this power to act by the influence of spatial things upon the mind (129).   We do not need to postulate a perceptive act of the transcendental mind or *Ego,* whereby empty space would be apprehended antecedently to any conscious act of empirical sense perception—even if we could conceive what such an *a priori* perceptive act, cognitive and yet unconscious, would be like.   We therefore simply deny the *consequentia* of Kant's argument : that in order to perceive an object, A, as to the right of B, we must first have apprehended empty space.

Thirdly, the argument proves too much ; for if, to apprehend things as extended and spatially related, we must have not only the *capacity* to do so, but also an *a priori* actual perception of *empty* space, *a pari* in order to have empirical sense perception of individual colours, sounds, tastes, smells, etc., we should need to have antecedently not only the *powers* of eliciting such perceptions but also *actual a priori* perceptions of *formal* (or so to speak, *empty*) colours, sounds, tastes, smells, etc.,—or at all events the *a priori* " forms " of the corresponding empirical perceptions, in whatever sense, other than that of mere powers or capacities, Kant understands such " forms ".   But Kant dis-

---

[1] As a matter of fact what Kant is thinking of all the time is the *abstract concept* of space : space as abstract and universal, which cannot be apprehended by *sense perception. Cf. infra,* pp. 193 *sqq.*

claims the need for such a multiplicity of forms on the part of the mind for apprehending colours, sounds, tastes, smells, etc. Therefore there is no need for such an *a priori* form for the perception of things as extended or spatial.

Fourthly, the space of which Kant was thinking as perceived *a priori* is *de facto* space *conceived in the abstract* by the understanding. Moreover, it is thus conceived not prior, but posterior in time, to our empirical sense perceptions of individual extended things. And finally, though derived from these latter perceptions, nevertheless, being abstract, it presents to the intellect relations which are absolutely necessary and universal and are not grounded in sense experience (69).

B. Kant's second argument is stated as follows:—

> Space is a necessary representation *a priori*, forming the very foundation of all external intuitions. It is impossible to imagine that there should be no space, though one might very well imagine that there should be space without objects to fill it. Space is therefore regarded as a condition of the possibility of phenomena, not as a determination produced by them; it is a representation *a priori* which necessarily precedes all external phenomena.[1]

This argument simply confounds the actual space or spatial relations of the extended "objects" or bodies which constitute the actually existing physical universe, with the possibility of these bodies and the possibility of their actual spatial relations. We can indeed think of the whole spatial or physical universe as *non-existent*, but having once experienced it as actual we cannot think of it as *not even possible:* we necessarily continue to think of it as possible, and by that very fact we necessarily continue to think of its spatial relations as possible : and this thought or concept of the mere possibility of a spatial universe is necessarily accompanied by the *imagination image* of what is called *ideal*, or more properly *imaginary*, space—indefinite, void, empty. The fact that it is impossible for us to rid ourselves of this representation of imaginary space only proves that we cannot rid ourselves of the activity of memory or reproductive imagination ;[2] it by no means proves that we must have perceived real and actual space *a priori*, and antecedently to our actual perception of bodies, or that when we think these as non-existent and merely possible we do not *eo ipso* think their

---

[1] *Critique*, p. 19. Note how intuitions and phenomena are identified.
[2] *Cf. Ontology*, § 84, pp. 320-1; MERCIER, *op. cit.*, pp. 389-91.

actually perceived spatial relations also as no longer actual but merely possible.[1]

The two preceding arguments purported to prove that our apprehension of space is *a priori;* the two following purport to prove that this apprehension is a *sense intuition* or *perception,* not a *conception* of the *understanding.*[2]

Before stating them, however, attention must be called to the possibility of discriminating, and the test or tests for discriminating, between that which is *per*ceived and that which is *con*ceived. Kant teaches[3] that in "the representation of a body," for instance, we can isolate what is reached by *conception,* "substance, force, divisibility, etc," from what is given in sensation and reached through *perception.* But this is not so ; for whatever we can perceive we can also conceive or think : the distinction between perception and thought or conception, so far as what they represent to our consciousness is concerned, consists in this, that *what we apprehend by the former as concrete and individual we apprehend by the latter as abstract and universal.* Even the most concrete and individual datum revealed to me in sense perception, *e.g.* "this individual instance of this particular shade of redness," I can and do also conceive or think of as "a particular *kind* of shade of redness of which this is an individual instance, and of which there are or can be an indefinite plurality of other instances".

A. Kant's first argument is as follows :—

Space is not a discursive or so-called general concept of the relation of things in general, but a pure intuition. For, first of all, we can imagine one space only, and if we speak of many spaces, we mean parts only of one and the same space. Nor can these parts be considered as antecedent to the one and all-embracing space and, as it were, its component parts out of which an aggregate is formed, but they can be thought of as existing within it only. Space is essentially one ; its multiplicity, and therefore the general concept of spaces in general, arises entirely from limitations. Hence it follows that, with respect to space, an intuition *a priori,* which is not empirical, must form the foundation of all conceptions of space. In the same manner all geometrical principles, *e.g.* "that in every triangle two sides together are greater than the third," are never to be derived from the general concepts of side and triangle, but from an intuition, and that *a priori,* with apodeictic certainty.[4]

---

[1] *Cf.* MAHER, *Psychology* (4th edit.), pp. 118-19.   [2] *Cf. supra,* p. 191, n.
[3] *Critique,* p. 17, quoted vol. i., § 51.   [4] *Ibid.,* pp. 19-20.

Here Kant's conclusion is not what we should expect, *viz.* that space is a *form* of *a priori* perception, but that it is an *actual a priori* perception. He argues that because imagined space is one, unique, numerically individual, whereof there cannot be a plurality of instances, it must be apprehended by *perception*, not conception; inasmuch as what is apprehended by *conception* is apprehended as universal, as having an indefinite plurality of instances. In other words, he uses the proper test to distinguish perception from conception. Unfortunately, however, he misapplies it. The actual process is precisely the one which he says it is *not*. We first perceive empirically, through visual, tactual, and motor sensations, a plurality of individual extended bodies in their individual spatial relations with one another. We do not and cannot perceive empirically more than limited portions of the whole physical or spatial universe. But our imagination can and does multiply these by extending or pushing out their limits indefinitely. Simultaneously our *thought* seizes the homogeneous extensional or spatial aspect of what is thus presented in imagination, and conceiving this aspect in the abstract, apart from the concrete, extended bodies in which it was presented, thus forms the abstract and universal concept of space. Accompanying this is the vague imagination image of a vast, indefinite void, the phantasm corresponding to the intellectual concept. It is *not* true, therefore, that we *perceive* space as a whole, first or last, *a priori* or otherwise; we *perceive* individual bodies with their individual extension and spatial relations. It is *not* true that "we can imagine one space only"; we imagine the individual perceived bodies and their spatial relations as forming one totality extending indefinitely. These "parts" *are* imagined "antecedent to the one all-embracing space," and the imagination of the latter *is* derived from that of the former by multiplication of the parts or extension of the limits. And meantime the abstractive process of thought or conception apprehends, even in the first empirical percept of a definite and limited plurality of extended and spatially related bodies, *the nature of space* as a universal,[1] as applicable to an indefinite plurality of such perceived instances, and as (like every other abstract and universal thought-object, *e.g. colouredness* in general) *one and homogeneous* in all its possible instances. Kant's statement that " space is essentially

[1] *Cf.* MAHER, *Psychology* (4th edit.), pp. 371-2.

one " is ambiguous, for it may mean (1) that space as a universal, *i.e.* as apprehended by abstract thought or conception, is one and homogeneous in all its instances (as is "colouredness," or any other universal, in all its instances); or (2) that the totality of spaces, or instances of space, forms numerically one whole or collection of parts or instances (just as the totality of colours forms numerically one collection of colours).[1]   But in the former sense its apprehension as a universal is not antecedent to the apprehension of its individual instances.   And in the latter sense it cannot possibly be perceived empirically, or imagined antecedently to empirical perception ; nor is there any need to suppose that it is or can be either perceived or conceived *a priori*, for it is really a totality of empirically imagined and conceived homogeneous parts or instances, and not a whole apprehended *a priori*, by the division of which we would come to apprehend, consciously and empirically, individual parts or instances of space in the concrete.

B. His second argument to prove space an *a priori* percept and not a concept is as follows :—

Space is represented as an infinite given quantity.   Now it is quite true that every concept is to be thought of as a representation, which is contained in an infinite number of different possible representations (as their common characteristic), and therefore comprehends them : but no concept, as such, can be thought as if it contained in itself an infinite number of representations. Nevertheless, space is so thought (for all parts of infinite space exist simultaneously).   Consequently the original representation of space is an intuition *a priori* and not a concept.[2]

In other words, though a concept implies an indefinite multitude of individuals which come under it, the elements which constitute the concept itself (objectively : the mental object as conceived) cannot be indefinite ; but the elements that constitute space are indefinite ; therefore it is a percept, not a concept.

The reply is that although the elements or "notes" which

[1] This is the elementary logical distinction between the intension and the extension of a concept. *Cf. Science of Logic*, i., pp. 48 *sqq.* The totality of individual instances of colour is of course a *discrete* quantity (*quantitas discreta*) or *multitude*, while the totality of individual instances of space is a *continuous* quantity (*quantitas continua*) or *magnitude* : any perceived finite space being not merely an *instance* of the conceived universal, an instance in which the nature of space is realized, but also (owing to the peculiar nature of space as indefinitely divisible) a part (itself indefinitely divisible) of a larger perceivable or imaginable space. *Cf. Science of Logic*, i., § 39, pp. 86-7.

[2] *Critique* (2nd edit.), p. 728.

13 *

constitute the *connotation* of a complex concept cannot be indefinite, still the conceived object may be of such a nature as to be seen to be indefinitely divisible into homogeneous integral parts —which parts form its *instances* or *denotation*. And this is true of space whether we think of it as finite or as indefinite. The argument confounds multiplicity of the notes or elements which give the *nature* of an object, *i.e.* the *intension* of the mental representation, with the indefinite multiplicity of instances of the object, *i.e.* the *extension* of the mental representation. Space is, no doubt, thought of as containing, or applying to, an indefinite multiplicity of parts or instances ; but it is likewise thought of as being in its *nature* comparatively simple, involving merely the notes of *quantity* and *relation*.

Space apprehended in the absence of limits, or as indefinite, cannot be an object of empirical perception : we only perceive extended bodies. Nor, indeed, can it be an object of empirical imagination, for the imagination must have some sense-element in its images, and when we are said to imagine empty space, what really happens is that we think away all perceived and imagined bodies and thus *conceive* empty space.

In contending that space must be a percept or intuition, and not a concept, Kant is clearly under the influence of the assumption that only in *intuition* is anything *given directly* to the mind ; that conception, since it represents a representation,[1] is twice removed from the phenomenon, which it is supposed to represent only mediately,—and three times removed from the extramental reality, the last remove rendering the latter unknowable.

133. SPACE NOT A PROPERTY OF MERE MENTAL APPEARANCES OR "PHENOMENA," BUT OF MATERIAL REALITIES.—The aim of the arguments just examined was to establish (1) that space is *a priori*, (2) that it is a pure *perception :* from which two characteristics it was to follow that space is a property not of things in themselves but only of phenomena or mental appearances. In drawing this latter conclusion[2] Kant gives another argument in support of the second characteristic,[3] an argument based on the supposed synthetic *a priori* (and at the same time intuitively evident) character of geometrical judgments. Since we have already shown this latter position to be untenable (63) we need not examine the argument in detail. But some points

---

[1] *Cf. Critique*, pp. 56-7, quoted vol. i., § 52, pp. 186-7.
[2] *Ibid.*, pp. 20-4.   [3] *Ibid.* (2nd edit.), pp. 728-9; *Prolegomena*, §§ 6-11.

in it are worthy of notice; and his attempt to infer from the supposed *a priori* and *perceptive* character of our apprehension of space his final conclusion that *space is a property of phenomena only, and not of things in themselves*, has also to be examined.

(1) Arguing from the character of geometrical judgments he admits that all such judgments are *intuitive* or *perceptive*.[1] This obliges him to apply the term *a priori* to perception as well as to judgment. Applied to perception it can have only a temporal sense and must mean " prior to all experience "; and, as Prichard remarks,[2] "since the object of perception is essentially individual,[3] the use of the term gives rise to the impossible task of explaining how a perception can take place prior to the actual experience of an individual in perception ".

(2) Kant contends that such a perception (of empty space) does take place, but that it can take place only if space, or the perception of space (which he identifies with space [4]), be a characteristic of our perceiving nature;[5] and since such perception does take place it must be such a characteristic.

(3) The question, How is it possible to *perceive* anything (in this case, empty space) *a priori*?—raising as it does the insuperable difficulty of perceiving an object before the object is given, —forces Kant, therefore, to hold that what we apprehend in such a perception can be only *our own nature as percipient beings*, or, in other words, the *mode* in which we must necessarily perceive objects when they are given (in empirical perception): the reason apparently being that *nothing else* but our own nature as percipient beings *is present to us* in such an *a priori* perception. " I can only know what is contained in the object in itself, if it is present and given to me "[6]—as it is in *empirical* perception, in which Kant allows the possibility of our knowing the given object as it is in itself,[7] though only with a *contingent, a posteriori* knowledge. In *a priori* perception, at all events, we can apprehend only *our own perceptive nature*, or the mode in which subse-

---

[1] *Prol.*, § 7.   [2] *Op. cit.*, p. 60 n.
[3] *Cf. Critique*, pp. 572-3.   [4] *Cf.* PRICHARD, p. 51 n.
[5] *Critique*, p. 729; *Prol.*, § 9 : " It is therefore possible only in one way for my perception to precede the actuality of the object and to take place as *a priori* knowledge, *viz. if it contains nothing but the form of sensibility, which precedes in me, the subject, all actual impressions through which I am affected by objects,*"—*apud* PRICHARD, p. 55.
[6] *Prol.*, § 9.
[7] This important admission (*ibid.*) has been referred to already—*supra*, p. 185, n.

quently the sensuous content given in empirical perception
must necessarily be apprehended.

(4) From this the final conclusion is plausibly inferred, *viz.* that
the sensuous datum or material which is given in empirical intuition, and which is *necessarily* apprehended therein as *spatial* (owing
to the mode of our perceiving nature being spatial *a priori*) must
be itself something exclusively mental, must be, and be apprehended as, a mental appearance or phenomenon, and cannot possibly be anything extramental or any thing-in-itself: for if in
perceiving empty space *a priori* we are apprehending a law of our
nature as perceptive, then our empirical perceptions, or objects
empirically perceived, are spatial only because by being mental
appearances they come under the *a priori mental* law ; while it
must on the other hand remain impossible to say whether objects
apart from perception, or things in themselves, are or are not
spatial.

Plausible, however, as the conclusion is, nevertheless it is (1)
neither the conclusion warranted by his supposition that we have
an *a priori* perception of empty space whereby we can discover
the rules of spatial relation (geometrical truths) which must
apply to all spatial objects subsequently (and empirically) perceived ; nor (2) is the conclusion even compatible with the supposition on which it is based.

For *firstly*, what is involved in the supposition that we have
such an apprehension of empty space as will yield the geometrical laws to which all empirically perceived objects must conform ?
It does *not* involve what Kant says it does, *viz.* that space is a
form of sensibility, or a mode or way in which objects must appear. It simply involves that space is the form of all perceivable
objects, or that all perceivable objects are spatial.[1]   For, provided
that perceivable objects *are* spatial,

"they must be subject to the laws of space, and if, therefore, we can discover these laws by a study of empty space, the only condition to be satisfied,
if the objects of subsequent perception are to conform to the laws which we
discover, is that all objects should be spatial. *Nothing is implied which
enables us to decide whether the objects are objects as they are in themselves
or objects as perceived ;* for in either case the required result follows. If in
empirical perception we apprehend objects only as they appear to us, and if

---

[1] That space is a form of objects (whether we call these *phenomena* or not) is
quite a different assertion from this other, with which Kant confounds it : that space
is a form of sensibility, or of our perception of objects.

space is the form of them as they appear to us, it will no doubt be true that the laws of spatial relation which we discover must apply to things as they appear to us. *But on the other hand, if in empirical perception we apprehend things as they are, and if space is their form, i.e. if things are spatial, it will be equally true that the laws discovered by geometry must apply to things as they are.*" [1]

Secondly, the conclusion that space is a characteristic of *phenomena* is really incompatible with the initial supposition that the truths of geometry imply an *a priori* spatial perception which turns out to be a perception of the mind's perceiving nature. For, strange though it may seem, Kant's account of this latter *a priori* perception implies that space is a characteristic of *things as they are in themselves!* In this way : When explaining how we can perceive the characteristics of an object *before* the object is given, he allows that if the thing or object were given, or were present to us (as in empirical perception), we could perceive the characteristics of it as it really is.[2] But if this is so, and if the objects given in empirical perception are given as spatial, as Kant allows that they are, then it follows that space is their real form and that the truths of geometry relate to them as they really are. But if so, Kant's presupposition would involve this, that in perceiving empty space *a priori* we should be perceiving a *real characteristic of things* in space before actually perceiving *the things ;* "and no doubt, Kant thinks this impossible ".[3] But, as Prichard justly maintains, no greater difficulty is really involved in it than in Kant's actual presupposition—that we perceive how objects will *appear*, before they *actually do appear :* " It is really just as difficult to hold that we can perceive a characteristic of things as they appear to us *before* they appear, as to hold that we can perceive a characteristic of them as they are in themselves *before* we perceive them ".[4]

The fact is, of course, that the necessary character of geometrical judgments does not presuppose a pure *a priori* perception of empty space. But even if it did, the paradox which such a perception presents to Kant—that of perceiving the characteristics an object must have, before the object itself is given—is really a paradox only because it is supposed that we *can* perceive the characteristics of the object *when* it is given, *i.e.* in empirical perception ; and since we can, and since the empirically perceived

[1] PRICHARD, p. 53 (italics ours).   [2] *Cf. supra*, pp. 185, 197.
[3] PRICHARD, p. 59.   [4] *Ibid.*

object is spatial, it follows that space must be a real characteristic of such an object. Hence Kant's final conclusion is incompatible with a portion of his initial supposition.

We referred above to the plausible character of Kant's conclusion that space can be a characteristic only of mental phenomena. The conclusion is equally plausible if we connect it directly with the absolutely necessary character of geometrical judgments, without postulating an *a priori* perception of empty space. For just as Kant argues from the *necessity* and *universality* of what he calls the principles underlying physics to the existence of *a priori conceptions*, and from the similar characteristics of mathematical judgments to the existence of *a priori perceptions*, so to he infers, in regard to both classes of judgments alike, that they cannot possibly be applicable to things in themselves, to reality, but only to mental phenomena. The argument for the phenomenal character of space would then be as follows : Space is obviously that to which geometrical judgments relate, and of which they formulate the necessary and universal laws. But since the necessity and universality of such judgments cannot be grounded on what is given *a posteriori* from without, in repeated empirical perceptions of bodies, the validity of such judgments can in nowise be defended on the assumption that space, of which they formulate the laws, is a thing in itself,—for how could a necessity of thought (which such judgments express) be binding on what is *ex hypothesi* independent of the nature of the mind ? If, however, that to which such judgments refer, *viz.* space, be merely a mental appearance, or apprehension, or perception, then it is at once intelligible how a necessity of thought could and should apply to that which is itself mental through and through.[1]

One fatal flaw in the argument as just stated is this : it assumes that *contingent, empirical, a posteriori* judgments can and do reveal real characteristics of the things given in empirical perception, and that the reason why *necessary, "a priori"* judgments cannot reveal real characteristics of the latter, but only characteristics of *something mental*, is precisely because the connexions they reveal are necessary and universal. But as we saw already (55), no such distinction can be drawn between necessary and contingent judgments. To question the *reality* of a connexion which we see to be necessary and which we think to be real, and

---

[1] *Cf.* vol. i., §§ 55, 94 ; *infra*, § 140.

to do so simply on the ground that it is necessary, is " to question the validity of thinking altogether, and to do this is implicitly to question the validity of our thought *about the nature of our own mind*, as well as the validity of thought about things independent of the mind ".[1]   What right, after all, have we to assume that we think or judge validly about *our perceptions* of things any more than about *things themselves?*

Furthermore, the assumption that space is something mental and not real, not a characteristic of things as they are but only of our mental representations of things, in no way helps to explain the necessary and universal validity of geometrical judgments.[2]   Kant thinks that it does because he confounds the *necessity* of apprehended spatial *law*, or relation, or connexion, with the *universal validity* of the *judgment* whereby we apprehend such law as necessary.

" No doubt [writes Prichard [3]], if it be a law OF OUR PERCEIVING NATURE that, whenever we perceive an object as a three-sided figure, the object AS PERCEIVED contains three angles, it follows that any object AS PERCEIVED [*i.e.* perceived as a three-sided figure] will conform to this law ; just as if it be a law OF THINGS AS THEY ARE IN THEMSELVES that three-sided figures contain three angles, all three-sided figures will IN THEMSELVES contain three angles.   But what has to be explained is the universal applicability, not of a law, but of a judgment about a law.   For Kant's real problem is to explain why *our judgment* that a three-sided figure must contain three angles must apply to all three-sided figures.   Of course if it be granted that in the judgment we apprehend the true law, the problem may be regarded as solved.   But how are we to know that what we judge *is* the true law?   The answer is in no way facilitated by the supposition that the judgment relates to our perceiving nature.   IT CAN JUST AS WELL BE URGED THAT WHAT WE THINK TO BE A NECESSITY OF OUR PERCEIVING NATURE IS NOT A NECESSITY OF IT AS THAT WHAT WE THINK TO BE A NECESSITY OF THINGS AS THEY ARE IN THEMSELVES IS NOT A NECESSITY OF THEM.[4]   The best, or rather the only possible, answer is simply that that of which we apprehend the necessity must be true, or, in other words, that we *must* accept the validity of thought. . . ."[5]   No vindication of a judgment in which we are conscious

---

[1] PRICHARD, p. 62 (italics ours).   [2] *Cf.* vol. i., § 55.
[3] *Op. cit.*, pp. 63, 65-6 (capitals ours).
[4] *Cf.* vol. i., § 59, where this objection is urged against the whole reasoning of the *Critique.*
[5] In other words, that which the intellect, reflecting on the data of human experience, is necessitated to think as involved in this experience, is *real* : what is given to the mind for its interpretation is real : and what is seen by the mind to be necessarily involved in the given is likewise real.   This is the thesis on which scholastics have at all times emphatically insisted : The proper object of intellect is reality : *Objectum intellectus est Ens* (*cf. Science of Logic*, ii., § 215, p. 58).   This

of a necessity could do more than take the problem a stage further back by basing it upon some other consciousness of a necessity, and since this latter judgment could be questioned for precisely the same reason, we should only be embarking upon an infinite process."

When, therefore, Kant thinks that he has solved " the original problem of the conformity of things to our minds " by the contention that the "things " about which we *judge* are not "things as they are in themselves" but "perceptions," "it can be forced upon him again, even after he thinks he has solved it, in the new form of that of the conformity within the mind of perceiving and thinking".[1] Of course Kant "solves" the problem, stated in this latter form, by the contention that just as what we *perceive* is not the thing in itself but a mental impression produced by the latter and made conformable to the mind's *perceiving nature* by the forms of sense perception, so what we *think* or *conceive* or *judge* is not the perception but the perception transfigured once more and made conformable with the mind's *thinking* or *judging* nature by the categories of the understanding : a solution which really empties the question of the validity of knowledge of all intelligible meaning by issuing in the "logical idealism " which identifies thought with its object and denies all "extra-logical" reality.[2]

134. KANT'S DOCTRINE OF TIME AS AN A PRIORI FORM OF "INTERNAL" PERCEPTION.—According to Kant *time* is no more a characteristic of things than space. Like space it is an *a priori* form of perception. The arguments[3] by which he seeks to establish this contention are, *mutatis mutandis*, the same as those on which he bases his doctrine of space, and therefore we need not reconsider them. What they should prove, apparently, is that time, like space, is an *a priori* form under which we perceive things. Kant, however, concludes from them that time is the *a priori* form under which we perceive *not* things, but *ourselves ;* for, he teaches, while space is the form of *external* sense perception,

does not imply that our spontaneous conviction as to the mind's capacity to attain to real truth must be assumed from the outset as a reasoned certitude, but only that the spontaneous conviction can be—and will be, if the mind proceeds carefully— transformed by reflection into a reasoned certitude (*cf.* chap. iii.) ; nor does it imply that the mind is infallible, but only that in the measure in which it interprets the given according to the laws of thought and the evidence of reality it will avoid error and attain to truth about reality.

[1] PRICHARD, p. 65.   [2] *Cf.* MERCIER, *op. cit.*, § 147, pp. 401-2 ; *supra*, § 110. *Critique*, pp. 24-33, 731.

time is the form of *internal* sense perception, or of the *internal sense*. Let us see what this can mean.

The distinction to which Kant endeavoured to give expression by the phrases "external sense" and "internal sense" is the familiar psychological distinction between the group of cognitive states or activities which make us immediately aware of what we call things and their qualities, and the cognitive activity whereby we become directly aware of the former activities as states or activities of our minds. The latter activity is, of course, the activity of *reflection* or *self-consciousness*. Locke,[1] distinguishing these two main sources of knowledge, called the former "sensation" and the latter "reflection,"—suggesting at the same time however, that the latter "though it be not sense as having nothing to do with external objects," is nevertheless "very like it [sense], and might properly enough be called internal sense". He realizes that it is not sense, because sense, as he understands the term, involves the operation upon the mind (through sense organs) of bodies existing externally, or independently of the mind, and the production of "perception" in the mind thereby. Yet he describes the activity in question in terms of sense, adding the adjective "internal"; the assumption being, apparently, that just as in direct cognition external things act on the mind and produce sensation-percepts, or what he calls "ideas of sensation," so in reflex cognition, where the mind contemplates its own activities, the mind acts upon itself and produces reflection-percepts, or what he calls "ideas of reflection".

Now Kant adopted this description of the facts in terms of "external sense" and "internal sense". For him, however, the term "sense" cannot mean the affecting of physical sense organs by bodies, but the affecting of the mind by things in themselves, *i.e.* things independent of the mind. "External sense" or "outer sense" is then, for Kant, the mind's capacity for receiving impressions ("receptivity of impressions") produced by things independent of the mind, and of becoming thereby aware of mental states or appearances or phenomena : the supposed things in themselves remaining unknowable. So too, the mind, in order to perceive itself and its own states or activities, must be affected by itself, by its own states or activities : it must have a capacity to be affected by its own states (parallel to its capacity to be affected by things independent of itself), and this capacity Kant

[1] *Essay*, ii., 1, §§ 2-4.

calls the internal sense.   Moreover, if the external sense does
not reveal things, but only sensations or representations or appearances produced by things, so too the internal sense cannot
reveal the mind itself or its states or activities, but only appearances produced by these : "and since time is a mode of relation
of these appearances, it is a determination not of ourselves [the
real or transcendental *Ego*], but only of the appearances due
to ourselves [the empirical, phenomenal *Ego*]," [1]—just as space is
a determination not of things [the real or transcendental *non-Ego*]
but only of the appearances due to things [the empirical or phenomenal universe]. Thus, then, through "external sense" we do not
know whether things in themselves are either spatial or temporal ;
we know the states or appearances produced by them in the mind
to be spatial, because by the *a priori* form of space we arrange
these appearances spatially ; but by the internal sense we do not
know these mental states to be really and in themselves *temporal*,
for we do not know these mental states *as they are in themselves*,[2]
or *in the real mind :* we only know the representations produced in our minds by these states or activities.   It is only
this second layer, so to speak, of representations—representations of *ourselves*, appearances produced *by the action of our own
mental states* upon our minds—that we can know to be really
temporal : inasmuch as time is the *a priori* form under which
alone *all* mental activities, states, appearances, etc., can be perceived or apprehended.

Now it will be manifest to anyone who follows Kant's line of
thought, as just indicated, that on his own principles he could
have had absolutely no ground for distinguishing between "external" and " internal " sense.   For, manifestly, if we cannot
know our real selves or minds, any more than real things, we
have no means of determining whether any given representation is due to " things " or to our "selves ".   To be consistent
he should ascribe *all* representations alike to "unknowable
reality," and recognize the mind's inability to distinguish this
latter into a transcendental *Ego* and a transcendental *non-Ego*, and
consequently to distinguish between "internal" and " external "
sense.

---

[1] PRICHARD, *op. cit.*, p. 107.

[2] Therefore it should follow that we do not know even these " phenomena " or
"mental appearances " to be *in themselves spatial :* it is only our (*a priori* " temporal ") representations of these representations that we could really know to be
(both) spatial (and temporal).

Not only, however, is the distinction between "external" and "internal" sense incompatible with the general theory that reality is in itself unknowable. It can also be shown, and this is more important still, that Kant's doctrine on the ideal or phenomenal character of space, and the consequent unknow-ability of *things* in themselves, *rests on the assumption that we can at least know our own minds, or our own mental states, as they really are in themselves,*—an assumption which, nevertheless, he flatly contradicts by his contention that time is an *a priori* form whereby alone we can perceive our own minds and their states *not as they really are,* but only as they appear under this form. For why does Kant hold that we cannot know things in them-selves, but only the "mental appearances" produced by them? Why does he hold that *space* cannot be a determination of things in themselves, but can only be a determination of phenomena or mental appearances? Because he accepts unquestioningly the fundamental postulate of Idealism that the mind cannot trans-cend itself to know the extramental, or what is independent of mind. But this at least implies that the mind *can* know the intramental, or what is dependent on mind, *i.e.* can know its own conscious states, representations, etc., *as these really are.* Other-wise what right has he to assert that *space* is mental?—or that any of the other supposed *a priori* factors of knowledge are mental? Therefore it appears that the mind can know its own states as they really are. But temporal succession is an essential characteristic of these states; therefore, since they are real, and are known as real, time, which is a characteristic of them, is likewise real, and is not merely an *a priori* form or mode under which or in which they are perceived.[1]

---

[1] *Cf.* Kant's own formulation of the argument as a difficulty against his doctrine of the *a priori* character of time: "Changes are real (this is proved by the change of our own representations, even if all external phenomena and their changes be denied). Changes, however, are possible in time only, and therefore time must be something real."—*Critique,* p. 29. And he rightly points out that the reason why people urge the objection particularly against the *a priori* character of *time* is that whatever about the extramental reality of *external, spatial* objects, "the reality of the object of our internal perceptions (the perception of my own self and of my own states) is clear immediately through our consciousness. The former might be merely phenomenal ['blosser Schein,' 'mere illusion'—*cf.* PRICHARD, p. 113], but the latter, according to their opinion, is undeniably something real."—*Critique,* p. 30. He thinks he answers the difficulty by pointing out that time *is* real as a *real* form of *our perception* of our own states: but the difficulty is that his own view of space as a form not of things but only of mental representations, implies that time is a real form and real characteristic of these representations themselves,

If, on the other hand, we do not and cannot know the real mind and its real states (and *time* as a real characteristic of them), then (1) we have no intelligible ground for distinguishing in knowledge some factors as belonging to (and contributed by) the mind or knowing subject, from other factors as belonging to (and contributed by) the supposed extramental reality in contrast with the knowing subject; and (2) even if we do inconsistently make the distinction, it would appear that what we can *know* is neither (*a*) real things, nor (*b*) our mental *spatial* arrangements of *sensations* supposed to be caused by such things, nor (*c*) any other *real* state whatsoever of our own minds, but (*d*) only *temporal* mental arrangements which constitute the empirical or phenomenal *Ego*, and which are arrangements of *spatial* sensations, these in turn (being now both temporal and spatial) constituting the phenomenal universe or *non-Ego*. Or rather, to be accurate we should say that all we have comprehended under the last head (*d*) is not itself *known*, but furnishes only the *data* or *material* of knowledge: since what we really *know* is a

and not merely of our perception of them. And from this difficulty there is really no escape for him: unless indeed by withdrawing his contention that space is a characteristic merely of mind-dependent appearances, and at the same time withdrawing the idealistic principle underlying it, *viz.* that the mind cannot know things or realities independent of itself,—in other words, by abandoning his general theory. *Cf.* MAHER, *Psychology* (4th edit.), p. 120: "A conscious state cannot have any *existence-in-itself* apart from what it is apprehended to be. Its *esse* is *percipi*. Since, then, mental states are as they are apprehended, and since they are apprehended as successive, they must form a real succession *in-themselves*. They cannot be timeless as they are non-spatial. But if so Kant's 'form of the internal sense'—the intuition of time—is extinguished." And Maher further argues that therefore time-succession must likewise be a real characteristic of the extramental world which causes these successive states: "As . . . there is a *real succession* in our ideas there is a true correlate to the notion of time. A sequence of changes being once admitted in our conscious states, an analogous succession of alterations cannot be denied to the external reality which acts upon us, and so we are justified in maintaining the objective reality of the notion"—p. 120. *Cf. ibid.*, pp. 474·5: "Consciousness affords at all events an *immediate* knowledge of my states and of myself in those states. There is no room for appearances or phenomena here; the mind, the object of knowledge, is really immediately *present* to itself."

In accordance with the view that time is an *a priori* form under which alone we can apprehend all mental representations whatsoever, Kant holds that "the concept of change, and with it the concept of motion (as change of place) is possible only through and in the representation of time; and that, if this representation were not intuitive (internal) *a priori*, no concept, whatever it be, could make us understand the possibility of change".—*Critique*, p. 721. This is an inversion of the facts. Time, apprehended in the manner in which Kant deals with it, is not a percept at all, but an abstract concept; and it is a concept based upon, and derived from, our perception of motion or change. *Cf. Ontology*, § 85, pp. 322-8.

synthesis of these mental materials with the *a priori* concepts *of the understanding*.

The argument, then, against Kant's view that time is an *a priori* form of our perception of our own mental states or activities, or, in other words, that it is a "form of internal sense intuition," is briefly this, that his own proof of the *phenomenality* of *space* (if we may coin the expression) implies the *reality* of *time*. As Prichard puts it, " Kant must at least concede that *we* undergo a succession of changing states, even if he holds that *things*, being independent of the mind, cannot be shown to undergo such a succession ; consequently he ought to allow that time is not a way in which we apprehend ourselves, but a real feature of our real states ".[1] Or, finally, to put the argument in the converse way, if Kant will not allow that we can apprehend any " real feature of our real states," or that we can therefore know time to be such, then he destroys the ground of his own contention that space is not a characteristic of things but only of mental representations or phenomena, for the ground of this contention is that whereas we cannot know things that are "external" or "independent of the mind," as they really are, we *can* know states that are "internal" or "dependent on the mind," as these states really are.

One final and fatal flaw in Kant's thesis that time is a form of our perceptions of events is this. He himself is forced to recognize that some temporal relations belong to the *physical events* which we perceive : that there are, in these, temporal successions, which, by virtue of their irreversibility, differ from mere successions of our perceptions : that we can apprehend this distinction in general, and apply it in detail so as to appre-hend some successions (*e.g.* that of the moon moving round the earth), as objective, from other successions (*e.g.* of our impres-sions as we survey the parts of a house), as subjective (*cf.* § 93). Hence time would not be a form or character of our perceptions exclusively, but also of things perceived. Of course if Kant were consistent he should see that his theory, by identifying perceptions with things perceived, makes it impossible to appre-hend, either in general or in detail, any such distinction between two classes of temporal successions.[2]

---

[1] *Op. cit.*, p. 114.   [2] *Cf.* PRICHARD, *op. cit*, p. 139.

PART V.

TRUTH AND CERTITUDE: THEIR CRITERIA AND MOTIVES.

CHAPTER XXII.

RETROSPECT. RELATIVIST THEORIES OF KNOWLEDGE.

135. THE RELATIVITY OF KNOWLEDGE. TRUE AND
FALSE RELATIVISMS.—The relativity involved in our *sense perception* of material reality (118, 121, 126) suggests the analogous
question as to whether there is also a relativity involved in *intellectual thought, i.e.* in conception and judgment, or knowledge
proper. There is one obvious sense, already indicated (126) in
which whatever is known intellectually must be relative to the
knower: in the sense, namely, that in order to be known it must
be manifested, or set in relation, or cognitively united, to the
intellect ; and that it can be known only in the measure in which
it is so manifested.

But sensist philosophers maintain that intellectual cognition
is of the same order as sense awareness (83-85); that, therefore,
just as the domain beyond sense consciousness is transformed by
a subjective factor in *perception*, so that we perceive it otherwise
than it is independently of conscious perception, so too this
domain, having been transformed by the subjective factor in the
process of *conception*, is conceived and judged intellectually,
otherwise than it is really and extramentally ; and that the *necessity* which characterizes our abstract judgments of the ideal
order is a merely subjective, psychological necessity, wholly relative to, and produced by, the *de facto* constitution of our minds
(40-44) : the upshot of which would be that all our intellectual
knowledge is relative in the sense that it can attain only to
subjectively wrought mental appearances of reality, and not at

all to reality as it is. This is the Positivist form of Relativism, as propounded by Comte, Mill, Spencer, Huxley, etc.[1]

Then, too, Kant and his followers have given such an account of the way in which objects arise in consciousness, and of the mental conditions under which they are perceived by sense and interpreted by intellect, that all objects of knowledge are made out to be mental products of subjective factors which so modify the extramental reality given in our cognitive processes that this reality cannot be known as it really is. If, therefore, our mental constitution and forms were different from what they are the known product would be likewise different from what it is : which is relativism in the sceptical or subjectivist sense over again.[2]

We, on the other hand, have repeatedly emphasized the fact (43, 44) that while *sense data* are partially dependent, for the qualities they reveal to consciousness, on the subjective factor which is the perceiver's own organic constitution, and are relative to this latter, so that *e.g.* sugar could conceivably taste bitter, or snow appear red, if our organic constitution as sentient beings were other than it is, on the other hand certain *objects of intellect* —*viz.* abstract relations between objective concepts abstracted from sense data,—are necessarily such as we judge them to be,— *e.g.* " the whole is greater than its part," " two and two are four," etc.,—not for *our* intellects alone, or *relatively* to our intellects merely, or because our intellects are so constituted, but *absolutely* and for all conceivable intellects (44). In other words, we have contended that through abstract intellectual conception and interpretation of concrete sense data, and intellectual inference from such data, we can attain to a knowledge which, as far as it goes and as far as it is true, attains to what reality is *absolutely*, *i.e.* not merely to how reality appears to *our* intellects, or to how it is *relatively* to the actual constitution of our intellects, but to what it is in itself, and what it must therefore be for *all* intellects.[3]

---

[1] *Cf.* JEANNIÈRE, *op. cit.*, p. 316.   [2] *Ibid.*, p. 317.

[3] Of course if there be other orders of finite intellects, besides the human intellect, *e.g.* purely spiritual intelligences, we can conceive their manner of apprehending reality only after the analogy of the human intellect : just as we can conceive the Divine Knowledge of reality only negatively and analogically by eliminating the imperfections of our own human mode of understanding (74). Pure spiritual intelligences would not have knowledge by abstract conception from data coming through organic sense channels, or by analytic and synthetic processes of judgment, or by discursive reasoning, but by some more perfect, more direct and intuitive, apprehension of the real (p. 15, n. 3). Their conceptions of reality, if we can so speak of them, would not be abstractive elaborations like ours. We have no positive con-

Now this contention is quite compatible with holding that the reason why we judge material reality to have such and such qualities is partly because our bodily sense organs (which are a part of material reality) are so constituted as to reveal these qualities to our intellects ; and with holding that if we had bodily sense organs otherwise constituted (or if material reality, of which they are portion, were otherwise constituted) we should apprehend material reality as having other qualities. Moreover, the contention is not independent of the assumption that all human intellects are similarly constituted, are of the same general order : the reason why men generally employ the same processes, and make use of the same ultimate concepts, in their interpretation of reality, is not only because the realities which are *objects* of intellectual knowledge manifests themselves similarly to all human intellects, but because the realities which are *subjects* of this knowledge, *viz.* human intellects themselves, are of the same order, or uniform in all men.[1] But the contention that intellectual knowledge can attain (inadequately of course) to the nature of reality as it is extramentally, does imply that this latter, as it manifests itself to, and is interpreted by, intellect, is not " moulded," " metamorphosed," " transformed," in the very pro-

---

ception of the nature of the purely spiritual cognitive processes whereby they would (intellectually) apprehend material reality with its spatial extension, solidity, shape, number, and other sense qualities; or by which they would apprehend our human conceptions and interpretations of material reality. What we mean, therefore, by saying that our *necessary* judgments are necessarily true for *all* intelligences is that such judgments so faithfully represent the nature of reality that by no intelligence, not even the Divine Intelligence, could reality be so apprehended as that our knowledge of it would appear false, that *e.g.* two and two would not be four, or the whole not be greater than its part.

[1] Nevertheless the ultimate reason why any individual man assents to immediately evident facts and principles, such as " I exist," " The whole is greater than its part," etc., as revealing to him *the existence and nature of reality*, is not because he finds all other men forming them and assenting to them (which would involve a vicious circle), but because he is conscious that reality forces these interpretations of itself upon *his* intellect, and because reflection shows him that there are on the side of his intellect no subjective factors the influence of which would cause his intellect to represent the reality otherwise than it is extramentally. If an individual man happens to have any *sense* faculty the organic structure and function of which are abnormal, —so that, *e.g.* a field of poppies appears to him as green,—he can, by reflection on his experiences, and comparison of them with those of other men, discover the defect and make allowance for it. If, however, the exercise of his *intellectual* faculty of interpretation and reflection is through any cause impeded, and therefore abnormal, so that he forms and asserts judgments that are manifestly self-contradictory or false, —as, *e.g.* that he is dead, or that he is a snake, or that his head is larger than his body,—he has obviously lost the power of exercising aright his intellectual faculty of judgment and reflection, and is, as we say, "mentally deranged," a "victim of delusions," " insane " (*cf.* §§ 119, 122, 126, *supra*).

cess of intellectual cognition, by any *mental* factors of which intellect is unaware, and for the influence of which, therefore, it cannot make allowance.[1]

This contention we have already vindicated, not by maintaining that the intellect passively and intuitively mirrors reality, for it does not; or by denying that it has specific modes or processes of cognition wherein it necessarily constructs purely subjective logical entities, *entia rationis*, and apprehends the real only through their instrumentality, for it has such modes (conception, abstraction, generalization, judgment, comparison, inference), and it does construct such purely subjective entities (abstractness, universality, and logical relations of all sorts); but by showing, on the one hand, that through the exercise of its power of reflective introspection on its own cognitive processes it can and does discriminate between the *real* which is *given* it to interpret, and its own subjective products, the various logical relations whereby it carries on this interpretation, *so that these subjective, "constructive" or "constitutive" factors of intellectual cognition do not unconsciously fuse with, and transform or transfigure,* the extramental reality which is given to intellect and which intellect interprets by means of them; and by showing, on the other hand, as against Kantism, that the various thought-objects which intellect comes into possession of through conscious experience, *i.e.* the (ultimate) empirical concepts or categories, and their intellectually apprehended differences, are furnished to consciousness not by an unconscious, subjective elaboration-process gratuitously ascribed to factors of the real or transcendental intellect, and supposed to be wrought upon a "given," extramental, and therefore transcendental and unknowable non-self reality, but that they are furnished by, and are manifestations of, this extramental reality itself.

[1] *Cf. Ontology,* § 3, p. 45; § 36, p. 140 n.; § 37, pp. 145-6; § 89, pp. 339-40; § 93, pp. 355-6. "It is true . . . that *if* the reality, or realities, which form the 'materials' of our knowledge, *were* 'metamorphosed' in the process of our 'knowing' them, our knowledge of them would be deceptive and misleading; nay, more, it is even true that though they were not *de facto* so 'metamorphosed,' still, if they *might be,* without our being aware of the metamorphosis, our knowledge would by this possibility be rendered entirely suspect—mere unreliable guesswork. But, then, we may fairly ask, have Kant's disciples any ground whatsoever for such a suspicion—any more than Descartes had for his suspicion that he might have been the sport of some malicious sprite rather than the creature of an All-Wise Creator?"—Art. "Appearance and Reality," *Irish Ecclesiastical Record,* Nov. 1908, p. 476.

14 *

136. EPISTEMOLOGICAL SIGNIFICANCE OF DISTINCTION
BETWEEN SENSE AND INTELLECT.—But, having thus justified
our rejection of the idealist form of relativism, it will be convenient here to meet explicitly the question, How is it that
although the modes in which material reality appear to *sense
consciousness* are partly relative to, and dependent on, subjective
sense factors, the modes which such reality are judged really to
have by *intellect*, and in general the characters ascribed by *intellectual knowledge* to *all* reality, whether in contingent judgments
concerning the existence of reality[1] or in necessary judgments
concerning its nature, appertain to these realities as they are
absolutely, independently of their being known, and do not rather
partly belong to the intellect, thus characterizing not the extramental reality as it really is, but only as it is "transformed" by
intellect,—which would be Idealism.

In the first place, then, it must be noted that mere sense
awareness or sense perception is not *knowledge ;* that it only
furnishes the data, the materials of knowledge, the data for
interpretation ; that knowledge begins with judgment or interpretation ; that mere sense awareness is not *knowledge* even of
the bare existence of something ; that *knowledge* of existence
begins with the *predication* of existence, and thus supposes the
intellectual concept of existence ; and that, *a fortiori*, knowledge
of the nature or essence of anything also involves intellectual
judgments, predicates, concepts.   We have already referred
(77) to the difficulty of separating, even by an effort of abstraction, the purely sense elements in our complex cognitive
experience, from the intellectual factors ; and we have noted
especially (114) the danger of confounding our *concepts* of the
sense qualities, particularly of the primary sense qualities, with
our *percepts* of these qualities, or with these qualities as perceived.   Yet if we are to analyse our cognitive experience
effectively we must make this effort of abstraction.

Secondly, we must not forget that it is by *intellectual* introspection, and by means of *concepts*, that we have been investigating our sensuous perceptive processes, and envisaging the
inarticulate, uninterpreted stream of conscious data presented
through those processes.

Thirdly, if there be a relativity of those sense data to the

---

[1] *I.e.* of contingent reality ; and in the one *necessary existential* judgment concerning the existence of the Necessary, Self-Existent Being.

self as perceiver, if they depend partially, for the qualities they reveal to sense consciousness, on the perceiver, this relativity and dependence are not unconscious; we are not unaware of it; we have discovered it by investigation of our perceptive processes. Such relativity and dependence, therefore, cannot mislead or deceive, cannot vitiate our *knowledge* of the sense qualities : we are aware of it and allow for it in our intellectual interpretation of the real nature of those sense qualities.

Fourthly, looking at this dependence of sense data and their qualities on the subjective or "self" factor in perception, and their consequent relativity to the self, we find that it is not a dependence of those data and their qualities on the self *as conscious*, or a relativity of them to the self as subject *of awareness*, but that it is a dependence of them on the self *as organic*, and a relativity of them to the organic structure and constitution and conditions of *the material or bodily sense organs* whereby they are revealed to consciousness. The relation of dependence is not between the mental and the extramental, between the subject and the object of awareness : both terms of the relation are extramental in the sense of objective to consciousness ; for the terms of the relation of dependence are respectively the whole domain of sense data and their qualities, the whole domain of "material" reality, on the one hand, and the special portion of this domain which is the perceiver's own body or sense organon on the other hand. The "subjective" or "self" factor, therefore to which perceived sense data and their qualities are "relative," and on which they are partially dependent for their perceived characters, is not a *mental* factor at all, not a factor of the self or subject *as cognitive*, but is a factor of that portion of *material* reality which is interpreted by intellect to be united, in the individuality of the human person, with the conscious, cognitive principle or "mind" of the knowing subject, and to be the extramental, material organon which directly subserves the process of sense perception, and the channel through which sense consciousness has immediately presented to it *all* sense data and qualities, both organic or "internal" and extra-organic or "external". Thus we see that the partial "subjectivity" of sense data and their qualities is not at all a "mental" subjectivity arising from any mental but sub-conscious (or *a priori*, *transcendental*) factors of the constitution of the self *as cognitive*, but that it is an "extramental" subjectivity arising from the *known and experienced* constitution of the self or subject *as organic.*

Idealists, of course, assuming both the organic and the extra-organic sense data to be psychic or mental states, must necessarily hold that the relativity and dependence in question have reference to *mental* factors of the conscious subject : and whether their *intellectual interpretation* of the whole matter is right, or the realist's intellectual interpretation, will depend on the verdict pronounced by introspective analysis of our *concepts*, regarding the *validity* (and the *origin* and *nature*, as throwing light on the validity) of these latter. But even some of the realist supporters of the theory of mediate sense perception appear to regard the relativity of perceived sense data and qualities as a relativity to *mental* factors of the perceiver (125, 127) ; or at least to miss the significance of the fact that the relativity is to subjective *organic* factors, and not to subjective *mental* factors, of the perceiver.

Fifthly, if sense data and their qualities *as perceived by sense* are relative to and dependent on merely the *organic* factors, but are not relative to or dependent on any *mental* factors of the conscious subject, neither are those sense data or qualities *as conceived by intellect* relative to any mental factors of the con-scious subject. While sense becomes aware of objects only through the functioning of bodily sense organs,—the sense faculties being organic faculties, so that perceptive acts are at once conscious (or mental) and organic (or bodily),—intellect apprehends objects by a cognitive process which is not organic, which is not the act of a bodily or material organ at all, which is "spiritual," *i.e.* subjectively independent of the organic con-stitution of the thinking and judging human subject. But intellect is a faculty of the same individual mind or soul which animates the body, and which, as animating the body, is also endowed with organic sense faculties. The objects, therefore, which intellect first apprehends, and which first stimulate *thought*, —*i.e.* conception, reflection, comparison, interpretation, inference, —are furnished to it by sense, are already data of our direct sense awareness. These it apprehends in a manner altogether foreign to sense : it can apprehend in them what sense cannot : for sense they are mere objects of awareness ; intellect can apprehend *what they are :* it can *reflect* on them, on how they came into consciousness, on the nature and conditions of the perception process ; and in judging *what they are* it can and does take cognizance of their partial dependence on the organism for what they appear to sense consciousness. It can thus judge *what they are really* because it can apprehend them apart from all the "material" qualities which characterize them as concrete, individual, felt data of sense consciousness; nay, every one of these felt characteristics themselves it can envisage *in the abstract* and thus apprehend *what each is*, naming them as "taste," "red-ness," "sound," "heat," "motion," "extensity," "plurality," "in-ternality" or "selfness," "externality" or "otherness," etc., etc.[1]

Furthermore, it can *reflect* on the concrete sense data, on the way they appear to sense-consciousness, on its own mode of apprehending them in the abstract, on the concrete data of direct intellectual consciousness (100), on the objects which by its own activity it discovers in and through those immediate data of consciousness,—thought-objects or objective concepts such as "being," "existence," "substance," "cause," "action," "re-lation," "matter," "spirit," "time," "space," etc., etc.; and it can see that while sense, in so far as it apprehends these objects, cannot interpret them, or apprehend them as such, but is merely aware of a chaotic, ever-changing domain of being, in which these realities are, but are for sense unmeaning and uninterpreted, intellect alone can apprehend *what these objects really are*, can give them a meaning, and can thereby attain to a *knowledge*, an

[1] And why? Because intellect is itself not a mere organic faculty of awareness (awareness of a something which no mere sense faculty can even know to be " material," but which is really material because *intellect* apprehends and interprets it to be really all that we understand by the "material" mode of being), but a faculty *cognitive of reality*, a faculty which apprehends real being *as such*, a " spiritual " faculty, therefore, which in its mode of apprehension transcends the mere inarticulate, brute mode of sense awareness, and "cognitively" possesses or apprehends its objects untrammelled by the organic factor of sense, so that *it knows* by reflection that they appear to it as they really are. All cognition, all awareness, is a reception of an object in a subject, an " apprehension " or " cognitive possession " of an object by a subject. The mode of apprehension, therefore, is determined by the nature, the mode of being, of the subject: *Quidquid recipitur, secundum modum recipientis recipitur.* Reflecting on *sense perception* and on *intellectual conception and interpretation*, we see that sense, being a conscious faculty of an organic, corporeal, material subject, can cognitively appropriate or apprehend reality only in so far as this is material, or characterized by the modes which characterize the perceiving subject as organic, that on the part of the sentient subject it is a mere direct awareness of sense data (some of which are subjective or organic and others extra-subjective or extra-organic) but is devoid of *reflection* or conscious *discrimination* or *recognition* or *interpretation* of them as subjective or objective; while *intellect*, being immaterial or spiritual, transcends the material mode of mere sense awareness, is not subjectively limited by organic factors, and therefore apprehends immaterially and apart from their material, concrete, sense qualities, the *real being* of material data, and apprehends also, in and through these, both the reality of these material modes of being themselves, and other really immaterial modes of being which lie entirely beyond the range of sense.

interpretation of the reality of this sense domain, the reality of the self as sentient and rational, and the reality of a domain of being which, though not accessible to sense, can be rationally inferred from the domain of sense as interpreted by intellect.

137. VALIDITY OF CONCEPTS REVIEWED.—Now, of course the really crucial question concerning the significance or knowledge-value of those intellectual processes is this: Are the elementary thought-objects or root-concepts,[1] which intellect employs in these processes, revelations or manifestations of the objectively and extramentally real?[2]   In other words, are they

[1] On the nature and value of these depends of course the knowledge-value of the *more complex* generic and specific concepts which intellect elaborates by the analytic and synthetic process of judgment.   (*Cf.* vol. i., § 73, p. 259.)

[2] We are quite aware that the analysis given above is based upon concepts, is carried on by means of concepts, is a series of inferences from concepts, and is therefore a procedure of the "dogmatic" order, which Kant *professes to deprecate as an invalid procedure* in epistemology, and which he *professes to reject* in favour of the "critical" or "transcendental" method of arguing from the subjective, *a priori* conditions of the possibility of concepts (*cf.* vol. i., p. 359, n. 5; PRICHARD, *op. cit.*, pp. 274-5, 300).   But he must have *concepts* of what these conditions are; and so, as we have seen (*ibid.*), his method in no way differs from the "dogmatic" method which he deprecates.   Nor could it; for no rational investigation can be carried on in any sphere except by using, and arguing from, concepts.   To endeavour to investigate the validity of intellectual knowledge without using concepts is even more absurd than endeavouring to determine the competence of a telescope for its work before turning it on the stars (PRICHARD, *op. cit.*, p. 3; vol. i., p. 209); for it amounts to undertaking a rational investigation without using one's reason.   It is impossible for anyone undertaking to investigate the validity and scope and limits of knowledge to blink the fact that throughout this testing process he has got to use the very instruments into the competence of which he is inquiring,—his own human powers and modes of perception, conception, judgment, reasoning, etc.   Nor can he explore the nature, origin, and validity of those root-concepts or categories on which the significance and worth of all his knowledge depend, without actually using those same concepts or categories in the process of critical introspection itself.   If, then, provisionally assuming his conceptions to be valid and their objects to be real, he finds that reflection justifies this assumption, he has attained to philosophical certitude.   Were he, even provisionally, to assume the opposite, he could not consistently take a single step forward in reflective introspection (*cf.* chap. iii.).   In order to get to work at all he must provisionally assume at least some of his conceptions, some of his modes of thought, some lines of investigation, to be valid, *i.e.* to reveal to him what is *true*, what is *really so*, what is *real:* as Kant, for instance, must have assumed the particular conceptions and modes of thought and lines of inference which he used in his *Critique*, to be valid; else of what value are the conclusions of the *Critique?* (*cf.* § 59).   On the other hand, should reflection, unfortunately, issue in a real doubt about the lawfulness of that provisional assumption, and about the possibility of justifying any of his spontaneous convictions, he will have fallen into theoretical scepticism (§§ 30, 31).   And should he persuade himself, as Kantists apparently do, that the concepts which he employs in the "theoretical" or "speculative" use of his reason *do not reveal reality*, it is not easy to see how he can persuade himself that the concepts he used in reaching this conclusion *are* valid,

given to the knowing mind or intellect in and with and through the direct data of sense consciousness, data which are intellectually interpreted by means of those concepts as constituting a real material universe, partly extra-subjective or extra-organic and partly subjective but organic ; and in and with and through the direct data of intellect itself, data interpreted by means of these concepts as constituting a suprasensible, rational, or intellectual knowing subject ?   Or again, in other words, can intellect convince itself, by introspective reflection, that reality, in the process of manifesting or revealing itself to intellect, and thus entering into cognitive relation or union with intellect, can present itself as it really is, so that intellect can distinguish reality *as it really is* from any subjective intellectual modes or relations which are added to it, on its presentation, from the side of the intellect, and which necessarily attach to the reality *as it is known*,—so that when intellect has thus discriminated between the *ens reale* and its own *entia rationis* in interpreting the real it can *ignore the relation of reality to itself*, as not transforming this reality in some unascertainable way and so for ever screening it off from intellect, but as allowing the reality to manifest itself as it is?   *Or, on the contrary*, do those elementary thought-objects, instead of being given to intellect objectively in and with the uninterpreted world that appears to direct consciousness, *come up into the conscious domain subjectively* and *from the side of the intellect itself*, where they must be latent as unconscious cognitive grooves or conditions, and emerge into consciousness only by uniting with the " extramental," objectively " given " world, to form a " product " which is neither *really* subjective nor *really* objective, neither *real* self nor *real* non-self, but is a *tertium quid* to which we give the title of "phenomenon" because it alone "appears" or "manifests itself" to the knowing mind in conscious experience?   This is the alternative embraced by Kantism ; and obviously if it be an accurate interpretation of the process of intellectual cognition the world known through such a process is relative to unknown and unknowable subjective mental factors in such a sense that the " known world " cannot possibly be the *real world as it really is*.   But where is the evidence for such an interpretation ?   Is it because *sense* cannot apprehend, in the domain which is given in our direct sense awareness, such ob-

and that the concepts which he employs in the " practical " use of his reason are also valid or capable of attaining to *reality as it is* (*cf.* §§ 56, 59).

jects as "existence," "essence," "substance," "cause," "relation," "distinction," "otherness," "externality," "motion,"
"extension," "space," "time," etc., etc.,—because sense cannot
interpret this domain,—because sense cannot *reflect* on its data
and consciously pronounce to itself *what they are*,—is it because
it takes *intellect* to do these things,—is this any reason, adequate
or inadequate, for asserting that these thought-objects are not
really *in* this "given" domain, that intellect is mistaken in thinking it detects them there, that instead of discovering them in this
domain it really projects them into this domain from an unknowable background of its own subjectivity, and that therefore
the whole intellectually known universe is a mere phenomenal
construction built up by the activity of intellectual thought
through the union of unknowable subjective factors of the *real
Ego* with equally unknowable factors of the *real non-Ego*,—a
construction, therefore, by knowing which the intellect does not
and cannot know *reality?*[1]   We must confess that neither in

[1] In every error there is a grain of truth—which makes the error plausible and
pernicious. The Kantian theory of knowledge misconceives, exaggerates and distorts a truth,—the truth, namely, that the human intellect has its specific modes of
apprehending reality, and that these cannot be the modes in which intellects other
than human, if such exist,—pure spiritual intelligences, for instance, not to speak
of the Divine Intellect,—apprehend reality. The human intellect apprehends
reality not intuitively and comprehensively, but piecemeal, discursively, inadequately. The reality directly given to consciousness in the stream of conscious experience it slowly interprets by abstracting partial aspects of this concrete whole:
it is a faculty which abstracts, compares, analyses, and synthesizes, divides, unifies,
generalizes, classifies,—thus forming specific and generic concepts, ultimate categories, and transcendental notions, expressive of the real. To say that intellects of
a different order from the human intellect would have other modes of apprehending
reality, and would apprehend it without our human apparatus of abstraction, conception, comparison, judgment, inference, etc., is not saying or implying that our
human conceptions do not apprehend reality as it really is. Again, *one* reason why
we have such conceptions—in number and in nature as we experience them, *e.g.* the
abstract conceptions known as the ultimate categories,—is of course because our
intellects are so constituted and not otherwise, because they are human intellects,
not angelic or divine. But this again by no means implies that those human conceptions do not reveal reality as it is, or that they reveal it otherwise than it is. It
only implies that we must not attribute the modes of these conceptions,—*i.e.* such
entia rationis as abstractness, universality, conceptual identities and distinctions,
modes of predication, negations and affirmations, and other such conceptual relations,—to the reality which we intellectually apprehend by means of them. And
moreover, there is *the other* reason why these conceptions *reveal the objective contents* which they do actually reveal,—the reason which is the ultimate, and indeed
the only rationally assignable ground of the nature of their actual contents,—*viz.*
that their contents *are real*, are *reality*, and that reality *is so*, and *is known to be so*
because it appears, manifests, and reveals itself so to the intellect conceiving it (135).
But apparently, because our modes of apprehending reality are modes of the human

the considerations just suggested, nor in any we have met else-where, can we see a particle of evidence for such an interpretation. In examining Kant's theory of conception and judgment we have already shown that the process of intellectual analysis which led him to such an interpretation is wholly unwarranted by the facts.[1]

138. TRUTH OF CONTINGENT JUDGMENTS ABSOLUTE.—The elementary thought-objects conceived by intellect, in and through the immediate data of direct consciousness, are therefore real; nor is their reality transformed or disfigured in any unascertain-able manner by any subjective intellectual factors in the process whereby they become related to intellect, and revealed or mani-fested to intellect, as objects of knowledge. Now, those thought-objects (and the more complex generic and specific con-cepts reached by synthesizing them) are employed to interpret (1) the domain of our immediate sense experience (the " material " universe, inorganic and organic,—including the self as organic); (2) the domain of consciousness, mind, sense, and intellect, revealed by intellectual reflection (the self as a conscious, mental, cognitive being or reality); and (3) the suprasensible or intelli-gible realities, and aspects of reality, involved in those two do-mains (*i.e.* the world of our mediate, inferential experience: things not immediately or intuitively apprehended whether by sense or by intellect: inferred realities: the natures and causes of things immediately experienced: suprasensible relations: laws of nature: ultimate efficient and final causes: the First Cause: Necessary Being). But conception is the abstract intellectual apprehension or representation of what is given or

---

intellect, because they have its limitations and are conditioned by its *de facto* con-stitution, because it is conceivable that intellects of another order would have other modes of apprehending reality, Kantists seem to think they have ground for infer-ring that these human modes of conception come between the intellect and reality, necessarily transfigure the reality apprehended, and are therefore not modes whereby the intellect apprehends reality at all, but are rather modes whereby the intellect *is prevented from* apprehending reality ! Kantists, of course, will maintain that this conclusion of theirs is the legitimate and only possible issue of an inquiry into the conditions under which intellect gets its objects. But we have seen that on the one hand the method of procedure which issues in this phenomenism is vitiated by a gratuitous assumption that prejudges the whole investigation, the assumption that mind cannot apprehend the extramental; and that on the other hand the whole inquiry overreaches and contradicts itself by adopting and assuming as valid the distinction between a *real self* and a *real non-self* in a real domain which is declared in the same breath to be absolute'y unknowable (*cf.* § 59).

[1] Chaps. vi., vii., xii.

presented in the concrete in direct consciousness. The abstractly conceived objects, or thought-objects, are identical (*quoad rem*, not *quoad modum*) with the intuitively apprehended data of direct consciousness. Let us therefore consider how it is that when an individual uses those concepts aright, *i.e.* when he forms a true judgment, that which he apprehends through such a judgment and such concepts not merely is *for him*, and relatively *to him*, as it appears to him, but is *really and absolutely and independently of him* as it is represented by him: so that, being really and absolutely so, it must appear similarly to, and be represented similarly by, all other human minds if they conceive and judge aright, and must be so even for all other possible intelligences if they apprehend aright.

Let us take first the concrete, contingent, singular judgments, whereby we assert the existence, and interpret the nature, of any material or sense datum—any portion of " material " reality. A man plucks a rose, holds it in his hand, smells it, and says, " This something which I see and feel and smell is a reality distinct from my conscious perception of it,—is really external to myself, —has the real scent which I smell, the real redness which I see, the real texture which I feel, the real size, shape, position, which I both see and feel ". Assuming that these judgments are really true, what is the meaning of saying that their truth is absolute, that what they assert is really so not merely for him but for all men and all minds? Or in order that this be so, in what sense must these judgments be understood? Asserting that the scent, colour, texture, size, shape, position, are *externally* real, is not asserting that these qualities as perceived are independent of an organic factor internal to him as perceiver; it is, however, asserting that they have an external reality which is independent of this organic factor, which persists even when unperceived, and which appears in the same way to all *normal* perceivers, inasmuch as the influence of the internal organic factor is the same in all other normal perceivers as in the actual individual normal perceiver: not that the external reality of the qualities is asserted merely to consist in their appearing thus to all normal perceivers, but rather to involve their capacity of so appearing and revealing their reality to *human minds* through the actualization of this capacity. Understood in this sense the assertion that such sense qualities are externally real is true absolutely, and not merely relatively to any individual mind which makes the assertion, for it means that their reality is known by the human intellect partially to consist in appearing as external scents, colours, textures, volumes, shapes, positions, etc., to the normal perceiver. Nay, it is true for all possible intelligences: for it does not imply that it is any function of these qualities to appear thus to intelligences of another order, not subserved by human sense organs;[1] but it does imply that whatsoever intelligence apprehends the nature of their reality, of the human subject, and of their mode of apprehension by the human subject, must likewise see that it is a part and function of their reality to appear as they do to the normally constituted human subject. In other words it implies that no intelligence apprehending their reality aright could apprehend in them anything that would contradict, or be incompatible with, this particular function of their reality: and this is true absolutely.

The same is true of our concepts and judgments of *all* sense qualities whether secondary or primary, of spatial and temporal relations, of externality and real distinction from the individual perceiving and knowing self or *Ego*. Any *true* judgment formulated by the individual human mind concerning these, is, when understood in the sense just explained, true *absolutely* and for all conceivable intelligences. Our conception of "externality" itself involves the concepts of "extension," "space" and "relation": it is the abstract intellectual apprehension of concrete, sensuously felt externality. Our concepts of *real* unity, individuality, plurality, identity, and distinction or otherness, are all derived from the data of direct sense consciousness,[2] and are therefore "properly" applicable only to "sensible" or "material" reality : but inasmuch as intellect apprehends them simply as modes of reality, in abstraction from the sensuous modes of their manifestation in direct consciousness (76), it can apply them "analogically" to the positively suprasensible modes of being the reality of which it discovers as necessarily implied by the reality of the data of sense.[3] Now the validity of all such concepts (as distinct from the validity of our concepts of *logical* relations, *entia rationis*) consists in this, that they reveal modes of real being, modes of reality ; and the truth of judgments in which they are rightly used means that reality is as it is interpreted by means of them. It is not meant that all

---

[1] It makes no assertion as to how realities apprehended by *us* through *sense* appear to, or are apprehended by, intelligences not subserved by sense : nor have we any positive and proper conception of the modes in which such intelligences apprehend sense realities,—or indeed suprasensible realities either.

[2] Has intellect any immediate intuition (by reflection on its own processes) of *positively suprasensible* or *spiritual* modes of reality, or are its apprehensions even of its own processes, as objects, apprehensions through concepts the contents of which are furnished by sense consciousness ? *Cf.* §§ 71, 74, 77, 100, 114.

[3] *Cf. Ontology*, §§ 26-8, 31, 34, 35, for the derivation of those concepts from the domain of *sense* reality to the domain of *intelligible* reality,—*i.e.* reality that is immaterial negatively (by abstraction) or positively (in its actual mode of being).

conceivable intelligences (*e.g.* pure spiritual intelligences) must apprehend reality only through such concepts and judgments, but only that by no conceivable intelligences could the realities which *human* intellects apprehend in these ways be truly apprehended as contradictory of, or incompatible with, what true *human* judgments represent these realities to be. Thus, all *true* judgments asserting the existence, qualities, and nature of the real domain, or any portion of the real domain, revealed to intellect through sense, are true absolutely and for all intelligences.

And this is so even of *contingent* judgments which assert or imply the actual existence of the objects interpreted through our concepts. A concept is said to be valid when its object is an *actual* or a *possible* reality. If the object of the concept is asserted, implicitly or explicitly, to exist *actually*, then the concept (carrying this implicit judgment with it) will not be valid, *i.e.* the judgment in which it is used will not be *true*, unless the object of the concept does actually exist, and is not a mere possibility. Now since intellect conceives the data of sense in the abstract, *i.e.* as to *what they are*, and apart from their actual existence, this latter is not included in the content of the abstract concept ; and furthermore, intellect can see that actual existence is not necessarily involved in *what they really are ;* [1] in other words it conceives and judges them to be *contingent* realities. Nevertheless when it judges *truly* that such or such a contingent reality does actually exist, this *contingent* judgment is *absolutely* and *necessarily* true *for all possible intelligences.* In this sense the truth even of contingent judgments is "necessary," "absolute," "universal " ; it is not relative to any individual intelligence but holds good necessarily and for all intelligences : "once true, true forever ".[2]

139. TRUTH OF NECESSARY JUDGMENTS ABSOLUTE.— Finally, over and above the implicit or explicit assertions of (contingent) *de facto* existence which may attach to our thought-objects, over and above the *contingent* judgments, whether individual or general, immediate or mediate, which assert the actual (contingent) existence of the objects we conceive,—we have, by contemplating those abstract thought-objects apart from their existence, and merely as possible essences, a whole domain of those ideal, *absolutely or metaphysically necessary*

---

[1] Through the data of direct experience intellect discovers, as necessarily implied by the actuality of those data, *one* reality to which *actual existence* must belong *essentially* : the Necessary, Self-Existent, Divine Being. But this Being also intellect apprehends only through concepts which, owing to their human mode of abstractness, present their object *without the note of actual existence*, concepts which, applying " properly " only to contingent beings, cannot give us " proper " or "intuitive " insight into the nature of the Necessary Being. " Existence," and "essence " or " nature," are for the human intellect, owing to its abstractive mode of attaining to reality, logically or conceptually distinct thought-objects : they remain so even in our concept of the " Necessarily Existing Essence or Being ": therefore even when seen to be necessarily identified in Him they give us no positive insight into what that Divine Nature must be which is Self-Existent.

[2] *Cf. Science of Logic*, i., § 80, p. 162

judgments, into the real significance of which we have already inquired (chaps. v.-viii.). As we have seen, English Subjectivism misinterprets their character (chap. v.). Kant had a juster appreciation of it; but by locating the ground of the necessity neither in the *non-Ego* as known, nor in the *Ego* as known, but in what he (gratuitously and unwarrantably) distinguished as the *subjective* or *self* domain of transcendental and unknowable reality, he reached an agnostic conclusion which, instead of explaining the character of such judgments, just left the problem where he had found it (chaps. vi., vii.). The Scholastic account of these judgments is that the human intellect can *understand* and *account to itself for* their characteristics of *absolute* necessity, immutability, universality, etc., by seeing that the realities which it apprehends through its concepts are apprehended *in abstraction from all the conditions which attach to the actual mode of their existence as contingent* (chap. viii.).

Does this imply that it is the human intellect that *creates* or *causes* these characteristics of the reality which it thus apprehends? Some would say *No*; for the human intellect itself, no less than all the direct data of consciousness which it apprehends in the abstract, is *a contingent reality*, and can know itself to be such; and no contingent reality can create or cause such properties as the *absolute* necessity, immutability, eternity, universality, etc., which intellect apprehends as characterizing the realities that are its objects : these characteristics, therefore, must be in the intellectually conceived realities, and must be in them *independently of our intellectual modes of apprehension*. But hence arise two difficulties. Firstly, if the realities we conceive by intellect are identically the realities we perceive by sense, such characteristics are certainly not in these realities *as revealed to sense*, but must be in these realities (*i.e.* in the sensible, material, physical universe) and nevertheless remain themselves unrevealed to sense : from which it remains unexplained how or why the intellect can attain to a knowledge of such characteristics.[1] And

---

[1] It is hardly an explanation to point out that the maxim, "*Nihil est in intellectu quod prius non fuerit in sensu*," must be qualified by "*nisi intellectus ipse*" : for this latter means precisely the intellect's own modes of thought, discovered by introspection ; whereas in the view under consideration the characteristics of possible essences (or "necessary" judgments) are *not* due to modes of intellectual apprehension, and are not in these essences *merely as intellectually apprehended* ; and moreover the characteristics in question clearly belong to objects *abstracted by intellect from the domain of sense*, e.g. to *quantitative* or *extensional* thought-objects such as a "whole" compared with its "part".

secondly, if these characteristics of necessity, immutability, eternity, etc., be interpreted not as arising from, and consequent on, our intellectual modes of conceiving and interpreting reality, but as being, so to speak, exclusively ontological, *i.e.* as appertaining to the reality (which is object of our thought) as it actually is, independently of our thought, then it is not easy to avoid the Platonic-Ontologistic inference that the reality which has such characteristics independently of thought, and which presents them to thought, cannot be the reality of the domain revealed to sense at all, but must be the transcendent reality of the Necessary, Eternal, Immutable, Self-Existing, Divine Being (70).

Others, therefore, answer the question proposed above in the affirmative. They say *Yes :* the absolute or metaphysical necessity-and-universality of our abstract judgments arises from the fact that these judgments are (objectively) relations between *aspects* of reality which are *conceived* by intellect *in the abstract*, as *abstract thought-objects* or essences. It is because the human intellect apprehends reality by conceiving it piecemeal, analytically, in abstract aspects, and by comparing, discriminating, and identifying these abstract aspects in judgment, that it sees reality *as so judged and interpreted* to have those *logical* relations— mentally or intellectually *static, fixed, changeless* relations—of identity or diversity, compatibility or incompatibility, when *related as subject and predicate* in our human "judgment"-mode of apprehending the real. They point out that these characteristics of necessity, universality, immutability, etc., are characteristics of "*abstract* essences," *i.e.* of aspects of reality *conceived in the abstract and* RELATED *to one another* IN JUDGMENT; that they are therefore properly characteristics of *judgments ;* that judgment is a mode in which the human intellect apprehends the real; that objectively the judgment reveals a reality, but only *through a logical relation ;* that the reality represented by the judgment is itself neither a "subject" nor a "predicate" nor a "relation between a subject and a predicate": the reality, itself, independently of thought, is not the relation itself, nor is it either term of the relation, for the terms are *abstract* concepts or thought-objects, and "abstractness" too is an *intentio logica*, a product of thought [1]; but the reality is given in, and forms the content of, our concepts; so that if our *complex* concepts are

[1] *Cf. Ontology*, § 87, pp. 334-6.

formed by inter-relating and synthesizing our *most elementary* concepts, and if our concepts are inter-related in judgments *under the influence of objective evidence and in accordance with the exigencies of their objective contents*,[1] these concepts and judgments faithfully represent, and give us a valid (if inadequate) insight into, reality : for *that which reality appears* to the human intellect thus interpreting it in the light of objective evidence is a function of *that which reality is in itself.*

140. SOME RELATIVIST DIFFICULTIES.—I. But now, if this latter view be correct, would it not appear that absolutely necessary judgments of the ideal order give us an insight rather into the constitution of our intellects than into the nature of reality,— just as in Kant's account of them?

Before meeting this objection we may observe, in reference to Kant, that according to his account they do not even give us an insight into the constitution of our own intellects, *i.e.* of the *real* intellect, or the *real Ego*, but only into *our mental representation* of the real *Ego*. And secondly, even waiving that point, his account gratuitously assumes the impossibility of discriminating the subjective or formal or logical elements from the objective or given or real elements in things intellectually known : and we have seen (chap. xii.) the breakdown of his own attempt to trace all the "affinities" which determine the ultimate conceptual divisions and classifications of the categories, to subjective, formal, *a priori* factors of conception. The Scholastic account, on the contrary, vindicates for intellectual reflection the power to discriminate between the *logical* attributes and relations which its own modes of apprehension necessarily attach to the given reality in its interpretation of this reality, and the *modes and attributes of real being*, which it represents to itself through these logical relations.

And now, as to objection itself: such judgments do undoubtedly give us an insight into the nature of our own intellects, but an insight which we get only by reflection. Nor is it true to say that they give in this insight *rather than* an insight into the nature of the reality represented in such judgments ; for what they give us primarily and directly—*e.g.* such judgments as " The whole is greater than its part," " Whatever happens has a cause," etc., etc.—is an insight into the nature of the reality

---

[1] The possibility and sources of *error*, of erroneous interpretations or representations of reality, will be dealt with later on.

represented by the various concepts so related.   And this, finally, is what we have now to fix our attention on.

When we say that such judgments represent *reality as it is*, —that, therefore, reality is *necessarily* as thus represented, inasmuch as it is represented as being *necessarily* such or such,—that these judgments are true not merely for all *human* minds but for *all conceivable intelligences*, that reality *must be* so for all conceivable intelligences,—what do we really mean ?   Do we mean that all conceivable intelligences,—pure spiritual intelligences, or the Divine Mind,—must apprehend reality through our human modes of abstract conception, intellectual analysis and synthesis, relating, comparing, generalizing, predicating or judging, etc. ? that they must have the same qualitative and quantitative concepts as we have? that *e.g.* they can apprehend what we designate " material " reality only through abstract concepts derived from sense qualities?   By no means ; for we have no proper or positive knowledge of the modes in which such intelligences would apprehend reality.[1]   What we do mean is simply that whatsoever intelligence apprehends reality, apprehending human beings and human minds as part of reality, cannot so apprehend it as to see it incompatible with, or contradictory of, its function of being what it is represented to be by human minds in the judgments referred to.   When, for instance, we say that " two and two *must be* four even for the Divine Mind " we do not at all mean that the Divine Mind apprehends reality by comparing abstract, quantitative concepts, but that the Divine mind sees all reality (including human minds) to be such that the human representation of an aspect of reality by the human judgment "two and two must be four " is for the human mind the right and proper representation of that aspect of reality : or sees the reality apprehended by the human mind, and the human mind apprehending it, to be such that a necessary function of reality is to appear to the human mind as it does in such a representation.   And when we reflect on our motive for assenting to the judgment "two and two must be four," and on what such a judgment means for us, we realize (1) that our *motive* for assenting to it is *not* because

---

[1] If, therefore, we consider the way in which the Divine Mind apprehends reality we have to think of the Divine Knowledge after the analogy of human knowledge : we have no other way in which to think of it. We know that our human concepts represent it only analogically and negatively : rather what it is not than what it is. But, allowing for this inadequacy of our concepts, the knowledge they give us is true as far as it goes. *Cf.* vol. i., §§ 66, 74, 75.

our intellect is so constituted (whether by custom or habit, or as a result of evolution, or by virtue of factors operating in an inscrutable domain of the real self) that it is forced to apprehend such a relation between its thought-objects,[1] but because reality, which reveals itself through our concepts, is so constituted that the abstract aspect of it revealed through the concept "two *plus* two" must be really identical with the aspect which reveals itself through the concept "four"; and (2) that its *meaning* is that the reality represented by the judgment is such that it is *rightly* represented in such a judgment by *a mind which has the judgment-mode of representing reality*, and that by no conceivable mind could it be (rightly) so apprehended as to conflict with its being thus represented by the human mind.

II. But—it will still be urged—if the human intellect were otherwise constituted "two *plus* two" might after all appear other than "four," just as sugar may, perhaps, taste not sweet and pleasant, but bitter and unpleasant, to the palates of some of the lower animals (43).

We reply: If by "otherwise constituted" we are to understand "so constituted as not to apprehend reality by means of such abstract concepts as we have *de facto*," then obviously there could be no question of such an intellect apprehending reality by comparing the abstract concept "two *plus* two" with the concept "four," and seeing a relation between them: in that case whatever way it would understand reality it could not so apprehend reality as to see it to be *wrongly* represented in a *human* intellect by such a judgment. If, on the other hand, "otherwise constituted" means simply that such an intellect would have our human modes of conceiving and judging, and could nevertheless judge "two *plus* two" to be other than "four," then it must be denied that such a judgment is possible to such an intellect rationally understanding the concepts in question; and it must furthermore be asserted that were such an intellect

---

[1] *De facto*, of course, the intellect is so constituted that (a) it has its own specific ways of apprehending the real, *e.g.* by abstract conception of the given concrete, by analysis and synthesis, judgment, reasoning, etc., and (b) that the given reality impels it (by cogent objective evidence) to use its judgment-mode of apprehension by applying a certain logical relation, *viz. affirmative* predication, and not its contradictory, to the reality given in the two abstract thought-objects or concepts, "two *plus* two" and "four". But all this is not the motive of our direct assent; it is discovered by reflection; and even when discovered, this knowledge of the real nature, processes and products of intellect does not affect the conviction that the judgment "two and two must be four" is a representation of reality.

per impossibile really to formulate and assent to such a judgment, the judgment would be erroneous, would misinterpret reality.

As to the false analogy drawn from the domain of sense, its misleading character has been already exposed (135-6). Sense does not judge; therefore sense does not *know*: it is incapable either of truth or error: it merely furnishes the materials for knowledge. Intellect alone judges; intellect alone can reflect: in its interpretation of sense data it can see and allow for the influence of the subjective, organic factor on the datum as perceived: it can, moreover, reflect on its own processes, on its own modes of cognition, and on the logical attributes and relations consequent on these modes; and *by distinguishing these from the given and interpreted reality* it can know the latter *as it is*, and can see that its own knowledge is *not vitiated by any intrusion of unknowable subjective factors between itself and the known reality*.

141. SCHOLASTICISM AND KANTIAN RELATIVISM.—The following is another general line of objection which would make out the scholastic theory of knowledge to be just as deeply tinged with subjective relativism as Kant's theory: How can the truth of knowledge be said to be absolute and independent of subjective intellectual factors if the absolute necessity and universality of judgments depend on the fact that the objects related in these judgments are *abstract?* Is not the "abstraction" whereby intellect conceives reality in the form of "abstract" concepts or thought-objects an intellectual function which subjectively moulds or transforms the given extramental reality just as the Kantian "application of the categories" does? Do not scholastics, therefore, by teaching that the necessity and universality of judgments are due to "abstraction," *eo ipso* teach that these characteristics are imposed on the extramental reality by a subjective intellectual function, and are therefore due to the *de facto* constitution of the intellect,—which, were it otherwise constituted, would understand or interpret the *same* reality *otherwise* than it does? And does not all this confirm the view that since in all "cognition" of the extramentally real this reality must be "mentalized" by a positive contribution of subjective or mental factors to the "known object," this object cannot possibly be reality as it is extramentally and independently of such contribution, but must always be a mental product essentially relative to the knowing subject?[1]

[1] *Cf.* JEANNIÈRE, *op. cit.*, p. 198.

From what was said above in reply to the first objection, in addition to our general criticism of Kant's theory, the student will have little difficulty in disposing of this plausible assimilation of the scholastic to the Kantian theory. There are very profound and irreconcilable oppositions between the scholastic theory of "abstraction" and the Kantian theory of the "application of the categories". Abstraction does not add or contribute a positive mental product to the given extramental reality; Kant's *a priori* forms do. Abstractness and consequent universality are logical entities, "*intentiones logicæ*," *modes of cognition*, which are known to be such, and are not attributed by the mind to the known extramental reality that forms the real *content* of our concepts (75, 76); the Kantian categories, on the contrary, are subjective, mental elements not consciously distinguishable from the extramental reality with which they are supposed to combine or blend for the construction or fabrication of the mental product which is the " known object ". From the scholastic theory that reality is known or interpreted by the human intellect only through abstract and universal concepts whose contents are fragmentary and partial aspects of reality, it follows indeed that even the fullest and truest human insight attainable into reality is imperfect and inadequate, but nevertheless that it is a genuine insight into reality in so far as the human judgments constituting it are true; whereas from Kant's theory it follows that our concepts and judgments could give us no insight whatever into reality, that it is simply an *illusion* to suppose that our "knowledge" attains to reality or reveals reality in any measure whatsoever. The scholastic theory imposes no mental characteristics on extramental reality; attributes none of its own subjective modes of cognition to the known and objective extramental reality; and in the necessary " mentalization " of the extramental it sees no process of mental construction or fabrication of a mental product or *tertium quid* distinct from the extramental reality, but simply a revelation, manifestation, presentation of reality to the knowing mind,— a presentation which, however, being gradual, piecemeal, fragmentary, demands that the presented data be *represented, reconstructed, reproduced* mentally, *interpreted, given a meaning*, by the analytic and synthetic processes of conception, judgment and reasoning, by which processes precisely our human understanding of reality is necessarily conditioned and mediated. In

Kant's theory, on the contrary, human knowing or understanding would consist not at all in a mental apprehension of reality, in a revelation of reality to the mind, but in the fabrication of a system of "objects of awareness," "phenomena" or "appearances," by the *a priori, transcendental,* and therefore unknowable co-operation of an unknowable *non-Ego*-reality with an equally unknowable *Ego*-reality, which latter, without knowing either itself or its helpmate, would be merely aware of the fabricated product.

The differences, therefore, between the scholastic and the Kantian theories of knowledge are fundamental in principle and far-reaching in their issues (56). Nevertheless the existence of certain more or less remarkable parallelisms and apparent affinities between the two theories has led to the formation of what might perhaps be called a "right wing" among Kant's followers themselves, and to an attempt on the part of some apologists of the Christian Philosophy of Theism to show that Kant's philosophy is wrongly interpreted by those who see in it the seeds of a subjectivism, relativism, scepticism, agnosticism, utterly incompatible with any intellectually sincere and genuine belief in God or Christianity. But apart altogether from the undeniable historical fact that Kant's philosophy has been almost universally interpreted in this latter sense,—in which it has proved itself a disastrous solvent of Christian faith and morals,—it can easily be shown that the coincidences of certain of Kant's doctrines with those of scholasticism are more apparent than real. And while justice demands full recognition for all that is true in his philosophy, as well as for the undeniable rectitude of his intentions and sincerity of his own religious beliefs, it is certainly more charitable to warn the student that Kant's whole system is indeed what it has been generally interpreted to be, and what it has proved itself to be in fact,—*viz.* a destructive solvent of human certitude,—than to mislead the student by forcing upon that system an interpretation which would read into it a body of sound principles which, unfortunately, are in reality alien to it. The following are the main points urged by those who would favour such an interpretation :—[1]

(a) It is said, for instance, that according to Kant we have *proper* knowledge only of what is found in *sense intuition;* but that scholastics also tell us we have *proper* concepts only of the data of sense : *Nihil est in intellectu quod prius non fuerit in sensu.*

(b) For Kant, all cognition the matter of which (*i.e.* subject and predicate) is not sensible is knowledge only in an *improper sense,* and may rightly be called *faith;* but according to scholastics, similarly, suprasensible realities can be known not *properly* but only *analogically.*

(c) According to Kant the mind has its laws of sense and intellect, laws which it applies to things in order that these be known : in sense perception it apprehends the given by applying to the latter the space-and-time conditions of its own sensibility ; and it interprets or understands sense intuitions by subsuming and synthesizing them under the categories which intellect ap-

[1] *Cf.* JEANNIÈRE, *op. cit.,* pp. 795-8.

plies to them : thus forming from the extramental, according to the laws of its own constitution, the mental domain which it comes to know. But scholasticism likewise teaches that in all cognition the extramental must be "mentalized": *cognitum est in cognoscente, secundum modum cognoscentis* (and *not secundum modum rei*) :[1] that the data of sense are relative to sense : that they are in intellect, yet otherwise than in sense, being there abstract and here concrete : that intellect understands them *componendo et dividendo, i.e.* only as moulded through a system of conceptual relations imposed upon them by intellect in the process of judgment.

(*d*) Kant did not regard the *a priori* forms and categories of cognition as produced by, or dependent on, the individual mind : they may be interpreted as embodied in the constitution of the mind by God. But scholastics likewise teach that the mind has its natural modes of functioning, its forms of knowing, with all their limitations, from the Creator.

(*e*) According to Kant the mind "constructs the object" which it knows ; but this is only another way of saying that the noumenon or extramental reality must be constructed or transposed into a phenomenon, a "something present to the mind," an *object*, in order to be known. But is not scholasticism in substantial agreement with this when it distinguishes between reality as extramental, or in its *esse reale*, and the mental representation, the *esse ideale*, the object present to mind and constituting the term of the mind's awareness ?

(*f*) The Kantian doctrine of the *Critique of Practical Reason*—the doctrine of the autonomy of the will and the categorical imperative—seems, indeed, the antithesis of the ethical teaching of scholasticism. But what Kant really proclaimed was the autonomy of the *Universal Reason*, not of the individual human person. Kant's "categorical imperative" is really a dictate of the Universal Reason, the Divine Intelligence, participated by the human intelligence. What Kant rejected, as incapable of ultimately grounding a moral obligation, was an order coming from a will as such and binding us by way of promise or threat. A promise or a threat can never ground a *duty*, but only a *sanction*. Reason alone can bind the conscience : and ultimately the Divine Reason. But in all this there is nothing antagonistic to, or incompatible with, Christian Ethics. It must, however, be admitted that Kant really, if unintentionally, pointed the way to unbelief by "relegating religion to the domain of personal affective needs and yearnings, and confidences built thereon, while at the same time reducing Christianity to a symbolism which empties the Sacred Scriptures of all dogmatic content ".[2]

In what we have already written the student will find the principles which will enable him to see the futile character of these attempts to reconcile Kantism with philosophical orthodoxy. To answer each of them explicitly here would be tedious and needless repetition. We may merely observe, with Jeannière,[3] that such a novel interpretation of Kantism would sound exceedingly strange to the vast majority of his disciples ; that for them this pretended discovery of Aristotle in Kant would be something like finding

[1] *Cf.* St. Thomas, *Summa Theol.*, I., 85, 5, ad 3,—*apud* Jeannière, *op. cit.*, p. 196, n. 1.

[2] *Cf. ibid.*, p. 197, n. 2.   [3] *Ibid.*, pp. 197-8.

the Koran in the Gospel of St. John ; and that anyhow it will be time enough
for us to reconsider our criticism of Kant when philosophers generally begin
to find Aristotle in his pages.

142. THE EVOLUTIONARY FORM OF RELATIVISM.—We
pointed out above (135) that the absolute character which we
claim for the truth of knowledge presupposes "that all human
intellects are similarly constituted . . . and make use of the
same ultimate concepts. . . ." And we saw that this presupposition, which is justified by experience, does not interfere with the
absolute character of the truth of knowledge (137, p. 218, n).
We also pointed out (136) that the organic relativity of the sense
qualities and nature of external, material reality to the perceiving
subject can be detected by intellectual reflection, and therefore,
being allowed for in our intellectual judgments, cannot destroy
the absolute character of the truth of these judgments. Finally
we emphasized the fact (136) that intellect is not a mere organic
faculty of awareness, but an inorganic or spiritual faculty which
apprehends what the object presented to it really is ;—which,
being spiritual or immaterial, can abstract from, and transcend,
the time-and-space limitations that characterize the concrete
mode of existence of the material things presented to it through
sense ;—which can therefore apprehend, *as they really are*, all the
presented aspects,—the dynamic and kinetic or *changing*, no less
than the *static* aspects, the *becoming* no less than the *being*,—of
the reality that is given to it for interpretation. By *true* intellectual knowledge of reality, interpretation of reality, insight
into reality, we therefore come into conscious, cognitive possession
of the real : so far as we know reality *truly*, we appropriate or
possess it mentally, "*intentionaliter*" ; we become cognitively
assimilated to, or identified with, the real. The individual
human intellect is assimilated to, or identified with, the real
by asserting in the *true* judgment that *what is is*, *what is not is
not*, what is permanent is permanent, what becomes or changes
becomes or changes, etc. In so far, therefore, as the individual
human intellect judges *truly* of the existence or nature of any
presented portion of reality, since by so judging it is so far
assimilated to the real, and since it is absolutely and necessarily
true that "what reality is, that it is," it necessarily follows that
what reality is thus truly pronounced to be by the individual
human intellect, that it must also be for *every* human intellect,

for *all* times and in *all* places : once true, true always and everywhere, and for all intellects.

Now directly opposed to this view of the absolute character of truth or true knowledge there is a widely prevalent form of relativism which extends the concept of "evolution" from the domain of material phenomena, organic and inorganic,—where it has been utilized to explain or render intelligible the distribution in space and succession in time of those physical realities,—to the human mind itself, to all its knowledge and all its objects, to all concepts and categories of the knowable, to all truths whether scientific, philosophical, ethical, or religious. According to this theory no truth or true knowledge is anything absolute or fixed or achieved or unchanging, but, on the contrary, all truth is in a state of continuous "making" or "*fieri*" or evolution : truth is always relative to the actual stage of evolution attained by the individual or by the human race generally : therefore, what is true for men in one age, or at one particular stage of their mental, social, ethical, or religious progress ceases to be true and becomes false and is supplanted by something different from, or even contradictory of and incompatible with, that former truth when men have reached a new stage of development,—the supplanting view or conception being now true for the time, but only to be supplanted in turn by some other conception of things.

The theory is, of course, not applied, even by its most extreme advocates, to the truth of judgments which merely express the existence or happening of things or events : for instance, to judgments formulating historical facts such as the defeat of Napoleon or the assassination of Julius Cæsar or the crucifixion of Christ or the existence of Alexander the Great : the truth of such judgments, they would admit, can never "evolve" into falsity. It is judgments interpreting the nature, meaning, significance, and implications of the "things" and "events" which make up the universe, that they have in mind : and more especially the *philosophical* judgments by which we seek to interpret the *ultimate significance* of human experience as a whole. There is, for instance, scarcely an intelligible sense in which it could be maintained that a stage of mental evolution may some time be reached in which what we now call the "truths" of mathematics would become "false" : the very most the theory might hazard in this direction would be the suggestion that pos-

sibly the human mind and its "objects" might so "evolve" that
the whole category of "quantity," as a mode or form of cognition
or of its objects, would disappear or be worked over into a totally
heterogeneous category of conscious experience. The theory is
more plausible when it points to the succession of scientific conceptions each of which prevailed for a time in the positive or
inductive sciences, only to be cast aside and replaced by others :
but here its plausibility depends on whether such conceptions or
hypotheses were "true" for those who accepted them, and while
they were accepted ; or, in other words, on whether the "truth"
of a judgment consists in its "suitability," on whether a judgment is "true" in so far as it "works,"—a notion of truth on
which we shall have more to say later.   It is, however, to *philosophical* judgments,—metaphyscial, ethical, and religious,—to
judgments regarding the great, outstanding problems of the
origin, nature, and destiny of man and the universe, and to the
religious beliefs and practices of the human race as determined
by such judgments, that the "evolution" theory of truth is
nowadays most persistently applied.   It is contended, for
instance, that although all the great religious (or philosophical and ethical) systems of history,—Confucianism, Buddhism,
Judaism, Christianity, Stoicism, Epicureanism, Mahomedanism,
Naturalism, Rationalism, Pantheism, Positivism, etc.—cannot all
be "true" at the same time, or in the same age and for the same
people, nevertheless each is true for the people who accept it in
the epoch during which it prevails, inasmuch as it harmonizes
with their mentality at that particular stage of their mental
evolution.   And it is suggested, furthermore, that this evolution
of ethical and religious truth is guided by certain spiritual laws
or impulses operating subconsciously in the mentality of the
human race and giving rise at intervals to the appearance of
great religious teachers,—"prophets," "saints," "heroes," etc.,—
who exercise a profound and salutary influence on the religious
beliefs of their fellow-men by elevating these beliefs to a higher
plane in the progressive evolution process.[1]

---

[1] *Cf.* JEANNIÈRE, *op. cit.*, pp. 318 *sqq.* This theory of the relative and evolutionary character of religious truth is the cardinal error of *Modernism*, propounded
by Loisy, Sabatier, Tyrrell, Le Roy, etc., and condemned by the late Pope Pius X.
in the Encyclical *Pascendi* and in the Decree *Lamentabili* (July 3rd, 1907). The
fifty-eighth proposition condemned in the Decree reads : "Veritas non est im-
mutabilis plus quam ipse homo, quippe quae cum ipso, in ipso et per ipsum evolvi-
tur". A modern pragmatist, F. C. SCHILLER, writing in the *Hibbert Journal* on

143. TRUTHS OVERLOOKED OR PERVERTED IN THE EVOLU-
TIONARY THEORY.—Before examining directly this widely prevalent and very erroneous and pernicious theory, let us point out
the principal truths which it has either lost sight of or else misconceived and perverted.

(1) The higher the nature of the knower the more perfect the
mode of cognition : hence the Divine Knowledge, and the knowledge of purely spiritual intelligences such as the angels, are more
perfect than our ·human modes of cognition.

(2) Human knowledge is obviously capable of increase,
growth, development, both in depth and in extent,—*intensive* and
extensive.   This is true both of the individual and of the race.
The universe is constantly yielding up new objects of knowledge
to human investigation.   Moreover, new implications of principles
or truths already known are being incessantly brought to light,
thus increasing the depth or intensity of our knowledge of such
principles.   To this process religious knowledge is no exception.
The Catholic Church recognizes a doctrinal development of
Christian dogma in this sense of a growth of human insight into
the Christian deposit of Divinely Revealed Truth.   It is the
function of Catholic Supernatural Theology to note and to pro-
mote this fuller understanding of the Christian Revelation ; and
nowhere has the character of this development been more clearly
expounded than in the well-known work of Cardinal Newman.
But such growth or development of knowledge, whether secular or
religious, whether scientific or philosophical, does not make knowledge " relative " or " changeable " in the sense (of the theory)
that what is at any time truth or true knowledge can ever become
false or erroneous.   This is too obvious to need enlargement.

(3) Language changes.   Languages progress and decay.
New discoveries necessitate the invention of new technical terms.
The conception of new hypotheses or theories in any domain of
human experience,—in physics, ethics, esthetics, philosophy,

the Encyclical *Pascendi* (October, 1908), rightly observes that Modernism' stands for
more than mere intellectual freedom, that it champions a new conception of truth,
the view, namely, that there is no such thing as absolute truth, and therefore no
such thing as religious dogmas absolutely and definitively true.   Similarly, LOISY,
Autour d'un petit livre (p. 150), writes : " If truth, so far as it is accessible to the
human intellect, were something absolute, and if revelation and dogma partook of
this character ; if not alone the object of knowledge were in itself eternal and immutable, but also the form assumed by that knowledge in human history, then indeed the assertions of the little book are more than rash, they are absurd and
impious ".—*apud* JEANNIÈRE, *l.c.*

religion,—similarly involves the finding of new forms of expression. This implies not only the constant formulation of hypotheses or theories *not yet established as true*, but a variety of *alternative formulations* of admitted facts and familiar truths. But mere change in the modes of formulating knowledge in language does not involve change in the knowledge, and certainly not such change—from true to false, or *vice versa*—as the present relativist theory contemplates.

(4) A widely prevalent and generally received *concept* or *conception* as to the nature of things in some domain of human experience may disappear and give place to a conception which seems a wider, fuller, deeper, more adequate mental apprehension or representation of the nature of the facts. But this by no means implies that the former conception was objectively valid or true and has now ceased to be so. If it was true, and if the new conception is also true, the change merely shows that the former, though true, was not adequate, and that the latter is also true and more adequate. Or it may be that the former, though helpful in many ways, is now discovered to have been false all the time, *i.e.* not to have represented even in an inadequate way the real state of things : as, for instance, the Ptolemaic compared with the Copernican astronomy. Or again, it may be that the new conception, perhaps after proving very useful as a working hypothesis for a time, may be afterwards proved to have been false and may lead to the reinstatement of the old, discarded conception, or some slight modification of it, as embodying after all a more accurate apprehension of the facts. We have an illustration of something like this in the quite recent reinstatement of *emission* theories in the place of *undulation* theories, as explanations of magnetic and electrical phenomena, in physical science. Now all such shifting and changing of hypotheses or conjectural interpretations of things, so far from supporting the view that *truth* or *true knowledge* is subject to change and evolution, rather militates against this view : for why should hypotheses be rejected except because they are discovered not to have been true, not to have been expressive of the real state of things? An hypothesis is a *conjectural* judgment or interpretation which may be true or false, which may be verified or proved erroneous by research.[1] It is therefore of the very nature of an hypothesis, as opposed

---

[1] *Cf. Science of Logic*, ii., Part IV., chap. v. WIND E, *The Church and Science* (London, C.T.S., 1917), chaps. v.-viii.

to an established truth, to be unstable, uncertain, subject to modification or to total rejection.

(5) Knowledge must be distinguished from its effects on men's minds, and on their character and conduct. Different truths' have different values; and the same truth has varying values for different types of mind. A truth which may have a profound influence on human progress at one epoch or in one part of the world may not be appreciated at another epoch or by another section of the human race. All depends on the *preparedness* of men's minds for its reception, on the mentality, the mental receptivity, of the epoch or section of humanity in question. All this is beyond doubt. It implies, however, not that truth or knowledge is itself relative, not that one and the same judgment is true for some and not true for others, or true at one time and not at another, but only that the *practical effects* of a certain item or body of knowledge, or insight into reality, on men's minds and lives, on their manners and customs, on their actions and institutions, vary from age to age and from clime to clime, according to the measure in which, from whatsoever causes, men are able or unable to appropriate the truth or knowledge in question, to give what Newman calls a *real* assent to it, to utilize it and act according to it. The human mind or intellect,—no less than the human will, the moral character, the whole man,—is undoubtedly capable of progress or " evolution," —as also, unfortunately and undeniably, of retrogression and decadence,—by the development, or by the disuse and atrophy, of its capacity of acquiring knowledge, which is its connatural perfection. And whether in the individual or in the community, nation, or society, the actual condition of this mentality, its comparative stagnation or progressiveness, will of course depend mainly on the opportunities offered by the whole intellectual atmosphere or environment. Hence in different parts of the world, and at different epochs in the world's history, we find different stages of intellectual development; and we find that, naturally, human institutions corresponding to one stage of development, and suitable to one state of society, will not adapt themselves to another. In this sense, and in this sense alone, may the human intellect be said to be subject to " evolution "; but evolution in this sense does not in the least imply that knowledge which is true, which represents " that which is," can ever " evolve " into falsity or error.

(6) Because the whole world of our direct cognitive experience is subject to change, because its reality consists not exclusively in "being" ("*esse*") but also in "becoming" ("*fieri*"),
the doubt may be raised whether it does not follow from this, as
a necessary corollary, that the truth of our knowledge also must
be essentially subject to change, and therefore be not absolute
but relative.   But the least reflection will show how groundless
such misgiving is.   For since it is assumed that we *know* the
reality thus experienced to be changing, and that therefore our
knowledge can attain to this process of change and represent it
faithfully (if inadequately), the difficulty is seen at once to be
self-destructive.   For if our knowledge represents any reality as
subject to change, or as actually changing, then in so far forth
as this reality *is* subject to change, or *is* actually changing, our
knowledge represents it aright and is therefore true.

(7) A still more transparent objection to the absolute and
immutable character of truth is that which arises from confusion
of time *in* predication with time *of* predication when there is
question of judgments concerning subjects which change with
time.[1]   Because the judgment "This fire is burning" is now
true, and will be false if repeated to-morrow when the fire will
have ceased burning, it is loosely said that "What is true to-day
will be false to-morrow".   But obviously to-morrow's judgment
will not be false if the predication be made of *the same* subject
as that of to-day's judgment, *i.e.* of the fire as it is to-day ; but to
refer the predicate to-morrow to this same subject, to-morrow's
judgment will have to be formulated in the past tense.   The
truth of a judgment, therefore, is not independent of "time *in*
predication," but it is independent of "the time *of* predication" :
"once true, true for ever".

144. CRITICISM OF THE THEORY.—Turning now to the
"evolutionist" theory of the relativity of knowledge, and granting their full force to the observations just made, we must assert,
in opposition to the theory, that (1) truth cannot vary for different minds, or in other words the same judgment cannot be true
for some men and false for others ; (2) truth cannot vary for
different times or places, or in other words the same judgment
cannot be true at one time or in one place and false at another
time or in another place ; (3) from the very nature of knowledge
and truth it is impossible that the human intellect, as subject

[1] *Cf. Science of Logic,* i., § 80, pp. 161-2.

of knowledge, be essentially, intrinsically, and in its nature so subject to evolution or change that what it once apprehends as true can ever become for it really false. Therefore the evolution theory of the relativity of knowledge is false, and in ultimate analysis unintelligible and destructive of the possibility of knowledge. Let us take up these points briefly and in order.

(1) Knowledge is contained in the true judgment. Now the judgment is a mental synthesis or comparison of concepts which asserts that something *is or is not, is so or is not so*. This affirmation or denial will be true if it be determined by the objective reality, and so represent mentally the real state of things ; otherwise the affirmation or denial will be false. In other words, it will be true if it conforms the mind with reality ; if not it will be false. Now, the reality, the real state of things, can be only *one* state of things ; it cannot be *two* or more mutually contradictory or incompatible states of things : therefore it cannot be truly represented in different minds by different and contradictory or incompatible judgments. Hence if it be known by different minds, *i.e.* truly represented by different minds, this can only be because the different minds are conformed with it by judging, interpreting, representing it *similarly*, by *the same* (affirmative or negative) judgment. Hence if a judgment be true for one mind it must be true for all minds.[1] This, in fact, is an essential property of truth or true knowledge : its *impersonality*, its *objectivity* to the individual mind. There is no knowledge unless there is conformity of thought or judgment with its object, which is reality : and such conformity that this identical thought or judgment arises in *every* mind in the act of knowing the reality which confronts it,—identical in spite of all individual divergences of personal taste or mentality.

(2) Practically the same consideration shows that the truth of a judgment cannot vary with time or place.

In concrete, contingent judgments, *i.e.* judgments of the " real " order (10), which make or imply assertions about matters of contingent fact, about the concrete existence or happening of things or events in time and space, we have seen already that if any such judgment is true, then *by a necessity of fact* it is true for all minds, at all times and in all places. " That Socrates

---

[1] *Cf.* St. Thomas : " Considerandum est quod veritas ex diversitate personarum non variatur, unde cum aliquis veritatem loquitur, vinci non potest, cum quocunque disputat ".—*In Job* xiii., l. 2,—*apud* Jeannière, *op. cit.*, p. 320 n.

existed " is true for all minds.   " That an eclipse of the sun will occur at such or such a date in the future" is likewise true for all minds if it is true for any mind, *i.e,* it is true for all of them alike, conditionally on the present order of the physical universe persisting until the eclipse takes places ; and if this condition be included in the judgment then the judgment is true for all minds absolutely,[1]—assuming, of course, that astronomers are right in the calculations whereby they predict such an eclipse.

In regard to abstract, necessary judgments of the "ideal" order,—*e.g.* the principle of contradiction, the principle of causality, the judgments of pure mathematics,—judgments which, being necessary, therefore hold good universally,—since we have already proved that what is revealed to the intellect through the abstract concepts compared in such judgments is *the nature of the objectively real,* including the nature of the intellect itself and its cognitive processes, it follows that if reality *has* the nature asserted in any such judgment by the individual intellect, in other words, if such a judgment is true, it must be true for all minds at all times and in all places.   For the individual judgment, assumed to be true, asserts that reality is *necessarily* such or such, independently of all actual conditions of the time-and-space mode of existence of reality ; but obviously if reality be necessarily such or such, independently of its actual modes of existence, it cannot be *truly* judged or represented to be otherwise by any mind at any time.

(3) There is a relation of the mind to reality, a relation which is *sui generis,* and which has always been understood to be the relation designated by the terms "cognition" or "knowledge" (6).   Being *sui generis* it cannot properly be defined ; but when we use the term "knowledge" simply and without qualification we mean *true* knowledge : and it has been universally understood to be a sort of mental appropriation or possession of the real, by a process which mentally reproduces or represents the real, and which thereby assimilates or conforms the mind with reality, or, again, which effects a conscious union or identification of the mind with reality.[2]   Now the individual knowing subject has many other relations with reality besides this particular relation ; and this particular kind of relation, or whole collection of such

---

[1] *Cf. Science of Logic,* ii., §§ 250, 257.

[2] *Cf.* St. Thomas : " Intelligibile in actu et intellectus in actu unum sunt " " Mens cognoscendo quodammodo fit omnia ".

relations, is one of a vast multitude of conditions,—processes, habits, and attitudes,—of the individual knowing subject in his concrete environment : these being the concomitants and consequences of the relation known as "knowledge". Now if certain philosophers have taken the terms "truth" and "knowledge," and used them in a new meaning, to designate some of these other concomitant or consequent relations between the knowing subject and his environment, rather than the relation of conformity between the intellect judging or interpreting reality and the reality so interpreted, this procedure of theirs by no means abolishes or suppresses or explains away the relation from which they wrested its traditional and recognized title of "truth" or "true knowledge," while it confuses the issues of Epistemology by fostering a misconception of its problems. Moreover, as we shall see, such relations as "suitability" or "usefulness" to human progress, "harmony" with the emotional, ethical and religious cravings of human nature, etc., cannot constitute truth or true knowledge, for they already suppose the possession of it. If, then, in the theory under consideration, truth or true knowledge be understood in the commonly received sense to signify the conformity of the judgments of the individual mind with reality, with *that which is*, a little reflection will show that the theory is unintelligible and self-destructive.

For (*a*), the theory itself is presumably put forward by its advocates *as true*, as the true explanation of what knowledge, or the truth of knowledge, consists in. But either knowledge is what this theory represents it to be, or it is not. If it is not, then the theory should be rejected without further consideration as false : and the alternative, scholastic view, that truth is something absolute and unchangeable, should be accepted. If, on the other hand, the theory is true, then this means, according to the theory itself, merely that the view of knowledge embodied in it happens to be the most acceptable and suitable, the one that "works best," for a particular section of human beings at a particular stage or epoch of their "mental evolution," though it may not be so, and may therefore be false, for other people or for other times. But whatever "knowledge" really and truly is, that it is and that it must be ; and if a certain theory of knowledge represents "knowledge" as being something other than it really is, and is therefore false for anyone at any time, the theory must be false simply and absolutely and without qualification. What is true must be true for all, whether it be impervious or unpalatable to few or to many; and what is false must be false for all whether it be embraced and cherished by few or by many.

Moreover (*b*), the real being which is the subject of knowledge, the human intellect in the present context, the intellect which in interpreting the world of conscious experience derives therefrom the concept of "evolution" or "progressive change," and considers this concept to be validly applicable to certain domains of this conscious experience, must see that the concept would not and could not be validly applicable to these domains if it did not reveal anything as to their real nature. But manifestly it could not reveal anything of the kind if the concept of "evolution" itself (no less than all other concepts) must be regarded as a mere ephemeral and changing product of an intellect likewise essentially subject to an unceasing process of "evolving" ever and always into something totally different from what it is at any particular stage of this process. On such a theory we could not possibly say that our concepts validly represent, or our judgments truly express, or our intellects really know, anything as to the nature of reality, of *that which is or happens.* At the very most there would be going on, in each conscious individual, a process of mere awareness in which the subjective representations—and the subject of the representations—would be for ever essentially changing, and in which it would be pure illusion and error for the conscious subject to think (if *per impossibile* he could think, *i.e.* conceive, judge, interpret) his conscious states to be "knowledge," *i.e.* to be true or genuine representations of reality. If there be truth or knowledge at all it must be that relation of intellect to reality, which expresses mentally *that which is or happens;* and if there be intellectual or rational cognition at all it must be the intellectual or rational process which establishes this relation. But what reality, or any portion of reality is, that it is—simply and absolutely. If reality exists, then it *does* exist. If reality changes, then it *does* change.—If the principle of identity is not absolute, there is an end of reason and intelligibility.—If, therefore, the mind conceives or judges reality, or any portion thereof, to exist or to happen or to be such and such, and if this mental state, so far as it goes, is true, *i.e.* if it rightly represents or expresses the real,—if the reality or portion thereof *does* exist or happen or *is* such and such,—then manifestly the judgment is true *absolutely,*—just as absolutely as it is true that "*whatever is is,*"—"*whatever is not is not,*"—"*whatever happens or changes does happen or change,*" etc.   Now the existence of such mental states and mental relations to reality, as those just referred to, is an undeniable fact, and it is to them the titles "truth" and "knowledge" properly belong,—whatever other conditions of the individual mind or of its environment, or relations of the individual mind to its environment, certain philosophers may have described under the guise of those titles.[1] Moreover, the relation called truth or true knowledge must, as we have just seen, be absolute and unchangeable if it is to be at all intelligible.   But this clearly involves that the concepts and judgments of the human intellect, its representations or interpretations of reality, must, in so far as they are true, be absolutely and immutably what they are.   And it is only by possessing such concepts and judgments that the human intellect can have truth or true knowledge at all.   Now, what is the necessary inference from all this as to the nature of the human intellect? Obviously, that inasmuch as it can think, conceive, judge, reason, reflect, etc., and thereby attain to some true knowledge of the real, it must be in its own nature,—as subject of knowledge, as a real being capable of knowing and actually possessed of knowledge, —it must be itself *essentially and in its substantial nature exempt from all such processes of substantial change or essential evolution as it may apprehend in the domain of sense experience.*   In other words, it must have itself a *suprasensible, essentially simple, immaterial or spiritual mode of being.*

Truth or true knowledge is indeed an endowment of the individual human intellect, but it has the undeniable and deeply significant peculiarity of being impersonal, objective,—of transcending the time and space limitations of the human individuality.   And thus it proves the human intellect, as the subject

[1] The distinction of truth or knowledge into two broadly different departments, *speculative* and *practical*, must not be misunderstood in the sense in which it would render certain of those theories plausible, as, for instance, Kant's theory of the knowledge of the *Practical Reason*.   The distinction does not lie in the truth or knowledge itself, but is based merely on *its effects*, *i.e.* on something extrinsic to it. There are not two essentially distinct mental processes or states included under those titles.   Considered as truth or true knowledge, the knowledge called "speculative" and that called "practical" are one and the same : mental insight into reality, the conformity of the mind judging with the reality interpreted.   But because the truth or knowledge embodied in some of our true judgments has a direct and immediate bearing on human conduct, practice, activity, while that of other judgments has no such immediate import for the ordering of our lives, knowledge of the former kind has been called "practical" and that of the latter kind "speculative".   *Cf. infra*, chap. xxv.

possessing it, to belong to a higher domain or order of reality than things which are merely objects but not subjects of knowledge, things which are "known" but are not themselves "knowers": the domain which we call "spiritual". Being objective and impersonal, knowledge would be wholly unintelligible and impossible if human intellects differed *essentially*, as subjects or possessors of knowledge, from one another, or if they were subject to an evolution process whereby they would evolve successively in the course of ages into *essentially* different forms or modes of being.

CHAPTER XXIII.

TRUTH AND EVIDENCE.

145. OBJECTIVITY AND TRUTH.—Our main concern hitherto in the course of our inquiries has been to vindicate the *objectivity* of knowledge, to show that knowledge can and does attain to *reality* as its object. But truth is something more than objectivity; for even though the objects apprehended by intellectual conception through sense perception be real, even though the root-concepts and derivative concepts which we use in all our judgments or interpretations of reality be themselves derived from reality and be aspects of reality, nevertheless our judgments are not always and necessarily true, not all of them represent reality accurately. Error is possible. And so the question arises as to the possibility and the means of assuring ourselves that our knowledge is *true*, of distinguishing with certitude between truth and error: the question of the *tests* or *criteria* of *truth* and the *grounds* or *motives* of *certitude*.

By the objectivity of knowledge Kant meant, as we have seen, the necessity, universality, uniformity, with which its judgments impose themselves on all minds: these judgments revealing "objects" or "phenomena" which were to be regarded as joint products of the unknowable, extramental reality and certain *a priori* forms of the mind. Thus reality is the *partial excitant* of knowledge, but not the *term* or *object* of knowledge. For scholastics, on the contrary, knowledge is objective in the sense that extramental reality is not only its partial excitant, but is also its object or term. That is to say that in sense perception the reality, by its action on the conscious subject, produces a conscious process or state by means of which the percipient is made aware of the reality present and given. This real sense datum is always concrete and complex. Its presence to consciousness arouses the activity of other cognitive faculties of the knowing subject: imagination, sensuous association and unification, sense memory. By means of these the knowing subject is capable of becoming aware of the perceived reality even in its absence. In this imagination-and-memory process what the subject immediately contemplates is a mental substitute of the reality, a mental "image" or "representation" of the temporally or spatially absent sense datum. But in man the presence of sense data arouses furthermore the higher or intellectual cognitive activity. This is essentially a power of analysing the concrete, complex sense data into abstract aspects called concepts or thought-objects. From the dawn of rational activity the human individual, concomitantly with acquiring the use of language, is laying up an ever increasing mental store of these thought-objects, and, associating them with language, is learning to use them as predicates whereby he interprets, in the rational process of judgment, the realities presented to him throughout the course of his experience. Now the individual's "concepts," whether in the subjective sense of "conception-processes" or in the objective sense of "thought-objects" (73), are not always actually in consciousness. But the processes certainly leave behind them, as psychic effects, some sort of intellectual modifications, by way of dispositions or habits, which account for what we call habitual knowledge. And the thought-objects themselves, from the simplest aspects revealed by abstractive analysis (*i.e.* the highest "categories") to the most complex intellectual syntheses resulting from the process of judgment, are thus possessed and retained by the subject as the content of all his "habitual" knowledge.

Now about all these thought-objects revealed to the individual intellect by the analytic and synthetic processes of conception and judgment, and about these processes themselves (or, rather, about the mental states, conditions, endowments, "products," resulting from the processes), we may inquire (1) whether, or in what sense, these thought-objects are *real*, are *realities?* and (2) whether, or in what sense, the mental possession of them, through the processes of conception and judgment, constitutes *truth*, or *true knowledge* of *reality?*

We have already shown that all thought-objects are *real* in the sense that the most simple and unanalysable of them, those of which our more complex concepts are rational syntheses and into which these are resolvable, are themselves aspects of reality. And we have also already expressed the view that these aspects of reality, whenever they are actually thought of, are *factors of reality immediately present to intellect :* that it is themselves, and not any intellectual " representations " or "substitutes " of them, that are the objects of the mind's contemplation :[1] that the *" species intelligibilis expressa "* or *"verbum mentale "* is, so far as these ultimate aspects of the real are concerned, not a mental substitute for them, an *"objectum quod concipitur,"* but a *" medium quo,"* a psychic means whereby they are consciously present to and apprehended by intellect (78).

But the mere conscious presence of such aspects of reality to intellect does not constitute knowledge. We have, accompanying mere conception, the process of judgment or interpretation, the process whereby the intellect is constantly analysing the concrete, complex reality, presented in direct conscious awareness, into intelligible aspects, factors, thought-objects, abstract concepts, and these again into simpler factors, thus amassing a mental store of predicates ; whereby it is constantly comparing these factors with one another and reuniting or synthesizing them into fuller and richer intelligible objects ; whereby it affirmatively or negatively predicates them of one another and of the successively occurring and recurring individual data of direct conscious experience, thus interpreting intellectually the nature of these data ; whereby it asserts certain tentative complexes to be impossible and therefore unreal, and others to be possible and therefore real ; whereby it asserts certain of them to be actually experienced and existing, and others to be unexperienced and not actually existent. Some of these judgments assert or deny the actual *existence* of certain conceived objects ; others abstract from the actual existence or non-existence of

---

[1] Since the faculty of *thought* proper, the intellect or reason or understanding, is a spiritual faculty, *i.e.* apprehends realities, which are its objects, apart from the time-and-space conditions of their actual material existence, it follows that in the process of conception (as also in judgment and reasoning) these realities can be *immediately present* as objects to intellect even though in their actual existence they be spatially and temporally remote from the thinker. When I *think* of the battle of Waterloo, or of my own death, or of the falls of Niagara, or the Seven Hills of Rome, there are, no doubt, corresponding imagination images in my sense consciousness. It is not these, however, but the *real* events and things themselves, that are *immediately present* to my *intellect* as *objects of thought,*—though the real things are spatially distant, and the real events temporally remote in the past and in the future respectively, so that none of them can be present to sense. This immediate presence *to intellect*, of realities which cannot be present *to sense*, is possible simply because the " presence of reality as object to intellect " is a mode of presence which transcends and is independent of the time-and-space limitations under which alone realities can be " present to sense ".

these, and make assertions about their *nature* or *essence*, their possibility or impossibility. Again, some judgments assert their objects (which are relations of necessity or incompatibility between concepts) to be absolutely *necessary* and universal ; others assert their objects to be *contingent*, definite, limited matters of fact.[1] But however we may classify judgments logically, it will be apparent from the nature of the judgment itself that it is a process of *interpreting*, and so *representing*, intelligibly reproducing or reconstructing, by successive intellectual analyses and syntheses, the whole domain of the real which is being gradually given or presented to us in the course of our direct conscious experience. In external and internal sense perception, and in direct intellectual intuition or consciousness (96), the real is being constantly presented to us as a vast problem for interpretation,— to have its significance gradually unfolded and rendered intelligible by our understanding through the intellectual processes of judgment and reasoning. If our judgments, so far as they go, represent reality rightly and accurately,—*i.e.* represent it as it really is and really demands to be represented and really ought to be represented,—thus putting the mind into conformity, concord, harmony with reality, then our judgments are true. A judgment which, so far as it goes, represents reality otherwise than it is, and, so far, puts the mind into a condition of positive disconformity or discord with reality, is on the contrary false.

146. DEFINITION OF TRUTH.—Hence the traditional scholastic definition of *logical truth*[2] or the *truth of knowledge* as "the conformity of the mind judging about reality, or of the mind's judgment about reality, with the reality to which the judgment refers".[3] But for the proper understanding of this definition certain points must be noted.

In the *first* place the conformity in question, like the relation which we call "cognition" or "knowledge," is *sui generis* and does not admit of illustration by analogies. It is not to be thought of as physical or photographic ; it has been described as "mental," "representative," "*intentionalis*".

---

[1] All *existential* judgments are *contingent*, except the judgment which asserts the existence of the Necessary Being.

[2] *Ontological* truth is reality itself considered as conformable and conformed with its mental type or archetype in some mind or intellect.—*Cf. Ontology*, §§ 40-3. *Moral* or *ethical* truth, or *veracity*, is the conformity of language with thought.— *Cf. Science of Logic*, ii., § 248.

[3] *Science of Logic, ibid.*

Secondly, it is not adequate : no one true judgment, and no accumulation of true judgments, can ever adequately conform the human mind with reality,—for the simple reason that the human mind is finite, imperfect, incapable of exhausting what is knowable in the real.   Hence, although a judgment is true when that which it expresses is really so, nevertheless it leaves the mind in *ignorance* of *further* knowledge about the real : this *absence* of *further mental conformity* with reality is sometimes spoken of as " *negative* discord " of the mind with reality : it is plainly different from the *positive* discord or want of conformity, produced by the *false* or *erroneous* judgment.

Thirdly, the conformity in which logical truth consists, is not to be found in the mere *sense* awareness produced by the presence of a *percept*, or in the mere *intellectual* awareness produced by the presence of a concept,[1] although both in perception and in conception there is a conscious relation of subject to object : it is only when the mind judges, affirms or denies a predicate (which may be either "existence " or some other abstract note or factor) of a subject, that there can be question of truth or error, *i.e.* of the concord or discord of the mental representation (which is the formal identification of predicate with subject, or separation of predicate from subject) with the objective reality so represented or interpreted.[2]   If judgment were the mere passive mirroring of reality in the mind, then, so far as reality thus revealed itself to mind there would be a necessary conformity of the latter with the former : there could be no question of error (17).   But judgment is no such passive mental assimilation of reality ; it is an active process of analysis and synthesis, an " *actus componendi et dividendi*," an intellectual fractioning or resolution of the stream of presented reality into abstract aspects, and an interpretation or mental representation or reconstruction of the presented reality

---

[1] Note the force of the expression " *mere* . . . awareness ": for both perception and conception are normally accompanied by the active, interpretative process of judgment, which process, of course, always establishes the relation of logical *truth* or *error*.

[2] Hence St. Thomas defines truth in these well-known terms : " Veritas intellectus est adaequatio rei et intellectus *secundum quod intellectus dicit esse quod est, vel non esse quod non est* ".—*Summa Contra Gentes*, I., q. 5.   And again : " Verum enim est *cum dicitur esse quod est vel non esse quod non est*. Falsum autem est *cum dicitur non esse quod est, vel esse quod non est* ".—*In Met.*, iv., L. 8.   These formulæ plainly reproduce Aristotle's definition : " Τὸ μὲν γὰρ λέγειν τὸ ὂν μὴ εἶναι ἢ τὸ μὴ ὂν εἶναι ψεῦδος, τὸ δὲ τὸ ὂν εἶναι καὶ τὸ μὴ ὂν μὴ εἶναι ἀληθές ". - *Met.*, iii., 7 (ed. Didot). *Cf. Science of Logic, ibid.*

by a series of mental comparisons of these aspects, mental affirmations or identifications, and mental denials or separations, of predicates and subjects.

Fourthly, in the definition we understand by "reality" ("*res*"), not of course the reality "as it is in itself" if by this phrase be meant "standing out of all relation to mind": we have already shown how absurd and self-contradictory it is to speak of true knowledge, or any knowledge, of "things as they are in themselves" in that sense (126, ii.). Against the conception of truth or true knowledge as the conformity of a mental state with an extramental reality considered as "in itself," or "unrelated to" and "independent of" mind, there is the unanswerable objection that on such a view we could never know any judgment to be true inasmuch as the extramental term of the relation of conformity would be *ex hypothesi* not present to mind, so that it could never be known whether the relation is one of conformity or not.

We mean, therefore, simply the extramental reality,—internal or external, *Ego* or *non-Ego*,—as it really is *when it stands related to the mind* by being "present" or "presented" to the mind in and through our direct perceptual and conceptual processes. Reality is presented to intellect through sense as a collection or series of individual data each of which is first apprehended intellectually through the transcendental concept of "thing," "being," "reality," individuated as "this thing," "this being," "this reality," "*hoc aliquid*," τόδε τί. Each such datum the intellect proceeds to "interpret" or "represent" by discovering in it, and identifying with it in affirmative judgments, previously conceived aspects of reality, specific and generic, and by denying other aspects or thought-objects of it in negative judgments: a process which likewise involves comparisons of these abstract aspects with one another and judgments asserting their mutual compatibility or incompatibility as factors of one and the same reality. The affirmative judgment pronounces two formally distinct concepts (subject and predicate) to be objectively and really identical; the negative judgment pronounces them to be diverse or separate, pronounces the predicate to be not really identical with the subject. The affirmative judgment is true if the identity represented by it expresses an objective, real identity (*e.g.* "Man is mortal"; "England declared war on Germany in August, 1914"); otherwise it is false (*e.g.* "The sun moves round the earth "; " The human soul is mortal "). Similarly the negative judgment is true if the diversity or non-identity represented by it expresses an objective, real diversity or non-identity (*e.g.* " Not all wars are just " ; " 1917 is not a leap-year ") ; otherwise it is false (*e.g.* " There is no God " ; " The human will is not free "). Hence judgment might also be defined as a mental act which represents a reality by objectively and really identifying formally distinct aspects of that reality (*affirmative*), or by objectively and really separating some thought-object (or aspect of reality) from that reality (*negative*). And the truth of a judgment might similarly be defined as the conformity of the identifying (*affirmative*) or discriminating (*negative*) representation with an objective and real identity or diversity, respectively.[1]

147. THE OBJECTIVE TERM OF THE TRUTH-RELATION IS EXTRAMENTAL, REAL, AND ATTAINABLE. KANT'S VIEW OF TRUTH.—Logical truth, therefore, is an attribute not of things in the absolute, or of objects of thought, but of judgments, *i.e.* of relations between objects of thought. The formal object of the act of judgment is a relation of identity or diversity between two formally distinct objective concepts or aspects of reality : *i.e.* what the mind apprehends, through the act of judgment, is a

---

[1] *Cf.* MGR. SENTROUL, *La Verité et le progrès du savoir*, in the *Revue néoscolastique*, May and August, 1911 (pp. 212-30, 305-28) : two very instructive articles, in which, however, the author's definitions apply only to affirmative judgments. Defining *logical truth* as " the conformity of a judgment with a real identity " (p. 177), and the judgment itself as " a real identification " (p. 305), he illustrates the latter description in the following terms : " The judgment (of the ideal, or of the existential order) declares that a thing (intrinsically possible or actually existing, and) signified by the subject (abstract or concrete, respectively) is identical with the thing that is signified l y the predicate. Take, for instance, this judgment of the ideal order : the triangle is a figure in which a circle can always be inscribed. To assert that judgment is to assert that once a triangle is realized in the existing world you have *ipso facto* a figure which is not only triangular (as the subject itself already states) but is also endowed with the property signified by the predicate. Or, take a judgment of the existential order : to assert that " this horse is young " is to assert that there is here a single being which is both " horse " and " young ". . . . It is in this sense that judgment is always a real identification. We prefer the term *real* to the term *objective* which seems to refer to the *formal object* of a cognition rather than to the reality signified by the cognition, and which in any case seems restricted rather to the identification proper to judgments of the ideal order " (p. 305). " Judgments which are not of the ideal order we prefer to describe as of the *existential* order rather than of the *real* order. The matter of designation is of minor importance provided we make our meaning clear : that all judgments are *real* identifications, and are either of the *ideal* or of the *existential* order " (*ibid.*, n. *Cf.* § 10. JEANNIÈRE, *op. cit.*, p. 310).

relation of real identity or of real diversity between the reality signified by the subject, and that signified by the predicate, of the judgment. Something " actually perceived or imagined reveals itself to thought as identical with another object already conceived by the intellect, so that the former must be placed under the extension of the latter, and the latter applied to the former. This attribution is the function of the act of judgment." Such are the terms in which Mercier describes the affirmative judgment.[1]   And after explaining briefly the nature of the "identity" or "agreement" expressed by the logical copula,[2] he says that "logical truth characterizes the judgment when the mind asserts the union or disunion of two terms in conformity with objective truth : the judgment is true when the mind unites terms which agree or disjoins terms which disagree; in the opposite event the judgment is erroneous".[3]   By the expression "objective truth" in this statement Mercier means "ontological truth," *i.e.* the reality itself as present or presented to the mind and as having a nature which can be "understood," "known," "represented" only by the affirmative and negative judgments, the real identifications and discriminations, which that nature demands.[4]   When the judgment, therefore, whether affirmative or negative, the real identification or separation of objective concepts or aspects of reality, takes place in conformity with the *real exigencies* of the datum presented for interpretation, with *what its concrete reality demands* as an *intelligible representation* of it, then the judgment is true; otherwise it is false.   "And if we are finally asked," he continues, "what are these exigencies whereby the subject demands from our intellects such or such attributes, and not others, we would reply that they spring *from the indivisible unity proper to each subject* and by virtue of which it presents itself to the mind with a certain group of attributes, rather than any other group, and consequently *demands such and*

---

[1] *Op. cit.*, § 13, p. 20. His whole treatment of the subject (§§ 10-17) marks a distinct advance from the traditional scholastic treatment which approached the question from an exclusively dogmatic and synthetic standpoint.
[2] *Cf. Science of Logic*, i., §§ 78-80; 99-109.   [3] *Op. cit.*, p. 26.
[4] The author rightly observes (*ibid.*, p. 24) that the objective or ontological truth of reality implies a relation of reality to some mind. Apart from such relation things have ontological truth only *fundamentally* or *potentially*, not *actually* or *formally*. As St. Thomas says (*De Veritate*, Q. i., a. 1),—"Etiamsi intellectus humanus non esset, adhuc res dicerentur verae in ordine ad intellectum divinum. Sed si uterque intellectus, quod est impossibile, intelligeretur auferri, nullomodo veritatis ratio remaneret ". *Cf. Ontology*, § 41.

such predicates to the exclusion of others.[1] But there reflection reaches its limit: for, as St. Thomas somewhere remarks, to demand why a man is a man is to ask an unmeaning question, 'quaerere cur homo est homo est nihil quaerere'." [2]

Thus, then, the reality with which the mind is conformed by a true judgment is on the one hand extramental or objective in the sense that it is something beyond, distinct from, and independent of the judicial, interpretative, representative act itself; [3] but on the other hand it is this something not as standing out of all cognitive relation to the knowing subject, but as present or presented to the knowing subject: and, consequently, since both terms of the truth-relation are consciously apprehended, the task of justifying our reflex conviction that we *know* some at least of our judgments to be true is at least not *prima facie* an impossible task.

Nor can it be objected that on this view both terms of the "truth" or "conformity" relation are subjective, and that therefore all truth, all knowledge is subjective,—which is Idealism. One term (the subjective or mental term) of the relation is the mental state produced by the judgment, or interpretation, or "representation". The other term is not a mental state, the state produced by the "presentation" of the reality to consciousness; nor is it this "presentation" itself, for this presentation itself is not an object but a process, just as the "representation" is not an object but a process: the whole process, both of presenting and representing, constitutes the *esse ideale* of the reality, or gives the reality its *esse ideale*, which *esse ideale* is not an object

---

[1] *Cf.* vol. i., § 92.

[2] *Ibid.*, p. 25 (italics ours). The student will recognize in those sentences an affirmation of the influence of objective "affinities" urged against Kant's formalism (vol. i., §§ 92, 93); and also of the doctrine that the truth of our judgments is determined, and our assent to them motived, by the ontological exigency of the presented reality to have certain predicates affirmed or denied of it,—in other words, by "objective evidence".

[3] This holds good even when the realities which we interpret are *our own judgments*, or our other conscious, mental processes. For these processes are also realities, and by introspective reflection we make them the objects of inquiry, investigation, interpretation, judgment, etc. The distinctive feature of the judicial act, the feature which characterizes it as a representation or interpretation of reality, and which has been described as its "objective reference" or its "claim to *truth*" (*cf. Science of Logic*, i., §§ 79, 80) has been emphasized in many modern definitions. Thus, BRADLEY defines judgment as "the act which refers an ideal content, recognized as such, to a reality beyond the act"; and BOSANQUET, as "the reference of a significant idea to a subject in reality by means of an identity of content between them" (*ibid.*, § 80).

of cognition or *objectum cognitum* at all, but is only the psychic means,—the *medium quo*,—by which the reality is mentally apprehended. The other term of the truth or knowledge relation, the objective or real term, is the *extramental reality itself* present or presented to consciousness immediately, *i.e.* without the intervention of any mentally fabricated product or object intervening as a substitute or *tertium quid* between the knowing mind and the known reality. And we have shown already that there is absolutely no ground for supposing that in the process of presentation or manifestation the reality is transformed or disfigured by any mental forms of the knowing subject. The reproach of Idealism against our definition of truth or true knowledge therefore falls to the ground.

When a judgment is true, the identification or discrimination which it makes is in conformity with what the intelligible nature of the presented reality demands: this latter so appears to intellect that it reveals subject and predicate as aspects of it and demands their identification, or as such that it demands the exclusion of the predicate from the subject which represents it. Not that the reality itself, apart from its relation or presence to the intellect, is formally an identity of distinct aspects (subject and predicate), or a unity which (as subject) formally excludes some aspect of reality (as predicate); for these identities, distinctions, comparisons, affirmations and denials are formally *logical relations*, forms or modes of thought, modalities of the judgment which is itself a form of thought. But that the reality presented for interpretation has an objective, real, ontological exigency, as intelligible, for representation by intellect through the instrumentality of such relations: these have their foundation in the presented reality; they are in it fundamentally, potentially; and it is precisely because of this that reality is *intelligible*, *i.e.* capable of being *known* or *understood* through our human modes of thought. We may err in judging, interpreting, representing the real; but when our judgments are true it is with *reality* that they are in conformity.

Now Kant likewise recognizes the distinction between truth and error in the judgments of our speculative reason (33, 125, 128-9). For him, too, the true judgment is the one that is in conformity with something,—something with which it ought to be in conformity. He admits, moreover, that this something is the same for all human minds, that the true judgment is necessarily and universally true because of its determination by, and conformity with, this something. But the necessity and universality are, as we have seen, subjective, because the "something" which determines them is subjective. In his view the "something" which is the standard of the conformity or truth of our judgments *is not reality*. For reality itself, in its presentation to the mind in perception and conception, is "moulded" into "objects" by transcendental, *a priori* forms *which belong to the mind's own constitution*. The true judgment, therefore, is the judgment which is in conformity with these mental products or objects; and it is in conformity with these when it expresses *what those transcendental, a priori mental laws demand* that the judgment should express. Truth, in the sense of conformity of our judgments with reality, is unattainable by the speculative reason, because reality is unknowable. But truth in the sense of conformity of our judgments with the laws which constitute our own understanding is attainable, because these determining principles of reason,—which likewise construct or create the universe of intelligible phenomena or appearances, —are discoverable by a critical investigation of the *a priori* conditions of the possibility of speculative knowledge.

Our criticism of this view is simply that such knowledge is not worthy of the name. If the object with which the true judgment is conformed, and into which it is supposed to give an insight, be not *reality*, then the judgment is not a form of *knowledge* at all. Kant's theory that the objects which determine our knowledge are not realities, but mental constructions, themselves determined by *a priori* forms of the mind, we have already seen to be fundamentally unsound and wholly indefensible. As Jeannière observes:[1] "The mental causality whereby we form and compare concepts does not consist in constructing reality, but in apprehending it through inadequate conceptions which we so co-ordinate with one another, according to ontological exigencies, that we gradually attain to the genuine knowledge which we embody in real definitions".

148. CRITERIA OF TRUTH AND MOTIVES OF CERTITUDE.— We have seen that reality is presented to intellect through perception and conception; that perception presents a consciously apprehended series of concrete, individual, complex and unanalysed realities; that the ultimate conceptual factors or thought-objects

[1] *Op. cit.*, p. 314.

which intellect apprehends in these data, which it builds up into more and more complex generic and specific concepts, and which it thus employs as predicates to interpret these data, are themselves abstract aspects of reality. Now when we form any judgment and assent to it as true, we are concomitantly (or "*in actu exercito*") aware of its truth, of its conformity with the reality which it interprets or represents, of what we may call its faithful compliance with the real exigencies of the presented datum.[1] And of course when we formulate any judgment and assent to it as true, our reason for doing so is because we see, or think we see, that the reality presented to us as subject of the judgment demands that the thought-object which is predicate be affirmed or denied of it as the case may be. If the relation which the judgment asserts be *clear* or *evident* to us, we are *convinced* that the judgment is true, we give it the firm assent known as *conviction* or *certitude* (7). If it is not quite clear or evident to us, but yet appears to be there objectively, we regard the judgment as *probable*, and give it the provisional assent known as *opinion*. If we cannot see, in the terms of the relation suggested by the judgment, any grounds for affirming or denying the relation, then we abstain, or should abstain, from formulating the judgment, suspend our assent, and thus adopt the attitude known as *doubt*. But among the judgments to which we assent as certainly true, or as probably true, there may be some that are really false. Hence arises the question : Have we any reliable test or tests for distinguishing truth from error ? Have we any reliable grounds or motives of certitude ?

A *test or criterion of truth* is anything that enables us to decide whether a judgment is true or false. Our cognitive faculties themselves—the higher cognitive faculty of intellect or reason ; the faculties of consciousness and memory ; the senses, external and internal—are the means, and the only means, at our disposal for discovering truth, if truth can be discovered : and intellect or reason, subserved by the other faculties, is of course the faculty which finally decides or judges in every case. In a

---

[1] Hence UEBERWEG'S definition of judgment as "the consciousness of the objective validity of a subjective union of conceptions whose forms are different but belong to each other". Similarly JOSEPH (*Introd. to Logic*, p. 147) writes : "All judgments, besides affirming or denying a predicate of a subject, affirm themselves as true. But a judgment which affirms itself as true claims to express, so far as it goes, the nature of things, the facts, or the reality of the universe." *Cf. Science of Logic*, i., § 80.

certain wide sense, therefore, our cognitive faculties may be called tests or criteria of truth. But only in a wide sense ; for what we mean properly by a test or criterion of truth is something which guides or directs the function of the judging faculty so that it will assert, and adhere or assent to, only true judgments : something in the judgment itself or the terms of the judgment, or connected and presented with these, which will show forth the judgment to be true, and thus elicit for it the firm or fixed assent of the intellect.

By a *motive of certitude* we mean whatever *moves*, determines, inclines the intellect to assent firmly to a judgment as true. Our judgments are intellectual acts which are caused, both as to their actual happening (*quoad exercitium actus*) and as to their affirmative or negative quality (*quoad specificationem actus*) by a variety of influences (10). These may be all described as *causes* of assent or belief. Some of them, however, are *subjective* or psychological, *i.e.* they are exerted on the intellect by the will, the temperament or mentality, the inclinations, likes and dislikes, passions, feelings, emotions, etc., of the individual judging or knowing subject (11, 12). They are *non-intellectual* in character. That is to say, they have no *direct* bearing on the truth of any judgment to which we assent, and do not help us to *discern* or *decide* its truth—except in so far as we may consider them, on reflection, to have perhaps a certain legitimate weight as tests or guides to the truth of the judgments to which they incline us to assent. From these subjective influences we can distinguish other causes or motives of our assent to any judgment as true, causes which we describe as *grounds* or *reasons* of our assent, motives which are directly *intellectual* inasmuch as they present themselves to the intellect in or with the terms of the judgment, and at least appear to be *objective*, to characterize the reality itself which is presented as object for interpretation. These appear at once as *reasons* of the truth of the judgment and as *grounds* or *motives* of our assent to it ; and they may be collectively catalogued under the comprehensive title of *evidence.*

From this it will appear that whatever is a "test or criterion of truth,"—whatever appears in or with the reality presented for interpretation, enabling us to form a true judgment about this reality,—is also *eo ipso* a ground of our assent to the judgment as true, or is in other words a "motive of certitude". But can we say, conversely, that whatever is a motive of certitude is also a test or criterion of truth? Well, since intellect is the judicial faculty, the faculty which elicits the only act that can put us formally in possession of truth, the faculty which in all cases must ultimately decide (as far as it can) whether a proposed judgment is true or not, the faculty which must ultimately give firm (certain) or provisional (probable) assent, or abstain from assenting, to the judgment as true,—we can say at least that the *intellectual* grounds or motives of certitude are also tests or criteria of truth; and of the non-intellectual motives or causes which may influence our assents we may say that they too are criteria or tests of truth in so far, but only in so far, as intellect, reflecting on them, can recognize in them indications, indexes, evidences, of the truth of the judgments to which they prompt our assent.

We have to inquire, then, whether by reflection we can discover in our spontaneous convictions (10), in the judgments to which we spontaneously assent as true, anything in the nature of grounds or motives which will justify us in accepting those judgments as true.

Having discussed in Part I. the scope and limits and method of our whole inquiry, and having rejected scepticism (36-39) as a prejudiced and unjustifiable issue thereof, we proceeded at some length in Part II., by an analysis of our cognitive processes, to vindicate for knowledge its claim to *real objectivity*. We there justified the contention that knowledge is objectively real, that it has for its objects realities; and in doing so we were guided throughout by the available *evidence*. It will not be difficult, now, to take the further step of showing by reflection that we have the means of convincing ourselves that some *true* knowledge of reality is attainable, that there are at our disposal adequate tests of truth and adequate grounds or motives of *reflex or reasoned certitude*.

In our opening chapter on the *Terms and Data of the Inquiry* we classified the judgments in which human knowledge is supposed to be contained (10) into (*a*) interpretations of immediate facts of our cognitive experience, (*b*) self-evident axioms, (*c*) deductions from the axioms, (*d*) inductions from the facts, and (*e*) judgments based on authority or testimony. In the same chapter (16) we noted among man's spontaneous certitudes certain universally entertained convictions which appear to have an intimate and even essential bearing on (*a*) his *physical* existence, (*b*) his *intellectual* life, (*c*) his nature and conduct as a *moral* being, and (*d*) as a *religious* being. Our inquiry into the criteria of truth and motives of certitude must take note of these classifications.

We also distinguished (11) between judgments to which our assent seems to be compelled and judgments to which we assent freely,—*i.e.* not because we cannot help assenting to them but because we see, or think we see, intellectually that the grounds, reasons, motives, for assenting to them as true exclude all prudent fear of error. The grounds of our assent to judgments of the former class are all purely intellectual ; and the judgments themselves are of the ideal order arising from analysis and comparison of abstract concepts. Such, for instance, are the judgments of pure mathematics, and the first principles of logic and metaphysics, *e.g.* the principles of contradiction and causality. They are all *in materia necessaria*, and the certitude we can have about them is called *metaphysical* certitude.[1] No philosophers have seriously questioned the rectitude of such judgments, or the propriety of forming them and giving them the full assent of certitude. But about this whole class of judgments a serious question can be and has been raised, whether, namely, they have any *real knowledge-value*, whether they give the mind a genuine insight into *reality*, whether, therefore, they embody *truth* in the traditionally accepted sense of this term (29, 30, 33). We have contended that they do, that the thesis of *Moderate Realism* gives the right interpretation of their significance (chap. ix.). But it is clear that while the intellectual grounds of our assent to those judgments themselves are cogent, and produce in us irresistible convictions, the intellectual grounds for the thesis of *Moderate Realism* are not of that cogent character. If they were the thesis in question could not have been rejected as it has been by many philosophers. Our conviction that Moderate Realism is true is a freely formed conviction (11) ; and our contention is that the grounds for its truth are such as to exclude all prudent fear of error. Thus we see that the intellectual grounds for the *real truth* or *real knowledge-value* of even " self-evident " judgments of the ideal order are not cogent, but are nevertheless reasonably sufficient for certitude.

In other words, the " objective evidence," which scholastics

[1] *Cf. Science of Logic*, ii., § 249.

maintain to be the "supreme criterion of truth" and the "ultimate motive of certitude," is—as regards our reasoned or reflex
or philosophical certitude concerning the real truth and real
knowledge-value of judgments of the ideal order—not indeed
cogent, but sufficient to exclude all prudent fear of error.   This
is worthy of note for two reasons.   Firstly, because it is mainly
in regard to men's ultimate philosophical convictions, their judgments about the origin, nature, and destiny of man and the
universe, about the "ultimate causes" of things, and about the
ultimate real worth and significance of our ordinary and scientific
knowledge,—rather than in regard to our inevitable acceptance
of those judgments and convictions themselves as a necessary
means of meeting the practical needs of life (7, 15, 17, 37, 38),
—that philosophers have assigned very different tests or criteria
of truth, and grounds or motives of certitude, as supreme and
ultimate.   And secondly, because the scholastic thesis, that
"objective evidence is the supreme criterion of truth and the
ultimate motive of certitude," seems to have been misunderstood
by many as implying that only intellectually cogent evidence is
a sufficient test of truth, and that the firm assent of certitude is
or ought to be confined to judgments for the truth of which such
intellectually cogent evidence is forthcoming.

On the contrary, however, scholastics recognize, besides
irresistible convictions, a much wider—and in many respects
philosophically more important—class of judgments for whose
truth the human mind can have grounds which, though not cogent, are so sufficient as to render the truth of these judgments
wholly *credible* (7, 11, 12, 35): motives which make such an
appeal to reason reflecting on them that it would be plainly *unreasonable* and at variance with the dictates of our *rational nature*
to refuse to such judgments the full and firm assent of certitude
(38).   The scholastic attitude is therefore intellectualist,—as
opposed to all systems which base human certitude regarding
the solutions of the great, fundamental (philosophical, ethical,
religious) problems on volitional, emotional, instinctive impulses,
etc.,—in the sense that it recognizes in the distinctive *cognitive*
faculty of our nature as *rational, viz. intellect* or *reason*, the ultimate court of appeal for deciding between truth and error.   But
it is not *narrowly* intellectualist in the sense of refusing to recognize any *evidential* value either in intellectual grounds that
fall short of logical cogency or in motives that do not appeal

directly to intellect but rather to our whole complex nature as human beings (14).

149. EVIDENCE AS THE SUPREME CRITERION OF TRUTH AND THE ULTIMATE MOTIVE OF CERTITUDE. When scholastics contend that evidence is a test of truth, and that it is indeed the supreme and ultimate criterion of all truth, what do they mean by the term *evidence*?

Etymologically the term designates the condition of a material object which is clearly visible (*e-videre*) to the eyes. An object which is thus clearly visible is *evident*. But the language descriptive of corporeal vision and its objects has been transferred to mental apprehension and its objects. Intellect or reason is the "eye" of the mind. Intellectual apprehension is a kind of "vision". And so whatever is objectively clear to the intellect is described as "evident," and the corresponding condition of the thought-object is described as its "evidence". Now the object of the intellectual act which attains to truth, the act of judgment, is a relation between two thought-objects, a relation that is *enunciable* by an act of affirmation or denial. To say that the truth of the judgment is evident is to say that in the objective reality which is being interpreted, in the whole concrete context of its objective presentation, the mind clearly sees or apprehends adequate ground for the relation whereby the reality is interpreted or represented in the act of judgment : and not only sees this ground, but is conscious that it asserts and assents to the relation *because* the ground of it is really there and really apprehended (67),—so that this condition of the reality, this "evidence" of the reality, is not only the reason of the truth of the judgment, the objective "deciding factor" or "test" or "criterion" of the truth of the judgment, but is also and *eo ipso* the "motive" of the mind's assent to the judgment.

But there are many kinds of evidence. (1) There is *perfect* or *cogent* evidence, and there is evidence which is not cogent or perfect but yet *sufficient* to reveal the relation asserted in the judgment, and consequently sufficient to gain for the judgment the firm assent of certitude excluding all prudent fear of error.

(2) There is *immediate* evidence and *mediate* evidence. If the ground of the relation of identity or diversity between subject and predicate, asserted in the judgment, be clearly revealed in these objective aspects themselves of the presented reality, then the judgment is said to be *immediately* evident or

self-evident: e.g. "two straight lines cannot enclose a space"; "this paper is white". If the ground of the relation is not manifest from an inspection of the compared aspects or thought-objects themselves, but only from relations already apprehended between them and other concepts, then the judgment is only *mediately* evident: *e.g.* "the three interior angles of a plane triangle are equal to two right angles"; "St. Peter suffered martyrdom". It is plain that mediate evidence implies and rests ultimately on immediate evidence, that the former cannot be an adequate test of truth or motive of certitude unless the latter is.

(3) We can distinguish between evidence of *fact*, of actual *existence* or *happening*, and evidence of *possibility* or *impossibility*, of *essential* relations between abstract aspects of reality : *i.e.* evidence for judgments of the *existential* order, and evidence for judgments of the *ideal* order. In the former, if the evidence of existence or happening is not immediate, *i.e.* if the reality of which it is predicated be not directly apprehended as existing or happening, then its existence or happening must be seen to be involved in some directly apprehended existence or happening. For example, I know that "Corn was sown in this field last Spring" because I see that "Corn is here and now growing in this field".

(4) Finally—not to mention less important distinctions—there is the distinction between *intrinsic* and *extrinsic* evidence for the truth of a judgment. The evidence is said to be intrinsic when the grounds of assent to the judgment as true are seen to lie immediately or mediately in the reality itself which the judgment interprets ; and in this case the assent is said to be an assent of *reason* or *science*. When the ground of our assent lies not in the interpreted reality itself, but in some testimony or authority which is considered to vouch sufficiently for the truth of the judgment, the evidence is said to be extrinsic ; and the assent is then described as an assent of *belief* or *faith* (10, *e*). It is clear that extrinsic evidence can be an adequate test of the truth of a judgment, and a sufficient motive of certitude, only when and because the testimony or authority on which we rely is already judged by us to have the requisite conditions for guaranteeing the truth of the judgment and grounding our firm assent thereto. These conditions, in the source of our information, are two in number, *viz. knowledge* and *veracity* ("*scientia* et *veracitas*"). In other words, before accepting a judgment on authority we must first be certain of these two other judgments,

"The authority in question is not deceived, but well-informed," and "The authority is not deceiving us, but is trustworthy". Now for the truth of these two judgments we must ultimately have adequate *intrinsic* evidence, *i.e.* evidence lying in the sub-ject-matter itself of these two judgments : for if we accepted these judgments also only on some other authority, the same question would arise about the credentials of this latter, and thus we should find ourselves involved in an endless regress. All extrinsic evidence therefore rests ultimately on intrinsic evidence, and cannot itself be the supreme test of truth or the ultimate motive of certitude.[1]

150. APPLICATIONS OF THE DOCTRINE TO MEDIATE EVI-DENCE.—(1) When, next, we come to apply the scholastic doctrine of evidence as the supreme criterion of truth and ulti-mate motive of certitude to the five classes of judgments referred to above (148), we shall find no special difficulty in the doctrine as applied to mediate evidence for deductive inferences from self-evident axioms of the ideal order. It will be admitted that in such a purely deductive science as, for instance, mathematics, if our conclusions are inferred in strict accordance with the logical canons of formally correct deductive reasoning, then these conclusions will give us a true or genuine insight into reality *in whatever sense the principles or axioms do so.* Hence it is some-times said that *conformity with axioms or principles*, as standards, is the test or criterion of the truth of such conclusions. And again it is said that *the logical canons of formally correct inference* are also tests or criteria of the truth of such conclusions : inas-much as the intellect, as long as it is guided by such canons, will derive from the principles only what is really involved in them. Both statements are correct. The self-evidence of the principles is the *norma* or *standard* by conformity with which the con-clusions are known to be evident and therefore true. And the canons of inference are means of realizing this conformity. They are, in a sense, tests of evidence : *i.e.* they help the intellect to test *mediate* evidence by resolving it into, and showing its con-tinuity with, *immediate* evidence. For at least in regard to judgments which are not immediately evident the intellect may err by mistaking *apparent* evidence for *real* evidence : and the canons of inference help it to avoid such mistakes.

[1] *Cf. Science of Logic*, ii., § 260. For the criteria and sources of historical knowledge and certitude, *cf. ibid.*, § 261.

In regard to deductive inference there is one point to be noted when we pass from the abstract domain of *pure* or *rational* demonstration to the concrete domain of *mixed* and *empiric* demonstration.[1]   In this domain we are applying abstract principles to concrete facts, and assuming that the facts really embody the principles: *i.e.* we are assuming the truth of some form of Realism as against Conceptualism and Nominalism. Therefore the mediate evidence on which the certitude of our conclusions is based includes the evidence on which the truth of Realism is grounded.   In other words, we know that these conclusions give us a true and genuine insight into reality only because and in so far as we are certain that our abstract concepts and principles are validly applicable to the concrete domain of our sense experience.

It will also be admitted that for the whole domain of *scientific conclusions* from purely *rational principles, intrinsic* evidence, mediate or immediate, must be forthcoming before the mind can give an assent of science to such judgments.   If the individual mind accepts them as true merely on the *extrinsic* evidence of human testimony, its assent is not an assent of *science* but of *belief* or *faith.*   It is only right and reasonable to seek for their intrinsic evidence before assenting to them.   In view of the persistent misrepresentation of scholasticism as teaching that even in the domain of purely rational truths authority is the ultimate basis of human certitude, we can only reiterate the genuine teaching of scholasticism that in this domain the appeal to authority is the weakest of all arguments.[2]   Of course, when an individual investigator derives some remote conclusion by a long and sustained effort of deductive reasoning from first principles, his assent to such a conclusion will be strengthened when he learns that other investigators have reached the same conclusion independently : conscious as he is of his own fallibility, this corroborative testimony will assure him that he has avoided mistakes and reasoned correctly.   In this sense it may be admitted that in the domain of purely rational, scientific investigation human testimony is a "confirming criterion" of truth.

[1] *Cf. Science of Logic,* ii., § 254 (*c*), p. 234.

[2] " Locus ab auctoritate quae fundatur super ratione humana est infirmissimus."—St. Thomas, *Summa Theol.,* I., Q. i., a. 8, ad 2.   *Cf. Science of Logic,* ii., pp. 251-2, for references to sources.

(2) All that has just been said about the scholastic doctrine of evidence as applied to deductions from principles is equally true of the same doctrine as applied to inductive generalizations from the individual facts of immediate sense experience. The *Logic of Induction* analyses the whole complex process whereby we can trace back to the *immediate* evidence for our interpretations of individual sense data the *mediate* evidence we have for inductively established laws or generalizations; it teaches us how to evaluate this evidence; it lays down the canons in accordance with which we reach physical or moral certitude about those generalizations through such evidence; it explores the scope and significance of the principle known as the *Uniformity of Nature*, which is involved in all inductive generalization from individual facts or phenomena; and it brings to light the ultimate rational grounds which justify our assent to this principle.[1] Hence all such general judgments as we can establish by induction, all generalizations for which we have sufficient (mediate) evidence to warrant a firm or certain assent, will be true, or genuinely representative of reality, *in whatever sense the self-evident principles of reason and the self-evident interpretations of sense facts* are representative of reality.

(3) Thirdly, our certitude about judgments which we receive on authority, on *extrinsic* evidence, is ultimately dependent on the *immediate intrinsic* evidence we have for the trustworthiness of the authority in each particular case. And not on that alone: but also on the sufficiency of the grounds or evidence which we have for our general spontaneous conviction that human testimony can be found to be really endowed with the characteristics of " knowledge " and " veracity " which make it trustworthy. But this latter conviction is based on repeated actual verifications of the trustworthiness of human testimony by the presence of immediate, intrinsic evidence for the truth of the judgments which that testimony has vouched for.

151. APPLICATION TO IMMEDIATE SENSE EVIDENCE.—All mediate evidence, therefore, depends ultimately for its value on that of immediate evidence; and of this we have two kinds : immediate sense evidence for our interpretations of the immediate data of sense experience, and immediate intellectual evidence for abstract axioms of the ideal order. By the former class of judgment we assert either (*a*) that some datum of sense ex-

[1] *Cf. Science of Logic*, ii., *passim.*

perience (*e.g.* "this seen-and-felt datum ") *exists, i.e.* objectively to ourselves perceiving it and as a reality independent of the subjective perception process ; or (*b*) also that it *is such or such*, as the predicate-concept represents it to be (*e.g.* that it is "a pen "). By the latter class of judgment we assert either (*a*) that some abstract thought-object (*e.g.* "a whole") is an objective reality, a real possibility of actual existence, distinct as such from our thinking, and not identical with, or a mere product or creation of, our thinking ; or also (*b*) that it *is such or such*, as the predicate-concept or thought-object represents it (*e.g.* that it is "greater than its part").[1]

Now we say that the immediate, intrinsic, objective evidence of what is present to the mind in such judgments is the ultimate test of their truth or conformity with reality, and the ultimate ground or motive of our certain assent to them. If this contention be well-grounded, then it is plain that such evidence will be also the supreme criterion of *all* truth and the ultimate motive of *all* human certitude, inasmuch as all judgments to which we assent on mediate evidence ultimately depend for their truth or knowledge-value on those to which we assent on immediate evidence. But to show that the contention is well-grounded we must understand clearly what it implies,—and what it does not imply.

(4) Let us take first the case of immediate *sense* evidence. By this we are to understand not the mere presentation of a datum to sense consciousness, but its presentation to intellect through sense perception. For since truth or knowledge proper is attained only through the intellectual act of interpretation or judgment, the evidence which is a criterion of the truth of the judgment, and a motive of our assent to the judgment, must be always a characteristic of *that which is presented to the intellect* for interpretation. Sense evidence is therefore a characteristic of the sense datum as presented to and apprehended by the intellect. Now we have already shown[2] that this datum can present itself to intellect through sense with characteristics (of "actual existence," "externality" or "otherness," "extensity," "shape," "colour," "taste," etc.) which (1) *compel* the intellect to

---

[1] Or such judgments may be negative: *e.g.* "There is no fireplace in this room "; " This paper is not blue " ; " Two and two are not five " ; " Two straight lines cannot enclose a space ".

[2] Chaps. xiv.-xxi., especially §§ 105, 109, 115, 122, 123, 127, 128.

judge *directly* and *spontaneously* that the datum *appears* to "exist" (independently of the cognitive process), to be "external," "material," "coloured," etc.; and which (2) can be seen by intellectual reflection on the whole cognitive process and its content to be such that those characteristics adequately ground and guarantee the truth of the *reflex* judgment that the datum *is really* what the spontaneous judgment pronounced it to be. But in vindicating the claims of such evidence to justify these conclusions a number of points must be noted.

First, the object apprehended by the judgment being a relation of real identity or non-identity, or, in other words, the judgment being a representation of the presented real datum through the medium of such a relation, the objective evidence in this datum is an apprehended quality or characteristic in it which grounds this relation, or what we have called an "ontological exigency" which demands that the datum be intellectually represented through the assertion of such a relation.

Secondly, even the direct, spontaneous judgment involves the use of abstract intellectual concepts as predicates ("existence," "externality," "extensity," "colour," etc., etc.), and their application to the datum apprehended in the concrete as subject. Therefore the reflex or philosophical justification of the real truth-claim of the direct judgment rests on the evidence whereby we have justified the thesis of Moderate Realism that those abstract concepts are derived from the concrete sense data, and are formed according to the apprehended real or ontological exigencies of the sense data.[1] We have already shown that while the *form* of intellectual conception,—*i.e.* the fact that the continuously presented stream or manifold of sense data is apprehended in the form of abstract and universal concepts, simple and complex, transcendental, generic and specific,—is determined by the nature of the human intellect as a power of "abstractive" cognition, the *matter* of its concepts is determined by the nature of the sense manifold in which this matter is seen to be embodied.

Thirdly, although the process by which the intellect forms its complex concepts from simpler factors, pronouncing such complexes to be real and objective possibilities of existence, and the process by which it applies them to actual sense data to interpret these latter as actual existences, are both conducted under the

---

[1] *Cf.* what was said above concerning the "real affinities" of the factors of our intellectual concepts, vol. i., §§ 88, 89, 91.

influence of what appears to be objective evidence, or to be in other words the real nature of the presented realities, nevertheless the intellect *is liable to error in both processes*. Leaving the fallibility of the former process for consideration below, let us fix our attention on the latter process : that by which we form such judgments as " This is a flower " ; " This flower is a rose " ; " This rose is red," etc. Now since, as we saw in dealing with sense perception, we may, from a variety of causes (*cf.* § 118), be mistaken in such immediate spontaneous judgments, the question arises whether or under what conditions the *"sense* evidence" of what a thing *appears* can be a *sufficient* ground for judging what the thing *really is*, or a sufficient motive for certain assent to such a judgment as true.   And the further question also arises, whether what the thing appears can ever be an *infallible* test of the truth of the judgment as to what the thing really is, and a *cogent* or *compelling* motive of assent to this judgment.

The answer to the first question is in the affirmative, but with these qualifications: provided we have by reflection convinced ourselves that in the case in point our perception is normal and accurate ; provided all the conditions, organic and external, for accurate perception are verified ; provided the mutually corrective and corroborative information of all the senses that can subserve the judgment have been actually availed of.[1]   If a person neglect the safeguards thus furnished by reflection, if he be unaware of their necessity, if through whatsoever cause he fail to make use of them, he is liable to mistake apparent evidence for real evidence, and thus to err in assenting to what he thinks to be a self-evident judgment of sense perception. And it may even happen that on the one hand, whether through inexperience or inadvertence, he may be at the time unable to avail of those safeguards, while on the other hand the apparent evidence may be such as there and then to *compel* his assent. Hence we have to recognize that there are errors which, for the time and for individual human minds, are inevitable (*cf.* § 16).

---

[1] Should we add also : "provided the observer has convinced himself that his spontaneous belief in the trustworthiness of his senses is philosophically justified" ? No ; not in the sense that he must have made a systematic study of this whole epistemological problem ; but only in the sense that should he happen to have encountered from any source any apparently serious reasons for doubt or misgiving as to the general trustworthiness of normal sense perception, he must of course have succeeded in convincing himself that those reasons were only apparent and not real reasons for doubting.

But in the faculty of intellectual reflection the human mind has the means of correcting such errors.

The answer to the second question is that when reflection has convinced us that our actual perception is normal and accurate, *i.e.* endowed with all the conditions requisite for trustworthiness, the evidence (of what the thing appears to be) persists often,— and, indeed, as a general rule,—so clear as to be a cogent or com-pelling motive of assent to the judgment that the thing really is such or such. When it does remain thus cogent it is an infallible test of truth in the sense that the intellect cannot be the victim of an illusion in yielding to it. The reflective process, whereby the observer judges that all the conditions of normal perception are present in the particular case, is of course dependent not merely on the evidence that the present perception is normal, but also on the evidence of what constitutes normal sense experience in himself and others. And although there can be cases in which he may err in forming this reflective, justifying judgment, there are certainly cases,—and they are the generality of cases,—in which the evidence for this judgment is so clearly cogent that he cannot be mistaken in interpreting his present sense perception as giving him certain knowledge that "this thing is really what it appears to him". We may say, therefore, that although the human mind is fallible in its interpretation of sense evidence, *i.e.* although the individual observer may err accidentally in judging that things really are as they appear ; and although there are even cases in which such error is for the time *inevitable ;* nevertheless there are cases in which error is *impossible, i.e.* in which all the conditions of normal and trustworthy ‚perception are so clearly present that it is physically impossible for the observer to mis-interpret the sense datum.[1]

To this, however, it may be objected that the individual ob-server is never *compelled* by the evidence to formulate or accept such a judgment as *e.g.* "This rose *is really* red," but only such a judgment as "This rose *appears* red *to all normal sense percep-*

[1] We say " physically impossible," because in any individual perception the Author of Nature may, for a higher, moral purpose, miraculously modify the normal physical appearances on which our interpretations of the extramental reality and nature of sense data are based. The consequent accidental deception of the indi-vidual is therefore metaphysically possible. But universal sense deception would be metaphysically impossible, because purposeless and incompatible with the Divine Wisdom and Veracity. *Cf. supra*, § 123. *Science of Logic*, ii., § 224, pp. 100-2, 112-13 ; § 250, pp. 220 1.

tion" (*cf.* 119, 123, 126). The reply of the ordinary man would be something to this effect : "It is just precisely because (1) this rose *appears* red to me, and because (2) I know my own perception to be normal, and this rose to appear red to all other possible normal perceivers, that I feel not only justified but compelled to judge that this rose *is really* red ". In other words the *cogency* or *compelling force* of sense *appearances* as evidence of *reality* can persist throughout the reflective process by which the intellect tests and determines the real evidential or truth-revealing value of these appearances.[1] The difficulties raised by sensists, phenomenists, or idealists, against the real validity of sense evidence cannot affect its natural cogency. Either these difficulties are seen to be really groundless and frivolous, in which case the irresistibly formed spontaneous judgment of perception is philosophically justified ; or else such difficulties will seem insuperable, in which case also the spontaneous judgment will continue to assert itself as a practical principle of action in spite of the supervening theoretical scepticism.

We may say, then, that the immediate evidence of actual *normal* sense perception is for the individual a sufficient criterion of the truth of the spontaneous judgments suggested by it, and an adequate motive for physical certitude as to the truth of those judgments. We are liable to misinterpret sense evidence, *i.e.* to be misled by appearances. Experience of such mistakes will teach us that not all apparent sense evidence is real evidence, but only such sense evidence as fulfils certain conditions which can be discovered by reflection on our past experiences. In other words our perception must be normal in order that its evidence be trustworthy. This, however, does not mean that explicit knowledge of its conformity with other people's perceptions is a prerequisite of our accepting it as trustworthy ; nor does it mean that such conformity is the test of its trustworthiness (126): for if the evidence furnished by the individual's own sense perception did not of itself guarantee the truth of his spontaneous interpretations of his sense data neither could any cumulation of such evidences guarantee it,—apart from the fact that it is only on the evidence of his own sense perceptions that he knows of the distinct and independent existence of other

---

[1] It is this cogency, or *vis insuperabilis*, which persists on reflection, that JEANNIÈRE sets down as one of the characteristics by which we can discern evidence to be *real—op. cit.*, p. 252.

human beings. It only means that his spontaneous interpretation of a particular portion of his sense experience, as revealing to
him other men having experiences similar to his own, helps him
to determine the conditions under which his own perceptions will
be trustworthy;[1] and that the experienced conformity of his
own perceptions with those of other people will be for him a
confirming criterion of the trustworthiness of his own sense perceptions.

Finally it may be noted that when we claim for immediate
sense evidence the prerogative of being the supreme criterion of
the truth of our conviction that a material universe exists in time
and space independently of our perception of it, and the ultimate
motive of our certitude as to the truth of that conviction, we do
not make this claim for immediate sense evidence *in itself, in
isolation from the evidence we have for the validity of our intellectual concepts, and for the truth of rational principles of the ideal
order.* From our treatment of the general problem of sense perception[2] it will be clear that the conviction[3] is philosophically
justified only by what we may perhaps appropriately describe as
the intellectual interpretation or *rationalization* of sense evidence
by the evidence of necessary principles of the ideal order. The
claim of this latter evidence to be, therefore, in ultimate analysis,
the supreme criterion of truth and the ultimate motive of human
certitude, we must now briefly examine.

152. APPLICATION TO IMMEDIATE INTELLECTUAL EVI-
DENCE OF PRINCIPLES OF THE IDEAL ORDER.—(5) In refuting Kant's theory that the mind is compelled from the
subjective side by *a priori* forms to effect the necessary and universal syntheses called axioms or principles (63-65), and in proving
that it is compelled rather from the *objective* side by *what it sees
in the presented reality*, in the content of its concepts (68),—we
have really proved that objective evidence is the criterion of the
truth of such principles and the motive of our assent to them.
What we there established explicitly was the *objectivity*, the real
objectivity, of those principles. But in *their* case objectivity is
really indistinguishable from truth. For the abstract thought-

---

[1] It is the same judicial faculty which judges spontaneously and by critical reflection; and in obedience to the same order of principles of interpretation and motives
of assent (24).

[2] Chaps. xiv. and xv., especially §§ 103-5, 109-11.

[3] And *a fortiori* whatever certain knowledge we may attain to concerning the
qualities and *nature* of the material universe.

objects which they compare, and pronounce to be necessarily
inclusive or exclusive of one another, are absolutely simple and
unanalysable. They are the ultimate terms of intellectual
analysis. Hence their mere presence to the intellect simultaneously (*e.g.* the presence of "2 + 2" and "4"; or "whole"
and "part"; or "straight line" and "shortest distance between
two points"; or "event" and "efficient cause"; or "veracity"
and "virtue"; or "responsibility" and "liberty"; etc., etc.),
necessitates the intuition of a *nexus* between them, and that in
virtue of *their apprehended content.* If the intellect apprehends
them at all it *necessarily* and *infallibly* apprehends the *nexus*
between them. That is to say, in the apprehension of axioms
or first principles of the ideal order intellect is infallible, even
though in forming its more complex concepts, and in deriving
remote conclusions from principles, it is fallible.[1] If, therefore,
those ultimate thought-objects are *aspects of reality,* *i.e.* if their
content is *real* and *given* through sense to intellect, then those
axiomatic syntheses or judgments are genuine intellectual representations of reality; they conform the mind with reality; they
are objectively, really and evidently true. But in dealing with
the relation of conception with perception, the relation of abstract
concepts with their concrete counterparts in sense consciousness,
we have shown that while the *form* of our concepts (*i.e.* their
abstractness and universality) is indeed a mode of apprehension
which springs from the nature of the human intellect,—and is
therefore an *intentio logica,* an *ens rationis* or mental construction,
—the matter of our concepts is *real,* is given to, and not constructed by intellect.[2] And in dealing with the relation between
sense perception and extramental reality we have shown our
concrete sense percepts to be manifestations or revelations of this
reality to our minds.[3] Hence those self-evident axioms or
principles give us a genuine insight into reality as it is in itself,
and not merely into mentally constructed "objects" or "phenomena". In other words they do not reveal merely the constitution of the human intellect (140); they reveal the nature of
reality: they are "*laws of reality,* laws to which whatever is
either actual or possible must conform, laws which are partial expressions of the *nature* or *essence* of *reality*".[4] Hence the self-

[1] *Cf.* § 68, iii., which should be re-read in connexion with the present context.
[2] *Cf.* § 69; chaps. ix. and xii.   [3] *Cf.* Part IV., *passim.*
[4] Vol. i., § 69, pp. 243-4.

evidence which compels the assent of the intellect to such axioms is the manifestation, to the mind, of objective reality or objective truth as being necessarily representable by the mind through such axioms (30-33).

153. "TESTING" EVIDENCE. INFALLIBILITY OF INTEL-LECT.—From those various applications of the doctrine that objective evidence is the supreme criterion of truth, and the ultimate basis of certitude (149-52), there emerge a number of important considerations which will help the student to appreciate the real meaning of the general thesis.

We have described objective evidence generally, whether mediate or immediate, as consisting in certain real or ontological exigencies of the datum presenting itself for interpretation to the intellect. That is to say, in the presented datum taken in its whole concrete context the intellect sees such nature or features or characteristics as demand that the datum be represented by the intellect through the affirmation or negation of some judicial *nexus* between concepts. Whether the suggested judgment be of the ideal order or the existential order, whether it be a judgment of science (based on the intrinsic character of the presented datum : intrinsic evidence) or a judgment of faith (based on testimony or authority extrinsic to the datum : extrinsic evidence), it will be evident if, and only if, the datum is apprehended as such that it either compels the intellect to form the judgment or else at least expels all prudent fear of error from the intellect forming and assenting to the judgment.

Hence it appears that the *evidence* for the judgment is *not really distinct from the reality which the judgment interprets*. Nor is it : it is this reality itself as revealing itself to the intellect ; or, in other words, it is the ontological truth of this reality. Evidence, as a criterion of truth, is not really distinct from the truth itself of which it is a criterion. Hence to say that evidence is the criterion of truth is really to say that truth is its own criterion : and this is in fact the force of the aphorism, *Verum index sui*. The test of the truth of the judgment (*logical* truth), the test of its conformity with the reality which it represents, is ultimately this reality itself revealing itself to the mind (*ontological* truth) as demanding such representation.

But while this disposes of the difficulty of the *diallelus*, urged by Montaigne (39, B) against the possibility of finding any ultimate criterion, it seems to involve the equally serious difficulty that evidence as a test of truth is practically useless. For to say that the ultimate test of the truth of any judgment by which we interpret or represent a reality is simply the clearness with which this reality reveals itself as representable (so to speak) by the judgment,—is not this assigning as a test something which itself needs to be tested ? What appears to be real evidence need not be real evidence ; what appears to be a real exigency of a given subject for a certain predicate need not be a real exigency : in a word, evidence itself seems to need testing, and what we desiderate is some instrument or means of testing it ; but evidence itself cannot be this means, and hence cannot be the ultimate criterion of truth or the ultimate motive of certitude (39, E).

This apparently serious difficulty is based largely on a misconception of the claim that is really made for evidence. The scholastic thesis does not at all imply that evidence is a sort of *open sesame* or magic charm lying ever ready at the disposal of the intellect for the discrimination of true from false judgments. It is no sort of automatic device which would exempt the intellect from the task of scrutinizing closely and laboriously its real data, of comparing, analysing, synthesizing, reflecting on these data, in order to represent and interpret them faithfully. It is only by such processes that the intellect can *lay bare their real exigencies, i.e.* the grounds or *evidence* in them for the judgments which will represent them rightly.   " Evidence itself seems to need testing : " yes, in the sense that appearances need to be scrutinized by intellect to bring to light their real significance, their real exigencies as data for interpretation, and thus to suggest the judgments which will really and truly represent the realities which have such appearances.   Intellect is the only "judicial instrument " we have for testing appearances, for interpreting the real significance of the modes in which, and the aspects under which, the presented reality appears.   Whether in doing so it is fallible or infallible, is an intelligible question : in doing so, in endeavouring to interpret or represent the given reality through judicial acts which assert what this reality is or is not, the intellect is objectively determined, guided, influenced by the clearness with which the appearing reality demands such representations, *i.e.* by its *evidence*.   But to talk of this evidence itself as being an *infallible* test of truth, or *infallible* motive of assent, is really just as unmeaning as to talk of the reality itself, or its ontological truth, as being infallible.   It is not really of the evidence, the objective determinant of the logical truth of the judgment, the objective motive of assent to the judgment, that we can predicate fallibility or infallibility ; but only of the intellectual faculty in the process of forming its judgments in conformity with what the presented reality, in so far as it is apprehended, really demands.

When it is said that " evidence itself needs testing," this may mean that the presented reality needs to have all its appearances in their whole concrete context scrutinized by intellect, so as to determine what *real* evidence is contained in the "apparent" evidence 'or "appearances " ; and this, of course, is quite true.[1] Or it may mean that mediate evidence needs to be tested by assuring ourselves that it is real evidence ; and this is equally true. To accept a judgment on *mediate* evidence (intrinsic or extrinsic), we must have *immediate* evidence (whether cogent or reasonably sufficient) that its truth is involved in some other judgment or judgments; if these are only mediately evident their connexion with other judgments must likewise be immediately evident ; and so on till we come to self-evident judgments. It is in such series of immediate evidences that mediate evidence consists. Thus it is the intellect that tests and evaluates mediate evidence,—aided by logical canons of interpretation and inference, canons which are already accepted by the intellect on their own evidence. We shall examine later the reasons, repeatedly noticed already, why the intellect is fallible or subject to error in carrying on this process.

But what about immediate cogent evidence? Is intellect infallible in yielding to such evidence and judging reality according to it? Or do we really need some other criterion to satisfy us as to the truth of the judgments to which it compels us to yield our assent?

We have already distinguished between immediate *sense* evidence for judgments of the existential order, judgments which interpret the immediate data of sense perception,[2]—and immediate

---

[1] We have already distinguished between the appearance of reality *to sense* and its appearance *to intellect* (125, 128). The latter appearance of course depends on the former. But intellect can scrutinize, and reflect upon, the sense appearance. It is only by so doing that intellect can detect in the sense appearance *real evidence*, *i.e.* the intellectual ground for interpreting what the sense datum *really is*. If the intellect judges spontaneously, unreflectively, hastily, according to the sense impressions, it is of course liable to error.

[2] To which we may add the evidence of consciousness for the existence of the conscious self or *Ego* (chap. xiii.).

18 *

intellectual evidence for abstract axioms of the ideal order. The individual human intellect, judging spontaneously according to *immediate sense evidence*, may err occasionally—and even for the time unavoidably—in its interpretations of individual sense data (151). But when it reflects on the relativity of sense data to the perceiver's organic conditions, and to external, spatial conditions (118); when it adverts to the consequent requirement that the perception must be normal in order that the spontaneous intellectual interpretation be true (119),—the individual intellect has always the power, by such reflection, to avoid or correct mistakes and so attain to true knowledge. Furthermore, when each individual learns that there has always prevailed among men a common, universal, unanimous assent to the spontaneous judgments that "an external material universe exists independently of their minds"; that "it really possesses the qualities revealed to them through their senses," etc.,—this observed fact is for each individual an unquestionable confirmation of the truth of such elementary, easy, and irresistibly formed spontaneous judgments (122). In other words, it confirms the trustworthiness of immediate sense evidence and establishes as a reasoned certitude the conviction that the human intellect is infallible in attaining to the truth embodied in such judgments. We refer, of course, only to the judgments which assert the broad fact of the mind-independent existence of the material universe and its qualities; not to the unreflecting judgments of "naïf dogmatism" concerning its nature in detail, some of which may be erroneous. And if doubts are raised, as they have been raised by idealists, concerning the real truth-value of men's uniform, spontaneous verdict on the broad fact itself, we have shown, by establishing the truth of Realism, that a reasonably careful, cautious and unprejudiced application of critical, reflective thought can dispel such doubts as really groundless.

Secondly, we have held that in assenting to abstract axioms of the ideal order the intellect is determined by immediate, cogent, objective evidence; that this is the supreme test of their truth and the ultimate motive of our assent to them; and that intellect is infallible in yielding assent to them on this motive (44; 68, III.; 152). We have already shown that the objective terms compared in such axioms are *aspects of reality*, that they reveal *reality* to the mind; furthermore, that they are simple, ultimate, unanalysable. If, therefore, it is reality that so reveals itself, then the real or ontological exigencies which such aspects involve, for the relations of identity or incompatibility expressed by these axioms, secure *eo ipso* the *truth* of the intellectual representations of the reality through these axioms. For these real exigencies of the objective terms constitute the real evidence of the relations established by intellect between them. And this real evidence is as clearly present to the intellect as the terms themselves. Either, therefore, the intellect does not apprehend the terms, *i.e.* the *reality*, at all, or it also and *eo ipso* necessarily and infallibly represents the reality by apprehending the relations.

154. REFLECTION SHOWS THE COGENT EVIDENCE FOR SPONTANEOUS ASSENTS TO BE SUFFICIENT EVIDENCE FOR REASONED CERTITUDE.—A few points, however, call for notice. First, when scholastics emphasize the doctrine that the immediate objective evidence of axioms of the ideal order is the supreme criterion of all truth and the ultimate motive of all human certitude, they are not to be understood as implying that the evidence we have for the judgments that are of the most profound importance to the human race can be reduced to such evidence (*cf.* 148). The *true* solutions of the great problems concerning the origin, nature, and destiny of man and the universe, concerning the immortality of the soul, the existence of God, the reality of the moral order, the obligation and sanctions of religion,—are, needless to say, not immediately evident. Indeed *no* solutions of these problems are immediately evident. Nor can the true solutions of them be deduced from self-evident axioms of the ideal order by any process of pure deductive reasoning, of which every step would be cogently self-evident (35) : such, for instance, as the reasoning employed in pure mathematics. Their solution involves *mixed* demonstration.[1] It therefore implies certitude about some judgments of the *existential* order ; it implies that abstract concepts and principles are validly applicable to the actually experienced order of concrete, existing things, *i.e.* it implies the truth of Moderate Realism ; and finally it implies well-grounded certitude on our part that in the actual process of applying concepts to percepts, of interpreting singulars by universals, of locating the intellectual abstract in the sense concrete, we are allowing ourselves to be guided by the *real evidence*, *i.e.* that we are representing or interpreting the reality presented to us for

---

[1] *Cf. Science of Logic*, ii., § 254, *c; supra,* § 154.

interpretation only according to its real or ontological exigencies and not otherwise.[1]   Now this evidence is by no means cogent. It can be sufficient to ground a firm or certain assent ; but, clearly, it allows wide scope for the exercise of prudence, care, and caution in conducting the intellectual processes of conception, judgment, generalization, induction, deduction, etc., through which alone we can hope to attain to a reasoned and reasonable certitude regarding the true solutions of the momentous problems referred to. There is nothing to justify the impression which one sometimes encounters concerning the scholastic doctrine of evidence (as the supreme criterion of truth and the ultimate motive of certitude), that this doctrine would make the attainment of human certitude on the ultimate problems of science, philosophy, and religion, a much simpler and easier matter than it really is ; or that it seems to imply that the evidence for these ultimate truths ought to be, and must be, and really is of the same cogent character as *e.g.* the evidence forthcoming in mathematical demonstrations. On the contrary, scholastics have always distinguished between cogent evidence for the truth of judgments and reasonably sufficient evidence for the credibility of judgments (11, 12, 38, 67); and they have always protested against the unreasonableness of demanding as a *universal* condition of certain assent to judgments in *every* domain the sort of cogent evidence which compels intellectual assent to asbtract axioms.[2]

The real reason why scholastics have emphasized the importance of the thesis that the " supreme criterion or test of true or genuine knowledge, and the ultimate motive of human certitude, is to be found in the intrinsic, immediate objective evidence of first principles of the ideal order," [3]—is not far to seek.

---

[1] It is this question of the possibility and grounds of certitude *about concrete matters* (especially in the domain of religion), or the possibility and legitimacy of applying abstract principles of the ideal order to the interpretation of concrete matters of fact and thus reaching certitude about such interpretations, that Cardinal Newman has examined in his *Grammar of Assent*.   His analysis, which is ably conducted on original lines, will at least convince the student that such certitude rests on evidential grounds which, so far from being intellectually cogent, call for the exercise of diligence, candour, caution and prudence, in appreciating their sufficiency for reasoned and reflex certitude.   But it is hardly too much to say that the author would have been materially assisted in his investigation by a fuller knowledge of the scholastic doctrine of Moderate Realism than he was in a position to bring to the investigation.

[2] *Cf. Science of Logic,* ii., § 203, p. 12; § 275, pp. 322-7.   *Cf.* vol. i., § 67, p. 234 n.

[3] Vol. i., § 67, p. 233 n.

It is simply because unless such evidence is a revelation *of reality* to the intellect, unless the intellect infallibly attains to true or faithful (if inadequate) representations of reality through the intuition of such principles, it cannot possibly attain to any truth, but is doomed to hopeless scepticism. And why? Because these principles are involved in every single item of what we regard as knowledge. They form the very warp and woof of all knowledge. They are implicit in all our judgments ; and all inference, all inductive generalizations from facts and all deductive explanations of facts, depend on them. Therefore the real truth-value of all our knowledge, *i.e.* its value as giving us a genuine insight into reality, depends altogether on whether the intellect, when its assent to such principles is compelled,—as all, even subjectivists and sceptics, admit that it is compelled,—thereby gets an insight into reality. And this in turn depends on whether the compelling factor is *objective evidence*, *i.e.* the *reality itself* presented as necessarily representable by intellect through such axiomatic judgments, as having and displaying a *real exigency* for such representation ; or whether on the contrary the compelling factor is a subjective influence which, whether conscious or unconscious, has no claim to any *evidential* value, *i.e.* to any significance as *manifesting reality* to the mind. From this it is clear that what scholastics describe as "evidence" would be useless as an index to *truth* and a motive of *certitude* (*i.e.* firm assent to judgments as *true*, as revealing *reality* to the mind), if it appeared on reflection either that the determining factor of the judicial *nexus* between our concepts were not objective, or that the concepts containing that determining factor (or sufficient ground) of the *nexus* were not themselves manifestations of reality.

In other words, the function of evidence, even of cogent immediate evidence, as revealing real truth and determining certitude, had to be vindicated against the suspicion cast upon it by subjectivists, and notably by Kant, in the manner in which we saw (29-35) that it is possible to raise such a suspicion. For there is a sense in which even self-evident judgments can be, and have been, doubted. It has been doubted whether what is called their "evidence" is indeed real evidence, *i.e.* whether what the mind *sees*, in assenting to them, is indeed reality,—whether it is a feature of reality that is representable and faithfully represented in and through them. Until such a doubt was removed the scholastic thesis in regard to evidence stood unproven. And how was such a doubt removed? By the whole process of introspective analysis which established the objectivity of the *nexus* in regard to our judgments, the reality of our concepts as propounded in Moderate Realism, and the reality of our percepts in regard to sense perception. And what was it that guided us in our investigations and determined our conclusions? At every stage in the process we reflected on what came into consciousness ; we examined the *appearances* of our data as critically and carefully as we could with a view to discovering their *real demands* upon our faculty of interpretation, *i.e.* their *real evidence*, and with a view to representing or interpreting them accordingly. The whole process was not a process of demonstration but of introspective analysis (33). And if it be described as a process of "testing" evidence, it must be observed that on the subjective side our testing "instrument" was intellect, and on the objective side we had no test for evidence *except evidence itself:* which means simply that we tried to judge *appearances* critically according to what we detected, in the appearing reality, as its real exigencies for intellectual interpretation, *i.e.* its *real evidence*.

This is what the human mind has to do in every department if it is to attain to truth and avoid error : it has to explore the data of experience, or how things appear, in order to discover, as far as it can, what intellectual interpretations they really call for, or what judgments will, as far as they go, truly represent what those things are. This applies equally to men's "common" knowledge, to their "scientific" knowledge, to their "philosophical" convictions, and to their "religious" convictions. The mind has certain possession of truth only in so far as it knows its judgments to be in conformity with *what reality demands* as its intellectual representations. Hence those real exigencies of things must be *clear* to the intellect before it can give a firm or certain assent to the judgments they call for : *i.e.* sufficiently clear either to compel assent or to be reasonably and prudently considered to yield adequate ground for assent. But though some of those exigencies are clear *ab initio*, most of them can be made clear only *gradually* and *by the sustained application of intellect* to the data of human experience. This is true especially of the evidence for the ethical and religious truths that are of the deepest import to human life.[1] Hence the fact that real objective evidence, or the manifestation of reality to the intellect, is the supreme test of truth and the ultimate motive of certitude, by no means dispenses the intellect from labour : "There is no royal road to knowledge". In the data of experience there is *potential* evidence, so to speak, for as much truth as the finite human mind can ever reach concerning man and the universe ; but this potential evidence must be made *actual* to the individual mind before it can "inform " the individual mind with truth ; and only by its own active application can the individual mind make this potential evidence actual.

---

[1] That is, for reasoned, reflex certitude in regard to such truths. Obviously, it is not by way of original research that the masses of mankind attain to their spontaneous ethical and religious convictions : they receive these on extrinsic evidence, by way of authority,—a vehicle which can have the requisite conditions for grounding firm or certain assent to its deliverances.

CHAPTER XXIV.

OTHER INTELLECTUALIST THEORIES OF CERTITUDE. TRADITIONALISM.

155. OTHER TESTS. SPENCER. DESCARTES. "CIRCULAR" THEORIES.—The conclusions we have reached in regard to the function and force of evidence will affect different types of mind differently. They show that the human intellect can attain to some truth [1] with reasoned certitude, provided it prudently follow its own natural dictates and assent firmly only to such judgments as it sees to be clearly called for by the real exigencies of the data presented for its interpretation. They therefore prove the attitude of Scepticism (chap. iv.) to be unreasonable. On the other hand they show that although the intellect is infallible in its assent to self-evident abstract axioms, and to self-evident interpretations of the immediate concrete data of conscious experience, it is not infallible in interpreting the truth-value or knowledge-value of such compelled spontaneous assents, or in interpreting the real nature either of the human mind itself or of the world that is given it for interpretation. Hence they account for the possibility of error,—and for its prevalence in regard to the solutions of those ultimate questions that are of the most profound import to man, the questions which constitute the domain of philosophy proper. Our conclusions are therefore in conformity with the broad and undeniable facts which emerge from the history of philosophy.

But there are many philosophers who will not allow that it is by the exercise of intellect or reason on the data of experience, —by interpreting these data and reasoning about them in the light of the demands which they make on this faculty reflecting on them,—that the human mind can or does attain to the possession of any truth and certitude, or at least to truth and certitude regarding the great questions of the origin, nature, and destiny of man and the universe. The anti-intellectualist or voluntarist

---

[1] To *how much* truth ? *Cf. infra*, § 173.

theories of knowledge, represented by Kant's *Practical Philo-sophy*, and in our own time by *Pragmatism* or *Humanism*, will be seen below (chap. xxv.) to involve a perversion of the right use of reason confronted with the problem of knowledge.

Again, there are philosophers who, apparently underrating and losing faith in the power of the human intellect to attain to a reasoned certitude on those same fundamental problems by scrutinizing the evidence furnished by the data of human ex-perience, contend that it is only by the aid of a supernatural Divine Revelation that man has attained, or can attain, to such certitude. This theory—known as Fideism or Traditionalism—will next claim our attention. In passing, however, from the subject of evidence as the criterion of truth, we may glance briefly here at a few theories, some of which are really only modifications of the scholastic theory, and others attempts to indicate some means *apparently* distinct from evidence itself, for testing the truth of judgments.

(1) We have already examined (43, 44) the test proposed by Spencer, as the supreme and ultimate criterion of the truth of a judgment, *viz.* the "inconceivability of its opposite"; and we saw that not all inconceivability is, as he contended, subjective, psychological, relative and merely negative. There is an incon-ceivability which springs from our direct and positive intuition of the real, ontological incompatibility of the terms compared in the "opposite" or "contradictory" of the judgment. Such, for instance, is the incompatibility of the subject "two straight lines" with the predicate "enclosing a space". Such, too, is the inconceivability of the contradictory of such a judgment as "two and two are four," or such a judgment as "I exist". Manifestly the test entitled "inconceivability of the opposite," *understood in this sense* of positively apprehended real and objective impossibility, is precisely the same as the scholastic test of immediate, cogent, objective evidence,—stated, however, in a needlessly indirect and possibly misleading manner: for such judgments are not seen to be true because their opposites are seen to be inconceivable, but rather their opposites are seen to be inconceivable because they themselves are seen to be objectively and necessarily true.

(2) We also saw (30, 34) that the first test adopted by Des-cartes was that known as the "clear and distinct idea": he could not doubt his own existence because he "saw very clearly that, in order to think, one must exist"; and so he accepted as a

general rule the test "that the things which we conceive very clearly and very distinctly are all true".[1] It is beyond doubt, too, that he accepted this test as guaranteeing the *objective truth* of the intuition of his own existence, and not merely in the Kantian sense of revealing this intuition as a *subjective* mental synthesis of conscious thought-products (30, 31). Now, if the test is understood in this objective sense,[2]—if it means that the clearly apprehended real exigency of a given conscious content to be represented by some definite judgment or interpretation, or the cogency with which it compels such a judgment, is to be taken as adequate ground for the *objective truth* of this judgment, —then the test is obviously identical with that described by scholastics as cogent, immediate, objective evidence. Where Descartes erred, therefore, was (*a*) in not applying the test impartially to other self-evident truths besides that of his own existence; (*b*) in thinking that it was not ultimate, in entertaining a serious doubt about its real validity, in imagining that its real validity needed to be vindicated by establishing its dependence on the Divine Veracity; and (*c*) in trying to prove the existence of God by employing principles and premises for the truth of which he had no other test than the one he had just declared to be unreliable (34).

(3) It is needless to point out that a reasoned knowledge of the *veracity of God* as the author of our faculties cannot possibly be for us the ultimate guarantee of the truth of our judgments : on such an assumption any and every attempted proof of God's existence would be a *petitio principii*.[3]

(4) The same is true of the theory according to which the ultimate guarantee of the truth of necessary principles of the ideal order would be not their objective self-evidence but the knowledge that they are expressions of the *Eternal Exemplar or Archetype Ideas in the Divine Mind*.[4] In the *ontological* order, of course, the Divine Essence is the ultimate ground of the necessary truth of such judgments.[5] But it is another thing altogether to contend that in the *logical* order we must *know* this dependence of truth on the Divine Intellect before we can have any reasoned certitude :[6] if this were so, reasoned certitude would be unattainable.

(5) Again, we have seen that the immediate disciples of Descartes, and notably MALEBRANCHE (80, 123), considering that even immediate sense evidence, as presented to the intellect, could give us no cognitive insight into the

[1] *Discours de la Méthode,—apud* MERCIER, *op. cit.*, pp. 213-14.
[2] *Cf.* vol. i., § 30, p. 112, n. 1.
[3] *Cf.* MERCIER, *op. cit.*, §§ 94-6, for critique of Descartes' arguments.
[4] *Ibid.*, § 100 ; *cf.* vol. i., §§ 69, 70, 80 ; *supra*, § 139.
[5] *Cf. Ontology*, § 20.   [6] MERCIER, *op. cit.*, § 101.

existence of contingent, material reality, *i.e.* reality *transcending* the *Ego* and *external* to the *Ego*, adopted the view that the only rational ground we have for assenting to judgments which affirm the existence and nature of material reality must be the conviction that such judgments are *intuitions of this reality in the Divine Mind decreeing its existence.* Not only does this theory confuse our knowledge of the *existence* of things with our knowledge of the *mode of their origin*,[1] but it likewise involves a *vicious circle* and renders all knowledge impossible. For we are certainly not conscious of seeing either the essences or the existences of contingent things in the Divine Mind. The existence of God has therefore to be proved. But in order to prove it the individual human being must be certain (*a*) of the objective and real truth of principles of the ideal order (on the ground of their immediate intellectual evidence), and (*b*) of his own existence as a *real, permanent, abiding*, contingent being, distinct from the flow of his conscious states. But he cannot consistently accept the evidence forthcoming for this latter conviction if he rejects the *similar* evidence furnished by sense perception for the real, permanent, abiding existence of a material reality distinct from his perception, and from himself the perceiver.[2]

In a similar way, when Berkeley (failing to see *how* the conscious subject can transcend his own conscious states, and apparently concluding that they cannot be transcended) denied that immediate sense evidence must be interpreted as revealing an external material reality whose real *esse* would be independent of its *percipi*, he was inconsistent in interpreting *any* of his conscious states as revealing, beyond themselves, anything in the nature of a real, permanent, abiding, substantial *Ego* or mind : an inconsistency which Hume was not slow to bring to light, and which he himself escaped only by drawing the logical conclusion of pan-phenomenism. From this intellectual morass Kant in turn tried to emerge ; but his effort was futile simply because he too misinterpreted the significance of objective evidence by clinging to the idealist postulate in the face of this same evidence.

156. CONSISTENCY AS A TEST OF TRUTH. RELATIVIST AND HEGELIAN CONCEPTIONS OF TRUTH AS CONSISTENCY.—Since, after all, evidence itself needs to be tested (153) ; or, at all events, since *real* evidence is nothing else than the reality itself clearly apprehended as intellectually representable by a certain judgment or synthesis of concepts, while on the other hand it is admitted that we may be mistaken in thinking that the presented reality does really demand such a judgment, and it is undeniable that judgments which some men regard as really evident others regard as inevident and doubtful,—would it not seem desirable, if it be possible, to call in the aid of some criterion which would be easier of application than evidence, and which would be at once a test both of truth and of evidence? Now such a criterion would be the *consistency, coherence, harmony* of all

---

[1] *Cf.* MERCIER, *op. cit.*, §§ 97-8.　　　　[2] *Cf. supra*, §§ 97, 100, 101, 111.

our judgments with one another. To determine when an *isolated* judgment is really evident and therefore true, when it is—as far as it goes—in conformity with reality, is often a difficult matter: the difficulty lying precisely in discovering what the "reality" is, or whether the judgment in question will faithfully represent it. Indeed, as we have seen, it might be and has been seriously questioned whether the mind can attain to reality in this absolute sense at all. But there is no such difficulty in determining whether a given judgment coheres or conflic ts with any portion or unit of the whole collection or system of judgments already accepted by men generally as true. In this way, the term with which each judgment would have to conform would be the whole system of universally accepted judgments: this system would in fact *be reality* in the only sense in which we can know reality. No doubt, the consistency of one judgment with another is not *truth*. Such fractional or partial consistency is consistency in the *narrower* sense of *mere* consistency; and it must be admitted that a whole series of judgments could be logically consistent with one another in that way and yet not true. The conformity of one judgment with another, or a limited group of others, is consistency in this narrower sense. But what can truth be, after all, but a *wider* consistency? The truth of each judgment would be its consistency with *the whole system* of accepted judgments; and the truth of the whole system would be the evident organic coherence and harmony of all its parts with one another. On this view, moreover, truth would still be the conformity of the mind judging or interpreting reality with the reality interpreted: for "reality," in the only sense in which we can intelligibly speak of reality as known or as object of knowledge, is reality as revealed in and through the whole system of judgments which are universally regarded as embodying knowledge. Nay, reality, in so far as it is known, is just this ever-growing system of mutually consistent and coherent interpretations of the data of human experience. If the truth of a judgment is the conformity it establishes between the mind and reality, this can only mean conformity with reality *in so far as reality is already known* (for it cannot mean conformity with an unknown reality); and reality is already known only in so far as it has manifested itself in the whole system of universally accepted judgments. Thus the consistency or coherence of our judgments in one harmonious system is at once the *criterium "constitutivum" veritatis* and the *criterium* "*manifestativum*" *veritatis*,—that which *constitutes* their truth and that which *reveals* their truth.

Such, in brief, is the claim put forward for "consistency" from different standpoints by advocates of the relativity of knowledge, such as Spencer and Mansel, and by supporters of the Hegelian philosophy, such as Wallace in his *Logic of Hegel*.[1] It contains a grain of truth amid much that is wholly erroneous and inadmissible.

The truth it contains is this: Consistency is obviously a *negative* test or essential condition of truth, in the sense that truth cannot contradict truth: if, therefore, it be *absent*, if two or more judgments are mutually contradictory or incompatible, we know that all of them cannot be true, and that possibly not even one of them is true. But it is not a *positive* test of truth inasmuch as it may be *present*, two or more judgments may be mutually compatible or consistent, and yet none of them may be true.

Now, the absence of consistency, as a negative test, is not a test distinct from evidence. For its dictate simply amounts to this: that if a judgment is clearly seen to be in itself or in its necessary implications incompatible with some other judgment *already known for certain to be true*, this is an evident sign that the former judgment cannot be really evident or true. But such inconsistency cannot be properly described as a test or criterion of evidence, for though it guides and helps us in determining that the judgment in question is lacking in real evidence, the inconsistency itself is not independent of evidence but is apprehended (if rightly apprehended) *only because it is itself evident*. Thus, the fact that a judgment appears to be incompatible with *already known truths*, simply causes us to *reflect*, to see if the inconsistency is really there, and if the judgment must be rejected as false. Similarly, if a judgment which appears to us to be evident is at the same time seen to conflict with *some view that is widely or commonly accepted as true*, this should cause us to reflect both on the evidence for the judgment and on the reasons and motives on account of which the view in question is accepted as true,—in order to ascertain, if we can, which is really evident.[2]

---

[1] *Cf.* RICKABY, *First Principles*, pp. 196-200. The Hegelian influence is evident in many comparatively recent works on Logic both in England and on the Continent.

[2] *Cf.* JEANNIÈRE, *op. cit.*, p. 252.

As to the positive consistency or coherence of a judgment with *what we otherwise know to be true* of its subject-matter, this, no doubt, has more or less weight as evidence of the truth of the judgment. The fact that a certain judgment or interpretation of the data of some domain of our experience harmonizes or fits in with what we already know about these data, and seems to amplify and extend our knowledge of them, or to give us a deeper insight into them,—this fact alone, so far as it goes, points to the truth of the judgment. But it can never *establish* the truth of the judgment unless and until this judgment be seen to be the *only possible* interpretation consistent with the data in question, *i.e.* unless and until it is seen to be necessarily involved in them and therefore logically inferrible from them : in which case we have simply a conclusion based on *mediate evidence.* This is the ordinary procedure in verifying inductive hypotheses. Now, physical science abounds in hypotheses of such a character that the only kind of evidence available, as pointing to their truth, lies in their harmony with, and their capacity to explain or account for, wide domains of physical facts. But this sort of cumulative evidence can never, strictly speaking, *establish the truth* of such hypotheses. It may give them that high degree of probability which warrants an assent of *practical certitude : i.e.* we are perfectly justified in giving a *provisional assent* to them, in accepting them as if their truth were established, in utilizing them and working on them as if we *knew* them to be true.[1] The test of "consistency" will carry us no farther than this ; and, so far, it is clear that its function in no way supplants that of objective evidence. But, as put forward above, it bears quite a different complexion, and involves claims which will not stand impartial scrutiny.

In the first place, the truth of a judgment is not its conformity with *other judgments* but its conformity with *reality.* Nor can reality be identified with the whole system of judgments universally accepted as forming a self-consistent or coherent whole or system. Furthermore, the reality which is the objective term of the conformity-relation of any individual judgment need not be reality *as already known through other judgments :* on the contrary, it is the reality as *now known through the individual judgment itself.* No doubt, when the judgment is *mediately*

---

[1] *Cf. Science of Logic,* ii., §§ 226-37, for illustrations of such hypotheses, and for account of the process of verifying inductive hypotheses generally.

evident this evidence will consist in the knowledge we already possess about the reality through other judgments, and the reality to which it conforms our minds will be the reality as already known.   But clearly this cannot be the case with *all* judgments, nor is it the case with immediately evident or self-evident judgments.   Unless there are some judgments through which we *begin to know* reality as it is, apart from what other judgments reveal about it, then either (*a*) we could never begin to have knowledge at all, or else (*b*) knowledge would have for its object not reality but only mental representations.   And this latter alternative is what the theory involves : that the individual mind, in judging, does not really transcend its own mental states : that these, of course, include other minds with similar states, but that all are phases of One Reality, and that this Reality can be said to be known precisely in so far as it is seen to be similarly represented in all individual minds (111).   To hold that (*a*) the truth of the individual judgment is its consistency with the whole system of accepted judgments, that (*b*) the truth of the whole system is precisely the coherence and harmony of its parts, and (*c*) that this whole system of mental relations *is reality*, —is to identify judgment with reality, the ideal with the real, thought with thing, logical with ontological, representations with things represented.   It is the theory of the immanence or relativity of knowledge, worked out into the only logical alternative to Solipsism, namely, Idealistic Monism.   But we have already justified the theory which contradicts this, namely, the realist view that the mind in its cognitive processes does transcend itself and attain to truth in the sense of *conformity with reality.*

In the second place, the contention that only those judgments are true, or expressive of reality (or, as the theory would have it, "constitutive" of reality), which are so necessarily inter-related and mutually coherent as to form a logically elaborated whole or system, is not only unproven, but is also palpably at variance with some of the very convictions which men universally accept as true.   In no other way could it be established than by showing that it is the only possible theory of truth and knowledge which renders intelligible the data of human experience.   But while there is another theory of knowledge and of reality which does render these data intelligible, namely, that which is embodied in the philosophy of Theism,[1] the present (Hegelian)

---

[1] *Cf. Science of Logic*, ii., §§ 215, 224, 231-2, 256-7.

conception is in conflict with even the most elementary verdicts of reason reflecting on the data of experience.[1] For although man can certainly effect partial systematizations of his knowledge, or of some of his knowledge, into what are called *sciences*, it cannot be maintained that knowledge is knowledge only in so far as it is elaborated into one single system of logically inter-related and metaphysically necessary judgments. If this were so, our ordinary existential judgments which interpret the con-crete, actual, contingent facts and happenings that form the data of experience, would not be knowledge at all. Nay, more, they would be erroneous: for according to the theory under consid-eration reality manifests itself in our individual human minds only as a Process which is at once Thought and Being evolving itself into a system of *absolutely or metaphysically necessary mental representations.* But *de facto* multitudes of judgments which men universally accept as true, as faithful interpretations of the data of experience, are also universally accepted as *contingent* judgments, and as representing their objects as contingent. The distinction between the facts of our experience as *contingent facts*, and the mutual relations of certain abstract objects of our thought as *necessary relations*, is a distinction which experience simply forces upon us by its evident reality, but for which, nevertheless, there is no room in the Hegelian theory. Finally, the human mind undeniably seeks to unify all its experience, to find an ultimate explanation of the whole universe of things, to account for its existence and nature by referring it to some adequate Explanatory Principle. But if it follows faithfully the evidence of the facts, the mind will be led certainly not to the monistic conception which contradicts its experience, but to the conception of a Transcendent Divine Being as Omnipotent Creator and All-Wise Ruler of the universe.

In the third place it may be pointed out that the "consist-ency" theory of truth seems to labour under a defect which, even were the theory otherwise faultless, would render it practically useless. For apparently, before we could be certain that any suggested judgment is true, we should need to have discovered its consistency, coherency, harmony, not merely with *some* of the judgments already included in the universally accepted system of mutually coherent (and therefore "true") judgments, but with

[1] *Cf. Science of Logic*, ii., §§ 215, 224, 231-2, 256-7.

the whole system itself. But to know this system would be, for any individual, an utter impossibility. Supporters of the theory would, of course, admit this, and merely reply that consequently all human truth is imperfect and relative: it is truth only " in the making ": it is subject to revision and readjustment: it is aiming at, and approximating to, an ideal that is indefinitely remote as to its complete attainment and realization. This erroneous conception of knowledge will be recognized as a deformation of the truth that no human knowledge gives an *adequate* insight into reality, that the human mind is finite and capable of progress in knowledge (143).

Finally, the theory we have been examining suggests and partly includes another and distinct criterion of truth, a test which has been advocated mainly by Traditionalists from their special standpoint: the theory that the ultimate test of the truth of (some, or all) human convictions is *the universal acceptance of such convictions by mankind generally.* This view we shall now examine in connexion with Traditionalism.

157. FIDEISM: HISTORICAL CAUSES.—If it be denied that reality, under the reflective scrutiny of the individual human mind, can by its own objective evidence produce therein some true and certain knowledge; if it be maintained that the individual human reason, following carefully and cautiously its own natural dictate to base its judgments and assents on the real evidence of the data of experience, cannot attain to reflex certitude in regard to the most urgent problems concerning man and the universe, the existence of a Supreme Being, the distinction of moral good and evil, human freedom and responsibility and immortality, the duty of religion, etc., etc.,—then there is no safe anchorage left for the mind in its search after truth. Nevertheless, men have at all times disagreed concerning the validity and adequacy of evidence as a test of truth and a motive of certitude ; and many have gone over to scepticism (chap. iv.). This issue others have sought to avoid, and mainly in one or other of two directions, *viz.* by seeking some satisfactory motive of certitude either (*a*) in some source extrinsic both to the object of the assent (the judgment) and to the individual mind (such as Divine revelation, tradition, the common voice or verdict of mankind), or (*b*) in a source extrinsic to the object of assent (and therefore non-intellectual), but intrinsic to the individual (such as a natural "sense" or "feeling" or "yearning" or

"instinct," or "need" or "will" to believe, etc.). Both of these attitudes have been broadly described as *Fideism*, because they have in common both the negative, anti-intellectualist element of distrust in the capacity of the individual human intellect to attain to truth, and the positive, dogmatic or anti-sceptical element of conviction that nevertheless certitude is attainable. But as to how it is to be attained they differ in the manner just indicated.[1]

The historical reasons for the appeal from the court of individual rational speculation to that of the collective voice of the race as the vehicle of an authoritative Divine revelation, are not far to seek. What does the history of purely rational speculation present but a medley of discordant voices? Or what effective power or authority has the philosopher to teach mankind the saving truths which he needs most urgently to know? To philosophize in isolation from, or without regard to, the authoritative teaching of supernatural, revealed religion, *i.e.* the Christian Religion, is worse than vain. The "free" exercise of the individual human reason is not constructive or conducive to certitude : it is rather destructive, corrosive, and leads only to doubts and negations : it raises many questions but can answer none. The pretension to solve by means of it the problems and enigmas of human existence is unnatural : and history testifies that every attempt of the kind has only led to scepticism and provoked a reaction in the direction of reposing human certitude ultimately either on faith in supernatural revelation or in subjective, affective instincts, prompting the individual to believe in defiance of the impotent negations of pure reason.

Thus, the sixteenth century revolt against the authoritative teachings of revealed religion, the proclamation of the absolute supremacy of "private judgment," and the cult of an excessive "rationalism," threw back the warring sects of Protestantism on a religion of purely personal beliefs which rested only on the shifting quicksands of individual feeling. Europe in the seventeenth and eighteenth centuries witnessed a widespread disin-

---

[1] MERCIER describes as *Fideists* only those who propound as the ultimate source of certitude faith on *extrinsic* grounds of revelation, tradition, the unanimous assent of the human race, etc. (*op. cit.*, §§ 61 *sqq.*). The title is equally, and perhaps more commonly, applied to those who take refuge ultimately in an *internal faith* prompted by non-intellectual motives and influences intrinsic to the individual. *Cf.* JEAN-NIÈRE, *op. cit.*, p. 260. The latter class of motives,—which are subjective,—will be examined in the next chapter.

tegration and decay of religious faith. The speculations of Rousseau, Voltaire and the encyclopedists, the spread of atheism and materialism, the withering influence of an unbridled "freedom of thought" and "liberty of conscience," the French Revolution with its apotheosis of "reason" and "liberty,"—were so many portents which, in Catholic circles, caused men to inquire anxiously if any sure defence could be discovered for the foundations of belief against the lamentable results of what they naturally regarded as the onslaughts of "individual reason" run riot.[1] And it is not surprising if some of these, losing all confidence in the power of this "individual reason," went too far in proclaiming the need of its total dethronement in order to place human certitude under the protecting ægis of faith. This in fact is what the French Traditionalists attempted. Already Jansenism had proclaimed the impotence of human reason unaided by supernatural grace. Already Pascal (1623-62) had given his verdict against both dogmatism and pyrrhonism, had dismissed Epictetus and Montaigne as equally futile, and had heralded the necessity of a primordial act of faith on the part of the individual human reason in search of truth.[2] And Huet, Bishop of Avranches (1630-1721), had proclaimed that without the aid of Divine Revelation the human mind cannot transcend mere probability.

With *De Bonald* (1754-1840) commences the line of traditionalists proper, including *De Lamennais* (1782-1854), *Bautain* (1795-1867), *Bonnetty* (1798-1879), *Ventura* (1792-1861),

---

[1] An anxiety which was accentuated by the conviction that the stability of social order is absolutely dependent on the general acceptance and public recognition of the great fundamental truths of religion and morality: the existence of a Supreme Being ; Divine Governance of the universe ; human freedom, responsibility and immortality ; Divine Sanctions for human conduct.

[2] *Cf.* MERCIER, *op. cit.*, §§ 61, 65. Pascal was not a sceptic, but a convinced and fervent believer in the truths of Christianity.· His *Pensées* is a work of apologetics rather than a philosophy. Reason, he holds, is impotent, and must recognize its impotence, to give us certitude concerning the fundamental truths of religion. We must begin by ignoring its questionings, and simply *believe* in God, Immortality, Revelation, and the Christian Religion. But why *must* we believe ? Not because reason can or does establish, on grounds of evidence, the credibility of those truths ; or because any extrinsic authority convinces us of their credibility (as the traditionalists contended later on) ; but because our whole nature prompts and forces us to believe them : the human heart, too, has reasons which lie beyond mere reason. Let us yield to them and believe those truths : then we shall understand how the Original Fall of man accounts for the imbecility of mere reason. Thus Pascal belongs to the subjectivist, affective school, rather than to the traditionalist school, of fideism.

and *Ubaghs* (1800-75). The two first-mentioned writers propound traditionalism in its most pronounced and extreme form, the others in a mitigated and milder form.

158. EXPOSITION OF TRADITIONALIST THEORIES.—A. According to *De Bonald*, the certain assent of the individual not only to the fundamental truths of religion, but to natural truths, is based not on their appeal to the individual human reason, but on the authority which the individual finds for them in the fact that they are accepted by mankind and delivered to him by his fellow-men in society. To Rousseau's assertion of the absolute self-sufficiency of the individual in isolation from society, De Bonald opposed not the mere *contradictory*, "that the individual is not wholly self-sufficient, that he is partly dependent on the social *milieu*," but the *contrary* counter-assertion, "that without society the individual is absolutely helpless, that he owes everything he has, intellectually and morally, to society": for society is the vehicle which hands down by tradition the Primitive Divine Revelation without which no knowledge is possible.

Of this the *first* and chief proof offered by De Bonald is the psychological proof based upon the origin of language. Man is physically incapable of thought without language, without words pronounced at least mentally. He has, no doubt, in his nature the power of thinking, but he cannot exercise it without words in which to clothe his ideas consciously. He could not attain even to the primordial certitude of Descartes' *Cogito, ergo sum*, were he not already in possession of words to make his thought consciously intelligible to himself. Hence the aphorism: *Il faut penser sa parole avant de pouvoir parler sa pensée:* we must think our words before we can consciously conceive (or mentally express to ourselves) our thought. But if this be true it is plain that man cannot possibly have ever invented language himself: for to do so he should think the language, but he cannot think without language. The alternative is that God must have endowed our first parents with the gift of rational speech. This language embodied and expressed the Primitive Divine Revelation, which, therefore, may be described as a natural revelation in distinction from the subsequent, supernatural revelations of the Old and the New Law. Tradition is the vehicle of all those revelations, and to them we owe all we know or can know: for it will be apparent that even our certitude of our own individual existence rests ultimately on the Authority which endowed us with the gift of rational speech through which alone we can consciously think our own existence.

A *second* and corroborative argument to prove that all our certitude, all our knowledge, natural and supernatural, physical and moral, secular and religious, rests ultimately on this basis of Divine Revelation, is drawn from such considerations as that each individual acquires all his knowledge only in and through and with language, which language he does not invent but receives or learns from his fellow-men ; that even the truths that are necessary for physical existence, about food, shelter, clothing, fire, etc. (15), are transmitted from parent to child ; that even of mathematical truths we are not really certain until we find them universally accepted ; that especially the fundamental truths of religion and morals,—the existence of God, the immortality of the soul, the reality of Divine sanctions for human conduct, etc., —are *de facto* accepted only on the Divine Authority of which tradition is the vehicle, and could not possibly impose themselves effectively on mankind if God had not revealed and imposed them, or if individual men were supposed *per impossibile* to have at any time discovered them unaided.

Since, therefore, all our spontaneous knowledge has been communicated to us by our fellow-men, since they are the channel through which it has come to us from God, since the Divine Authority is our only and all-sufficient ground for accepting it, the starting-point of all philosophical reflection on this knowledge must not be a "*dubito*" but a "*credo*".   And philosophical reflection must not take the form of an impossible and impracticable effort of the individual reason to show any truth to be attainable by the independent activity of the individual reason ; rather it must take the form of a recognition *ab initio* that all our knowledge has been communicated by God to mankind, and has been handed down to us through the vehicle of tradition. In other words, there can be no such thing as a rational philosophy apart from Faith, but rather all true philosophy will be a religious apologetic, a defence of the whole system of divinely revealed truth.

B. The teaching of *De Lamennais* is the same in principle as that of De Bonald.   Its main feature is the substitution of the dictate of the *common sense* of human nature ("la doctrine du *sens commun*, fondée sur la nature de l'homme") for that of the *individual reason* ("*sens privé*," "*sens particulier*," "*raison indi-*

viduelle"), and the contention that the *supreme test of truth* is not the evidential appeal of things to individual intellect but the *common agreement of the human race* ("*le consentement commun*") in accepting and assenting to judgments as true,—the verdict of universal human reason (*i.e.* of mankind generally) as to what is true ("*la raison générale*" : "sensus communis humani generis" : "concors auctoritas hominum"). In his *Essai sur l'indifférence en matière de religion,* he claims to trace the prevalent religious indifference of his time to the pretension that the individual man, by his own unaided reason, independently of his fellow-men and of what he learns from them, can attain to truth by the Cartesian way of following the "evidence" of things, or "what appears clear" in things. But he cannot : contradictories "appear clear" to different individuals. The individual reason is fallible : it must be guided by the collective reason ("*la raison générale*") which is the real voice of man's nature, and which alone is infallible because it is ultimately the voice of the Divine Reason, being the organon or instrument through which God transmits from generation to generation the truth which in the beginning He revealed to our first parents. Certitude, therefore, is not to be sought in the dictate of the individual mind, but outside it in the concordant dictate or common assent of the collective mind. And hence "we must of necessity begin by faith".[1]

The supreme criterion of the truth of any judgment must be its conformity with the common verdict or assent of mankind. Without faith in this common dictate we can be certain of nothing : individual reason can only doubt. But nature forces us to believe. The use of reason and of language implies many invincible beliefs, *e.g.* belief in the connexion of language with thought ; and the necessity of language for thought implies the intellectual dependence of the individual on the community, on society, on the human intercourse which teaches him all he knows (*cf.* De Bonald). Futhermore, "we have only to open our eyes to see that in discerning the true and the false we are naturally guided by the common assent of men".[2] The existence of God is proved by this common belief of mankind : a belief which is the living and abiding witness of God's revelation of Himself to

---

[1] "We must [each] say *I believe that God exists* before we can reasonably say *I exist.*"—*Défense de l'essai sur l'indifférence,* etc., p. 571 (*apud* MERCIER, *op. cit.,* § 64, p. 134).

[2] *Défense,* etc., pp. 612-13—*apud* MERCIER, *l.c.,* p. 138.

men.   Therefore belief in Divine Revelation as the source of the
knowledge expressed and transmitted in the universal assents
of collective human reason is the ultimate basis of all human
certitude.

The system thus barely outlined is defended by De Lamennais with an abundant wealth of argument and illustration.   (*a*)
To prove the impotence of the individual mind, reasoning by itself and without recognizing the need of faith, he appeals to the
errors and contradictions of philosophers in every age (39, A).
(*b*) In the conflict of human opinions and beliefs, where, he asks,
are we to turn for an arbiter?   To the individual reason?   Impossible.   The atheist will claim that his individual reason is as
worthy of consideration as that of the believer.   No; the only
possible arbiter is *authority*,—the authority of the common sense
or assent of mankind.[1]   (*c*) Not only is the acceptance of this
authority a psychological necessity, but it is just as much a psychological necessity to *believe* first in order to use one's reason at
all.   When we commence to reflect critically on our convictions,
we find that they all imply belief and came by belief: through intercourse with, and belief in, our fellow-men.   Many of these beliefs are invincible, and at first inexplicable.   But when we reflect
on their origin and on the grounds of their validity, we find that
they have their only possible source and ground in the unanimous dictate or voice of the human race speaking authoritatively
to the individual, bearing witness to him of a Divine Teacher,
acting as the organon or vehicle of His teaching, and thus revealing to him that Divine Authority which he is thereupon inevitably forced to recognize as the ultimate ground and motive of all
truth and certitude.

C. According to the milder form of traditionalism, sometimes
called *semi-traditionalism*, an original Divine Revelation, transmitted by tradition through human society as its *organon*, is not
required for natural knowledge and certitude about secular,
mundane, material things: such knowledge lies within reach of
the individual human reason.   But for all our concepts of the

---

[1] And that this *is* the real arbiter we find borne out by the fact that it is the most
highly gifted men intellectually who are the most diffident of the power of the individual mind and the most prompt to consult the common verdict of men generally ;
by the fact that our assent to an " evident " truth is strengthened by our knowledge
that men generally assent to it ; and by the fact that men regard it as *folly* in the
individual to set up his *ipse dixit* in opposition to the common conviction. *Cf.*
Défense, etc., pp. 589, 625-6—*apud* MERCIER, *op. cit.*, p. 136.

immaterial, spiritual, moral, and *religious* domain of realities,[1] for attaining to the knowledge of God, immortality, the moral law and a future life, the individual mind is absolutely and essentially dependent on the Divine teaching thus communicated to it through society. It is from such Divine source that each individual *de facto* acquires these convictions, through *belief* in the testimony of society transmitting this deposit of revealed truth. *When the individual is enlightened* by the possession of these truths through faith, he can *then* indeed accomplish the task of formulating a *rational demonstration or proof* of them, and, *a fortiori*, of showing that no reasoning or argumentation of atheists, agnostics, or unbelievers can avail to disprove them. But he could not accomplish this task had his individual reason been left isolated and thrown on its own native resources, had it not been illumined, developed, "informed," by the "social teaching," the "*institutio socialis*," through which it first acquired its heritage of moral and religious concepts and convictions.

In the "social formation" of the individual mind, the process thus held to be necessary to enable the individual mind to reach a *reasoned* or *demonstrated* knowledge and certitude of God's existence, human immortality, etc., *language* was held to be not indeed an endowment that essentially implied a Divine Revelation (as De Bonald had contended), but to be an essential condition for the use of reason, an indispensable excitant for provoking, stimulating, calling forth intellectual thought.

A more important and debatable point concerning the "*institutio socialis*" which those writers claimed to be necessary for the individual man before he could *rationally prove* the *preambula fidei*—God's existence (and Veracity) and the fact of Revelation—or reach a *reasoned certitude* concerning them, was this : Did such "*institutio*," such didactic and educative (doctrinal and moral) influence of society on the individual, essentially involve, in the minds of those writers,—or does it essentially involve in reality,—that mankind should have been taught, enlightened, instructed *ab initio* by a positive Divine Revelation?—so that unless or until such Revelation were made to mankind the human race could never attain or have attained (by the unaided power of reason) to a knowledge of the Creator, of man's own dependence on the Creator, and of his consequent moral and religious duties towards the Creator? And on such a hypothesis, would such knowledge be only a "natural" knowledge, and the religion based on it a "natural" religion?—as distinct from the "supernatural" knowledge, which, according to the teaching of the Catholic Church, was *de facto* communicated to man in the original, the Mosaic, and the Christian Revelations, and from "supernatural" religion based on the teaching or content of those Revelations. This point will recur for consideration at a later stage (163).

[1] Vestiges of *ontologism* are found mingled with this later form of traditionalism.

159. GENERAL CRITICISM OF TRADITIONALIST THEORIES.—
We shall see in the course of our criticism (infra, 163) that there
is much that is useful and true and undeniable in what has been
written by supporters of those fideist and traditionalist theories.
Nevertheless their fundamental contention is profoundly erroneous,
and indeed destructive of all human certitude. This contention
is that human certitude rests ultimately on faith in a Divinely
Delivered Revelation, and that the supreme test of truth must be
the Divine Authority as manifested in the common assents or
collective dictates of mankind.   With this position we shall deal
in a general argument ; after which the special forms of general
theory, and the special reasons alleged in support of it, will come
up for consideration.

General Argument against Fideism and Traditionalism.—
Extrinsic authority cannot possibly be the ultimate motive of
certitude or the supreme criterion of truth ; nor, therefore, can
the first and fundamental assent of the individual intellect or
reason be an assent of faith, an act of belief, grounded on extrinsic
authority [149 (4), 150 (3)].   Accordingly the traditionalist theory
is erroneous.   The theory proclaims the necessity and adequacy of
belief or faith as an ultimate ground of certitude, on the assumption that no grounds of intrinsic objective evidence are or can be
adequate.   But, apart from the fact that this assumption is itself
indefensible,—since, as we have shown (149-54), such evidence
precisely is the adequate ultimate ground of certitude,—the
alternative offered by traditionalism is an impossible alternative.
For, when the individual assents to the truth of a judgment
on the ground of extrinsic authority, whether human or Divine,
his intellectual attitude towards such authority must assume one
or other of two alternative forms ; he must either assent blindly,
or else he assents because he is convinced on grounds of intellectual evidence that such authority is trustworthy and that what
it proposes for his belief is therefore evidently credible.   But a
blind assent, a blind faith, elicited by the believer in the absence
of adequate intellectual evidence, adequate grounds of reason, for
the trustworthiness of the authority, cannot be ultimately reasonable—nay, it cannot, on reflection, be ultimately possible psychologically—for a being endowed as man is with the judicial,
reflective faculty of reason or intellect, before the bar of which
he must, nolens volens, summon all the motives of his assents,
and by which he must judge the adequacy of these motives

if his assents are to be what they ought to be, *viz. reasonable,* or in conformity with his nature as a rational being.[1] Therefore the other alternative imposes itself. He must be intellectually convinced of the trustworthiness of the authority on which he believes. But how? If he invoke an antecedent authority for this trustworthiness,—as he may, indeed, in a particular case,—he only pushes back the problem one step. And he must avoid the futility of an endless regress (149-50). Hence for every judgment which he accepts on extrinsic authority the individual believer must rely *ultimately* on *intrinsic objective evidence* for the trustworthiness of the authority, evidence accumulated and apprehended and judged to be sufficient by the *exercise of his own individual reason.*[2] Therefore the act of belief or faith, on extrinsic authority, cannot possibly be *first* if it is to be reasonable: it must be preceded by acts of assent to judgments on intrinsic objective evidence.

Faith in Divine Revelation, if it is to be a reasonable faith, presupposes in the individual believer the certain conviction that God exists; that if He has made a revelation to mankind such revelation is credible inasmuch as God can neither deceive nor be deceived; that He has made such revelation. And certitude as to this latter fact means certitude that God has positively intervened in the course of human history. It means certitude

---

[1] To the supposition that the exercise of the individual's reason must be preceded by faith inasmuch as otherwise it would lead away from faith rather than conduce to faith, Bourdaloue replies that such an attitude is the negation of faith, for "the faith of the Christian is not at all a mere acquiescence in believing, or a simple surrender of reason, but a reasonable acquiescence and submission; and if this acquiescence, this submission, were not reasonable, it would be no longer a virtue. But how could it be reasonable if reason had no part in it?" (*Pensées sur divers sujets de religion et de morale—apud* MERCIER, *op. cit.,* § 68, p. 146). And similarly Fénélon writes: "Were we to suppose that faith comes to man through the heart, independently of reason, through a blind impulse of grace, without rational investigation of the authority to which we must bow in believing mysteries, we should run the risk of making Christianity a mere fanaticism, and representing Christians as [blind, unreasoning] enthusiasts. Nothing would be more dangerous to peace and right order among men; nothing could render religion more despicable and hateful" (*Lettre V sur la religion,—apud* MERCIER, *ibid.*).

[2] A person may, for instance, believe in (say) the resurrection of the body because he believes that God has revealed it: he believes that he has God's authority for it because the teaching authority of the Church assures him that he has; he believes that the Church does vouch for this and is trustworthy in vouching for it because he has been so informed by his parents, or educators, or religious teachers, etc.; and he takes their teaching or testimony as trustworthy *because his knowledge and experience of them furnish him with adequate intrinsic objective evidence of the reliability of their teaching or testimony.*

on these four questions : Where has God spoken? When did He speak? To whom? And in what manner? But manifestly it is only by the use of his own reason, brought to bear upon the facts of his experience, and interpreting them in the light of the objective evidence presented by them, that the individual can attain to those various rational convictions,—which he must have before he can reasonably believe in any revelation, and which are therefore called the *preambula fidei*. As St. Thomas puts it, "The individual would not believe the subject matters of faith unless he saw them to be credible".[1]

160. EXAMINATION OF DE BONALD'S THEORY. — The premisses of the argument based on the origin of language are unproven, and at least in part erroneous; and the conclusion drawn from them does not follow logically from them. God is, of course, the author of human language in the sense that He is author of all creation; but it is not proven that He did not, or could not, leave man to form rational speech for himself by his natural faculties under pressure of natural and social needs. De Bonald contends that language must precede thought; but, without going into the psychology of the connexion, we can see at all events that thought must be prior to language—if not by priority of time, certainly by priority of nature. For words that did not embody and express thoughts would not be language, but mere sounds, mere parrot-cries. Therefore, however God may have given language to man, whether immediately or mediately,—*i.e.* whether by giving him a ready-made

---

[1] " Ea quae subsunt fidei aliquis non crederet nisi videret ea esse credenda."— *Summa Theol.*, II.[2] Q. 1, a. 4, ad 2. Although reason has not to see positively the intrinsic evidence for the truths of faith, nevertheless it is needed to enable us to believe in a reasonable manner, in a manner suited to our nature as intelligent beings : " Fides non habet inquisitionem rationis naturalis demonstrantis id quod creditur : habet tamen inquisitionem quamdam eorum, per quae inducitur homo ad credendum ; puta quia sunt dicta a Deo et miraculis confirmata ".—*Ibid.*, Q. II. a. 1, ad 1. Similarly St. Augustine, explaining the sense in which faith must precede rational investigation of revealed truths, says that the reasonableness of this primacy *must be apparent to reason*. Faith in the mysteries of revealed religion cleanses the heart, fosters humility and reverence, and thus induces the disposition which enables the believer to apply his reason profitably and fruitfully to the contemplation and appreciation of such mysteries : " Ut ergo in quibusdam rebus ad doctrinam salutarem pertinentibus, quas ratione nondum percipere valemus, sed aliquando valebimus, fides praecedat rationem, qua cor mundetur, ut magnae rationis capiat et perferat lucem, *hoc utique rationis est*. Et ideo rationabiliter dictum est per Prophetam : 'Nisi credideritis non intelligetis'. . . . Si igitur rationabile est, ut ad magna quaedam, quae capi nondum possunt, fides praecedat rationem, procul dubio *quantulacumque ratio quae hoc persuadet etiam ipsa antecedit fidem*."—Epist. 120, 3 (italics ours).

language, so to speak, or by endowing him with the faculties and organs for forming and utilizing language,—He must first have given him ideas or the faculties for forming ideas. And since we see men universally forming their own ideas from the data of conscious experience; and moulding, developing, modifying language according to their progressive needs,—if in the beginning, by an exceptional privilege of the Creator, they received their thoughts and language otherwise, the *onus* of proving such a privilege to have been accorded to our first parents lies on those who contend that it was. And they have not proved it.

But even granting that such a privilege were accorded to our first parents, that ideas and language were divinely communicated to them *ab initio*, it does not follow, as De Bonald contends, that language is or can be the infallible vehicle of a divinely revealed deposit of knowledge. For in the first place neither ideas nor their verbal expressions constitute *knowledge ;* neither ideas nor words are true or false. Judgments alone embody knowledge; and hence judgments too,—ready-made and *a priori* syntheses of ideas,—must have been divinely communicated *ab initio*. Secondly, even if this were so, the transmission of ideas, or rather of language which expresses them, does not involve the transmission of the *judgments, i.e.* of the *knowledge*, of which such ideas are the elementary factors or materials. For it is notorious that the possession of the same ideas and the same language by men does not by any means involve their possession of the same convictions or beliefs. Thirdly, granting that God communicated words and ideas and even judgments, to our first parents, does this necessarily involve a Divine *Revelation*, calling for an act or exercise of *faith* on their part? *Not necessarily ;* for God could have communicated the knowledge not as *Revealer*, but as *Teacher, Instructor ;* not as an *Authority* demanding *belief*, but as an *Instructor* aiding pupils *to learn*, to apply their mental faculties to the interpretation of experience, so that they would gradually acquire a *rational* and *reasoned* knowledge on grounds of natural evidence, and without being called upon to elicit a single act of faith.[1]

As to the considerations urged in De Bonald's second argument (158), they are in the main true; but they do not

---

[1] *Cf.* St. Thomas, *De Veritate*, Q. XI, a. 1,—*apud* Mercier, *op. cit.*, § 70, whose line of argument we have merely paraphrased above.

warrant his conclusion. It is true that children believe before
they understand; that men hold *on authority* practically all the
convictions on which the physical, intellectual, moral, and religious well-being of the individual and of society depends (15) ;
that the truths which make for social order and well-being could
not be attained with sufficient facility and universality were their
discovery at the mercy of unaided individual initiative ; that,
even were they attainable by the vast majority, they could not
impose themselves on mankind with the efficacy needed for
social order were there no authority to impose and sanction
them. All this, however, merely proves the *practical* insufficiency
of the isolated individual reason, and the *practical* necessity of
social conditions and moral and religious guidance for the individual in order that man be enabled to work out his destiny
in conformity with his nature. But that has nothing to do with
the *critical* question raised by *reflection* on all the data of experience, including those very facts themselves. For the facts
just mentioned concern the order of *spontaneous* human assents.
And as soon as human reason comes to maturity in the individual, as soon as he realizes the errors, deceptions, discordant
and conflicting views, which prevail in that external social, intellectual, moral and religious *milieu* on the authority of which
he has hitherto accepted his own convictions, his individual
reason must inevitably take the initiative and proceed to inquire
into the credentials of that external authority in all its shapes
and forms. He becomes conscious that it is due to his nature
and dignity as a rational being to inquire into those credentials.
He sees that it would be unreasonable for him to give a final
and definitive assent to all generally accepted propositions merely
because they are generally accepted ; that the argument based
on the value or authority of universal agreement has only a
provisional value. Nor will it suffice for him to hold this general
agreement, with De Lamennais, to be infallible, as being the
voice of human nature; or, in other words, to suppose human
nature to be rightly and wisely constituted for the discovery of
truth, and error to be only accidental. For he must still ask
himself these further questions :—

If I consider this general agreement to be in any measure infallible, what rational ground have I for thinking that it is ? Why
do men generally assent to any propositions as true ? How can I
be sure that human nature or human reason, whether collectively

or individually, does or can attain to any truth? If it does, is it by some automatic process like breathing? Is it protected from error by an apparatus of reflex movements like those whereby the animal organism instinctively avoids what is hurtful? Clearly not ; for the attainment of truth and the avoidance of error can be only the work of reason, of judgment; and ultimately of the *individual's* reason, since certain knowledge, if it exists at all, exists in *individual* minds.

The individual has therefore to seek, in his own experience and its data, an ultimate test of truth, an ultimate motive that will justify his spontaneous intellectual assents, including those which he has heretofore grounded provisionally on extrinsic authority. Extrinsic authority itself, therefore, cannot be this test or this motive. " The authority of society and tradition is a provisional motive, a very widely operative motive, of spontaneous assents; reflecting reason subjects the affirmations of authority to the test of criticism in order to reject such as are prompted by prejudices and to bring to light the deeper motive of those that really put reason in possession of the truth ".[1] That underlying and ultimate motive is, as we have seen, intrinsic objective evidence.

161. THEORY OF DE LAMENNAIS EXAMINED. GENERAL ASSENT AS A TEST OF TRUTH.—The " general assent " to which we have just referred, De Lamennais proclaims to be the ultimate test of truth. We have seen how he regards it as the infallible index of Divinely revealed truth, and contrasts its dictates with the "unreliable" and mutually contradictory deliverances of the individual reason (the " *sens privé* "). But this " universal dictate" cannot possibly be the ultimate test of truth, nor can it possibly supplant, by its appeal to the individual reason, the function of intrinsic objective evidence.

If each of two individual disputants, *e.g.* the atheist and the believer, insists that his own interpretation of facts judged in the light of evidence is the right one, they may indeed appeal in the first place, if they so desire, to the general verdict of mankind on the matter in dispute. But such appeal will not and cannot of itself settle the question. For the atheist will not recognize, and the believer ought not to recognize, this general verdict as conclusive unless and until its authority is seen by its objective evidence to be a sure guarantee of truth : a point which can be

---

[1] MERCIER, *op. cit.*, § 70.

decided for each only by the exercise of his individual reason judging the credentials of that authority.

Nor can it be said that those universal dictates of the voice of human nature, those truths of " common sense," are beyond dispute, so that their rejection would be an abdication of reason. For if this general assent be put forward as an *authority* to which we are expected to yield unquestioning submission, it will be easy to point out that its testimony should not be accepted without reserve. Did not men for ages universally assent to the solidity of the heavens, and to the view that the sun moves around the earth? The most, then, that can be said is that universal belief creates a presumption in favour of truth, that we should be slower to believe it to be in the wrong than to be in the right; but *of itself* it cannot reasonably demand an assent of reasoned certitude from the individual.

If, however, the general verdict is put forward rather as a *sign* or *index* of the tendency of man's rational nature to assent to those generally accepted propositions as true,—and this seems to be what De Lamennais intended,—then indeed such common agreement can be *a* criterion of truth, though *not the ultimate criterion.* It can be a criterion in this indirect way. When in any particular case of common agreement we can convince ourselves by investigation that this agreement is not due to such accidental causes of error as prejudice, precipitancy, want of reflection, mal-observation, etc. ; and when, moreover, we see that it concerns some matter of grave import to man's nature and destiny,[1]—then we can conclude that the universal dictate or verdict in question is reached through the uniform and normal functioning, in each individual, of human nature as intelligent or rational. And from this,—unless we gratuitously conclude,

---

[1] Such are the convictions referred to in vol. i., § 15, as "truths of common sense". Among them might be enumerated, for instance, the conviction that the human mind is capable of attaining to some true knowledge of things; that an external material universe exists independently of human minds; that the universe is not chaotic but manifests order and furnishes evidence of design, purpose, intelligence; that there is a moral order and that the distinction between a morally right and a morally wrong is inseparable from human conduct and rooted in man's nature; that man is a free and responsible agent; that in man's actual experience of himself and the universe there are evidences which point to the actual existence of an unseen, suprasensible or spiritual domain of reality, to man's dependence on Higher Powers, to life after death, to the existence of a Supreme, Intelligent Author and Ruler of the Universe, to man's religious worship of this Supreme Being as a duty that is consonant with human nature and dictated by man's natural reason.

with the universal sceptic (ch. iv.), that men generally, in attaining to such universal convictions by the normal and natural functioning of human reason, are blindly yielding to impulses that are rationally unjustifiable,—we must infer the only other alternative conclusion, *viz.* that such examples of the universal accord of human intelligences as we have in those general dictates or verdicts must be due to the *manifestation of truth* or the *presentation of reality* to all intelligences alike. And in making this inference we are asserting *rational or intellectual evidence to be the ultimate basis of truth and certitude.* For we are simply interpreting the "common agreement" as an index of the presence of *intrinsic objective evidence* for the dictates or judgments in which men thus universally agree ; and as being thus a secondary criterion subordinate to the objective evidence the presence of which it indicates. In this way the "general assent" is merely an index that the objective evidence of the truth of the judgment assented to is really there and is really apprehended by each individual of the assenting masses. It must be because the truth of the judgment is borne in upon each by its intrinsic objective evidence that all agree in assenting to it. Thus, even in cases in which common assent is a criterion of truth it is subordinate to objective evidence as the supreme and ultimate criterion.

There are these other considerations also, which show that "common assent" cannot be an ultimate test, and must itself rest on objective evidence. How can the individual know (1) that any given judgment *has* the common assent of mankind ? (2) that this common assent, if forthcoming, is not really due in the case to some accidental cause of general deception, since many beliefs that were, morally speaking, universal for centuries have nevertheless been proved erroneous ? (3) that the common assent, even when the possibility of accidental deception is satisfactorily excluded,—as it can be in certain classes of assents, by virtue of the intimate connexion of their subject-matter with the essential conditions and natural needs of human existence (15),—is really a reliable test of the truth of the judgment assented to ?[1] It

---

[1] That in such cases (15) it is a reliable test, is not self-evident, but requires proof. And the proof cannot lie merely in the fact that the assent is, morally speaking, universal ; but in the answer to the question : Why is it universal? The universality of the assent merely creates a presumption in favour of the truth of the judgment assented to. But the individual must look to the nature of the judgment itself. He must weigh the objective evidential appeal which, in its whole concrete

is clear that until he decides those questions for himself he cannot make rational use of the criterion of "common assent".
And it is equally clear that he can decide them only by the
exercise of his own individual reason, and that the decision must
be based upon the intrinsic objective evidence furnished by their
subject-matter to his own individual reason.

It might be urged,—and it seems to have been thought by
the traditionalists,—that there is as it were some special virtue in
human reason taken collectively, in "*la raison générale*," which
is not in human reason taken individually, something which makes
the former infallible, or at least safe and reliable, where the
latter is unsafe and unreliable.   Such a suggestion gains plausibility from the undeniable fact that in the search for truth, in
the progressive discovery and proof of truth, many minds are
better than one ; that individuals learn from their fellow-men
most of what they know ; that mankind is in possession of an
accumulated heritage of truth (not, however, unmixed with error)
of which individuals are in varying degrees the sharers; and so on.
But, nevertheless, the suggestion will not bear analysis, and
cannot achieve the object for which it is made.   For the attainment of truth and certitude is not the work of an impersonal
human intelligence, conceived after the manner of the Averroists ;
nor of human reason existing as a universal *a parte rei*, as extreme
realism would have it : nor do traditionalists mean anything like
that by the "*raison générale*" or "common sense" of the race.
The attainment of truth and certitude is the work of individual
human minds ; knowledge is an attribute only of individual minds.
If, therefore, there is not in human minds, taken individually, any
native power or capacity to attain to a certain knowledge of
truth, neither can such power or capacity be forthcoming in the
collectivity : if each of them is essentially unreliable, no conceivable collection of them can be reliable, much less infallible.   But
it is the collection that traditionalists denote by "common sense,"
or "*la raison générale*".   By proclaiming, therefore, the power-

context, it makes to his own individual reason : part of that evidential appeal coming,
of course, from the fact that the judgment is generally accepted by mankind.   If
he sees, on reflection, that there is adequate *intrinsic* evidence for its truth, and that
this is the reason why people generally assent to it, he will have satisfied himself
not only that the judgment in question is true, but that the common assent of mankind to it, and to other similar judgments, is a reasonably safe and reliable test of
the truth of such judgments.   But he must see at the same time that this latter test
does not supplant, but rather presupposes as ultimate, the intrinsic evidential appeal
of the judgment to the individual reason.

lessness of the individual reason, they strike equally at the universal or collective reason. And in fact they do disfigure it and deprive it of the essential attributes of intelligence or rationality by proclaiming its function to be merely that of an organon or vehicle for the transmission of a body of Divinely revealed judgments, while denying to human reason individually, and therefore also collectively, the right to demand or the power to find any rational justification for its assents by scrutinizing the evidence, whether intrinsic or extrinsic, for the truth of the judgments assented to.   In ultimate analysis it is really an abdication of reason on the part of the individual to assent to any judgment merely because he finds everyone else assenting to it. For each and for all alike the ulterior question must inevitably arise : Why do any of them or all of them assent to it ?   And the answer must be, either because they have rational grounds of evidence for so assenting, or because they choose to assent in the absence of such grounds, that is, *blindly* and *unreasonably*. In other words, the ultimate choice must always be between a rational assent based on grounds of objective intellectual evidence, or a blind, instinctive assent which, in a being endowed with the reflective faculty of intelligence, must inevitably terminate in universal doubt and scepticism.

162. "COMMON SENSE" AS A CRITERION : THE SCOTTISH SCHOOL. NATURAL INTELLIGENCE AND CONCRETE EVIDENCE. —On the meaning of the expressions "common sense" and "truths of common sense," a further word of explanation is, however, necessary.   They have been used extensively by certain philosophers of the Scottish school, notably by *Reid* (1710-96), *Oswald* (1727-93), *Beattie* (1735-1803), and *Dugald Stewart* (1753-1828).   Against the scepticism of Hume, for instance, Reid emphasizes the futility and unreasonableness of questioning "principles that are self-evident," principles of which "every man who has common sense is a competent judge ".[1]   Now by " common sense" Reid meant simply what is sometimes also described as " good sense " or the faculty of sound judgment : in other words human reason or intelligence as brought to bear, in its sane and normal functioning, on the objective evidence whereby a large collection of convictions is borne in upon men generally as objectively true.   And this aggregate of primordial convictions

[1] Reid's *Works*, ed. by *Hamilton*, p. 442,—*apud* TURNER, *History of Philosophy*, p. 594.

20 *

or principles or "truths of common sense " (*i.e.* truths reached by the functioning of the faculty called "common sense ") has been sometimes itself described by metonymy as "common sense," *i.e.* the collective common sense of the human race. Subjectively, then, "common sense " would mean simply the individual's intellectual faculty appreciating the immediate objective evidence furnished by the data submitted to it by experience; and objectively it would mean the collection of judgments reached by our intellectual apprehension of their immediate, intrinsic, objective evidence. Now it is clear that to set down "common sense " in the former meaning as the faculty whereby the individual must ultimately discern truth from falsity is to give expression to the traditional teaching of scholasticism. And it is equally clear that to set down "common sense " in the latter meaning as the supreme objective test of truth and ultimate motive of certitude is also to repeat in a different terminology the scholastic teaching in regard to the respective rôles of objective evidence and "common assent " (the "sensus communis humani generis," the "consentement commun " of De Lamennais) in determining the assent of the individual reason to judgments as certainly and evidently true. The only reserve to be made in regard to the teaching of the Scottish philosophers is that in their reaction against the scepticism of Hume they advocated a somewhat excessive dogmatism in claiming that those "self-evident principles " of "common sense " should be totally exempted from all critical questioning.

But not all of the convictions universally entertained by mankind (15), and usually described as "truths of common sense," [1] are self-evident, or immediately evident, or impose themselves *cogently* on the mind of the individual like the axioms of mathematics or the abstract principles of logic and metaphysics. Some of them are convictions which can be and are *de facto* reached by the ordinary man, not through a perception of them as self-evidently true, nor "by any sustained and elaborate train of logical reasoning " (15) from abstract self-evident principles, "but by an easy, direct, and half-unconscious movement " of thought whereby they are interpreted as evidently *credible* or worthy of the full and certain assent of a prudent man, a man endowed with "common sense " or a sound faculty of judgment.[2] This argues that adequate intellectual evidence of their truth is

[1] *Cf. supra,* p. 304, n. [2] *Cf.* vol. i., § 15, pp. 59-61, 63-4.

objectively forthcoming, even although they "have not the *self-evidence* of axioms on the one hand, nor admit of the rigorous demonstration of a theorem of geometry on the other".[1] It means that the human intellect, confronted with the data of human experience (both of the self and of the external universe), and considering the facts of this experience in their entire concrete context, can and does see in it grounds for certain judgments or interpretations of its significance, grounds which intellect rightly regards as reasonably sufficient to warrant an assent of certitude to those judgments even though these grounds be incapable of such adequate verbal formulation as would do full justice to their evidential value.

It is this difficulty of explicitly formulating the evidence in such cases, and of analysing satisfactorily the complex, cumulative process through which it determines intellectual assent, that has prompted many writers to postulate special innate inclinations in the intellect to form such assents (15), or to appear to postulate a special "sense" or "instinct" for attaining to them,[2] or to speak of them as "instinctive," "innate," "inborn," etc. (15). What we may call the *purely logical* use of the intellect in apprehending the truth of cogently self-evident abstract axioms and deductively demonstrated abstract conclusions from such axioms, is consciously different from its function of apprehending and assenting to certain other judgments of "common sense," the truth of which it sees to be necessarily implied in its actual cognitive experience : to such judgments, for instance, as that reality is in some measure intelligible, that the mind is capable of attaining and does attain to some true knowledge, that there is a uniformity or orderliness in the universe, that it is possible to distinguish between dreaming and waking experience, that not all reputed knowledge is illusion, that there is a morally right and a morally wrong in human conduct, that the sensible is not co-extensive with the real, that man himself and the visible universe are not self-existent or self-explaining, but dependent on some Higher Power, to whom, therefore, man owes the natural duty of religious worship,—and so forth. These assents, or some of them, may be called " beliefs " (6) or " postulates "; but, however they be designated, the important point to note is this, that it is by his *intellectual* faculty as a *rational, reflecting* being, that man gives these assents, and

[1] Vol. i., § 67, p. 234 n.   [2] *Ibid.*

only in virtue of objective grounds or motives which are directly or indirectly evidential (148). If this is recognized and admitted there can be no danger of misunderstanding in describing such function of the intellect as " instinctive " or "natural " or "spontaneous," any more than there is in Newman's terminology when in his *Grammar of Assent* he speaks of "Natural Inference " and the "Illative Sense ". But if it is denied that such assents are given by the individual reason, if it is maintained that they are given without any reference to the voice or dictate of reason, that they are not amenable to the bar of reflecting reason, that reason is powerless to pronounce them to be objectively true and valid interpretations of reality, then, in the mind of a being endowed with reason they are inevitably doomed to wither into scepticism.

The spontaneous beliefs that are universally prevalent in the human race include certain elementary moral and religious convictions[1] which the individual usually receives on authority : convictions as to his own nature and destiny, such as belief in human freedom and responsibility, in ethical distinctions and ethical sanctions, in life after death, in the dependence of the universe on the Ruling Power of a Divinity, and in man's subjection to this Divinity. It is not contended that in the various forms assumed by these beliefs in the course of human history they are unmixed with errors : it is only *as to their substance* that they are universally prevalent. Nor is it contended that *even as to their substance* they have the same sort of immediate evidence, as *e.g.* mathematical axioms. The objects which they present to the human intelligence are of a different order from abstract thought-objects in the category of quantity. They are judgments which have an intimate practical bearing on human life and conduct. Their evidential appeal to the individual human intelligence must therefore consist in the intellectually apprehended fact that the real nature of man and the universe as revealed in human experience,—in other words the real or ontological exigency of this experience (152-4),—manifests them to the individual intelligence as the true interpretations of this experience. So far as the substance of these spontaneous convictions is concerned, this evidence may rightly be said to be immediate, for, as already observed, " it can hardly be denied that they seem to come natural to the human intelligence, that

[1] *Cf.* vol. i., § 15, pp. 62-6.

they are felt to satisfy not only a moral and religious, but also an intellectual need of our nature, that our reason promptly appreciates the grounds of those beliefs, and is inclined spontaneously and unquestioningly to accept those grounds as satisfactory and convincing ".[1]   When we bring those spontaneous judgments before the bar of reflecting reason, the fact that in their substance they have received the universal spontaneous assent of mankind will be strong presumptive evidence that in substance they are objectively true.   And, furthermore, their spontaneously apprehended harmony with our *whole* nature, —not merely with our nature as intellectual or rational beings, but with the religious and moral and esthetic yearnings and needs and dictates of our nature,—will likewise be rightly adjudged by reason as part of the evidence on which we can base a reasoned or reflex certitude of their truth.[2]   How far the natural, unaided reason of the individual can attain to such certitude concerning them is a point to which we shall recur presently (163).   What we wish to observe here is that if reflection on the general data of human experience were to lead necessarily to the anti-intellectualist attitude [3] that the spontaneous convictions on which religion and morality depend,—convictions concerning God's existence, and human freedom and immortality,—cannot be apprehended by man's *intellect* to be *objectively true*, or justified and vindicated on grounds of *evidence* by man's reason reflecting on them, but must either be accepted *without adequate rational grounds* (and merely to satisfy a blind, instinctive "need" or "impulse" of our nature, or "will to believe"),—or else not be accepted at all,—then reason could hardly be prevented, as in fact it has not been prevented where such an attitude prevails, from delivering as its final dictate the verdict that *ethical and religious beliefs are merely a matter of personal feeling or sentiment*, but that *their objective and real significance is unknown and unknowable.*   From such speculative agnosticism the practical tendency of human nature is downward, towards materialism.   *Facilis descensus averni.*

163. MODIFIED TRADITIONALISM. ITS SOUL OF TRUTH. TRADITIONALISM, RATIONALISM, AND CATHOLIC TEACHING.—

[1] *Cf.* vol. i., § 15, p. 65.
[2] It is this real function of motives which are not directly intellectual that is misconceived and exaggerated in the anti-intellectualist theories to be examined later (ch. xxv.).
[3] *Cf.* n. 2.

The later traditionalists [1] endeavoured to emphasize the divergence of their own teaching from that of De Bonald and De Lamennais.[2] No doubt there are minor differences; but the erroneous contention is still retained that the reception of the fundamental truths of natural religion and morality *on authority* by the individual is an essential prerequisite condition for that right " use of reason " by which the individual will then be able to " prove " such truths : this authority being ultimately that of a primitive Divine Revelation of which human society is the organon or vehicle. This contention is erroneous. For although *de facto* it is of course through the teaching of his fellow-men that the individual usually, if not indeed invariably, first receives and assents to the judgments which assert the existence of God, the spirituality and immortality of the soul, human freedom and responsibility, etc., nevertheless it is not true either (1) that this social authority *must be* in ultimate analysis the authority of God manifested in a primitive Divine Revelation and transmitted by tradition, or (2) that, even if it were so, the individual, reflecting on the grounds of these judgments, would have to declare them *undiscoverable* by human reason *independently of Divine Revelation*, and accessible only through such Revelation.

When the individual comes to reflect on the authority which he had for accepting them as true from his teachers, he sees that his acceptance of them was reasonable because, and only because, his reason told him that such authority was an adequate motive for accepting them. But reflection does not show him that in regard to those judgments the teaching of his fellow-men *must be* simply a traditional testimony to the fact of a Divine Authority manifesting itself in a Primitive Revelation. He may indeed raise the question *of fact:* How did men *de facto* first

---

[1] *Supra*, § 157, p. 293 ; § 158, C, pp. 296-7.

[2] The philosophical teaching of De Lamennais had been censured by Pope Gregory XVI. in the Encyclical *Singulari nos* (July 15th, 1834). *Cf. Catholic Encyclopedia*, vol. viii., p. 764.[2] In 1855 the Sacred Congregation of the Index proposed the following propositions to Bonnetty for acceptance : " (1) Ratiocinatio Dei existentiam, animae spiritualitatem, hominis libertatem, cum certitudine probare potest ; (2) *Fides posterior est ratione*, proindeque ad probandam existentiam Dei contra atheos, ad probandam animae rationalis spiritualitatem et libertatem contra naturalismi et fatalismi sectatores, allegari convenienter non potest ; (3) *Rationis usus fidem praecedit*, et ad eam, ope revelationis et gratiae, conducit,"—*apud* JEANNIÈRE, *op. cit.*, p. 267. In 1870 the Vatican Council condemned Traditionalism in the canon : " Si quis dixerit, Deum unum et verum, Creatorem et Dominum nostrum, per ea, quae facta sunt, naturali rationis humanae lumine certo cognosci non posse, anathema sit."—Can. II. De Rev., 1.

come to believe in the existence of God, the freedom and moral responsibility of man, the spirituality and immortality of the soul, the possibility and the fact of a Divine Revelation or Revelations? But whatever answer he may reach in regard to the way in which men *de facto* first came to believe in each of these particular judgments,—about which more presently,—there is another question which reflection must raise and answer, namely, How is *he*[1] certain that any judgments accepted by him on extrinsic authority are really and objectively true? Manifestly, if his certitude is worthy of the name, if it is the firm assent of a reasoning, intelligent being, the answer must be : Because *by the exercise of his individual reason* he has convinced himself that the authority on which he accepts the judgments furnishes a reasonably adequate guarantee of their truth. And this holds whether the authority be human or divine. If he has human authority for believing that certain judgments have been *de facto* revealed by God and vouched for by Divine Authority, he must, in order to give a reasonable assent to them, have convinced himself *by the use of his own reason* that he has adequate objective evidence for the trustworthiness of that human authority. In no conceivable case, therefore, does the exercise of faith (or assent on extrinsic authority) precede *some* use of individual reason and *some* rational appreciation of objective evidence. If faith on extrinsic authority is to be reasonable,—and unless it is it cannot stand the test of reason reflecting on it,—it must always imply such an exercise of individual reason as will convince the believer that the extrinsic authority is really there and is really adequate to ground the firm or certain assent of the intellect to that for which it vouches.

The later traditionalists sought to show that it is one thing to *discover* a truth, and another thing altogether to *prove* or *defend* it when discovered : the insinuation being that the individual reason is unable to discover such truths as those referred to above, but is able, when enlightened and disciplined and brought to its full use by the knowledge of them (through Revelation transmitted by tradition), to prove and defend them. In this contention there is both an error and an unproven assumption.

The error lies in the supposition that there is an essential difference, a difference in principle or in kind, between the pro-

---

[1] And the same question must be answered by every human individual for himself concerning his own beliefs.

cess by which the individual discovers a truth for himself and
the process by which he learns it from others or communicates
it to others. No doubt it is far easier to learn from others than
to discover for one's self: so much is undeniable. But the
difference is one of *degree*,—of more or less ease, expedition,
efficacy, convenience. It is not a difference of kind. The individual, whether he be discoverer, learner, or teacher, uses the
same intellectual faculty, follows the same intellectual laws,
employs the same concepts, starts from the same premisses, goes
through the same inferences and reaches the same conclusions.[1]

The unproven assumption is that the traditional communication of the truths in question from society to the individual, the
communication or "*institutio socialis*" (158, C) which is supposed
to be essential for the full development of his reason, implies
an original Divine Revelation.[2] But we have shown already,
against De Bonald (160), that it does not necessarily imply a
Divine *Revelation*. Nor, in fact, can it be shown necessarily to
imply any *direct* intervention of God as *Teacher* or *Instructor ;*
and not rather merely the indirect and natural Divine Teaching
which consists in God's endowment of man with the faculty of
reason.

It is, of course, an undeniable fact that the natural development of the
individual's faculties of thought and expression are conditioned by acquisition
of language and by social intercourse with his fellow-men : that the unnatural event of complete isolation would leave him in a "savage" state : that
he is naturally a "social animal". When, therefore, we speak of "the
natural light of human reason"[3] or the " natural power or capacity of human
reason," the reference is not to the individual in an unnatural, solitary,
isolated condition, but to the individual in human society, and to the intellectual capacity of the ordinary or average member of human society.
Now it is a fact of universal history that a part of the actual enlightenment for
which the individual is indebted to his social condition consists in the communication to him of the religious beliefs which are in substance universally
prevalent : beliefs concerning immortality, an unseen world, an influence of
Divine Powers on mundane things, and man's dependence on such Powers.
It is, moreover, a fact that the Catholic faith includes the belief that God
did *de facto* make an Original Revelation to our first parents, and that *de
facto* its content was in part transmitted from them to posterity,—although
gradually disfigured and corrupted by accretions of error. Now the later
traditionalists appear to have contended not only that such moral and religious truths as have prevailed at least in substance universally throughout

[1] *Cf.* MERCIER, *op. cit.*, § 72, pp. 157-8 ; *Science of Logic*, ii., § 204, pp. 14-16.
[2] *Cf. supra*, p. 297.   [3] *Cf.* Canon of Vatican Council, *supra*, p. 312, n. 2.

human history come *de facto* from that original Divine Revelation, but also that *only through the enlightening influence of such divinely communicated truths* could human reason, whether individually or collectively, *have the capacity of establishing and defending these truths by rational demonstration* (158, C).

If this contention be examined from the standpoint of the believing Catholic, it must be regarded as confounding the natural with the supernatural. For no positive Divine Revelation, or communication of knowledge by God to man, is "natural" or due to human nature as such. Although, therefore, the human race has been *de facto* (according to Catholic teaching) raised to a supernatural end, and has been made from the beginning the recipient of religious knowledge supernaturally communicated by Divine Revelation ; although, moreover, (according to Catholic teaching) human reason, whether regarded individually or collectively, has been *de facto* aided in its purely natural investigation of such fundamental problems as the existence of God, the immortality of the soul, the conditions and sanctions of the moral order, the rational grounds and duties of religion, by the universal transmission of at least some portion of that original Divine Teaching ; and although, finally, it is with man in this actual condition that the Catholic Church is concerned in its teaching, and not with the hypothetical condition of man in what is referred to as "the state of pure nature,"—nevertheless the Vatican Council, in teaching that man can attain to certain knowledge of the existence of "one true God, our Creator and Lord " by " the natural light of human reason," brought to bear on " the things that are made," [1] defined that it is within the natural competence of men generally, exercising their reason on the data of human experience, and *without the supernatural aid of any Divine Revelation*, to reach a certain knowledge of God's existence.

But over against the error of Traditionalism, which it thus condemned for unduly depreciating the power of natural reason, there is the opposite error of Rationalism which claims an undue and erroneous extension of this power. According to this general system,—which has many different forms, —not only can natural reason demonstrate the *preambula fidei*, not only has it the right and the duty to explore the authenticity of alleged Divine Revelations,—and the possibility of Revelation, Miracles, and Supernatural Religion generally,—but natural reason can of itself attain to the discovery and understanding of whatever moral and religious truths it is right or reasonable for man to accept and profess. Against this system the general Catholic teaching is that, considering the nature of men as history and experience reveal them in the mass with all the material tendencies of their passions, prejudices, and preoccupations, *the firm possession and preservation and transmission of* such *a body of religious truths* as would enable mankind to discharge substantially the essential duties of natural religion, and preserve the human race from grave religious ignorance, errors and superstitions, and gross moral decadence, *would be morally impossible without the assistance of some positive Divine Teaching or Revelation :* in other words, that for the effective practice of the natural duties of religion by mankind, and for the continuous substantial observance of the natural moral law by the human race *the aid of a positive Divine Revelation is morally necessary.* It can scarcely be denied

[1] " Ea quae facta sunt."—Rom. i. 20.

that this teaching embodies a sound and reasonable interpretation, indeed the only reasonable interpretation, of the universal data of human experience.[1] This is the truth which Traditionalism overstated in its vigorous reaction against the anti-social teaching of Rousseau and the doctrinaire Rationalism which proclaimed the absolute self-sufficiency of the individual (157). The individual reason considered in itself, apart from the educative influence of society and the *magisterium* of tradition, is not the imaginary self-sufficient being of Rousseau and the Rationalists. But neither is it, on the other hand, the helpless and imbecile creature that Traditionalists would make it. It was right and proper for the Traditionalists to protest against the contemporary deification of the individual reason, and to proclaim the reasonableness of recognizing and respecting the authority of the social *magisterium* which is extrinsic to the individual. But nevertheless the individual has the inalienable right to question the credentials of such authority. In matters that are within its own competence it must not bow blindly and unquestioningly. In such matters, as St. Thomas has pointed out, *locus ab auctoritate est infirmissimus:* the argument from authority is the weakest of all arguments. Hence in fact, though not in intention, Traditionalism did a real disservice to the cause of truth by its attempt to subordinate the function of the individual reason to the function of tradition as the vehicle of extrinsic Divine Authority.

Mercier puts the general argument against the "extrinsicist theory of certitude," propounded by Traditionalism, in this striking manner:[2] "It is involved," he says, "either in the fallacy logicians call *ignoratio elenchi*, or in a contradiction. On the one hand, it asserts that reason is incapable of rationally demonstrating the fundamental theses of natural religion : the existence of God, the distinction of good and evil, a future life. On the other hand, it asserts that we are certain of these theses because God has revealed them and humanity has accepted them. But such a position confronts its advocates with one or other of two alternatives. For we can say to them : Either you have *reasons* for admitting that God has revealed these doctrines, that He cannot teach error, that humanity is a reliable organon for the transmission of revealed truths ; and if you do you are reinstating the function of *rational* proof which a moment ago you rejected, *i.e.* you are contradicting yourself. Or else, you accept those theses *without reason*, thereby committing yourself to blind faith ; and thus for a philosophical problem, which of its nature demands a rational solution, you bring forward a solution which

[1] *Cf.* St. Thomas, *Summa Contra Gentes*, I., c. iv. ; Mercier, *op. cit.*, § 73, p. 159.
[2] *Op. cit.*, p. 161.

is not rational, *i.e.* you are misconceiving the nature of the point at issue."

Finally, if we look at the whole matter of the relation of individual reason to extrinsic authority, if we consider the attitude of traditionalists, rationalists, and orthodox catholics in regard to it, from the general standpoint of reflecting reason,—which is the attitude of the philosopher,—it will, of course, be obvious that the philosopher must have, by the use of his own reasoning powers, attained to the certain knowledge that man is a free, moral, and responsible agent, that the human soul is spiritual and immortal, that a Supreme, Infinite Being exists, on Whom man and the universe are dependent, that a Divine Revelation of truth by God to man is possible, and that if actual it can be discerned as genuine and authentic, before he can usefully proceed to investigate the credentials of any such alleged Revelation in human history, or explore any philosophical system which, like Traditionalism, presupposes the truth of the Christian Revelation and the Christian Religion.

To reach a reasoned certitude in regard to the true solutions of those fundamental problems concerning God, freedom, immortality, etc., must be ultimately the achievement of the human intellect considering the data of experience in the light of the objective evidence furnished by those data to the intellect. But many philosophers reject this statement, and try to base such certitude ultimately on grounds other than intellectual. Attempts of this kind we now purpose to examine.

CHAPTER XXV.

ANTI-INTELLECTUALIST THEORIES. KANT'S MORAL DOGMATISM.
PRAGMATISM AND HUMANISM.

164. SOME ILLUSTRATIONS OF ANTI-INTELLECTUALIST
THEORIES OF CERTITUDE. GENERAL ARGUMENT AGAINST
SENTIMENTALIST AND VOLUNTARIST THEORIES.—We have
seen (162) how Reid with the Scottish school of philosophers
opposed to the scepticism of Hume the indubitable character of
the " principles of common sense," but without analysing and
justifying the intrinsic reasons of the common assent of men to
such principles, or meeting boldly the attacks of scepticism on
the claims of intellectual evidence. If, however, the individual
intelligence fails to justify its assents positively on grounds of
evidence, its ultimate dictate will be scepticism. This was felt
by a French student of the Scottish philosophy, *Theodore Jouffroy*
(1796-1842), who, concluding that truth is unattainable by *reason*,
maintained that scepticism can be and ought to be avoided by
believing in spite of reason, and thus basing human certitude on
" an act of faith, blind but irresistible, in man's power to attain
to truth ".[1]   This is what is known as the theory of " blind
faith ".

Already, in Germany, *Jacobi* (1743-1819), admitting the
main conclusion of Kant's *Critique of Pure Reason*, that the
human " understanding " (*Verstand*) cannot transcend the limits
of sense experience, proclaimed that man is endowed with a
higher faculty than this " understanding " which reasons logically
from the data of sense. This higher faculty (*Vernunft:* " reason ")
works in a hidden, mysterious way in the suprasensible domain
of the true, the good, and the beautiful, as a sort of spiritual feeling
or *sentiment (Geistesgefühl)*.   It is prior to, and deeper than, all
reasoning : we cannot seize or analyse it : we simply *believe*
in it and accept its dictates.   It has not to do with *phenomena*
but gets us into contact with *noumena*, with reality.   Through

---

[1] *Cf.* TURNER, *History of Philosophy*, p. 608 ; MERCIER, *op. cit.*, § 80, pp. 176-7.

it we escape scepticism and rise superior to all the doubts and limitations of the mere logical faculty, the understanding.[1]

Thus, human certitude is based ultimately not on any intelligent apprehension of reality as object of the human understanding, but on an inevident dictate of sentiment or feeling. This "philosophy of sentiment,"—sentiment or feeling variously described as "rational," "moral," "esthetic," "religious," "spiritual,"—was widely espoused after Kant's time as superior to the so-called "reasoned" systems with their alleged impossible and deceptive claims for the supremacy of intellectual evidence as the basis of certitude.[2]

Although "feeling" or "sentiment" can scarcely claim to be a third department of mental life, adequately distinct from the domain of "cognition," and from "appetite" or "conation," still the distinction has been widely recognized since the eighteenth century (46); and accordingly the theories which base human certitude ultimately on sentiment or feeling are distinguished from the "voluntarist" theories, which, following the moral dogmatism of Kant's *Critique of Practical Reason*, seek the ultimate basis of certitude in the domain of the *will*. In all voluntarist theories the mental act which reaches beyond mere appearances and attains to reality is not an act of intellectual apprehension, not an assent of reason, but an act of *belief*, motived or determined by the will. Of this we have a minor illustration in the French modification of the main or Kantian theory,—the "neo-criticism" and "philosophy of belief" propounded by *Renouvier* (b. 1818).[3] Kant, as we shall see, formulated three postulates for the practical reason. Renouvier and the neo-Kantians contend that underlying *all* demonstration there is a postulate, at the root of every assent there is a belief accorded to a free dictate of the will. "According to the classic *intellectualism* certitude is caused by the necessitating action of objective evidence on the intelligence; according to *the philosophy of belief*, on the contrary, it is in ultimate analysis

[1] This so-called higher faculty, distinct from intellect or understanding, is an arbitrary fiction. Its postulation, by Jacobi, is due to this philosopher's defective psychological analysis of the origin of our intellectual knowledge of the positively immaterial or suprasensible domain of reality. All our knowledge of this domain is attained by intellect through analogical concepts derived from the domain of sense. *Cf.* MERCIER, *op. cit.*, § 85, pp. 190-1 ; vol. i., ch. ix.

[2] *Ibid.*, § 79, pp. 175-6.

[3] *Cf.* UEBERWEG-HEINZE, *Geschichte der Philosophie*, iv., pp. 396 *sqq.*; MERCIER, *op. cit.*, § 81, pp. 177-80; § 87, p. 198.

the will, with all its concrete, personal springs of action, that must and does freely determine all certitude, whether spontaneous or reflex, and which consequently establishes the fundamental distinction between truth and error." [1]   But they do not openly go so far as formally to identify truth and error with the respective objects of our likes and dislikes. Rather they look to "a general accord of thinkers" as at least a provisional criterion of truth. Such truth and certitude as are thus attainable are, of course, not absolute or objective, but only relative and subjective and moral : something like the "probabilities" of Carneades and Cicero (37). But we must be content with them, as the best attainable. It is plain, they argue, that there is no discoverable objective standard which would be a sure test of absolute truth : because even amongst the most sincere and highly gifted thinkers we find mutually contradictory views, some regarding as false and inevident the very judgments which others proclaim to be evidently credible and true. And finally we can see by reflection and experience that there is no single judgment, however "self-evident," against which reason cannot raise doubts and difficulties. Unless, therefore, the will freely interpose to arrest reflection and stifle doubt, there can be no certitude. So that certitude is ultimately a matter not of the reason but of the will.

We have given those few illustrations of anti-intellectualist theories of knowledge and certitude in order to reveal the general drift of such theories. We can now offer a general argument in criticism of the attitude and implications revealed in them : an argument which will tell equally against Kant's philosophy of the Practical Reason, against Pragmatism, and all similar tendencies in more recent philosophy.

All such theories may be described—by reason of their opposition to absolute scepticism, and their rejection of intellectually objective tests of truth and motives of certitude—as forms of "subjectivist dogmatism". However they may differ among themselves in detail, they all agree in basing human certitude—at least concerning the fundamental metaphysical, moral and religious convictions that are of deepest import to mankind—not on *intellectual* grounds, on motives which reflecting reason can or ought to evaluate, but on motives which determine assent or belief by their exclusive appeal to *affective* needs, impulses,

---

[1] MERCIER, *op. cit.*, p. 179.

instincts, of the thinking subject. For all of them alike the last word of critical philosophy must be sought not in *objective evidence*, not in the appeal of reality to the intellect, but in its *subjective* influence on *affective* dispositions of the soul.

Now, no affective disposition or inclination of man's nature, whatever form it may take, or however it be described, can issue a dictate which will be accepted, or ought to be accepted by man, —constituted as he is, and endowed as he is with the reflective faculty of reason, intellect, intelligence,—as the supreme and ultimate motive of certitude.

For the subjective source, the affective disposition of will, or feeling, or sentiment, from which such dictate emanates, must issue this dictate either *blindly*, or else only because and in so far as it is itself *enlightened.*

But if it acts *blindly* it cannot reasonably and *de jure* satisfy, and *de facto* it does not under the test of reflection satisfy, a being endowed with the faculty of rational reflection on the grounds and motives of his assents. He may be inclined instinctively to trust those natural tendencies ; he may earnestly wish to safeguard the fundamental moral and religious convictions which are so intimately bound up with man's individual and social dignity and well-being. But endowed as he is with the power of rational reflection he cannot reasonably rest in an instinctive trust in such natural tendencies, wishes, desires, etc. ; he cannot help inquiring how and why they are there, or how and why they are what they are. His nature as a rational being impels him to seek *enlightenment* regarding those tendencies, and regarding the real value or validity, the real credibility and grounds and truth, of the judgments which they dictate : and, should he in this reflective inquiry fail to find satisfactory *reasons* for what they dictate, should they prove blind, impervious to intellect, unjustifiable before the bar of reflecting reason, he could not possibly escape the issue of universal scepticism.

If, on the other hand, the dictates of those affective tendencies be *enlightened*, in other words if reason precedes and guides them, if they are reasonable and reasoned, justifiable and justified, this must be because there is intellectual insight into the sufficiency of their grounds and motives, because in other words the grounds and motives of such dictates do ultimately make an adequate evidential appeal (153-4) to intellect, so that such dictates are ultimately based on a motive of the intellectual order. But in this case certitude is ultimately based not subjectively on the dictate of an affective tendency, but objectively on the evidential appeal of the content of the judgment to the intellect which apprehends and assents to it as true. And so, subjectivist dogmatism is abandoned.

We see, then, that for a being endowed as man is with the faculty of intellectual reflection, the ultimate motive of certitude cannot be of the subjective, psychological, non-intellectual, affective order : that subjectivist dogmatism can be only another name for scepticism.

165. VOLUNTARIST OBJECTIONS. MISCONCEPTION OF INTELLECTUALISM.—Supporters of this anti-intellectualist dogmatism seem to regard it as the only possible alternative to the extreme or narrow intellectualism (148) which would accord to human intelligence or reason the mere function of assenting to *cogently* self-evident abstract principles, and to conclusions inferred by rigorous deductive inference from such principles. But the "classic intellectualism" according to which certitude is caused only by "the necessitating action of objective evidence on the intelligence" (163), is not that of scholasticism. It is rather the type of intellectualism revealed in the excessively deductive and *a-priorist* speculations of Descartes, Leibniz, Spinoza, Ferrier, etc.,[1] in the Hegelian dialectic, and in the utilization of scientific inference according to mathematical and mechanical principles and methods by the positivists and phenomenists in constructing their purely mechanical philosophy of the universe as a phenomenon. But to this erroneous intellectualism the "voluntarist" or "affective" theory of certitude is not the only alternative. The scholastic theory of objective evidence embodies the true form of intellectualism, the form which recognizes and assigns their rightful function to the affective tendencies of human nature as having a real, if indirect, evidential value which intellect can appraise as objective evidence for the truth of their dictates. This doctrine, as propounded in Chapter xxiii., §§ 148-54, really forestalls the arguments on which "affective" or "voluntarist" theories rely, by showing that these theories are not really implied or necessitated by the class of considerations to which they appeal. Renouvier, for instance, appeals to the contradictory affirmations of sincere thinkers, and to the possibility of raising rational difficulties against even the most "self-evident" proposi-

[1] *Cf.* vol. i., § 35, p. 128, n. 3.

tions, as forcing upon us the conclusion that certitude must be ultimately determined by a free act of the will. But no such conclusion is legitimate: and in fact the conclusion drawn is self-contradictory, for a *free* act of the will is an act of *intelligent* decision, an act of choice *enlightened* by *rational* apprehension of the sufficiency of its grounds.[1] And if certitude is determined ultimately by a blind, capricious, instinctive determination of our nature, such certitude is, as we saw in our general argument above, a condition of mind which cannot but issue in absolute scepticism. The truth of course is that in the appreciation of evidence, in the examination of doubts and difficulties against a judgment, in the sustained effort of voluntary intellectual attention, in the consideration of *pros* and *cons* where the evidence is not cogent, and where the assent when given will be *freely* elicited (11-13), a man must make that use of reason which is known as the exercise of *prudence* in determining whether or when the evidence for the truth of the judgment is such as to warrant a *firm* or *certain* assent which will exclude all *prudent fear of error*. But so far from this being an abdication of the claims of reason or intellect to the demands of a blind, instinctive or affective voluntarism, it is a clear assertion of the supreme control of intellect in estimating the rightful evidential value of those subordinate tendencies. It is true, moreover, that individuals may suffer constitutionally from what is known as *pusillanimity* or *intellectual indecision* (37), and that this is accountable for some men's unreasonable negations and lapses into agnosticism ; just as the opposite defect, excessive haste, impulsiveness, dogmatism, is also accountable for widely prevalent errors. But the prevalence of such errors, and of their causes, even among "sincere thinkers," is not a legitimate reason for pronouncing the human intellect to be radically incapable of attaining to any truth (39, A); or for making the futile attempt to avoid scepticism by taking refuge in the so-called "certitude" of an "affective" or "voluntarist" assent which is avowedly *non-rational*, and therefore really *irrational*.

The absence of intellectual accord among men, as to the certain intellectual possession of any truth, is exaggerated by the advocates of subjectivist theories in their zeal to belittle the competence of the human intellect. There are truths which all sane men *spontaneously* accept as self-evident, and which on

[1] *Cf.* Mercier, *op. cit.*, § 87, p. 198.

21 *

reflection they continue so to accept, truths in respect to which intellect is infallible (44, 68, 153, 154). Not that it is impossible for the human intellect to investigate critically their real import or truth value (32), or even for individual minds to err in conducting this delicate process—whether through prejudice, prepossessions, inattention to pertinent evidence, defective or inadequate consideration of evidence—and so to drift into an attitude of avowed or concealed theoretical scepticism (37). But such abnormal use of the intellect is quite consistent with the view that there are truths to which the intellect in its normal use can attain infallibly. And the fact that such speculative sceptics, in order to live at all, must act in direct contradiction and defiance of their sceptical professions, and as if they believed quite a multitude of judgments (15) to be objectively true and certain, is a sufficient proof that their intellectual attitude is unsound, abnormal and unnatural.

It must, however, be acknowledged that the judgments which are really self-evident, and those that can be inferred from them by cogent logical inference, do not include certain judgments which are of the very deepest import to human life. The existence of God, the spirituality and immortality of the soul, the reality of human freedom and the implications of moral responsibility, the natural duty of religion, the possibility and the fact of supernatural or revealed religion,—are theses to the truth of which the intellect is not compelled to assent. The evidence on which they are based is not found by rational investigation to be cogent. They are the subject-matter of *freely formed* convictions (11-13), reached by *a posteriori* consideration of the immediate facts of experience. Now, since they are theses which have a direct and intimate bearing on human nature it is but natural that among the facts which have an evidential value in determining their truth, and which therefore demand rational consideration, we must include all the natural mental instincts, inclinations and needs of man,—whether intellectual, volitional, emotional or affective. That is to say, we must rationally recognize in these a certain evidential value, as pointing to the objective truth of the convictions towards which they impel us : just as we must recognize an evidential value in the universal acceptance of the substance of such convictions (160) by the human race. Thus, in establishing and justifying a reasoned certitude for such affirmations as the existence of God, the spirituality and immortality of the soul, human freedom and moral responsibility, etc., the argument from the universal assent of mankind to at least the substance of those affirmations must be recognized to create a more or less strong presumption in favour of their truth ; although it must not be taken as in itself conclusive, or as exempting us from raising and answering the question why such assents are universal.

When we do raise this question we find that we can point to many broad facts which are in the nature of direct intellectual evidence, and which suffice to justify rationally the certitude of men's spontaneous assents to those universal affirmations : such, for instance, as the great broad fact of order in the universe as indicating the existence of a Supreme Ruling Intelligence. If the evidential demand of the complex, concrete facts of experience on the human *intelligence*, for certain interpretations of what is implied by these facts, though it be really felt and operative, yet cannot be adequately expressed in any verbal formulæ ; and if on that account we choose to describe the assents which they call forth as springing from an "intellectual instinct" (15, 161),—this is not denying that such motives of assent belong to the intellectual or objectively evidential order.

But another undeniably operative factor in eliciting those universally prevalent spontaneous assents to the reality of a future life, to the existence of a Divinity, to the righteousness of Divine sanctions for human conduct, etc., is their *felt* harmony with the *affective* needs, yearnings and aspirations of human nature. The natural human yearning for immortality, for happiness, for a final adjustment of the rights and wrongs of earthly existence, is as universal as man's sense of his finiteness and dependence on Higher Powers. Now the affective or voluntarist theory would base such certitude as we can have concerning the truth of those or any other convictions *exclusively* upon their harmony with the dictates of such affective yearnings or aspirations : thus making all religion a matter of feeling or sentiment. Such procedure is rationally indefensible. But it is another thing altogether, by rational reflection on the harmony of such assents with the affective needs and aspirations of human nature, to recognize in this harmony a certain weight of objective evidence pointing to the presumptive truth of those assents, and to the credibility of that which they affirm. In this there is no abandonment of sound and reasonable intellectualism. For by such procedure we are simply recognizing those affective factors as interpretatively or indirectly intellectual ; we are only interpreting their objective evidential value for intellect. No doubt their evidential value is only secondary if considered apart from the main data which we find within us and around us for rational demonstration of human freedom and responsibility, the spirituality and immortality of the soul, and the existence of a Supreme Being. And no doubt this evidential value can be erroneously overrated. When, for instance, it is asserted that there can be no natural faculty without its adequate object, no really natural need or yearning wholly aimless or doomed to complete frustration ; and when it is pointed out that human yearnings for immortality, for happiness, for righteousness, for moral perfection, for communion with the Divine, the Infinite, the All-Perfect, appear from the abiding universality of their manifestations to be implanted in human nature itself, as distinct from accidental, ephemeral inclinations and impulses : if it be inferred that therefore it is certain that God exists, that the soul is immortal, etc., the inferences are quite too sweeping, and reason will promptly demand justification of the major assertions concerning the non-frustration of yearnings that are universal and natural. But if we consider such facts of the affective order, such yearnings in so far as they are really universal and natural, and the harmony of the conclusions in question with their dictates,—if we consider those facts in the light of all the other evidence we have for those conclusions, and the conclusions themselves as explaining, accounting for the yearnings, and rendering their dictates intelligible, then we can hardly fail to see in those yearnings presumptive and corroborative objective evidence of the truth of those fundamental convictions which underlie religion and morality, and which offer the only satisfactory rational explanation of the nature and destiny of man and the universe.

Those reflections suggest, perhaps, the soul of truth there is in the voluntarist and affective theories of certitude. But they point to the conclusion that it is reason ultimately, and not feeling or sentiment, that must have the last word in determining and justifying our assents : a conclusion *to the justice of which the advocates of such theories unconsciously bear testimony by their own zealous use of their intellectual powers in elaborating their rational exposition and defence of those theories.*

166. KANT'S MORAL DOGMATISM OF THE PRACTICAL REASON. —The most influential subjectivist theory of certitude is undoubtedly the "moral dogmatism" of Kant. Hume had inferred from Sensism the impossibility of any knowledge of absolutely universal and necessary truths. Against this conclusion Kant's *Critique of Pure Reason* had asserted, and started from, the undeniable fact of the existence of such knowledge. So, too, English Sensism had endeavoured to reduce moral obligation or duty to an egoistic, utilitarian dictate of self-interest. And against this Kant's *Critique of Practical Reason* asserted, and started from, the undeniable fact of the existence of a moral law that is utterly irreducible to any such dictate.

Is not duty often in conflict with the inclinations of self-interest? To explain duty, therefore, as springing from any such motive is to attempt the impossible. The English and Scottish moralists had imagined that a "moral sense," inclining the human heart to benevolence, sympathy, enlightened self-interest, could adequately account for the growth and development in man of the consciousness of duty, the sense of moral obligation. This Kant regarded as utterly erroneous and destructive of morality. A person may be sincere and truthful and honourable from the motive of an enlightened self-interest in his own good name and reputation. But the moral law dictates that he be sincere and truthful and honourable even at the sacrifice of his own personal interest and reputation. Its dictate is above all personal interests, superior to all individual considerations, exempt from all particular conditions : it is an unconditional or *categorical imperative.*

Moreover, the moral law as such simply dictates that we *do the right because it is the right,* without prescribing the objects or contents of our individual moral acts. In other words it is a *pure form*, which says simply : Do your duty because it is your duty. The theory of the moral act he calls a *metaphysic :* the "metaphysic of morals ".

The dictate of the moral law, then, is wholly disinterested : it does not seek any end ulterior to itself : it commands the right for sake of the right. It is *its own end.* Moreover, transcending as it does all individual interests, it is a *universal* law, and is capable of formulation in absolute or universal terms. For instance : *So act that the maxim of your conduct can prevail as a universal law.* Further, the moral law forbids that the will be subordinate, as a means to an end, by seeking any good beyond the moral act itself. Hence also : *Act always so that human nature, whether in yourself or in others, be always an end, not a means.* A will that would pursue an ideal of goodness extrinsic or foreign to itself would be *heteronomous*, or subject to an alien law ; but the moral law is *autonomous :* the practical reason, or will, finds in itself the true law of its own proper activity. Hence this final Kantian expression of the moral law as the form of moral conduct : *Consider the idea of the will of every rational being as the idea of a will dictating universal laws.*

Armed with this apparently lofty and stoic conception of the moral law, Kant asks himself what does it imply. What "postulates of the practical reason " are inseparable from it ? There are three such postulates.

The first is *freedom of the will.* If I *ought* to act morally, it must be that I *can.* Thus in the logical order moral responsibility implies human freedom as its *ratio cognoscendi*, while in the ontological order freedom precedes responsibility as its *ratio essendi.*

The second implication of the moral law is the *immortality of the soul.* And why or how ? For this reason and in this wise : The moral law dictates duty for duty's sake and forbids us to subordinate duty to the attainment of happiness. On the contrary, duty often demands the sacrifice of personal interest, well-being, happiness, satisfaction. Nevertheless reason revolts, and rightly revolts, against the idea that duty and happiness be for ever separated. Does not the notion of the *supreme good* imply *all* good, and therefore the union of the good which is *righteousness* with the good which is *happiness ?* But such union cannot be realized in the conditions of man's moral life here on earth. There must, therefore, be a future state of existence in which the soul can attain ever more fully to the moral ideal, where it can taste and enjoy, without however having sought, the happiness which must reward its fidelity to duty.

The third postulate of morality is the *existence of God.* For when the soul shall enjoy the reward of its virtue, when duty and happiness coincide, when the *bonum supremum* will be the *bonum consummatum,* such consummation of the universal order can only be conceived to be the work of an All-Powerful and All-Holy Will. There must be a God : the author of the physical order and the moral order, of the world of sense and the world of intellect, of the domain of appearances or phenomena and the domain of realities or noumena, Who will unify all in one universal and indefectible harmony.

Such, then, are the affirmations of the practical reason : the moral law exists as an absolute dictate, a *categorical imperative ;* its conditions are freedom, immortality, and God's existence. And *religion, based upon morality,* derives its legitimate sway over man, its authority and its credentials, *from the practical reason.*

But what are those affirmations of the practical reason worth ? What are *their* credentials and authority? They are *not* based on *knowledge,* but on a *need or dictate of the will.*

Knowledge is the achievement of man's *speculative reason* (46). But it is confined to phenomena which occur in space and time and are subject to the absolute determinism of the law of universal causation. Man's speculative reason can attain to no *knowledge* either of a substantial soul exempt in its acts from the absolute determinism of physical antecedents and capable of surviving bodily death, or of an Absolute Being transcending the phenomenal universe (46, 54). It may, and indeed must, *think* them, but only as problematic : it cannot know them to be *real.* Neither, however, can it know them to be *unreal.* Know-. ledge has simply nothing to say of them. Nevertheless we will, and cannot help willing, the morally good ; and therefore we believe, and cannot help believing, what this implies. Conse- quently we will, and have *a natural need to will,* that there be a free and immortal soul in man, and that God, the Supreme Good, exist ; and we believe, and cannot help believing, in the reality of what the will thus dictates to be real. The foundation, there- fore, of moral or ethical certitude, and of religious faith, is *the*

need of our nature to give credence to certain ideas. By nature we
are endowed with *will* or *practical reason*, the seat or source or
principle of moral conduct. Moral conduct is a fact; so is its
source or principle. They are of our very nature. In the
dictate of moral conduct we find certain necessary implications :
human freedom and immortality, and the existence of God.
This dictate of our nature as moral beings furnishes each of us
individually with a motive that is subjectively sufficient for
believing in the reality of these implications : though their objective reality falls necessarily beyond the scope of our *knowledge ;*
their reality cannot possibly be an object of knowledge. Kant
admits this expressly. "All faith," he says,[1] "is an assent that
is subjectively sufficient, but conscious of its objective insufficiency ; faith therefore is opposed to knowledge."

Nor can this consciousness that God, freedom and immortality are unknowable, unattainable by the speculative reason,
militate against the personal certitude of our belief in them as
realities : for reflection on the speculative reason shows that such
realities, being suprasensible, cannot possibly be its objects,
cannot belong to the sphere of knowledge or science. The
Critique of Pure Reason established this. Its achievement in
regard to them was to "remove *knowledge* in order to make
room for *belief* ":[2] and thus "to render a signal service to
humanity by removing morality and religion from the domain
of science and from the consequent corroding influence of
scientific doubt".[3] The limits of the scientific knowledge attainable by the speculative reason being thus duly recognized, the
primacy of the practical reason, the supremacy of its influence
in determining the certitude of personal belief in those suprasensible realities, is manifest. For the dictate of the practical
reason, the categorical imperative of conscience, implies and
demands belief in God, freedom and immortality, as realities ;
and at the same time this dictate (with all that it involves)
transcends the sensible or phenomenal domain of the speculative
reason and attains by way of belief to the real or noumenal domain of being.[4] Thus, then, the scepticism or phenomenism

[1] *Qu'est-ce que s'orienter dans la pensée.* Edited in the *Mélanges de Logique.—*
apud MERCIER, *op. cit.*, § 77, p. 173. Mercier's exposition (*ibid.*) has been closely
followed in the text above.
[2] *Critique of Pure Reason*, Pref. pp. xxx and xxi (tr. MÜLLER, pp. 700-1), quoted
above, vol. i., § 46, p. 172, n. 1.
[3] Vol. i., § 46, p. 172 ; *cf.* § 56, pp. 199-200.   [4] *Cf.* vol. i., § 46, p. 172.

of the speculative reason is seen to be a condition of, and a preparation for, the moral dogmatism of the practical reason.

167. CRITIQUE OF MORAL DOGMATISM. THE "CATE-
GORICAL IMPERATIVE" AND ITS IMPLICATIONS.—Kant's intentions were good. He wished to defend man's fundamental
religious and moral beliefs against the attacks made upon them
in the name of science. The aim of the *Critique of Practical
Reason* was to show up the error of identifying duty with self-
interest after the manner of the British moralists; to vindicate
the real existence of a moral law, or dictate of duty, absolute in
character and universal in its authority; to show, consistently
with the principles and conclusions of the *Critique of Pure
Reason*, that the certitude of our belief in God, freedom and
immortality, is sufficiently grounded in the subjective, practical
human need of such belief as necessitated by the dictate of the
practical reason interpreting the implications of the imperative
of duty revealed in our moral conscience; that the primacy of
this practical dictate, or need of the will to believe, its supremacy
in transcending the limits of the mere knowledge-verdicts of the
speculative reason, reveals this practical need or dictate as the
subjectively adequate and only possible ultimate basis of human
certitude in realities of the suprasensible, moral and religious
order.

If, therefore, we can show that Kant's method of vindicating
the reality of a moral obligation superior to all self-interest is a
failure; that such obligation cannot be grounded on any need
or dictate of our nature so long as the speculative reason is debarred from seeking or finding objective grounds for it; that he
cannot validly or consistently derive from such a dictate of duty
the three conclusions proposed for our belief concerning God,
freedom and immortality; and finally, that his two *Critiques*
are, in fact if not in intention, mutually inconsistent and contradictory, that the conflict between them is inevitable, essential,
fundamental,—it will be sufficiently clear that so far from
achieving what he wished and intended, his effort to defend
human certitude only leads once more to the wilderness of
scepticism.

I. *The deduction of the categorical imperative as pure universal
form or law of moral conduct fails to establish a real and effective
moral obligation.* Kant's moral dogmatism is avowedly concerned with existing realities, with the moral conduct of actual

men : its aim is to establish an effective moral obligation. Its method precludes its doing so. And for this reason : from abstract judgments of the ideal order it is impossible to deduce an affirmation concerning an existence. But the categorical imperative is an abstract formula of the ideal order. Therefore the actual existence of an effective moral obligation (and of its three ontological conditions) cannot be deduced from the categorical imperative.[1]

What Kant expresses in such a variety of formulæ as the moral law is not an object of actual experience, but an *abstraction*. Examine the formulæ given above. They are all *abstract* and *universal*. Kant has confused *the abstract formulation of certain conditions of morality with proof or vindication of the fact of moral obligation*. We need not examine those conditions on their merits. The stoic rigorism of some of them is not above criticism. But such as they are, where are they to be found ? Disinterestedness, for example, as a condition of moral conduct, —where is it realized ? Where, if not in the concrete acts of men's individual wills ? And so of the other veritable conditions of morality. But the acts of the will are elicited *in view of an end :* without an end in view there would be no "motive" of action, and consequently no action. If the end is in conformity with man's rational nature the act is morally good ; otherwise it is not. From such concrete data, embodied in concrete moral acts, reason abstracts the *conditions essential* for a morally good act, and then erects them into a universal norm or standard or criterion of moral acts. But the abstract formulation of such a standard or rule is not the proof of *a real and effective moral obligation*. The conditions or circumstances by the presence of which the existence of a duty or obligation are revealed to us do not *constitute* the *real and effective obligation*. To be morally obliged or bound in duty and to act accordingly, implies this : that we wish an end absolutely, that we see a definite act to be necessary for the realization of this end, and that we freely will or elicit to perform the act as a means to the end. But, then, the question at once arises : *Is there* any end which imposes itself absolutely on the will ? And if so, what is it ? It is for man's *intelligence*, for his *reason*, to find out. And so we pass from the

---

[1] The attempt to make such an inference is compared by Taine to an attempt to hang one's hat on the painted image of a nail in the wall.—*Cf.* Mercier, *op. cit.*, § 86, pp. 191-2.

domain of action to that of speculation, from the dictate of duty
by the practical reason to the analysis of this dictate by the speculative reason.   And, contrary to Kant's contention, the primacy
inevitably passes from the former to the latter.

Nor does Kant's actual procedure fail to betray an unconscious indication of this inevitable *denouement*.   "So act that
human nature be never a means, but always an end."   In other
words: "Subordinate your personal interest to the good of
humanity, and will this always as supreme end".   But *why*
should I?   Is the good of humanity the supreme end of life,
the supreme determinant of my conduct?   A question which it
is obviously the task of the speculative reason or intellect to
answer by rational reflection and investigation.

Again, look at Kant's account of the categorical imperative.
Man's moral conscience, it is alleged, reveals an absolute or categorical imperative which must be interpreted as the dictate of
an autonomous will.   But the dictate of duty *de facto* revealed
by introspection is not revealed, and cannot be interpreted, as
imposed autonomously by the will or practical reason.   An
"autonomous" will is one that should necessarily will its own
perfection, finding in itself the adequate object of its volition,
wholly uninfluenced by any end or object or motive outside or
extrinsic to itself.   But only the Will that is Divine, Infinite,
All-Perfect, can will in this way.   The will of the human individual is not thus self-moved or self-sufficient.   Nor can it will *in
vacuo*, as it were.   It must will this or that or the other concrete
end presented to it by the intellect as a good : only by such good,
as "motive," can it be solicited or "moved" from its state of
indetermination to elicit any definite, specific act of volition.
And such is the law of every will that is contingent and finite.
Only the Will that is Imperfectible, All-Perfect, Infinite, "*Actus
Purus*," can elicit a self-originated volition, an absolute beginning of activity.   Thus Kant's doctrine of the human will as
autonomous really deifies the human will.

II. *Kant's postulates of the Practical Reason cannot be validly
or consistently deduced from the categorical imperative or dictate
of moral duty.*

A. And first as to his doctrine of freedom.   How can he
speak of *free acts* of man after concluding in the *Critique of Pure
Reason* that whatever happens in space and time is ruled by
the absolute determinism of phenomenal antecedents according

to the law of physical causation? How can determinism prevail universally in the world of space and time if a *free* principle,
residing in the noumenal domain of the real human will, can
intervene in the flow of physical events and break their physically
determined continuity? Either there is no real relation between
the two domains, the noumenal domain of free volitional action
and the phenomenal domain of physical determinism, or there
is such relation. If there is none such, if free volition is confined to the noumenal world, how can it serve to explain the
actual moral conduct of men in the actual world of space and
time? When Kant argues, and rightly, that "you must" implies "you can," it is because he sees in any such definite, concrete human act as *e.g.* telling the truth at one's own expense,
an exercise of moral conduct, and infers as a necessary implication of this act the *freedom* of the man to tell the truth rather
than lie. But this is bringing down freedom from the noumenal
domain and admitting its real relation, its real contact, with
man's actions in the physical domain of space and time. And
what now becomes of the universal determinism? Kant, as
we have seen already, tried to face this difficulty.[1] But how?
By taking the soul in two senses, as the noumenal *Ego* and as
the phenomenal *Ego*, as a noumenal reality for belief and as a
phenomenal object for knowledge. By recognition of this distinction, he says, "we can without any contradiction think of the
same will when phenomenal (in visible actions) as necessarily
conforming to the law of nature, and so far, *not free*, and yet,
on the other hand, when belonging to a thing by itself, as
not subject to that law of nature, and therefore *free*".[2] But
how "without any contradiction"? Is the contradiction not
palpable? Kant denies that there is any contradiction; and
his reason for the denial is that while the speculative reason can
know the will only *as phenomenal* (and not free), it can *think* the
will *as noumenal* (and free), and therefore cannot deny the
possibility of free will as noumenal, while the practical reason
demands free will as a noumenon and justifies our *belief* in it as
really free: to which he would add the further plea that contradiction can be only between conflicting "knowledges," or
conflicting "beliefs," but is unintelligible and impossible as between any "knowledge" and any "belief," inasmuch as these

---

[1] *Cf.* vol. i., § 54, p. 193.
[2] *Critique* (Pref. to 2nd edit.), p. 699—quoted vol. i., *ibid.*

are wholly separate and mutually exclusive domains of human
experience. But all this is of no avail. For firstly, on his own
theory he *ought* to judge *human* free will to be *an impossibility.*
The *human* will, on his own admission, is the will that conditions
the moral acts of men, acts that are performed in the physical
world of space and time. He might, indeed, judge to be
possible a world of unknown and unknowable beings endowed
with free will, beings wholly apart from the world of human
experience. But how can he, without inevitable contradiction,
judge free will to be possible and operative in the actual moral
conduct of human beings existing and acting in this world of
human experience, if he holds all the events in this world, including the moral acts of men, to be rigidly and adequately
determined by their physical or phenomenal antecedents? And
secondly, is there in man only one *Ego*, one *will*, considered
under two different aspects?[1] If so, the contradiction is there:
such *Ego* or *will* cannot be both free and not free: nor will it
remove the contradiction, or satisfy us as rational beings, to be
told that we only *know* the will as not free, but can transcend this
knowledge by *believing* the will to be free, and console ourselves
with the thought that it is belief, not knowledge, that attains to the
reality of things.[2] Or is it that there are two real and really
distinct domains of reality, the one including the noumenal *Ego*
or *will*, and the other including the visible universe of men and
things? If this were so, and if the former had no influence on
or in the latter, then it is not about the former that reasonable
men will trouble themselves, but about the actual men and things
of human experience.[3] While if the noumenal (free) will has a
real influence on the flow of events in the phenomenal universe
the contradiction of maintaining this universe to be ruled by
rigid determinism remains inevitable.

B. Kant's attempt to infer the immortality of the soul from
the dictate of moral duty is inconsistent with his own principles.
His argument comes to this, that although morally right conduct
is essentially disinterested, and can never be in view of happiness,
nevertheless reflection on the notions of virtue and happiness
shows that there is an evident incompatibility in conceiving

---

[1] *Cf.* § 129, *supra*, for Kant's erection of phenomena into " secondary " realities.
[2] In other words the speculative reason of man will inevitably assert, and rightly
assert, its claim to primacy, to explore all the motives and grounds, whether subjective or objective, of all human beliefs or assents, and to evaluate these accordingly.
[3] *Cf.* MAHER, *Psychology*, chap. xxii., pp. 474-5.

virtue to be for ever divorced from happiness ; and since they are often divorced in the present life, where the lot of the just man is so allied with suffering, there must be a future life where virtue will have its reward.

But if it were *analytically evident*, from mere consideration of the notions, that virtue and unhappiness are incompatible, as Kant contends, then such analysis should enable us to see that virtue and happiness are essentially inseparable. But they are not, as indeed Kant himself admits and experience of life abundantly proves. If, therefore, the one does involve the other, the connexion must be proved or made clear *synthetically*. But it cannot according to Kant's own principles, for the *Critique of Pure Reason* teaches that *synthetic judgments are valid only within the limits of sense experience*, while the soul and a future life fall beyond these limits.

As a matter of fact the belief that virtuous conduct will have its reward, or ought to have its reward, is not a belief the validity of which is self-evidently valid. That it will have its reward requires to be proved. And that it ought to have its reward,— well, perhaps, the persuasion is no more than an illusion, prompted by the wish that is father to the thought? These difficulties can, of course, be solved, and the general argument from duty to immortality defended as valid. But Kant's doctrine concerning the scope and validity of the judgments that must enter into such an argument precludes Kant himself from all right to use it. His claim that the practical reason, being above the laws that govern the speculative reason, can use the argument legitimately to ground *belief* in immortality, we shall examine below (168).

C. In inferring the existence of God from the categorical imperative Kant employs the principle of causality inconsistently with his own teaching as to the limits of the valid application of this principle. The union of righteousness and happiness in a perfect and consummated good must, he argues, ultimately take place. But it can take place only if brought about by a Supreme Being, a Sovereign Legislator of the moral order, Who wills to realize the *bonum consummatum*. Therefore such Supreme Being exists.

But what can such inference avail, if the principle of causality is not objectively valid or applicable beyond the domain of phenomena ?

Before considering Kant's claim to the lawfulness of such reasoning in support of our *belief* in the postulates of the *practical reason,*—a point which belongs to the relation between the two *Critiques,*—we may note here a few other obvious defects in his procedure. From his stoic conception of moral duty he totally excludes the motive of happiness. Man's desire for happiness is natural. Moreover the virtuous man deserves, merits happiness, as the reward of well-doing : even on Kant's admission. Nay, more, a man is bound to be virtuous, and so to render himself worthy of happiness. And yet Kant would have it that if a man desires the happiness which he ought by his conduct to deserve, such desire of his cannot be a morally good act inasmuch as it is wanting in the essential element of disinterestedness ! The truth of course is that while disinterestedness is a perfection of the moral act, the full measure of disinterestedness which would exclude all consideration of self and all thought of individual well-being is not essential to morally righteous conduct.

Again, the unquenchable aspirations of man towards an ideal of moral goodness, beauty, righteousness, above and beyond the satisfactions of individual interests ; his inborn reverence, respect, admiration for this ideal,— are boldly emphasized in Kant's theory. " Two things," he exclaims, " fill the soul with admiration and respect, the starry heaven above us and the moral law within us." This is undeniably so. But then both of them alike raise problems for the human mind. What is the import or significance of such feelings ? It is all very well to say : " I wish, I desire, that the moral order be respected ; I experience an imperative need to respect it ; my nature impels me to respect it ; the moral dignity of man, the good of humanity, etc., demand it ". All that only *raises* a problem (and not quite accurately, thus expressed), but does not solve it. What right have I to assume *a priori* that such needs, impulses, aspirations are not illusory ? How do I know that the subordination of my personal satisfactions to a dictate of duty or a moral law is right or reasonable, and not a mere self-deception ? Therefore I must seek and find, *by rational investigation* of my own nature and the universe and what they imply, a *rational basis* for, and justification of, those moral dictates in obedience to which I am expected to shape my conduct and direct my life. And so we find ourselves once more led to the thesis of intellectualism, that man can attain to a reasoned certitude regarding his spontaneous assents, whether these be speculative or moral or religious, if, and only if, he can find for such assents a ground or motive that will be objectively valid under the scrutiny of reflecting reason. Natural promptings of the will, aspirations of the heart, impulses of feeling and sentiment, may serve as immediate motives of spontaneous assents, and as provisional practical guides of conduct ; but the ultimate ground of human certitude must be approved by reflecting reason, and with reflecting reason the last word on certitude must ever rest.

168. THE TWO CRITIQUES COMPARED. INCONSISTENCIES OF KANT'S SYSTEM AS A WHOLE.—The student of Kant will be struck by the fact that both of Kant's *Critiques* are *reasoned,* that both are works of the same individual human intellect, exploring, interpreting, arguing, reasoning, apparently in the same

way and according to the same general laws which guide and govern rational processes. When examining the first *Critique* we had occasion more than once to notice certain inconsistencies and certain peculiar problems it suggested concerning its own scope and significance.[1] We have now briefly to compare the two *Critiques* with a view to seeing whether their conclusions conform at least to the negative test of consistency (156) in considering their claim to acceptance as forming a satisfactory philosophy of human experience as a whole.

For a time it was thought by many that it was only when he realized the destructive bearings of the first *Critique* upon the fundamental moral and religious beliefs of mankind that Kant tried to avert the impending disastrous consequences by seeking a new basis for those beliefs in his second *Critique;* that he had not conceived and intended from the beginning the destruction of the "ancient metaphysics" as a necessary preparation for the transference of the basis of those beliefs from the scientific domain to the domain of the will, or regarded this transference itself as the only sure way of defending religion and morality against the sceptical attacks of reason. But from Kant's correspondence it appears that he had before him throughout,[2] the whole general outline of the system embodied in the two *Critiques*, and that therefore he always regarded their respective conclusions not only as mutually compatible, but as mutually complementary and as forming together one logical and perfectly consistent whole. That his intention was the very reverse of sceptical or destructive of moral and religious certitude is beyond all question. And that he could have regarded the two *Critiques* as mutually complementary is also intelligible. For the conflict between them is *de facto* not quite explicit and obvious.

When Kant set himself to the task of meeting the scepticism of Hume he was probably impressed by the formula with which Leibniz had countered the empiricism of Locke: "Nihil est in intellectu quod prius non fuerit in sensu, *nisi intellectus ipse*" (71). While sense experience is of objects allied to material conditions of time-and-space phenomena, reflection on our intellectual activity reveals this as determining the necessary, *a priori* judgments of science, and as thereby disclosing an intelligible world which is beyond the control of positive science altogether.

[1] *Cf.* especially vol. i., § 59; also §§ 46, 54, 56, 58.
[2] *Cf.* MERCIER, *op. cit.*, § 109, pp. 247-50.

When, therefore, the dictate of moral duty reveals itself in man's conscience as absolute, it cannot on the one hand ground itself on principles of the speculative reason which are concerned only with the scientific knowledge of the objects of sense experience, but neither on the other hand has it anything to fear from them since it is wholly beyond the range of their proper sphere of application.   The conflict, therefore, between the two *Critiques* is not direct or apparent.

But is the conflict between their directive principles nevertheless really there?   It certainly is; and by an inevitable logical necessity.

What, for instance, can be the significance of the distinction between the *speculative reason* and the *practical reason?* [1]   Are they two distinct faculties?   There appears to be no ground whatever for thinking so.   They are rather two aspects or domains of the activity of the human intelligence (or intellect, understanding, reason).   They are simply one and the same human intelligence, conceiving, judging, reasoning, in the domain of speculative reality (or "things"), and of practical reality (or "acts"), respectively.   The theoretical or speculative reason, then, would be intellect employed in the investigation of *that which is ;* and the practical reason would be the same intellect employed in the investigation of *that which ought to be*—or, human conduct in its ethical aspect.

But if so, this single faculty must in all its functions be subject to the same general laws.   If, as theoretical or speculative, it can attain only to sense phenomena, it should as practical

---

[1] Kant sometimes seems to identify what he calls the *practical reason* with the *will*, or again, at times, with man's moral *conscience.*   But the will, considered in itself, is not a cognitive faculty at all, not a faculty which *apprehends* or *judges* or *assents* or *reasons :* hence it has been described as of itself a " blind " faculty : its function is to will, desire, " intend " ends, to "choose" means, etc., *under the enlightening influence* of the higher cognitive faculty, the *intellect,* manifesting objects as " good ".   Hence Kant must rather have meant by the practical reason the faculty which discerns, judges, dictates, reasons, and delivers verdicts, concerning objects of the practical or moral order, human acts and human conduct, *i.e.* concerning matters in which the exercise of free will is directly involved.   The question is, then, is such faculty distinct from the intellect or reason which judges speculative matters ?   And the same question applies to man's moral *conscience.*   Conscience, as a faculty, is universally regarded by scholastics, and indeed by philosophers generally, as the intellect itself dictating a judgment concerning the lawfulness or unlawfulness of a definite act to be there and then performed or avoided by the person judging.   While the special aptitude of the intellect to discern the truth of first principles of the moral order has been described by scholastics and others as *synderesis* (15).   *Cf. supra*, p. 243 n.

have the same confines. On the other hand, if, as practical, it can attain to the *realities* of the domain of moral duty, so should it, as speculative, be able to attain to the *realities* of the domain of sense. Concerned as we are with only a single faculty, man's intelligence or reason, there can be only two alternative answers to the inevitable question : Can it attain to reality or can it not? We must choose one : we cannot choose both.

If it can, inasmuch as moral duty both transcends phenomenal conditions and is an object of certitude, why cannot substances and causes be also "noumena" or metaphysical realities likewise transcending phenomenal conditions, and be therefore objects of certitude on the same title as the realities of the moral order?

If it cannot, for the reason that, owing to the absence of phenomenal or sensible matter whereby alone reality could "be given" or "appear," the spontaneity of the intellect endeavouring to apprehend it would be without an "object," why should the reality called the "categorical imperative," or the realities supposed to be implied by it, be capable of certain attainment, seeing that they too are not presented in "sensible matter" as "objects"?

Kant, however, made the fatal mistake of endeavouring to show that the intellect cannot attain to certitude about substances and causes, that the supposed metaphysical knowledge of these is an illusion, whereas the knowledge embodied in physics and mathematics is genuine ; and his only way of making this negation plausible was by contending that genuine scientific certitude is confined to phenomena that fall within the limits of sense experience,—to the sense appearances which are the objects of physics and mathematics. But having taken up this position he could escape the sensism and scepticism of Hume only by maintaining the reality of a world beyond the scope of sense, a purely intelligible domain, and the possibility of attaining to certitude concerning it. The question, however, then was : How can such certain attainment be possible. After he had declared that the human intellect cannot attain to certitude about any reality, that all its necessary and universal judgments reveal merely mental phenomena or sense appearances moulded by the forms of its own activity,[1] how was he to get it into certain

---

[1] First it was represented as attaining to certitude as to how the reality *which directly affects us in external and internal sensation* (the "noumenon *of experi-*

contact with the purely intelligible, real or noumenal domain of being?

He tried to do so by seizing on one single fact of his own consciousness, assuming a similar fact to be present in every other person's consciousness, and by analysing *rationally* its implications. This fact was the concept or notion, which he found within his mind, of moral duty, moral obligation, moral law. This content of his consciousness he interpreted,—not very accurately, as we saw above, but no matter,—as a "categorical imperative," *i.e.* an *absolute* dictate *binding necessarily and universally.* But, granting all that, the reader will surely ask what possible use could *Kant* make of it for *grounding certitude about reality*, seeing that he had just declared all necessary and universal judgments, all notions or concepts, to be capable of manifesting either (1) merely *mental products* of subjective, *a priori* forms with sensuously given materials, where there are such materials, or else (2) mere empty mental *forms* themselves, mere regulative modes of the mind's activity, where there are no such sensuous materials, modes which it would be an illusion (according to his own teaching) to mistake for realities. Either those moral notions and dictates are revealed to us, and apprehended by us (as *de*

---

ence" : the real external world and the real *Ego*: what the "ancient metaphysics" called *material* substances or subjects, and *material* causes or agencies) *appears*; then as attaining to certitude only about *mental phenomena* or appearances, which were thus, as secondary entities (129), distinguished and isolated from their corresponding "noumena of experience": so that these latter were thus made just as remote from the intellect as the "metaphysical noumena," God, the soul, freedom, immortality, the moral order, the realities to which the three ideas of the pure speculative reason point. Nevertheless, Kant in places distinguishes and contrasts those two sets of noumena, as to their certain attainability by the human intellect. *Cf.* MERCIER, *op. cit.*, § 144, p. 397: "Kant often contrasts knowledge of the noumena of experience with knowledge of metaphysical reality. Why? Can I know the empirical noumenon, or can I not? If I cannot, where is the use of contrasting my ignorance of it with my ignorance of metaphysical reality. If on the other hand the empirical real, or noumenon of experience, does lie within the scope of my knowledge, why can I not pass from certitude regarding such empirical realities to certitude concerning metaphysical realities, seeing especially that *ex hypothesi* the latter are a necessary condition of the existence of the former."

The reader will recognize, in what are here referred to as "noumena of experience" and "metaphysical realities" respectively, the intelligible realities of the domain of sense (*sensibilia per accidens*: material substances and causes), of which we have proper concepts, and intelligible realities transcending the domain of sense (spiritual substances and causes; the human soul as free, spiritual and immortal; pure spirits; God), of which our concepts are only analogical (*supra*, § 114, p. 76, n. 1; pp. 80-1; § 125, pp. 143-4). And in *the rational inferribility of the latter from the former* he will see the fundamental reason of the possibility of a speculative metaphysics, and the condemnation of Kant's metaphysical agnosticism.

facto they are), *in the concrete, individual data of our conscious experience,*—in our individual moral feelings, sentiments, impulses, choices, decisions, etc., as these arise in our direct consciousness : but if so, they can (on Kant's theory) reveal just mere mental phenomena, pure and simple, like our other concepts and judgments ; and the objective reality of the noumenon which they suggest to us remains exactly as doubtful and unattainable as that of any other noumenon of experience. Or else those moral notions and dictates are *devoid of all empirical content,* independent of anything revealed in the consciousness of our actual moral life, objects of pure intellectual intuition. But then, if it is alleged that *because they are such* they manifest *realities* to us, and that we thus *attain to certitude about reality,* (1) why can we not have, *a pari,* a similar intellectual certitude of suprasensible realities through the (speculative) concepts and judgments we form regarding substance, cause, soul, spirit, God ? And secondly, (2) is it not inconsistent of Kant to claim the power of attaining to certitude about reality for the very faculty of intellect to which he had already repeatedly denied all such power ? Why should not such reputed attainment of suprasensible reality be still an illusion ? Why should it not still be *de facto* only the thought or idea of a mere empty mental form ? And finally, (3) even supposing it to be a certain attainment to reality, the insuperable difficulty would still remain of either leaving one of the noumenal realities, which is human freedom, up in the clouds of a Platonic *mundus intelligibilis,* or else bringing it down to the concrete world of actual human experience, to the inevitable destruction of the universal determinism which on Kant's own theory prevails there.[1]

It is sometimes urged,—and this will be our last point,—that while the certitude attainable by the speculative exercise of reason is conditioned by external experience, the certitude attainable by its practical exercise is conditioned only by internal experience. Or, to put it in another way, " human experience, taken in its totality . . . has two distinct starting-points : *sense* data, the subject-matter of scientific knowledge ; and the *categorical imperative* of conscience, the basis of moral and religious beliefs ".[2] And this being so, may not analysis of each of these domains show us that though *certitude* concerning *reality* is unattainable by reason proceeding from the former starting-point by way of external (speculative) experience, it is attainable by reason proceeding from the second by way of internal (practical, moral) experience ? May not such analysis lead us to the conclusion that

[1] *Cf. supra,* pp. 332-4. [2] Vol. i., § 46, p. 172.

the *sense* data of consciousness which reveal to reason the *physical* domain, and the *suprasensible* data of conscience which reveal the *moral* and *religious* domains, are totally heterogeneous and mutually isolated for reason? If, then, it be shown that reason can ground the certitude of its moral and religious *beliefs* in *reality* on the latter set of data, and that through the former set it can attain to *knowledge*, but only of *phenomena*, not of reality, is not moral and religious certitude thereby made absolutely proof against the sceptical inroads of science?

In this plea for Kantism we have a plausible mixture of good intentions and bad philosophy. But its plausibility is destroyed even by Kant's own teachings. The only point we need notice in it is the insinuation that, from the point of view of human certitude about reality, different values attach to the two sources of experience. But what *are* the two sources referred to? Not internal and external experience, in the sense of consciousness of the *Ego* and awareness of an external universe. For we have seen[1] that Kant holds all our consciousness of what goes on in the *Ego* to be conditioned by our awareness of an external, spatial universe; and that, moreover, both the spatial or external and the temporal or internal data can, according to his theory, reveal only mental phenomena, and not realities. The distinction, therefore, which he seeks to establish between two sources of our experience, must be the distinction between conscious data of the physical order and conscious data of the moral order. But neither can this effectively serve his purpose; and for two reasons.

Firstly, because the moral data from which he derives the categorical imperative and its implications, being *data of conscious experience*,[2] should on his own theory reveal only mental phenomena, only an "empirical" *Ego*, and not any reality. For after all the individual man has only one mind, one consciousness, the processes and data of which must therefore conform to the same law so far as their value for certitude or insight into reality is concerned.

And *secondly*, the heterogeneity of the two domains of conscious data is not absolute; nor can they be rightly or reasonably held to form two totally isolated and separate domains of mental life. Moral concepts and judgments are of course different from our concepts and interpretations of physical or sense data. They are not derived or derivable from the immediate data of any of the *senses:* just as concepts of the domain of one sense cannot be derived from the data of another sense : the concept of *colour*, for instance, cannot be derived from the *auditory* data of consciousness. But moral concepts and principles are nevertheless derived from other concrete, individual data revealed in our conscious experience. Conscious impulses, aspirations, sentiments, affective and volitional tendencies, choices, decisions, feelings of responsibility, duty, obligation, of regret, remorse, shame, or of the approval of conscience for our conduct,—these are all concrete individual facts or data of direct consciousness or intuition,—not of sense consciousness, of course, but of intellectual consciousness (95), consciousness of the higher or intellectual and volitional departments of our mental life. It is from such concrete, individual, conscious data, directly revealed to each of us in his own mental

---

[1] Vol. i., § 61, p. 214, n. 1; *supra*, § 97, p. 7, n. 4; § 100, p. 15; § 134, pp. 202-5.

[2] *Cf.* Vol. i., § 56, pp. 199-200.

life, externated in his own moral conduct, and inferred to be also in his fellow-men from similar externations apprehended in their moral conduct,—it is from such data that we derive the concepts of duty, responsibility, moral obligation, moral sanctions, etc., which enter into all moral principles, dictates and judgments. The "ought" of moral conduct is, of course, not a datum of sense. It is, however, a datum of intellect. Nor is it given to intellect, or apprehended by intellect, *in* the data of sense,—any more than God, or the free, spiritual, and immortal soul, or the intellect itself, or the will, are given *in* sense data. It is, however, given to intellect in our immediate intellectual awareness of the conscious, suprasensible, or spiritual activities, yearnings, aspirations, impulses, of our own intellect and will, as a specific characteristic of these data. Our intellectual apprehension of it as a thought-object, and of other thought-objects of the same suprasensible order, we have already asserted to be *mediated by sense,* inasmuch as we consider *all* our suprasensible mental activities to be conditioned by the prior operation of sense perception and sense consciousness. This we believe to be the proper interpretation of Locke's aphorism as qualified by Leibniz (71, 74, 100, 105, 114). But even if the conscious data to which the concept of the "ought" with all its implications applies, could be attained by an intellectual intuition that would be in no way conditioned by sense, and even if the "ought" as a concept were a pure *a priori* form applied by the mind to such data, consistency would demand that its function and application obey the same laws, and be subject to the same limitations, as the other *a priori* forms of the mind (for those moral data *are* data *of human consciousness,* and the concept of the "ought" *is* a concept *of the human intellect*) : but then the concept and its implications could enable us to attain merely to phenomena, and not to reality.

As a matter of fact the concept of moral obligation, and all other moral concepts, are formed by the human intellect through the same procedure, and in obedience to the same laws, as are revealed in its formation of speculative concepts. The notion of moral obligation is a complex notion. On analysis it reveals a necessary relation as obtaining between a free act and an end which imposes itself absolutely on the will. Analyse in turn the judgment which asserts this relation and you will find in it the categories of *relation, final cause, action, efficient causality.* And there we are back into the domain of the "speculative reason". Nor can the postulates of the practical reason be established if the principle of causality be denied objective and real validity.

The attempt, therefore, to vindicate consistency for Kant's thought as expressed in the two *Critiques* is found to break down hopelessly. The splitting up of the human intellect into two separate faculties, and of the whole domain of human experience into two water-tight compartments of "knowledge" and "belief," will not and cannot satisfy human reason reflecting on the grounds of its spontaneous assents. For "belief," no less than "knowledge," is an assent. If, therefore, it has no grounds that reason can *see and pronounce to be objectively valid,* it is not a "reasonable belief," an *obsequium rationabile.* Religious belief must then cease to be intellectual, doctrinal, dogmatic,[1] and degenerate into a mere sentimental pietism. It will be the

---

[1] *Cf. supra,* § 141, p. 231, (*f*), where it was pointed out that Kant's theory necessarily reduces Christianity (and indeed all positive religion) to a mere symbolism.

non-dogmatic religion which eschews all "creed" and identifies itself with moral righteousness. But moral conduct, in turn,—being based on a subjective dictate of duty, a dictate that is alleged to emanate from the "autonomous" will of the individual, *i.e.* from an authority for which the individual's *reason* can find no objectively valid credentials,—must inevitably tend to lose its character as *duty* and to become a matter of individual feeling or caprice. For the binding force of an obligation is incompatible with its being self-imposed, and equally incompatible with its having no credentials that reason can recognize and accept as adequate.

Moral Dogmatism was to foster men's moral and religious beliefs by justly limiting the scope of knowledge ; by destroying the ancient pretensions of the human mind to knowledge of the metaphysical, moral and religious domains ; by grounding those beliefs, among the ruins of the speculative reason, on a foundation that was to have nothing to fear from the impotent attacks of its castigated knowledge. But Moral Dogmatism was all the while itself an effort of that same human mind or reason, playing itself a suicidal trick which really involved those beliefs in the same abyss of agnosticism in which it sought to bury knowledge. The history of religion and morals during the last century under the influence of a widely prevalent anti-intellectualism bears out only too well the justice of our strictures on such a philosophical attitude towards human certitude.

169. LATER ANTI-INTELLECTUALIST THEORIES : SOCIAL DOGMATISM. CHRISTIAN APOLOGETICS.—The attitude of Fideism, which combines distrust of reason with attempts to ground certitude ultimately on non-rational motives, finds expression in certain recent tendencies which we purpose now briefly to examine. Some of them, which we may conveniently describe under the title of " Social Pragmatism "[1] or " Social Dogmatism,"[2] seek to combine the extrinsic motive of social authority with the intrinsic motive of individual moral and religious instincts or needs. Others, considering such knowledge as is attained by the speculative exercise of reason to be merely symbolic, to consist of contingent, hypothetical, regulative formulæ, more or less conventionally adopted, and serving the practical purpose of helping us to orient ourselves intellectually in the concrete stream of our conscious experience,[3] think that it is not

It necessarily leads to the religious indifferentism which sees in all positive religious systems mere specimens of " religious experience," or varying manifestations of the religious sentiment that is rooted in human nature. As to the interpretation there suggested (*ibid.*), by which Kant's " categorical imperative " would be the dictate of the *Divine Reason* revealed in the human conscience, it is in open and explicit contradiction with Kant's own language ; and anyhow it would leave the existence of God as Kant left it, an unsolved and (in his view) insoluble problem.

[1] *Cf.* JEANNIÈRE, *op. cit.*, pp. 280 *sqq.*   [2] *Cf.* MERCIER, *op. cit.*, p. 180.
[3] So, for instance, MACH, POINCARÉ, BOUTROUX, MILHAUD, etc.—*cf.* JEANNIÈRE, *op. cit.*, pp. 277-9.

by such knowledge but by some sort of immediate vital intuition that we attain to a true and genuine contact with reality.[1] Others, finally, pondering on the nature and significance of our assents, whether in the form of "knowledge" or in the form of "belief," have concluded that their real *truth*, their real knowledge-value, does not and cannot consist in their giving us any speculative insight into reality, or in their "conforming the mind with reality" according to the old notion of truth ; but that it consists rather in their *suitability*, their *practical* worth or value, their *utility*, the success with which they "work," with which they enable us to perfect and develop the essential conditions and purposes of human existence : so that truth would not be absolute but relative, and its ultimate criterion would be the *practical* test of usefulness or suitability to human progress. This is *Pragmatism* or *Humanism*.

As illustrative of the first of those general tendencies we may take the theories of *Mr. A. Balfour* and *Mr. W. H. Mallock* in England, and of *M. F. Brunetière* in France. Mr. Balfour in his *Foundations of Belief* (1895), as in his later occasional incursions from the domain of politics into that of philosophical speculation, admits that the logical use of the speculative reason on the data of experience, as illustrated in contemporary scientific philosophies, which he labels as "Naturalism," leads to the negation of religion and morality,—to agnosticism. Yet he does not boldly question their principles or methods, but merely observes that they rest on indemonstrable and inevident postulates ; and then goes on to contend that since men cannot and will not and ought not to abandon religious and moral beliefs, an adequate motive for these beliefs must be found. But what adequate cause or motive can be found ? Their immediate cause or motive is the combined influence of all the factors which constitute man's social environment and make up the " psychological atmosphere " in which his mental life is steeped and formed. " Non-rational causes " these are, if you will ; but, then, man cannot and does not live (his intellectual, moral, religious life) on reasons alone : " certitude is found to be the child not of reason, but of custom ". Man must hold to his beliefs despite the " rational " negations of agnosticism not by attempting the hopelessly difficult if not impossible task of rationalizing these beliefs ; nor by attempting the

[1] Notably BERGSON and his disciples ; and LE ROY in the domain of Catholic apologetics,—*ibid.*

equally hopeless task of finding adequate rational grounds for the
authority of the various social institutions whether civil or religious which propound these beliefs to him as true; but by reflecting that on the one hand if the authority of the extrinsic social
milieu from which he has received them is not evident to reason
neither are the·postulates underlying the agnostic philosophy
of Naturalism, and that on the other hand it is only right and
proper and natural for him to trust the instinctive " non-rational "
impulses and yearnings of his soul, and so to hold firmly to moral
and religious beliefs,—beliefs which so obviously harmonize with
all that is best and noblest in man's nature, and the loss of which
would degrade man to an unnatural condition of mere animality.

Notwithstanding the unquestionable excellence of Mr. Balfour's intentions his achievement is not likely to advance the
cause he has at heart.   His polemic against Naturalism has been
rather unceremoniously summarized by somebody in these terms :
Naturalism is false : so is my philosophy : but as my philosophy
is less false than Naturalism it ought to have the preference.[1]
There is much justice in the summing up.   For *de facto* his
philosophy is false: and for the general reason already given
against fideism or sentimentalism in any form (164).   From the
point of view of *reason* moral and religious assents would, on his
theory, be admittedly not assents of *certitude* but of a *prudent
probabilism*.   How, then, is their superior probability, as compared with the agnostic affirmations of Naturalism, to be transformed into certitude, into the firm assent of faith ?   *By an
appeal to subjective feeling or sentiment, to the will to believe.*   But
no such feeling or sentiment can be the ultimate ground of certitude in a being who can summon it to show its credentials
before the bar of reflecting reason.   And equally futile is the
appeal to such extrinsic social influences as are not directly
rational, influences that are *motives* or *causes*, but not *reasons*, of
assent.   Why should I yield to such social influences, or to such
instinctive, subjective feelings, until I know that what they
prompt me to believe is true ?   " You should believe ; you should
trust your faculties ; you should trust the moral and religious
promptings of your nature."   Yes, certainly, *when I convince myself that there are reasonable grounds for my doing so ;* but not
sooner.   I refuse to abdicate my dignity as a rational being by
believing or trusting blindly.   I will use my reason to discover

[1] *Cf.* MERCIER, *op. cit.*, § 88, p. 200,

satisfactory objective grounds for believing : such grounds will be the ultimate test of the truth of what I am to believe ; they will be the ultimate motive of my certitude ; then will my belief be a reasonable belief, an *obsequium rationabile.*

" But surely," it will be urged, "the masses of mankind, the millions of men in every age, who believe in a moral law, in immortality, in a Divine Lawgiver, etc., *de facto* hold these beliefs *without ever troubling* to *explore rationally,* and *pronounce to be a reasonably adequate ground of assent,* the combination of extrinsic social influences and intrinsic individual impulses and instincts which determine those beliefs ? Nor could they hope to accomplish such a process of rationalization if they attempted it. Therefore it would be unreasonable to expect it of them ; and the *reasonable* course for them rather is to follow the higher instincts of their nature as moral and religious beings, and to trust in the reliability of the universal social authority when it dictates beliefs that accord so admirably with these instincts."

We have met this plea before. It mingles false assumptions with an *ignoratio elenchi.* Moral and religious beliefs are *de facto* held by men in widely different ways. We have not to defend all these ways. Some of the actual beliefs are partly or wholly false *in their contents.* And some of them, even in so far as they are true in substance or content, are no better than superstitions *on account of the irrational ways in which they are held :* ways that are in direct conflict with man's nature as a rational being : ways that are tantamount to a denial of the fundamental fact of man's rationality. Our task is to point out the only rational, and therefore the only right and true, way of holding them. When the individual holds such beliefs because he is rationally convinced, rationally certain, that he has adequate grounds for their credibility, for the truth of what they propose to him, then and then only does he believe rightly and rationally. For, as St. Thomas says, " Ea quae subsunt fidei . . . aliquis non crederet nisi videret ea esse credenda " ; and not only would the individual *de facto* refuse, but he would be right in refusing, to " believe them unless he saw them to be credible ". And this brings us to the false assumptions and the *ignoratio elenchi* involved in the plea we are considering.

In the first place the duty of the epistemologist, in setting forth a theory of certitude, is not to indicate the provisional, actual or *de facto* grounds of men's spontaneous beliefs, but to discover what rational reflection declares to be *de jure* and neces-sarily the ultimate ground of them. And secondly, the alleged impossibility, for individual men generally, of finding a reason-ably adequate rational basis for their beliefs, and so making these beliefs reflex and reasoned, is based on the false assumption that in order to do so the individual must have explored and solved all the possible objections that human reason can urge against their credibility and truth. But this is by no means necessary. Provided that the beliefs are objectively true; and provided the individual sees on the one hand adequate objective evidence of their credibility,—which the man of average intelligence can *de facto* easily see both within him and around him, in his own nature, in the world of his experience, and in the light which those truths throw both on his own nature and on the world around him : for *truth* makes to the human intelligence an ob-jective evidential appeal which is not forthcoming in the case of *error ;*—and provided, finally, he can meet and settle satis-factorily, according to the measure of his capacity and oppor-tunities, such difficulties as may *de facto* happen to arise against the credibility of what he believes,—then the certitude of his belief *is* a reflex, reasoned and reasonable certitude.

To all this, however, we must add, in explanation of the wide errors and contradictions and conflicting beliefs that *de facto* prevail throughout the world in the moral and religious domains, the doctrine already stated (163), that the aid of a positive Divine Revelation is, morally speaking, necessary for the preservation of moral and religious truth among men. Moreover, what we have just said concerning the possibility of a reasoned religious belief for the average individual applies primarily of course to the individual who has been brought up in the possession and profession of *true* religious belief. And finally, those who are in full and certain possession of the Christian re-ligion in its authentic form know that *de facto* the only true religion for the human race is this *supernatural* religion, that God has *de facto* given to man a supernatural destiny, that He has *de facto* raised man to a supernatural end, that *Faith* in the truths which He has revealed concerning this super-natural end and destiny is a *gratuitous Divine gift*, that it is not attained by man's unaided natural powers but Divinely given, and that when given it can be preserved and made operative only by the free co-operation of man's reason and will with the supernatural grace by which Faith enlightens and strengthens him.

W. H. Mallock, in a volume published in 1903, *Religion as a Credible Doctrine: a Study of the Fundamental Difficulty*, con-fronts the affirmations of agnosticism with those of man's moral and religious consciousness, and concludes that since the affirmations of each domain are rationally inconsistent in themselves, and rationally incompatible with those of the other domain, neither set can be accepted on grounds of reason. But history teaches that the true progress of humanity is bound up with fidelity to the dictates of the moral and religious instinct. Let us therefore obey this instinct ; let us recognize the co-existence of those two rationally irreconcilable orders of experience: let us have the wisdom to bow to the inevitable "synthesis of contradictories," and try to make the most of it.

This is not a solution of any problem, but a verdict of despair: a recommendation to stifle reason and embrace a moral dogmatism that is admittedly in conflict with reason. So long as men have any regard for the dignity of their reason they will not agree to stifle reflection and live by instinct. Nor, even if they try to believe by instinct, can they prevent reason from operating on those beliefs, and so leading either to reasoned certitude or to scepticism.

M. Brunetière, a well-known French Catholic writer and apologist, defends religious and moral beliefs on lines not unlike those followed by Mr. Balfour. Noting that all the really great philosophers considered the practical question of those beliefs as the problem of supreme concern for humanity ; and pointing out that this question, even when it appears as a *social* or a *moral* question, is always and fundamentally a *religious* question, he himself contends that the ground of religious belief can never be fully accredited or vindicated by purely rational investigation. We have in our nature an ineradicable "need to believe". But we cannot find in our nature, even in our nature as rational, whether in the individual or in the collectivity, any adequate authority for what we are to believe. There must be, then, extrinsic to man and superior to man, some such authority. Where is it and how are we to recognize it? We can recognize it by the unique and extraordinary civilizing, moralizing, elevating, ennobling effect of its teaching on the human race: it is the Christian Religion, the Catholic Church. *Ex fructibus eorum cognoscetis eos.* It can be judged by its fruits, and will stand the test. We do not need and we cannot wait for strict rational demonstration of the justice of its claims. Life is too short for indulging in the luxury of rationalizing through and through the beliefs on which our social, moral and religious well-being

depends.   The philosophies speak with conflicting voices on the
grounds of these beliefs.   What we need is an authority which we
can recognize as responding to our highest needs by its manifest
efficacy in fostering these beliefs among men.   And such an
authority we have in the Catholic Church.

Thus, M. Brunetière subscribes to the Traditionalist verdict
on the practical incompetence of the individual reason face to face
with the problem of orienting ourselves aright in the actual
warring world of creeds and no-creeds.   He does not, however,
adopt as the test of decision the Traditionalist criterion of a
Divine Authority revealed in the magisterium of social tradition,
but rather *what serves the higher interests of humanity :* an index
which, for him, points immediately to Christianity; whereas for
Mr. Balfour it only pointed to the vague mass of moral and religious influences felt in our social environment.

This mode of grounding moral and religious beliefs is entirely unsatisfactory.   It is open to anyone to assail it on such
lines as these : Granted that history shows the influence of Christianity to be wholly beneficent, am I therefore *bound* to accept
its moral and religious teaching?   It may be good; it may be
the best : but show me that I am morally *bound* to accept the
good, or the best.   If I happen to be a utilitarian, or a hedonist,
why should I abandon my utilitarian ethical system, or my hedonist programme of self-gratification, and espouse Christianity?   If
these are wrong, and if it is right, you must prove it : you must
show your reasons.   But this precisely is seeking *a rational
basis for moral and religious belief.*   You appeal to what Christianity has done for the progress of humanity.   Progress towards
what?   What is the end or aim of human life?   You think that
humanity really profits and is really served by accepting the
religious teaching and submitting to the moral code of Christianity.   But what if I disagree ; if with Schopenhauer or
Nietzsche I hold the Christian conception of human society and
human nature and human destiny to be no better than an illusion ; if, in fine, I hold it folly to sacrifice individual pleasure,
present and attainable, to an ideal of some social good that
is future and problematical?   Who is to decide between us?
Reason alone can decide; your reason and my reason.   And
whether we succeed in coming to an agreement or not, one thing
at least is clear : that the ultimate decision of all such questions
must be reached by reason, or else never reached.   Between

reasoned certitude and scepticism there may indeed be a battle-ground, but there can be no resting-place.

Before passing to the consideration of Pragmatism we may conveniently notice here the philosophical aspect of a rather remarkable and more or less original method which many recent Catholic apologists in France have adopted for the vindication and defence of the fundamental beliefs of the Christian religion. As a method of apologetics it is known as the *Method of Immanence* and also, by reason of its philosophical content, as the *Philosophy of Action*.[1] Chief among those who have advocated and used the method are Père Gratry, Ollé-Laprune, Blondel, Brunetière, Fonsegrive and Père Laberthonnière.

The purely intellectual defence of Christianity as a supernatural, revealed religion, on extrinsic grounds of historical evidence, these writers admit to be necessary : it cannot be superseded. But in itself it is not adequate : it needs to be supplemented, to be made persuasive and operative, especially for the mentality of our own time, by showing how admirably the whole content of the Christian religion appeals to and harmonizes with all the needs and yearnings and aspirations of the human heart. In fact mere intellect, mere reason, will not of itself suffice, to impose religious certitude from without, as it were, upon the individual, or to win from him a real and living and operative assent to religious truth. We must go for the truth, as Plato said, *with our whole soul.* It is not by intellect alone, but also by the will, the heart, the feelings, aspirations, instincts of our nature, that we possess and realize in ourselves religious truth. Nay, it is primarily by these that we attain to it. It is by following our natural instincts and aspirations and obeying our will to believe, that we find Christianity,—not wholly without us, but partly within us, in the *anima naturaliter Christiana.* And it is by *living* up to it, by experiencing its elevating and purifying influence upon us, that we really and efficaciously attain to the certain conviction of its truth. The rôle of intellect or reason, as regards what we may call, with Newman, the engendering of a "*real* assent" to Christianity, is but secondary and subsidiary : the primacy is with the will. *Non in dialectica complacuit Deo salvum facere populum suum.* We cannot argue men into Christianity by intellectual evidences. Let us rather show them the content of Christianity as alone capable of satisfying the veritable needs and instincts of their nature. Let us realize ourselves, and help them to realize, that while Christianity is supernatural, while it transcends our mere nature, illuminating and elevating it *from without,* there is nevertheless a true and real sense in which it is not alien or foreign to our nature, in which we find it *within* us, inasmuch as it not only adequately corresponds to nature and perfects nature, but is also the *natural* complement of nature in the actually verified hypothesis of God's having created and intended man for a supernatural end and destiny. The supernatural is *ex supposito* natural. Does not St. Thomas say[2] that grace and faith are "natural" gifts,—not absolutely, of course, seeing that they are gratuitous gifts which God might not have conferred on humanity,— but consequently on the Divine Bounty, whereby they are *de facto* real

---

[1] From M. BLONDEL's work, *L'Action*, published in 1893.
[2] *Summa Theol.*, II^a, II^{ae}, Q. I., a. 4, ad 4.

accompaniments of human nature in its actual condition? This being so, should we not find the real and effective motive for Christian belief by looking *within* man, in the human heart itself, in its moral and religious instincts, aspirations, needs and yearnings, and argue the truth of Christianity from its perfect accord with these? Such is the *psychological* or *immanent* method of Christian apologetics.[1]

As an apologetic method it has no direct concern for the philosopher. It has undoubted merits from that practical standpoint as an aid to, and complement of, the intellectual defence of objective and historical Christian evidences. Christianity effects a harmony between two great facts—the external fact of a positive, historical, Divine Revelation, and the internal fact of the moral and religious aspirations of the human soul. But the consciousness of these aspirations, and the experienced fact of their finding the fullest satisfaction in certain religious beliefs,—those, namely, of Christianity,— must of necessity raise a problem for the individual intellect, the problem of investigating the objective credentials of doctrinal Christianity. And until the believer or seeker finds these to be rationally adequate, he cannot find intellectual repose, the repose of conviction or certitude, in the mere consciousness that assent to those doctrines satisfies certain instincts and yearnings of his nature.

From the strictly philosophical standpoint of a theory of certitude, the method of immanence misinterprets and inverts the respective functions of intellect and will in the attainment of certitude concerning religious and moral beliefs. It exaggerates the rôle of the will, the heart, the affective side of man's nature, and is thus unduly anti-intellectualist. We have already explained (159) the true sense of the priority of faith to reason,—as a purifier of the heart, as subduing human passion, as illuminating the intellect, and thus disposing man to make a prudent and reverent use of his reason in contact with the revealed mysteries of Faith. There is a true sense in the practical exhortation to seek truth " with our whole soul ". It is entirely intelligible and acceptable if we understand it to mean that we should love the truth, long to find it, apply ourselves zealously and perseveringly to the search for it, and brace up our *will* to apply our *intelligence* to the discovery of it.[2] But it also may bear a sense that is false and unacceptable and unintelligible : and that is, if it be taken to mean that it is the will rather than the intellect that discovers and assents to truth. When we find the truth we should no doubt love and embrace it and live up to it. But it is intellect, and only intellect, that finds and assents to truth and keep us in possession of truth. We have already (12) considered the influence of the will on our " free " convictions, and have noted that its influence on assent, even when direct and immediate, is an influence which, expelling imprudent fear of error, commands *the intellect to elicit the act of assent*, the act which puts us in possession of the truth. But will is not itself a cognitive faculty : its proper object is not *the true* but *the good, i.e.* the already apprehended good. To arrogate to the will, therefore, or to the affective and emotional springs of mental action, the discovery of truth, is the anti-

[1] *Cf.* MERCIER, *op. cit.*, §§ 83, 89, 90 (pp. 187-9 ; 204-8).

[2] St. Augustine says, " Sapientia et veritas *nisi totis animi viribus concupiscatur*, nullo modo inveniri poterit ". *Cf. Science of Logic*, ii., § 275, pp. 326-7.

intellectualist error of voluntarism. The *Method of Immanence, the Philosophy of Action*, would apparently accord the primacy to will, not to intellect, in the matter of truth and certitude. In so far as it does it must be rejected as erroneous.

170. OUTLINE OF PRAGMATISM AND HUMANISM.—Among the philosophies which, since Kant's time, have employed the "speculative" reason for its own dethronement, the latest fashion is undoubtedly that known as *Pragmatism* or *Humanism*. Though of quite recent origin it has to its credit a very extensive output of literature,[1] on the Continent, in England, and in America—its *locus originis*. Its principal exponents are, in America, *C. S. Peirce, W. James*, and *J. Dewey*; in England, *F. C. S. Schiller;* in France, *Bergson (psychological* direction), *Boutroux (critical* direction—of Poincaré and Milhaud), *Le Roy* (combining both directions in the "new philosophy") and *Wilbois;* and in Italy, *Papini.*

It is frankly anti-intellectualist, advocating as the sole test of truth the *practical* test of *utility* in a very broad sense. It is therefore voluntarist inasmuch as the "utility" of a judgment, its "bonum *utile*," is not immediately an object of intellect but of will. It has not, however, sprung from any preoccupation or concern with the defence of moral and religious beliefs, but rather from a teleological consideration of the function and purpose of thought and knowledge in man,—a consideration itself prompted by the influence of the *evolution* concept in biological science.[2] For Pragmatism all truth is essentially relative, provisional, transformable (142, 143).

It was first propounded by C. S. Peirce as a *method* of ending the sterile controversies with which the speculative reason is ever impeding the real progress of the human mind. The *sense* of any proposition, and hence its truth or falsity, must be judged by the mental habit it induces, the effect it has *in action*, its *pragmatic* or *working* value : hence the title *Pragmatism*. The truth or knowledge-value of a proposition is not at all any insight it is supposed to give us into things, but simply its relation of utility to human life.[3]

---

[1] For adequate bibliography, *cf.* JEANNIÈRE, *op. cit.*, pp. 269-71, whose treatment in the main we have followed.

[2] *Cf.* NOËL, Art. in the *Revue néo-scolastique*, 1911, p. 46.

[3] Such a view involves, of course, the abolition of Metaphysics in its traditional sense of a speculative study of the real. Hence the severity of Pragmatist strictures on Metaphysics, and the anxiety of Pragmatists to discourage such research. Here

James develops this notion and applies it to religious beliefs, especially in his *Varieties of Religious Experience*. All human functions, not excluding the intellectual function of cognition or belief, are essentially subservient to practical interests, to life, conduct, behaviour. Assent is essentially teleological, purposive, ordained to action. Religious beliefs, like all beliefs, have their truth-value in the degree of their utility to human existence. This doctrine he seeks to confirm by the consideration that (*a*) *de facto* the cognitive function *reveals* nothing for certain,—as witness the contradictions of the metaphysicians who use reason in the attempt to lay bare *reality* by exploring *evidence*,—and that (*b*) *de jure* concepts can disclose nothing certain about reality (*cf.* Bergson). Hence Pragmatism is more than a method : it is a *doctrine*, a *theory of knowledge*. For it teaches that the *truth* of a judgment does not consist in its giving us *any insight into what things really are*, but in its *working value*, in *its utility as prompting and leading to action that is beneficial or helpful to human progress*. Similarly, Dewey holds all cognition to involve a feeling of expectation or anticipation : by the satisfaction (or otherwise) of which, in the event, the truth-value of the cognition is determined.

Schiller enlarged this doctrine into a system called *Humanism*, applying it to every department of human speculation and action. When we reflect on the relation between these two functions of man, between what intellect conceives by way of theory or theories on the data of experience, and what it dictates to us to do, or how to live in and through this experience, we find four possible interpretations of this relation : (1) Intellect in its practical dictate is a lower and derivative form of the intellect as speculative (a view ascribed by Schiller to *Plato*); (2) they are mutually irreducible, but the speculative is the higher (*Aristotle*); (3) they are mutually irreducible, but the practical holds the primacy (*Kant*); (4) the speculative is a lower and derivative form of the practical (*Humanist Pragmatism*). For Humanism, then, the truth of a proposition would be its utility to man : and man would thus be the measure of truth.[1]

is a typical illustration : " Metaphysics has hitherto been a piece of amusement for idle minds, a sort of game at chess ; and the *ratio essendi* of Pragmatism is to make a clean sweep of the propositions of ontology, nearly all of which are senseless rubbish, where words are defined by words and so on without ever reaching any real concept ".—*The Monist*, April, 1905, p. 171,—*apud* JEANNIÈRE, *op. cit.*, p. 273 n.

[1] *Cf. The Humanism of Protagoras*, in *Mind*, April, 1911.

It is not, however, utility to *the individual* that is the test, but utility to society, to men generally. Look at the *general results* of any belief on human progress ; that is the test : *Ex fructibus eorum cognoscetis eos.* A proposition is not true merely because to act on it would suit *some individual utility :* " it could not gain currency as effectively true, unless it somehow afforded satisfaction socially ".[1] But social utility can evolve and change. A belief that " suited " men generally at one time may cease to serve them any longer ; may indeed disserve them and be repudiated. Hence the belief *was* true, but *has become* false [2] (142, 144). In defence of this view of truth and its criterion Schiller seeks to show (1) that the intellectualist conception of truth as mental insight into reality, or cognitive assimilation of reality, issues in contradictions and cannot account for error ; (2) that no proposition can have any significance as true or false unless in relation to the practical issues involved in believing it : by these alone can its truth-claim be tested, and only in relation to these is such claim at all intelligible ;[3] (3) that *psychological analysis* proves man to be always, in all his thinking and judging functions, influenced by affective motives or interests prompted by biologically evolved tendencies and impulses of an instinctively utilitarian order.[4]

In France, Boutroux, Milhaud, Poincaré,—and in Germany, Simmel, Mach, Hertz, Ostwald, etc.,—among others, had proclaimed that the theoretical science attained by reason is but a system of contingent, conventional conceptions formulated by reason for the convenience of our practical manipulation or utili-

---

[1] SCHILLER, *Error*, p. 10,—*apud* JEANNIÈRE, *op. cit.*, p. 276, n. 3.

[2] " Truth and error . . . are continuous, as history shows. Either may develop out of the other, and both are rooted in the same problems of knowing, which are ultimately problems of living. The ' truths ' of one generation become the ' errors ' of the next, when it has achieved more valuable and efficient modes of interpreting and manipulating the apparent ' facts,' which the new ' truths ' are continuously transforming. And conversely, what is now scouted as ' error ' may hereafter become the fruitful parent of a long progeny of truths."—*Error*, p. 11,—*apud* JEANNIÈRE, p. 277, n. 1.

[3] Every true or false proposition is relevant to an intention. Error is never accepted as such, but always presents itself as a *truth-claim :* " Truth-claims that have worked badly are those condemned as ' errors '; those which have worked well are those accepted as ' truths ' ".—*Error,—apud* JEANNIÈRE, *op. cit.*, p. 276 n.

[4] " Purpose, interest, desire, emotion, satisfaction, are more essential to thinking than steam is to a steam-engine. . . . Without these psychological conditions, thinking disappears, and with it presumably Logic."—*The Rationalistic Conception of Truth (Proceedings of the Aristotelian Society*, 1909, p. 83),—*apud* JEANNIÈRE, *l.c.*, n. 2.

23 *

zation of experience: symbolizing results and anticipations of experience but not attaining to the real. Then Bergson, in his *Matière et Memoire* (1897), *Essai sur les données immediates de la conscience* (1889), and *L'Évolution Créatrice* (1907), gradually formulated the view that intellectual cognition gives us, in its abstract, isolated, fixed and static thought-objects, only evanescent and kaleidoscopic glances at a reality which is essentially dynamic, continuous and fluent (86); that this intellectual mode of cognition is exclusively practical in its purpose and function, evolved in order to enable us to adapt our action to our environment, and not at all to inform us as to what reality really is; that the mistake of intellectualism has been to interpret this essentially practical function as a representation that attains to reality itself; that in so far as we attain to reality at all, we do so not by intellect, but by an active, sympathetic identification of ourselves with the *dynamic process* or *fieri* of our immediate vital experience; that this immediate vital experience of reality as a dynamic process (*élan vital*) or evolution that is *sui generis*, at once thought and action (*la Pensée-Action, les Idées-Forces*), may be described as *intuitional*, as a *vital intuition* (at once conscious, volitional, affective, dynamic),—in opposition to the static, abstract, intellectual, logical, conceptual and judicial processes which were wrongly supposed to give us a genuine speculative insight into reality, whereas they are only practical aids to the vital process wherein we attain to reality by feeling and living it.

Le Roy combined the conception of scientific laws as mere practical inventions of the intellect, with Bergson's intuition theory, to form a "new philosophy" in which the test of practical vital experience would supplant that of intellectual evidence in the discerning of truth. The "truths" or laws arrived at by speculation are not representative of the real: they are simply aids to the concrete, complex, vital process in which alone reality is attained,—not by contemplating it but by living it.[1] That is

---

[1] " Vivre une vérité consiste à en faire un object de vie interieure auquel on croit, dont on se nourrit, que l'on pratique et que l'on aime au point d'unifer en lui toute son âme : *est vraie* définitivement ce qui résiste à l'épreuve d'une telle vie. . . .

" Au fond le seul critère c'est la vie. Est évident d'abord tout ce qui est vécu à chaque instant par nous : images, affections, sentiments, idées ou actes, pris en eux-mêmes et en tant que faits. Est ensuite évident par le progrès de la pensée, tout ce qui . . . résiste á l'épreuve de la pratique, peut être assimilé par nous, converti en notre substance, integré á notre moi, organisé avec l'ensemble de notre vie. Ainsi l'évidence appartient à ce qui se montre capable de durée. Rien n'est évident de soi, mais tout peut le devenir."—*Un positivisme nouveau* (in the *Revue de Métaph. et Morale*, 1901),—*apud* JEANNIÈRE, *op. cit.*, p. 279, n. 2.

true which stands the test of life's experience, which is felt to assimilate itself in this process ; while that is *false* which does not work, which is rejected, repudiated by this experience. Thus the agreement of the French school with the American and English Pragmatism and Humanism is apparent. How a belief works is the test of its truth. By the extension of this theory to revealed dogma Le Roy attempted a new theology which was condemned as incompatible with orthodox Christian belief.[1]

In Italy, Papini interpreted Pragmatism as a method from the standpoint of which every conceivable philosophical theory or system could be seen to have its share of *truth, viz.* by considering all theories and systems *sub specie actionis, i.e.* as possessing a greater or less degree of *practical value or utility* in the progressive evolution of humanity : a value which, apparently, would be tested and determined automatically by the touchstone of experience, sifting the wheat from the chaff, assimilating the "useful" or "true" and rejecting the "noxious" or "erroneous". This interpretation W. James has felicitously described as "the corridor-theory" of truth.

171. GENERAL ARGUMENTS AGAINST PRAGMATISM.—Such in brief outline is Pragmatism or Humanism. Its advocates would admit that it is by rational, intellectual reflection on the facts of experience that they have formed these conclusions as to what truth, knowledge, belief and certitude really are. Whatever, therefore, be the nature of the truth-claim which they make for Pragmatism itself,[2] it will be as lawful for us to use

---

[1] *Cf.* § 142, p. 234 n.

[2] Do they put forward Pragmatism as *true* in the ordinary sense of this term, *i.e.* as giving us a genuine insight into what knowledge, belief, certitude, etc., really are ?—or only as true in their own sense, *i.e.* as a theory that is useful, helpful, suitable, that works well for the time being, but that may possibly have to be scrapped as no longer "true" at some future stage of man's mental evolution ? Propounders of anti-intellectualist theories of certitude,—theories which, like evolutionism, relativism (142-5), voluntarism, sentimentalism, moral dogmatism, etc., give their verdict *against* the validity of the absolute truth-claim which the speculative reason makes for its "knowledge"-achievements,—must find themselves in a peculiar position when they put forward any such theory for acceptance as a philosophical or reasoned solution of the problem of certitude. For if they put forward any such theory as a *true* solution of the problem, then since the theory itself proclaims truth and certitude *not* to be matters determinable *by intellect*, its own truth and certitude, its own worth as a solution, seems to be placed beyond the pale of rational discussion and intellectual criticism. If, on the other hand, they allow that the theory, being itself a product of speculative intellectual or rational reflection, is fairly open to rational criticism, and must stand or fall by the verdict of such criticism, they seem to be *eo ipso* giving away their whole position. We

358 THEORY OF KNOWLEDGE

our reason in criticizing the theory as for its advocates to use theirs in propounding and recommending it. We are justified, therefore, in offering the following criticisms.

1. All these Pragmatist or Humanist theories contain a destructive and a constructive portion. On the destructive or negative side they seek to show that intellect, in its speculative application to the data of experience, is unable to attain to truth about reality ; that the traditional conception of truth as intellectual insight into reality, or conformity of the mind with reality, is indefensible ; that the supposed possibility of attaining to truth *as absolute* is an illusion ; that truth is essentially relative and transformable ; that no criterion of truth or motive of certitude, appealing to mere intellect as objectively valid, or reputed by intellect to be objectively valid, is so in reality ; that accordingly the general intellectualist position must be abandoned as untenable. Secondly, it is as a necessary consequence of all this that on the ruins of the demolished intellectualism the human mind must, in obedience to the imperative need which it feels, construct a theory which will give some better and more acceptable and satisfactory account of the facts of its experience : an account in which, of necessity, the import of its own processes and products,—*truth, knowledge, belief, certitude,*—will be quite different from that which was attached to them by intellectualism. Hence the proposed Pragmatism, with its novel interpretations of all those mental functions and attainments. But in the course of our inquiry we hope we have gradually shown that no such abandonment of intellectualism is either necessary or justifiable ; that the difficulties urged against it from whatsoever source are not by any means insuperable ; that if in fact they were, and if intellect were in fact compelled to confess that truth, belief, knowledge, certitude, as understood by intellect itself, were unattainable, or unjustifiable before the bar of its own critical reflection, no other possible account of them and no other possible way of grounding them could avail in the least to save the human mind from blank and hopeless scepticism. Therefore we see the supposition on which the necessity of Pragmatism or any similar theory is based, to be not only unverified but positively erroneous ; and we see also that if such

have already called attention more than once to the inconsistency into which they are thus forced by this unavoidable dilemma. *Cf.* vol. i., § 59; *supra*, §§ 144 (3, a); 167-8.

a theory were really necessary the futility of its purpose would be already intellectually apprehended in the very act by which reflecting reason would become aware of that necessity.

We have already refuted the Kantian demolition of the speculative reason,—a demolition which some Pragmatists assume as having been *de facto* effectual. Moreover, the contention of such writers as Mach, Boutroux, Poincaré, etc., that intellectual knowledge and concepts have a *merely* regulative and practical value,—and the contention of Bergson, that, being *static*, they give us no insight into a reality which is *dynamic* and *fluent*,—are based upon considerations which merely show (1) that such knowledge is imperfect, inadequate, not comprehensive or exhaustive of the content of the real; (2) that all knowledge, even the most speculative, is ultimately in some way "tendential" or responsive and complementary to some natural need. Cognition is, of course, subservient to life, is a means of providing for human needs. But (*a*) among these needs is the *appetitus sciendi*, man's natural, inborn desire for knowledge,—and for speculative knowledge of *what things are*, as well as practical knowledge of *what use they are*. And furthermore (*b*) we can obviously avail of knowledge to serve human needs only in so far as it *is* knowledge, *i.e.* in so far as it gives us at least some real if partial and inadequate insight into *what things are*.

II. According to the Pragmatist view, truth is something essentially relative, evolving, transformable. But we have already shown, in our analysis of relativist theories of truth (142-4), that the evolutionist conception simply destroys truth, is self-contradictory, and in the end unintelligible (144, 3, *b*). And in the same context we pointed out the real facts and truths (143) which the evolution theory distorts and misinterprets.

Moreover, Pragmatism, by wresting the *terms* "truth" and "knowledge" from the thought-objects which those terms have traditionally denoted, and which they are still currently and properly understood to denote, and by applying these terms to *other* and quite distinct thought-objects,—to *other* conditions or attitudes of the individual mind in its concrete environment (144, 3), —has *left unsolved* the *real* problem of the nature of that peculiar and *sui generis* relation called the knowledge- or truth-relation: having merely misstated and displaced this problem instead of solving it.

172. THE PRAGMATIST CRITERION EXAMINED. SPECIAL ARGUMENT OUTLINED.—The criterion of *utility* in its relation to *truth* is capable of two interpretations: either as meaning (*a*) that the *utility* of a judgment or belief *is* its *truth*, so that truth would not be conformity of the judgment or belief *with things or reality*, but its conformity or harmony with *the progress or*

development of human life or existence in all its amplitude ; or as
meaning (*b*) that the utility of the judgment or belief is not
identically the truth of this belief, but is only a criterion or sign
or index revealing and vindicating the truth of the belief,—the
truth of this being still its conformity with reality. This latter
meaning would then leave two alternatives : either that the conformity of the belief with things, *i.e.* its truth, remains unknowable, or that it can be known.

Moreover, understood as a criterion, utility might be proposed
as a *universal* criterion, so that no human judgment of any kind
or on any subject could be accepted as true unless it passed this
test ; or as a *partial* criterion, *i.e.* a criterion to be used for some
particular domain of human beliefs, *e.g.* for general doctrines or
systems that have a direct bearing on human conduct by reason
of their affirmation or denial of God, freedom, immortality, moral
duty, etc.

Then, again, utility propounded as a criterion of truth may
be either *individual* or *social.* For *utility* is a relative term, intelligible only in relation to an end, to the attainment of a good.
And by the social or general good will be meant the realization
of the supreme perfection or ultimate end of human existence
generally, whatever this may be, and everything that really con-
tributes thereto.

Finally, the criterion of utility is a test that is understood
not to be applicable to any judgment or belief *a priori*, but only
a posteriori, i.e. by actual experience of the *success* or otherwise
of the belief, of *how it works out* in practice.

In the light of these distinctions we can now formulate our
third main argument against Pragmatism.

III. We do not deny that the practical issues of a belief can
create a presumption for or against its truth, that the " fruits " of
a doctrine can be even a criterion, a *subsidiary* test, of its truth
or falsity, *i.e.* its *practical* fruits : for of course if speculatively
false conclusions follow logically from any doctrine as antecedent, this is a *certain* index that the doctrine is false.[1]   But in
some measure the truth or otherwise of doctrines that have or
ought to have a bearing on human conduct can be judged by
their moral consequences.   Let us see how, and how far.

Firstly, man ought to find in his fundamental beliefs, in his
" philosophy of life," his general " world-outlook " or " *Weltan-*

[1] *Cf. Science of Logic*, i., pp. 296-7 ; ii., p. 313.

schauung," principles whereby to guide and direct his conduct : all philosophy should embody an *Ethic* or *practical philosophy*, a philosophy of conduct. Hence if any philosophy contains no directive principles, throws no light on the problem of conduct (*e.g.* Scepticism ; Agnosticism), or contains ethical principles the application of which would do violence to man's moral nature, subvert the whole moral order and lead to moral chaos, *e.g.* by opening the way to murder, suicide, fraud, injustice, sexual immorality, etc. (as would Atheism ; Materialism ; Evolutionism or the survival of the fittest, meaning the *strongest*, with the Nietzschean corollary that *Might is Right*, etc.),—such philosophy cannot be sound or true but must have something rotten in it. Yet, obviously, the test is not ultimate, for it assumes that we know (otherwise and independently) what kind of conduct is right, and what kind is criminal : which implies knowledge of the real nature, destiny, and end of man.

Hence, secondly, it yields only a presumption, or a practical confirmation, of the truth or falsity of doctrines. The moral issues of a system, therefore, should arouse inquiry, stimulate reflection, and urge us to verify by speculative investigation the conclusion they suggest to us regarding the truth or falsity of the system.

Thirdly, when the moral issues of a philosophy are perverse, noxious, disastrous, scholastics use thus "*argumentum ex consectariis*,"—this discerning of systems by their fruits : "*ex fructibus eorum cognoscetis eos*,"—as a *negative, indirect* and *confirmatory* argument in refutation of such systems. It is an argument which can have much force and can make a strong and effective appeal to right-minded people. But for grounding human certitude it can never be ultimate.

Pragmatism, however, goes much farther than all this, for (*a*) it identifies the truth of a judgment or belief with its utility ; (*b*) it denies that truth in the sense of conformity of the judgment with reality is *intellectually attainable* ; (*c*) it holds that the *only and universal* test of the truth of a judgment, *i.e.* of its real conformity or harmony with the veritable needs of human life and existence, is to be found by *living* it, by experiencing *how it works*, whether it *succeeds* by being assimilated, incorporated in the progressive current of human existence, or *fails* by being rejected and eliminated from among the beliefs that are found really helpful and beneficent. Against all of which we assert that *experienced utility is neither identical with truth, nor is it*

the only or the adequate test of truth, nor is the Pragmatist applica-
tion of it any more than a misleading evasion of the real problem
as to the ultimate ground and motive of human certitude.

What do Pragmatists mean by the *utility* of a belief, its
suitability, its *working-value*, its *success*, the *character of its*
practical issues, its *harmony with the process and purpose of human*
existence?[1] We are told that a belief or judgment is true if it
verifies or realizes what those and other similar expressions imply. But what *do* they imply? They are all relative to an end.
They are all unintelligible unless in reference to an end,—and
to a *known end*, to something *certainly known to be an end*, a
good, a perfection, a something really worthy of attainment. A
belief is true if it proves useful, suitable, workable, successful.
But useful, etc., *for what?* For helping, developing, enlarging,
perfecting human life and existence generally? But what *is* the
end or object or aim of human existence? Until I know *this*
how am I to know whether the "actual working" of a belief is
good or bad, successful or unsuccessful? How am I to judge
of a means unless and until I know the nature of the end to
which it is a means? And how can I discover the supreme,
essential end or perfection of human nature, and the veritable
goal of human existence, unless by the *use of my intellect or reason*
on the data of experience. But there we are back into the "intellectualism," and "metaphysics" which it was the *raison d'être*
of Pragmatism to demolish.

Apparently any doctrine that is widely received, and which
therefore "works," at least in the measure in which it is received
and "lived" by mankind,—be it Agnosticism, Atheism,
Materialism, Hedonism, or what not,—is *true* in that same
measure, inasmuch as in that measure it is actually assimilated
into the current or process of human existence: as the "corridor-
theory" explicitly admits. But if that be so, then,—and this is

[1] While admitting the difficulty—from the very nature of the theory—which
Pragmatists must feel in attaining to a clearly conceived and clearly expressed
presentation of their views (which is partly a task for the poor, belittled, derivative evolution-product which is the intellect!); and while admitting and admiring
the felicity of expression with which many of their writers, especially the late W.
James, can charm their readers,—we can understand the chorus of complaint that
has arisen about the *vagueness and obscurity* of the pragmatist teaching. According
to M. A. O. LOVEJOY, Pragmatism is a "Protean entity," of which he enumerates
no less than *thirteen* distinct forms! *Cf.* PÈRE BLANCHE, *Rev. des Sc. phil. et théol.*,
1909, p. 97.—quoted by JEANNIÈRE, *op. cit.*, p. 286, n.; also *Journal of Philos.*,
Psychol. and Scient. Meth., 1909, pp. 5-12; 29-39,—*ibid.*

possibly the underlying thought in the minds of pragmatists,—
the actual process of human life or existence, as it goes on in
time and space, is *its own end.* But this, too, is an *intellectual*
thesis ; and, what is more, it is one the truth or falsity of which
obviously cannot be tested by the Pragmatist criterion. So, then,
Pragmatism has postulates which escape its net and must be
sifted by the reflecting intellect.

Or is it that not all the *actual* phases or currents in the flow
of human existence are useful or beneficial thereto, that some
do *not* make for its perfection, that not all *change* is *evolution, i.e.*
progress or movement towards the good, towards perfection ?
But this implies that, at any particular stage, the life-process
as it actually goes on is not an end in itself, but a tendency or
movement towards some ulterior good. Perhaps, however, this
ulterior good consists in the indefinite progress, development,
evolution of life itself into ever greater largeness and fullness
of expression ? But the very concept of evolution, progress,
development, implies the concept of a *good, towards which the
movement is.* If there is indefinite movement or change *with no
purpose or goal beyond itself*, the distinction between evolution
and devolution, progression and retrogression, amelioration and
deterioration, simply disappears as unmeaning and unintelligible
for want of a goal or term as standard by which to determine
what change is progress and what change is decay. Hence the
pragmatist criterion of the *experienced success of a belief* in helping, developing, forwarding, enlarging, perfecting human existence, will not itself " work," and cannot itself even begin to be
applied, *until we know* whether human life has a purpose, whether
there is a *good* towards which it moves, and *what* this good is :
for only then can we judge what movements, what conduct, what
beliefs, tend to develop and perfect life, and what ones tend in
the opposite direction. But how can we know these things ?
Only by intellect, if at all. They are some of the problems of
metaphysics ; and their solution is a " piece of amusement "[1] in
which pragmatists might profitably indulge.

Again : if it is only by the actual "living" of a belief that
men generally can discover its "truth" by assimilating it with
their "vital experience," or its "falsity" by rejecting or eliminating it from their "vital experience" ; if its truth or falsity *consists in* the relation it gets to "vital experience" through this

---

[1] *Cf. supra,* p. 353, n. 3.

alternative process, and is always relative to the actual stage of human progress at which this sifting process is going on; and if also the whole general human movement,—or the whole cosmic movement, with which all human vital experience, intellectual or intuitional, is one and continuous,[1]—be the whole of (the ever-evolving) reality, and be an end in itself,—does it not follow that *all* beliefs, while entertained by any one and in any degree operative, are *eo ipso* true? And moreover, do not these questions inevitably arise: Are not all beliefs and all conduct equally right or equally wrong? Is it not that whatever is, is right? or rather that right and wrong become unintelligible? Is man really responsible and free? or is the process of perpetual change, or "*fieri*," in which reality is supposed to consist, subject to a rigid and blind determinism? Once more, these are all questions for which we must find an answer *before* the test proposed by pragmatists can be intelligently reduced to practice. They are questions which the Pragmatist test cannot decide, and which must be decided, if at all, by intellect interpreting the data of experience.

Finally, if we apply to beliefs the test of *success*, of harmonizing or not harmonizing with the progressive development of our human activity, it must be remembered that no small department of that activity is *intellectual ;* and, what is more, that intellect exercises—and that as rational beings we should not try to prevent it, and cannot succeed even if we try to prevent it, from exercising—a supreme suzerainty over all other domains of mental life and action. If a belief cannot be "assimilated" or "lived" because it is intellectually incompatible with some already accepted belief, is this failure a *practical* issue which determines the falsity of the former belief? If so,—and the pragmatist cannot consistently deny it,—the whole intellectual domain becomes *practical*, and the *intellectual failure* of any belief becomes the index of its falsity. But the *intellectual failure* of a belief to impose itself arises from its apprehended incompatibility with other judgments known to be true, or from its opposition to the objective evidence of the data of experience, or from its want of adequate objective grounds for intellectual assent. The Pragmatist test, therefore, as applied to the domain of intellectual needs and functions and interests, becomes the test demanded by intellectualism, *viz.* objective evidence. Now there is an

---

[1] *Cf.* BERGSON, *passim.*

exceedingly wide department of human judgments, belief in which can have no other human interest to test them than this purely intellectual kind of success or failure : all purely speculative judgments the knowledge of which can have no other cause than man's intellectual desire for knowledge, and no other practical effect or interest (by which to test " how they work ") than the satisfaction of this natural *cupiditas sciendi*. And if, further, intellect will *nolens volens* assert its supremacy over *all* our beliefs, and its right to judge all their sources and motives, then the intellectual test of objective evidence must remain supreme and ultimate.

Will the pragmatist meet all the considerations we have been so far urging against his position by the rejoinder that even though they may be intellectually unanswerable, still, being dictated by speculative intellectual reflection, they do not and cannot effectually assail a theory of certitude such as his, a theory which teaches that certitude can neither be vindicated nor destroyed by any effort of the intellect ; that it is not a matter for the intellect at all ; that truth and knowledge and belief and certitude are things that can be appreciated and tested only by " living " them, by feeling and experiencing how they work, and not at all by intellect speculatively discussing or exploring or disputing about them? Well, if he does we must leave him so. For of course there can be no discussion with one who appeals *from* reason. But we cannot keep remembering, and neither can the pragmatist, that in putting forward his theory as a philosophical theory, he himself has battled for its acceptance not merely by eloquent and persuasive appeals to the feelings and emotions, the will and the sentiments, and all the affective chords of the human heart, but by reasoned and logical appeals to the human intellect, and by free recourse to the armoury of a keen dialectic,— in the hope of not merely persuading but convincing. Moreover, a *philosophical* theory must be a *reasoned* theory : at least in the sense that it must show grounds which the human intelligence will pronounce to be reasonably adequate for its credibility, for its acceptance by intelligent beings. We take it, therefore, that the pragmatist will allow that his theory *is* open to the influence of such criticisms as have just been set forth.

And when, finally, we consider the gravity of the issues at stake,—the foundations of the intellectual, moral and religious life of man,—we cannot help thinking that the anti-intellectualist attitude, which is that of Pragmatism in common with the other subjectivist theories, voluntarist and sentimentalist, suggests an extremely imprudent decision to the inquiring mind. For it says, in effect : " You can't find out anything for certain about the reality of things. You need not attempt the task of exploring them intellectually, by rational reflection : such a task would be futile, would be labour in vain. Rather trust your own instincts, follow your own feelings, obey your own mental impulses and inclinations, hearken to your own aspirations and yearnings, be faithful to what you feel to be the true and the good and the right,—conscious that you cannot really *know* for certain what these are, and resigned to your inevitable limitations. Even against this counsel, your troublesome reflecting reason may raise *reasons* that seem to forbid your following it. But, then, reason has no *sure* course itself to point out to you, no counsel to offer against which it will not itself raise similar reasons. What then? *Il faut vivre.* You must decide, you cannot live without deciding. So take the counsel I offer you." And this is the advice of the philosopher, the expert, to the untrained inquirer. The latter might possibly have the courage or the curiosity to ask : " How do you know that reason cannot find out for certain what things *really* are, and what *is* the right course?" But the chances are that he will rather say : "You ought to know ; I will follow your advice ". *And the advice given is wrong.* How much more momentous and disastrous are the effects likely to be than in this roughly parallel case from the physical order ?—A grown-up person offers a draught to a thirsty child and says : " Drink this, you are thirsty. It is the only drink available. I do not know and I cannot find out what exactly it is ; nor do I know but it may possibly disagree with you. However, you are very thirsty : you must have something to drink ; so you may as well chance it if you find it agreeable. Taste it." And the thirsty child tastes, finds it agreeable, drinks it off. *And the draught was poison.*

173. CONCLUSION. POSSIBILITY AND SOURCES OF ERROR. THE PROBLEMS OF EPISTEMOLOGY.—The human mind, then, can attain to reasoned and objectively grounded certitude. But it is neither omniscient nor infallible. It can increase its knowledge, but without ever exhausting or comprehending the totality of things. It is, and must remain, in ignorance of much ; for it is finite. Not only so, but it is imperfect : it can and does *err.* We have seen that error is both a possibility and a fact (9, 16). A false or erroneous judgment is one which represents things otherwise than they really are, and which, therefore, *pro tanto*, puts the mind in positive discord or disconformity with reality ; and the mental state or condition of error is the firm adherence of the mind to such a judgment as true.

The *possibility* of error lies in the fact that human cognition is not a mere passive intuition or mirroring of reality (17, 22, 75, 118, 128, 136, 145) by the mind, but an active process whereby the mind abstracts successive aspects of the given reality, analyses and synthesizes, separates and reunites, these aspects, thus gradually interpreting or representing intelligibly to itself, or reconstructing intelligibly for itself, the presented reality (91, iii.). Our main task has been *first* to investigate the *objective reality* of these mental data, to establish the *real objectivity* of knowledge ; and *secondly*, to investigate the mental process of interpreting or representing the given reality : to vindicate the possibility and indicate the tests or criteria of *true* representations or *true* knowledge. We thus distinguished between the *real objectivity* and the *truth* of knowledge (17, 22, 75, 145); and we endeavoured to show that in the reality which presents itself objectively to the human mind the intellect can apprehend adequate objective evidential grounds for the certain truth of some of its interpretations of this reality. Especially in the chapter (xxxiii.) on *Truth and Evidence* we explored, and tried to vindicate, the possibility of transforming the various classes of our spontaneous assents and beliefs (148) into reasoned, reflex convictions by the application of the test of *Objective Evidence* (154). But from that chapter, as well as from the whole course of the inquiry, the student will have learned that the attainment of such certitude is possible only by a careful, cautious, prudent and patient application of intellect to the data of experience; that intellect is infallible only within such narrow limits as include the very starting points of knowledge, and with an infallibility that can be realized only by reflection (153); that, therefore, it requires a judicious and well-balanced use of this faculty to forestall and ward off error, to avoid acquiescence in serious errors, and to correct such errors as may, through the imperfections and limitations that are incidental to human existence, have crept into our spontaneous assents (153). Referring to the "testing" of evidence (153), we saw that while the *total* avoidance of such spontaneous errors is, perhaps, humanly impossible, it is nevertheless possible to avoid *reflex and deliberate adherence*, after due reflection, to a judgment as true which is really false. And the reason is that on the one hand if the judgment is really false there cannot be *real objective evidence* for it: in that case the reality does not and cannot furnish objective grounds which the intellect can prudently judge to be adequate for *certain* assent to the judgment as true; while on the other hand intellect is precisely a faculty *of reflection*, of discerning between real and putative or apparent grounds of assent, and so of giving a certain assent only when it can prudently judge the grounds of such assent to be real and really adequate. *No erroneous assent can be*, therefore, after due reflection and in spite of such reflection, *absolutely necessary, or absolutely unavoidable by the human mind.*[1] For assent can be and ought to be measured by the evidential value of the grounds for it. Hence the intellect can avoid *error* by giving only a *provisional* or *probable* assent, or

---

[1] *Cf.* JEANNIÈRE, *op. cit.*, p. 342.

by suspending assent altogether and remaining in *doubt* or *ignorance*, according to the objective requirements of the presented reality. But this implies the *prudent* use of the intellect, a use which depends on many influences extrinsic to the intellect itself.

Recognizing, then, the possibility and the fact of error, we might propose to inquire into *its actual causes*. But here again we may be very brief, for the student will doubtlessly have detected the main causes of the prevalence of errors among men from the course of our inquiry.[1] They are for the most part undue haste or precipitancy in assenting; the irksomeness of doubt as compared with the satisfaction of assent; sloth, or neglect to apply the mind sufficiently to the task of investigating and sifting evidence; permission of undue influence of the will, the passions and emotions, likes and dislikes, on the intellectual function itself of judging and assenting. From what was said in the opening chapter (11-15) concerning the influence of the will on our assents, and concerning voluntarist theories of certitude in the present closing chapter, it must be apparent that this whole mass of subjective, instinctive, volitional, emotional, affective influences on the distinctively intellectual function of *knowing, judging, assenting, believing*, is very considerable. And it is to the undue preponderance of those influences that much error must be ascribed. Intellect is itself an "undetermined" or "indifferent" faculty. It must be determined to elicit the act of assent. On those influences the intellect can reflect; and, though "subjective" or appertaining to the "self," they may be considered objectively, or as objects, by intellect, and, as such, may have a certain value as evidential, which the intellect can appraise (148). But if the total objective evidence, including such indirectly objective evidential value as those subjective influences may be judged to have, is not adequate, not sufficient to exclude all prudent fear of error and thus determine the firm or certain assent of the intellect; and if nevertheless the intellect *does* give its assent,—then it must be because it has

---

[1] It is one of the functions of *Logic*, as a practical science, to train and help the mind to avoid error by exploring, analysing and laying bare its various sources and causes. *Cf. Science of Logic*, ii., Part v., chap. iii., especially the suggestive treatment of the subject of *Fallacies* by Bacon and by J. S. Mill (*ibid.*, § 272). Some of the fallacies incident to method (§ 275),—those, namely, that bear on *Demonstration, Explanation, Assumption of Axioms and Postulates*,—raise issues that are distinctly epistemological. We may, therefore, refer the student here to what we have already said upon them, *op. cit.*, pp. 315-37.

allowed itself to be determined not by evidence but by the blind or inevidential influence of those subjective factors. And it is thus that error can and does arise.

But in addition to all those sources of error there is to be taken into account also the very illusive but very real and potent influence of what we may call the intellectual and moral environment or "climate" in which the individual has been brought up from infancy: the influences that have formed his whole mentality, his "receptiveness" or "preparedness" for the evidential appeal of truth to his intellect: the spontaneous beliefs and convictions in which he has been trained: his "prejudices," conscious and unconscious, whether they happen to be objectively true or objectively erroneous: his moral habits and character: his "inherited" religious beliefs, whether these happen to be true or false; and so on. What an enormous influence all these factors will have,—when we come to the case of the actual individual man in his concrete surroundings,—in determining just how far, and with what measure of success, he will avoid error, and attain to truth! In dealing with Traditionalism (158-62) we touched upon this question of the actual individual in human society: on the question whether, or under what conditions, the average individual human being can attain to certitude concerning the great problems that count most: his own nature, end, and destiny; God, freedom, morality, religion, immortality. There we found ourselves face to face with the question of *Christian Evidences*, of God's actual dispensations to mankind: with the problem of a Supernatural Revelation, involving the gratuitousness of the gift of Supernatural Faith, its necessity for the attainment of man's Supernatural End, and the mystery of God's Providence in the communication of that saving Faith to individual men. And there we must leave that momentous question of fact, with all its mysterious implications, to be dealt with by the Christian apologist and theologian.

Well, we have seen at any rate that the human mind, with all its limitations, can give to itself a reasonable account of itself; and can satisfy itself fully that *Reality is its object*, that to some measure of *truth about reality* it can *certainly attain*. Was not this our appointed task? Or have we to determine, further, *to how much truth* can the human mind attain? No; this is not for us to determine in Epistemology, except in principle and in broad outline. To show that the attainment of *some* true and

certain knowledge is possible concerning the data which constitute
the various departments of human experience: to vindicate a
reasoned certitude that the human mind can reach *some* degree
of genuine insight into the real nature of man and the universe:
to justify by critical introspective analysis the principles and presuppositions involved in *knowing*: to distinguish between right
and wrong methods of interpreting and appraising the grounds
on which human convictions are based (whether these be spontaneous or reflex; whether they be called "knowledges," or
"beliefs"; whether they be "ordinary," "scientific," "philosophical," "ethical," or "religious"): to show that the human mind
can increase its knowledge both in extent and in depth: and to
indicate in principle the means and methods of such progress,—
these are the duties of the epistemologist, rather than to decide
e.g. whether or not any suggested interpretation of any portion
of human experience is or is not true.

The historian marshals the evidence for certitude about past
facts; but the epistemologist shows that assent based on human
authority is reasonable.   The physical scientist is constantly extending the domain of our "knowledge" concerning the material
universe; but the epistemologist proves that such knowledge is
indeed a genuine insight into the reality of a material universe
which exists independently of our perception of it.   The psychologist,—assuming the capacity of the mind to discover the existence, and reach some certain knowledge of the nature, of a
hyperphysical or suprasensible domain of reality,—explores the
origin, nature and destiny of the human soul; but the epistemologist has to examine, and if so be to justify, that assumption.
The metaphysician, or philosopher, or theologian seeks the
ultimate causes and reasons which will explain or make intelligible the totality of direct human experience: he infers from the
data of this experience that a Supreme Being exists, that He
created and conserves and rules the universe, that He has revealed
Himself to man, that man depends on Him and owes Him the
worship He demands, that ethical distinctions of right and wrong
in human conduct are grounded on man's relations to the Deity,
etc., etc.; but the epistemologist must explore the validity of the
mental processes (of perception, conception, judgment, inference)
by which such investigations are prosecuted and such conclusions
reached.   Moreover, the masses of mankind have ethical and religious convictions of some sort: convictions which differ widely

in detail but have certain fundamental elements in common : convictions, too, which the masses of men profess and hold because they have, so to speak, inherited them, or been born into them, having received them on the authority of their parents, elders, teachers, etc. But the epistemologist, though he has not to decide which of these are true, or which false, has nevertheless to say whether or not there can be any truth-value or knowledge-value proper in convictions of such an order, concerning such a domain of objects : he has to say whether this domain of so-called "invisible or suprasensible realities," or "the unseen world" as it is also termed, is indeed a domain about the reality and existence of which man can have *certain knowledge*, or only conjectural knowledge, or only instinctive hopes and fears that have no sufficient ground in his nature as a rational being. And if man can attain to a certain knowledge of God and immortality and a future life, the epistemologist has to show that the rational principles and methods by which he attains to it, and the grounds on which he bases it, are in fact reliable.

Such are the tasks to which we have been devoting our attention throughout the course of the inquiry which we now bring to a close. That our investigations may have proved helpful to the student of such serious and engrossing problems is our very earnest hope.

INDEX TO VOLUME II.[1]

[1] The numbers refer to the pages. For references to the main topics of the volume, which are not included in the Index, the reader will please consult the Table of Contents.

373

www.ingramcontent.com/pod-product-compliance
Lightning Source LLC
Chambersburg PA
CBHW020212290326
41948CB00001B/20

* 9 7 8 3 8 6 8 3 8 2 8 2 2 *